Received On:

P9-BYJ-485

Ballard Branch

Seattle

NO LONGER PROPERTY OF
SEATTLE PUBLIC LIBRARY

"All you've got to do is decide to go
and the hardest part is over.

So go!"

TONY WHEELER, COFOUNDER – LONELY PLANET

THIS EDITION WRITTEN AND RESEARCHED BY

Brendan Sainsbury,
Celeste Brash

Contents

(left) Museum of Pop Culture p84

(above) Grizzly bear, Woodland Park Zoo p145

(right) Seattle Great Wheel p49

Welcome to Seattle

Blink and it's changed: Seattle can be that ephemeral. Welcome to a city that pushes the envelope, embraces new trends and plots a path toward the future.

Local Flavor

First time in Seattle? Cut to the chase and make a beeline for its proverbial pantry: Pike Place Market. Founded in 1907 to fortify locals with fresh Northwest produce, the market's long-held mantra of 'meet the producer' still echoes enthusiastically around a city where every restaurateur worth their salt knows the name of their fishmonger and the biography of the cow that made yesterday's burgers. It doesn't take long to realize that you've arrived in a maelstrom of educated palates and wildly experimental chefs who are willing to fuse American cuisine with just about anything – as long as it's local.

A United States of Neighborhoods

Visitors setting out to explore Seattle with a blank canvas should think of the city as a United States of Neighborhoods, or – to put it in more human terms – a family of affectionate but sometimes errant siblings. There's the aloof, elegant one (Queen Anne), the cool, edgy one (Capitol Hill), the weird, bearded one (Fremont), the independently minded Scandinavian one (Ballard), the grizzled old grandfather (Pioneer Square) and the precocious adolescent still carving out its identity (South Lake Union). You'll never fully understand Seattle until you've visited them all.

Micro-businesses

To outsiders, Seattle is an industrious creator of macro-brands. To insiders, it's a city of micro-businesses and boundary-pushing grassroots movements. For proof, dip into the third-wave coffee shops, the microbreweries with their casual tasting rooms, or the cozy informal bookstores that remain rock solid in a city that spawned Amazon. Then there are the latest national trends that Seattle has helped create: craft cider, pot shops, micro-distilleries, specialist pie-makers, homemade ice cream and fledgling nano-breweries. Walk the streets and scour the neighborhoods; there's far more to this city than Starbucks' vanilla lattes and Boeing airplanes.

A Walk on the Weird Side

Just because it nurtured tech giants Microsoft and Amazon, it doesn't mean that Seattle hasn't got an arty side. Cross its urban grid and you'll find all kinds of freakish apparitions: a rocket sticking out of a shoe shop; a museum resembling a smashed-up electric guitar; glass orbs in wooden canoes; a statue of Lenin; a mural made of used chewing gum; and a museum dedicated to antique pinball machines (which you can still play). No, you haven't over-indulged in some powerful (legal) marijuana. You've just worked out that Seattle is far more bohemian than beige.

XUANLU WANG / SHUTTERSTOCK ©

Why I Love Seattle

By Brendan Sainsbury, Writer

My knowledge of Seattle pre-2000 can be summed up in one word: 'grunge.' A product of my generation, I grew up admiring the city from afar by connecting with its music, unaware of 95% of what it had to offer. A move from London, UK to BC, Canada in 2004 quickly changed the configuration. Regular sorties south of the 49th parallel taught me that there isn't just one Seattle, there are at least 10 of them – mini-cities personified in neighborhoods full of shifting moods and weird subcultures that satisfied pretty much every taste I had.

For more about our writers, see p256.

Top: Space Needle (p80) and the Seattle skyline

Seattle's
Top 10

Pike Place Market *(p42)*

1 Way more than just a market, 110-year-old Pike Place is a living community, a cabaret show, a way of life and an intrinsic piece of Seattle's soul. Strolling through its clamorous, sometimes chaotic thoroughfares, you simply couldn't be in any other city. There are fish that fly, shops that look like they've sprung from a Harry Potter movie, an art wall made out of chewing gum, and a multitude of classic old buskers jamming acoustic versions of AC/DC songs outside the world's oldest Starbucks. Pure magic!

👁 *Downtown, Pike Place & Waterfront*

Space Needle *(p80)*

2 The city icon that is as synonymous with Seattle as the letters S-E-A-T-T-L-E was built for the 1962 World's Fair, and its novel revolving restaurant and bold futuristic design have proved durable. Although it's no longer Seattle's tallest structure, one million annual visitors still squeeze into the Space Needle's slick, speedy elevators to enjoy views that are best described as sublime. Granted, tickets are expensive and you might have to fight off the odd tourist or three, but stop complaining and get in line: this is an essential Seattle pilgrimage.

👁 *Belltown & Seattle Center*

CHICUBUS / SHUTTERSTOCK ©

Museum of Pop Culture *(p84)*

3 Paying homage to the left-handed, guitar-burning musical genius that was Jimi Hendrix, Paul Allen's architecturally bizarre Museum of Pop Culture is an apt memorial to a region that has been a powerful musical innovator since the days of local boy Bing Crosby. Come and see the legends and how they were created, from Hendrix to Kurt Cobain, or experiment with your own riffs in the interactive Sound Lab. Marrying Captain Kirk with Nirvana Kurt is the on-site 'Icons of Science Fiction' exhibit, where *Star Trek* meets *Doctor Who*.

👁 *Belltown & Seattle Center*

Puget Sound Ferries *(p177)*

4 Tap the average Seattleite about their most cherished weekend excursion and they could surprise you with a dark horse – a cheap and simple ride on the commuter ferry across Puget Sound to Bainbridge Island. There's nothing quite like being surrounded by water and seeing Seattle's famous skyline disappearing in the ferry's foamy wake, the only commentary the cry of the seagulls and the only entertainment the comedic antics of escaping families bound for a day out on the Olympic Peninsula.

🚶 *Day Trips from Seattle*

Public Art *(p143)*

5 Seattle likes to display its art out in the open with no holds barred. Sculptures and statues decorate parks, streets and squares, from the weird (a stone troll underneath a bridge), to the iconic (Hendrix in classic rock-and-roll pose), to the downright provocative (a statue of Vladimir Lenin). The city even has its own sculpture park, an outpost of the Seattle Art Museum that spreads its works across a beautifully landscaped outdoor space overlooking glassy Elliott Bay. ABOVE: OLYMPIC SCULPTURE PARK (P85)

👁 *Belltown & Seattle Center*

Discovery Park *(p155)*

6 Seattle justifies its 'Emerald City' moniker in the rugged confines of 534-acre Discovery Park, a one-time military installation reborn as a textbook example of urban sustainability. Speckled with Douglas fir trees, hunting eagles, log-littered beaches and wild meadows, it resembles a lonely tract of Pacific Northwestern wilderness picked up and dropped into the middle of a crowded metropolitan area. Come here for breathing space, coexistence with nature, and a chance to slow down and reflect on the magic that lured people to Seattle in the first place.

🏃 *Ballard & Discovery Park*

Belltown Dining *(p86)*

7 Belltown, the high-spirited neighborhood where flannel-shirted grunge groupies once practiced their stage-dives, is now better known for its restaurants – cramming over 100 of them into a strip abutting downtown. Considered a microcosm of Seattle's gastronomic scene, this UN of food places a strong emphasis on 'locavore' cuisine, showcasing ingredients from Seattle's adjacent waters and farms. Look out for artisan bakeries, sushi, creative pizzas, Basque-style tapas, Greek fusion, seafood from Pike Place Market and homemade pasta, served around communal tables.

🍴 *Belltown & Seattle Center*

ROMAN KHOMLYAK / SHUTTERSTOCK ©

Coffee Culture *(p27)*

8 Welcome to the new Vienna. Seattle practically invented modern North American coffee culture, thanks to a small store in Pike Place Market that went global: Starbucks. But, while the rest of the world has been quick to lap up the green mermaid logo and its multiple coffee-related inventions, Seattle has moved on. Starbucks is merely the froth on the cappuccino in a city where hundreds of small-scale micro-roasteries, cafes, baristas and knowledgeable caffeine connoisseurs continue to experiment and innovate.

🍷 *Drinking & Nightlife*

Beer Culture in Ballard *(p164)*

9 A one-time fishing village founded by Nordic immigrants, the Ballard neighborhood has been reincarnated as Seattle's beer capital with enough bars to satisfy a city in its own right. Boldly experimental, Ballard's small breweries concoct big flavors that are served in a cornucopia of drinking establishments. There are nano-breweries, brewpubs, old-school biker hangouts, tasting rooms, whiskey bars, sports bars, dives peddling rock, and bars with book corners. Bonus: once you're done with the booze, you can immerse yourself in Ballard's unique Nordic Heritage Museum and a necklace of waterside parks.

🍷 *Ballard & Discovery Park*

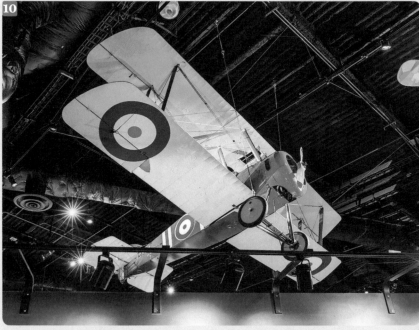

Museum of Flight *(p169)*

10 Even people with absolutely no interest in aviation have been known to blink in quiet astonishment at the recently refurbished Museum of Flight, which tells the tale of how humankind got from the Wright Brothers to the first moon landing in less than 66 years. Get ready for an exciting jet-propelled journey through war, peace, space rockets and inspired engineering, eloquently related with the aid of film, words, flight simulators, famous decommissioned aircraft, and a man called William E Boeing.

👁 *Georgetown & West Seattle*

What's New

Pot Shops

It took a while, but 20 months after the passing of Initiative 502, the law that legalized marijuana in Washington State, Seattle opened its first recreational pot shop, Cannabis City. Since then, the pot shop map has expanded to include nearly two dozen stores, although marijuana use in public is still restricted. Read up on the law before you arrive or join a tour with leading marijuana experts, Kush Tourism. (p129)

Micro-Distilleries

Since the relaxing of state laws in 2008, micro-distilleries have proliferated in Seattle. Many operators, such as SoDo whiskey-maker Westland, have tasting rooms and run factory tours. (p77)

Craft Cider

The US is developing a taste for hard cider and, not surprisingly, Seattle, with its proximity to the bulk of the nation's apple crop, is leading the way at places like Schilling Cider House. (p149)

Pike Place Market Extension

Pike Place Market is undergoing its first major extension since the 1970s with new stalls, shops and landscaped terraces over-looking the waterfront. The extension is due to open in 2017. (p42)

Starbucks Reserve Roastery

An unexpected new development from global coffee giant Starbucks, this multifari-ous coffee emporium in Capitol Hill appears to be surfing on the coffee industry's third wave. (p115)

Filson

This beautifully designed new store in SoDo is the latest offering from one of Seattle's oldest outfitters, which first made its name during the Klondike gold rush. (p76)

Public Transportation

Getting around Seattle has become a lot easier with a new streetcar and an extended light-rail line (serving Capitol Hill and the U District). (p199)

Amazon Tower I

The online shopping behemoth's Seattle HQ keeps growing, most recently in the Denny Triangle with the completion of the first of three sleek new towers in 2015. (p85)

KEXP

One of the finest indie radio stations in the US opened a new recording and broadcasting space in the Seattle Center in 2016. The campus also includes a venue for live music performances. (p93)

Amazon Books

Somewhat ironically, the world's largest online retailer opened its first brick-and-mortar bookstore in the U District in 2015. Inside, you can engage in the good old-fashioned joy of shelf browsing. (p139)

For more recommendations and reviews, see **lonelyplanet. com/seattle**

Need to Know

For more information, see Survival Guide (p211)

Currency
US dollar ($)

Language
English

Visas
Visa requirements vary widely for entry to the US and are liable to change. For up-to-date information, check www.travel.state.gov.

Money
ATMs are widely available. Credit cards are accepted at most hotels, restaurants and shops.

Cell Phones
The US uses CDMA-800 and GSM-1900 bands. SIM cards are relatively easy to obtain.

Time
Pacific Standard Time (GMT/UTC minus eight hours)

Tourist Information
Visit Seattle (Map p232; 📞20 6-461-5800; www.visitseattle.org; cnr Pike St & 7th Ave; ⊙9am-5pm daily Jun-Sep, Mon-Fri Oct-May; 🚇Westlake) The main tourist information center is located in the Washington State Convention Center in downtown.

Daily Costs
Budget: Less than $125
➡ Dorm bed in a hostel: $25–35

➡ Pike Place Market take-out snacks: $3–6

➡ Certain days at museums: free

➡ Public transportation average fare: $2.50

Midrange: $125–250
➡ Online deal at a no-frills hotel: $120–170

➡ Pub, bakery or sandwich bar meal: around $10

➡ Cheap tickets for sports games: from $12

➡ Short taxi trip: $10–12

Top End: More than $250
➡ Downtown hotel room: more than $200

➡ Meal at innovative Capitol Hill restaurant: from $50

➡ Tickets to the theater or a concert: from $40

Advance Planning
One month before Start looking at options for car rental, accommodations, tours and train tickets.

Two weeks before If you're hoping to see a particular performance or game, whether it's the Mariners or the opera, it's wise to buy tickets in advance.

One to two days before Book popular restaurants in advance. Search the *Stranger* and the *Seattle Times* for upcoming art and entertainment listings.

Useful Websites
The Stranger (www.thestranger.com) Seattle's best newspaper for entertainment listings – and it's free.

Seattle Weekly (www.seattleweekly.com) The city's other free newspaper can be picked up in coffee bars or from metal street-side dispensers.

Not for Tourists (www.notfortourists.com/seattle.aspx) Irreverent reviews and neighborhood commentaries.

Real Change (www.realchangenews.org) Weekly newspaper sold on the streets for and by homeless people.

Lonely Planet (www.lonelyplanet.com/seattle) Destination information, hotel bookings, traveler forum and more.

WHEN TO GO

Winter is dreary. Spring brings a few gorgeous days. July to September is dry, sunny and the best time to visit. Early fall has more changeable weather.

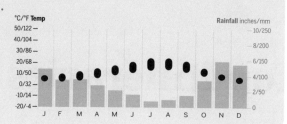

°C/°F **Temp**
50/122 —
40/104 —
30/86 —
20/68 —
10/50 —
0/32 —
-10/14 —
-20/-4 —

Rainfall inches/mm
— 10/250
— 8/200
— 6/150
— 4/100
— 2/50
— 0

J F M A M J J A S O N D

Arriving in Seattle

Sea-Tac International Airport (SEA) Link light rail connects to downtown Seattle in 30 minutes; shuttle buses stop on the 3rd floor of the airport garage and cost from $18 one way; taxis cost from $42 to downtown (25 minutes).

King Street Station Situated in Pioneer Square and on the cusp of downtown with good, fast links to practically everywhere in the city. Use light rail to Westlake in the heart of downtown or take the streetcar to First Hill (both fares $2.25).

The Piers Metro buses 24 and 19 connect Pier 91 in Magnolia with downtown via the Seattle Center. Fares are a flat $2.75. Shuttle Express links piers 66 and 91 with Sea-Tac airport ($22) or downtown ($12). Washington State Ferries dock at Pier 52 in downtown Seattle.

For much more on **arrival** see p212

Getting Around

There is a large and growing network of public transportation in Seattle.

➡ **Bus** Run by King County Metro Transit on a wide number of routes. Buses are pay-as-you-enter and cost a peak-time flat fee of $2.75/1.50 per adult/child.

➡ **Light Rail** Regular all-day service on one line between Sea-Tac airport and the University of Washington via downtown.

➡ **Streetcar** Two lines. South Lake Union line runs from Westlake Center to South Lake Union every 15 minutes. First Hill line runs from Pioneer Square to Capitol Hill. Fares are $2.25/1.50 per adult/child.

➡ **Water Taxi** Runs between Pier 50 on the waterfront to West Seattle; daily in summer, weekdays only in winter.

➡ **Taxi** Initial charge $2.60, then $2.70 per mile.

For much more on **getting around** see p214

Sleeping

Seattle has a quartet of good economical hostels: one in downtown, one in Belltown, one in the International District, and one a little further out in Fremont. Aside from dorms, they also offer private rooms. You'll find few good hotels for under $100 a night unless you're willing to share a bathroom/toilet. For good bargains in the $100 to $170 range, including reliable Holiday Inns, Best Westerns and Quality Inns, look around Belltown and Lower Queen Anne. There has been a recent increase in boutique hotels. Capitol Hill has some excellent B&Bs. Big chains and more expensive options, many of which are encased in their own mini-skyscrapers, are spread around downtown.

Useful Websites

➡ **Lonely Planet** (www.lonelyplanet.com/seattle) Recommendations and bookings.

➡ **Seattle Bed & Breakfast Association** (www.lodginginseattle.com) Portal of the city's 20 best B&Bs.

For much more on **sleeping** see p187

WHAT TO TAKE

➡ US plug/adapter if coming from outside the Americas.

➡ Umbrella and light rain jacket – it rains a lot from October to May.

➡ Good walking shoes for possible forays into Seattle's surrounding countryside.

Top Itineraries

Day One

Pike Place (p40)

Early birds catch more than worms at **Pike Place Market**. Arrive promptly at 9am for some real-life street theater at market roll call before wandering over to the Main Arcade to see the lippy fish throwers warming up. Spend the morning getting lost, browsing, tasting, buying and bantering with the producers, but don't miss the **gum wall** or Rachel the pig. Afterwards, be sure to wander down to the new market extension overlooking the waterfront.

> **Lunch** Grab a tub of mac 'n' cheese at Beecher's Handmade Cheese (p50).

Downtown & Waterfront (p40)

Duck under the soon-to-be-demolished Alaskan Way Viaduct to access Seattle's waterfront. Be a tourist and head for the **Aquarium** on Pier 59, or become a local and jump on a **Puget Sound ferry** just for the ride. Allow a good hour to browse the latest exhibits at **Seattle Art Museum** (SAM) on the western edge of downtown.

> **Dinner** Ivar's Acres of Clams (p55), a fish-and-chip institution since 1938.

Pioneer Square (p63)

Head to Pioneer Square for a drink in the amiable sports bar **Fuel** before hitting the **Comedy Underground**, where even poker-faced *misérables* have been known to break into uncontrollable giggles.

Day Two

Seattle Center (p78)

Resist the lure of the Seattle Center no longer. After a cursory orientation of the complex, opt first for the crystallized magnificence of **Chihuly Garden & Glass**. If you buy a joint-admission ticket you can zip up the adjacent **Space Needle** afterward for equally dazzling views.

> **Lunch** Divert into Belltown for lunch at lauded bistro, Tilikum Place Cafe (p89).

Seattle Center (p78)

After lunch, enjoy glittering Elliott Bay views and giant, imaginative art at the **Olympic Sculpture Park** before returning to the Seattle Center for an afternoon of rock-and-roll nostalgia at the **EMP Museum**. Anyone who has ever picked up an instrument will require at least an hour to twiddle guitar knobs in the Sound Lab on the 3rd floor. Stroll along 6th Ave afterward and pop into the **Assembly Hall** for a cup of coffee and a free game of pool.

> **Dinner** Decamp for a plate of home-made pasta to Tavolàta (p88).

Belltown (p78)

Start off with a game of pinball in **Shorty's**. If you like your bars divey, stay put. If you want to see what's going on in Seattle's new micro-distilling universe, hit the **Whisky Bar** and order a Westland single malt before checking out what band is playing at the **Crocodile**.

COURTESY OF CHIHULY GARDEN AND GLASS ©

Chihuly Garden & Glass (p82)

Day Three

Pioneer Square (p63)

 Start the morning like a true Seattleite with a latte in **Zeitgeist**, possibly the city's best indie coffee shop. Cross the road, admiring 1890s redbrick architecture, and visit the entertaining, educational and free **Klondike Gold Rush National Historical Park**. If there's time, take a gilded-age elevator up the **Smith Tower** before lunch.

> **Lunch** Hit the International District for dim sum in Jade Garden (p72).

International District (p63)

In the Asian-flavored ID, call in on its most famous sight, the **Wing Luke Museum**, and its most esoteric, the **Pinball Museum** (for a quick game), before imbibing tea and Japanese American history in the **Panama Hotel Tea & Coffee House**. From here, climb up through genteel First Hill to Capitol Hill.

> **Dinner** Join Seattle's locavore culture at Capitol Hill's Sitka & Spruce (p114).

Capitol Hill (p108)

Spontaneous evenings in Capitol Hill start early and go on till late. Warm up on the Pike–Pine corridor with a craft cocktail in **Sun Liquor Distillery** before heading over to **Optimism Brewing Co** for a straight-from-the-beer-vat microbrew. Those with high alcohol thresholds can keep mixing at **Capitol Cider**. Those with a penchant for cool indie music delivered live should check out **Neumo's**.

Day Four

Lake Union (p96)

 Time for a journey through Seattle's outer neighborhoods. Start the morning in South Lake Union, where a lakeside park hosts the **Museum of History & Industry**, a roller-coaster journey through Seattle's past. If there's time afterward, pop into the **Center for Wooden Boats** to plan future sailing sorties.

> **Lunch** Eat at Serious Biscuit (p101), owned by celebrity chef Tom Douglas.

Fremont (p141)

Stroll through Westlake along the **Cheshiahud Loop**, or flag a bus to take you to Fremont. Soon after crossing the Fremont Bridge, you'll spy *Waiting for the Interurban* and plenty of other whimsical sculptures. It would be foolish to leave Fremont without a visit to **Theo Chocolate Factory**. Share coffee with the locals afterward at **Milstead & Co** before hitting the **Burke-Gilman Trail** (or getting a bus) to Ballard.

> **Dinner** Go Mexican at La Carta de Oaxaca (p162) in Ballard Ave NW.

Ballard (p153)

 If weather permits, stroll out to **Hiram M Chittenden Locks** for sunset, before returning to Ballard Ave to experience the neighborhood's self-contained nightlife. There's no friendlier beer nook than **Populuxe Brewing**, a pioneering nano-brewery. More rambunctious is **King's Hardware**. Louder still is the **Tractor Tavern**, a legendary hive of indie rock and alt-country music.

If You Like...

Sculpture & Statues

Olympic Sculpture Park Modern sculpture set against the natural backdrop of Elliott Bay; a Seattle Art Museum outpost. (p85)

Pioneer Square Park Totem Pole An icon of Native American culture with a colorful backstory. (p66)

Fremont Troll The scary stone monster that lives under the Fremont bridge. (p143)

Chihuly Garden & Glass Dale Chihuly's intricate glass art blends seamlessly with flowers and reeds in the Seattle Center. (p82)

Hendrix Statue Beloved monument to one of the greatest rockers to have ever picked up an electric guitar. (p110)

Offbeat Stuff

Gum Wall Get rid of your chewing gum and contribute to Seattle's biggest (and most unhygienic) art wall. (p47)

Fish Throwers Watch huge salmon flying through the air at Pike Place Market. (p42)

Statue of Lenin Come and pay your respects, or hurl a few insults, at Vladimir Ilyich Ulyanov, aka Lenin. (p143)

Solstice Cyclists Fremont's Solstice Fair includes an artsy parade, where nude cyclists pedal through the neighborhood. (p21)

Hat 'n' Boots This giant cowboy hat and boots once embellished a Washington gas station. (p170)

GLENN R. MCGLOUGHLIN / SHUTTERSTOCK ©

Pioneer Square Park totem pole (p66)

Free Stuff

Boat Rides on Lake Union Free sailing trips at 10am Sunday at the Center for Wooden Boats; first come, first served. (p99)

Music in Pike Place Everyone from concert violinists to punk poets busk for free at Pike Place Market. (p42)

Occidental Park This refurbished Pioneer Square park offers free outdoor games, including chess and table tennis. (p66)

Borrow a Bike Numerous hotels offer free bikes, so grab some wheels and hit the beautiful Burke-Gilman Trail. (p140)

Public Art Viewing all of Seattle's alfresco art, including the Olympic Sculpture Park, costs precisely zero dollars. (p85)

Green Lake Park A favorite for runners, personal trainers and artistically tattooed sunbathers. (p145)

Fremont Public Sculpture Fremont's sculptures are an eclectic amalgamation of the scary, the politically incorrect and the, well, weird. (p143)

Bill & Melinda Gates Foundation Visitor Center See what one of the world's richest families does with their money. (p86)

Museums

Seattle Art Museum A leading player in modern and ethnic art, with an enviable Native American collection. (p46)

Klondike Gold Rush National Historical Park Interactive museum that details Seattle's role in the 1897 gold fever that gripped the Yukon. (p67)

Museum of History & Industry Seattle's boom-bust history laid out in an erstwhile armory building on the shores of Lake Union. (p98)

Chihuly Garden & Glass Tacoma-born Dale Chihuly honored (at last) in a dazzling glass-art display beneath the Space Needle. (p82)

Museum of Pop Culture Super-modern rock-and-roll museum that lets you play on some of the exhibits. (p84)

Nordic Heritage Museum Seattle's history isn't complete until you've traced the immigration stories at this illuminating Ballard outpost. (p157)

Green Spaces

Green Lake Park Amateur athletics track? Body-beautiful competition? Giant alfresco community center? Green Lake Park is where it all happens. (p145)

Volunteer Park Follow Millionaires Row to this elegant park on Capitol Hill, where a water tower offers panoramic views. (p110)

Discovery Park Former military installation that became a park in the 1970s; retains an element of wilderness lacking elsewhere. (p155)

Washington Park Arboretum Pleasant green corridor that bisects Seattle's eastern neighborhoods with multiple paths and a Japanese garden. (p124)

Views

Columbia Center The highest human-made view in Seattle can be seen for just over $14. (p48)

PLAN YOUR TRIP IF YOU LIKE...

For more top Seattle spots, see the following:
⇒ Eating (p24)
⇒ Drinking & Nightlife (p27)
⇒ Entertainment (p29)
⇒ Sports & Activities (p31)
⇒ Shopping (p34)

Space Needle The (expensive) rite of passage for every tourist since 1962. (p80)

Kerry Park Climb to this park in Seattle's salubrious Queen Anne quarter and watch the sun set. (p99)

Mt Rainier A volcano with killer views – fitness, bravery and a decent pair of crampons essential. (p184)

Architecture

Pioneer Square The homogeneous historic quarter where Seattle was born guards the city's most valuable architectural legacy. (p65)

Queen Anne Hilly, well-to-do neighborhood with fine residential houses designed in the elegant Queen Anne revivalist style. (p39)

Seattle Central Library A 21st-century architectural marvel that looks like a giant diamond dropped from outer space. (p47)

EMP Museum Frank Gehry allegedly designed this avant-garde building to resemble one of Hendrix' smashed guitars. (p84)

Month by Month

TOP EVENTS

Seattle International Film Festival, May to June

Fremont Solstice Fair, June

Seafair, June to August

Viking Days, August

Bumbershoot, September

January

The year starts with a hangover and flurries of snow. Plan indoor activities or bring your skis and head to the nearby mountains.

✨ Chinese New Year

Beginning toward the end of January or at the start of February and lasting for two weeks, the year's first big ethnic festival (www.cidbia.org) takes place in the International District with parades, firecrackers, fireworks and plenty of food.

February

Those who haven't jetted off to Hawaii hunker down for another overcast month. Scour the internet for hotel deals and book a night at the theater.

✨ Northwest Flower & Garden Show

Usually held the second week of February, this popular garden show (www.gardenshow.com) hosted in the Washington State Convention Center includes lectures, seminars, demos and children's activities.

March

The odd warm day can see restaurants opening their patios, but more often than not rain persists. St Patrick's Day provides a good excuse to shrug off the long, hard winter.

☆ Moisture Festival

This increasingly prominent comedy/varietè festival (www.moisturefestival.com) takes place over four weeks from mid-March to mid-April. The quirkfest is spread around four venues including Teatro ZinZanni, Nordo's Culinarium and its HQ, the Hale's Palladium at Hale's Ales Brewery in Fremont.

April

Bargain hunters still seek deals as the aroma of spring is detected in Seattle's parks and gardens.

✨ Cherry Blossom & Japanese Cultural Festival

A celebration of Japanese heritage, including performances of music, dance and drama, this festival (www.cherryblossomfest.org) is usually held in late April. It's part of the Seattle Center's series of multicultural festivals, dubbed Festál.

May

People start hitting the waterside attractions. Visit before Memorial Day (last Monday in May): this could be your last chance for a hotel deal as the shoulder season begins.

☆ Seattle International Film Festival

Held over three weeks from mid-May to early June, this prestigious film festival (www.siff.net) uses a half-dozen cinemas to screen over 400 movies. Major venues include the SIFF Cinema Uptown in Lower Queen Anne and the festival's own dedicated SIFF Film Center in the Seattle Center.

June

Showers can linger in the early part of June, but summer's in the post. With the rise in temperatures comes a rise in bizarre behavior.

🎭 Fremont Solstice Fair

Off-kilter Fremont offers a June fair (www.fremontfair. com) with live music, food and crafts, and the overtly artsy Solstice Parade, where human-powered floats and – ahem – nude cyclists trickle through the neighborhood in a lively tribute to quirkiness.

July

Peak temperatures (75°F/24°C) and peak prices mark Seattle's peak season, when you'd be wise to book ahead for pretty much everything.

🎭 Seafair

Huge crowds attend the Seafair (www.seafair.com) festival held on the water from mid-June to mid-August, with a pirate's landing, a torchlight parade, an air show, a music marathon and even a Milk Carton Derby (look it up!).

August

Salmon bakes, street fairs and lazy beach afternoons give August a laid-back feel. But school's out, so expect ubiquitous cries of excited kids.

🎭 Viking Days

Citizens of Ballard rediscover their inner Viking and celebrate Seattle's Scandinavian heritage in the grounds of the Nordic Heritage Museum at the so-called Viking Days.

🎭 Hempfest

Seattle's Hempfest (www. hempfest.org) is a large annual festival that began as a kind of stoner's convention in 1991, but has since morphed into a full-on celebration of marijuana culture attended by over 100,000. It's held in Myrtle Edwards Park on the waterfront on the third weekend in August.

September

The best month to visit? Possibly. Once Bumbershoot's over, the tourists go home and hotel prices deflate, but the weather usually remains sunny and relatively warm until early October.

☆ Bumbershoot

A fair few people would say Bumbershoot (www.bumbershoot.com) is Seattle's finest festival with major arts and cultural events at Seattle Center over the Labor Day weekend. Bank on live music, comedy, theater, visual arts and dance; but also bank on crowds and hotels stuffed to capacity.

October

There's the possibility of an Indian summer in the first half of the month when the start of the shoulder season brings cheaper prices. As the clouds roll in, people get out to celebrate Halloween.

☆ TWIST: Seattle Queer Film Festival

This popular film festival (www.threedollarbillcinema. org) shows new queer-themed movies from directors worldwide. It's curated by the Three Dollar Bill Cinema and held at various venues.

November

November can be a dismal month for weather, but most sights stay open and, with low season kicking in, some hotels slash their prices to half summer rates.

🎭 Best of the Northwest

The Best of the Northwest (www.nwartalliance.org) art and fine craft show is held in Magnuson Park in the Sand Point neighborhood just north of the U District. It showcases artists and designers of all genres from jewelry to glass.

December

Seattle's surrounding ski resorts open up, making the city a good urban base for snow-related activities. Hotel prices continue to drop along with the temperatures.

🎭 Winterfest

Seattle Center holds a month-long celebration of holiday traditions from around the globe, starting with Winter Worldfest, a massive concert and dance performance, and continuing with exhibits, dances, concerts and ice skating (www.seattlecenter.com/winterfest).

With Kids

Take it easy, overworked parent. Seattle will entertain, pacify and often educate your energetic kid(s) without them even realizing it. Some of the attractions are obvious – a children's theater and a zoo. Others are more serendipitous: don't miss the pinball museum or the exciting urban theater of Pike Place Market.

DANITA DELIMONT / GETTY IMAGES ©

Children's Museum (p86)

Where to Eat

Most restaurants in Seattle are kid-friendly. The only places where you're likely to see 'No Minors' signs is in pubs, gastropubs and dive bars (notwithstanding, many pubs will serve families as long as you don't sit at the bar). Some places introduce a no-kids policy after 10pm. Pike Place Market has the widest selection of cheap, immediately available food and is a fun place to hang out and eat.

You'll struggle to find anyone (kid or adult) who doesn't fall instantly in love with the mac 'n' cheese cartons sold at Beecher's Handmade Cheese (p50) or the flaky pastries rolled before your eyes at Piroshky Piroshky (p52). Elsewhere, Pie (p146) in Fremont cooks up some excellent crusty fare, and Belltown's La Vita é Bella (p89) is a traditional family-friendly Italian trattoria. Every youthful visitor to Seattle should be allowed at least one 'treat' from Top Pot Hand-Forged Doughnuts (p86) – preferably for breakfast. Ivar's Acres of Clams (p55) makes a good post-aquarium fish-and-chips lunch. Watch out for the hungry seagulls!

Tours

Seattle by Foot (p61)

Offers a special Seattle Kids Tour, two hours of educational fun involving art, music and chocolate. Prices are from $100 per family. Reserve ahead.

Ride the Ducks of Seattle (p95)

A local version of a popular national brand famous for its use of amphibious buses on land and water. Its standard 90-minute Seattle tour takes in Pike Place, Pioneer Square, the waterfront, the Seattle Center and Fremont, before going for a quick dip in Lake Union. Drivers add humorous commentary.

Outdoor Activities

Discovery Park (p155)

There are sometimes organized nature walks in the park; check schedules at the Environmental Learning Center.

Otherwise this giant green space has a kids' play area, wonderful beachcombing opportunities and several miles of safe trails.

Hiram M Chittenden Locks (p156)

Watch the boats traverse the locks and see the fish ladder. The adjacent park is good for a picnic, weather permitting.

Center for Wooden Boats (p99)

You can sail model boats on the pond in Lake Union Park at weekends from 11am to 2pm. The center also offers free sailboat rides (first come, first served) on Lake Union on Sunday (sign-up from 10am).

Cycling the Burke-Gilman Trail

Recycled Cycles (p140) in the U District rents trail-a-bikes or trailers (chariots) so you can cycle safely with your kids.

Alki Beach Park (p170)

The main part of West Seattle's beach is sandy – ideal for sandcastle building and all of those other timeworn seaside pleasures. There are good tide pools further west around the lighthouse.

RYAN C SLIMAK / SHUTTERSTOCK ©

Starfish at Alki Beach (p170)

keyboards, and even form their own band for the special 'On Stage' feature. The elevator ride in the Space Needle (p80) is an adventure and there are plenty of things to press at the top.

Seattle Center

The Seattle Center has the most concentrated stash of kid-friendly activities, including the professional Seattle Children's Theater (p94; performances Thursday to Sunday) and the Children's Museum (p86; better for the under 10s). In the summer, balloon-twisters, singers and dancers entertain the crowds alfresco. Aside from the interesting and educational permanent displays, the Pacific Science Center (p86) has some excellent touring exhibits. Past shows have included Harry Potter movie memorabilia and King Tutankhamun's jewels. In the Museum of Pop Culture (p84) you could fill an afternoon in the Sound Lab, where adults and kids can requisition drum kits, guitars and

Rainy-Day Activities

Seattle Pinball Museum (p69)

Pay $10 to $13 for unlimited use of several dozen pinball machines (stools are available for the vertically challenged and snacks are sold). The catch: getting your kid out afterward!

Museum of Flight (p169)

Huge museum with plenty of interactive exhibits, including a flight simulator.

Museum of History & Industry (p98)

Learn about Seattle's past through film, music, quizzes and questions.

RICHARD ROSS / GETTY IMAGES ©

Risotto featuring Seattle's renowned local seafood

Eating

If you want to get a real taste for eating in Seattle, dip your metaphorical finger into Pike Place Market. This clamorous confederation of small-time farmers, artisan bakers, cheese producers, fishers and family-run fruit stalls is the gastronomic bonanza that every locavore dreams about, and its cheap, sustainable, locally produced food ends up on the tables of just about every Seattle restaurant that matters.

What is Northwest Cuisine?

A lot of Seattle's gourmet restaurants describe their food as 'Northwest cuisine.' Its cornerstone is high-quality regional ingredients that grow abundantly in Washington State: seafood so fresh it squirms, fat berries freshly plucked, mushrooms dug out of the rich soil and a cornucopia of fruit and vegetables. Another distinguishing feature is pan-Asian cooking, often referred to as Pacific Rim cuisine or fusion food. The blending of American or European standards with ingredients from Asia, it results in some unusual combi-

nations – don't be surprised if you get wasabi on your French fries.

Things Seattle Does Well

Surrounded by water, Seattle is an obvious powerhouse of fresh seafood. Local favorites include Dungeness crab, salmon, halibut, oysters, spot prawns and clams.

Although it's not one of the most cosmopolitan cities in the US, Seattle has a sizable Chinese population and a strong selection of dim sum restaurants in the International District (ID). The ID also harbors a good cluster of Vietnamese restaurants in its 'Little Saigon' quarter.

Seattle's Italian restaurants are often highly progressive, many of them specializing in regional food such as Roman or Piedmontese. Chef Ethan Stowell has successfully married Italian cuisine with Northwest traditions and popularized the use of homemade pasta.

Other genres in which Seattle excels are bakeries (a by-product of its cafe culture), Japanese food (the sushi is unwaveringly good) and – perhaps surprisingly – spicy Ethiopian food; the bulk of the East African restaurants are in the Central District (CD). Many visitors from the South comment on the dearth of Mexican restaurants, but the city (especially Ballard) has experienced a rash of recent openings. While the Indian fare can't compete with that found in Vancouver, the appearance of Nirmal's (p72) in Pioneer Square has upped the ante.

Seattle also loves a good steak – especially one that's led a happy, grass-fed life on a farm just outside of town. The city's latest food fashion is crusty sweet or savory pies, with several new restaurants dedicating themselves exclusively to the genre.

Mold-Breaking Chefs

Tom Douglas The biggest name on the Seattle food scene, Douglas helped define what people mean when they talk about Northwest cuisine. He opened his first restaurant, Dahlia, in 1989 and has since followed it with 16 more. Douglas won the prestigious James Beard Award for Best Restaurateur in 2012 and once battled Masaharu Morimoto in an episode of *Iron Chef America* – and won.

Ethan Stowell With 12 Seattle restaurants, Stowell is now considered an established star. His specialty is marrying creative Italian cuisine with classic Northwest ingredients, especially seafood.

Matt Dillon Seattle's most devotedly sustainable chef owns a farm on Vashon Island and is a strong proponent of food foraging. In 2012 he shared James Beard honors with Tom Douglas when he won the Best Northwest Chef award. His don't-miss restaurant is Sitka & Spruce (p114), where pretty much all the ingredients are local.

Eating by Neighborhood

➡ **Downtown, Pike Place & Waterfront (p50)** Enjoy fine dining in downtown; grab cheap, on-the-go, artisan food at Pike Place Market.

NEED TO KNOW

Price Ranges

The following price ranges refer to the average cost of a main dish:

$ less than $15

$$ $15–$25

$$$ more than $25

Opening Hours

Breakfast is typically served from 7am to 11am, brunch from 7am to 3pm, lunch from 11:30am to 2:30pm and dinner from 5:30pm to 10pm.

Reservations

Most Seattle restaurants don't require bookings, but the hot new places fill up quickly, so it's best to call ahead or book online if you want to be sure to avoid disappointment.

Tipping

Tips are not figured into the check at a restaurant. In general, 15% is the baseline tip, but 20% is usually more appropriate, 25% if you enjoyed the service.

➡ **Pioneer Square, International District & SoDo (p70)** New veg-friendly bistros and old steakhouses dot Pioneer Square; Vietnamese food and dim sum characterize the ID.

➡ **Belltown & Seattle Center (p86)** Vies with Capitol Hill for Seattle's best selection of restaurants covering every genre and budget.

➡ **Capitol Hill & First Hill (p112)** All over the map, with Seattle's hottest chefs competing alongside the next big thing.

➡ **The CD, Madrona & Madison Park (p125)** A plateful of surprises that'll satisfy everyone from French haute cuisine snobs to soul-food purists.

➡ **U District (p134)** Cheap, no-frills, ethnic food that's kind to vegetarians.

➡ **Green Lake & Fremont (p146)** Fremont specializes in unusual noncorporate fast food; Green Lake exhibits warm, family-friendly restaurants.

➡ **Ballard & Discovery Park (p158)** Seafood, with some cool Mexican places making an interesting cameo.

Lonely Planet's Top Choices

Sitka & Spruce (p114) If you had to sum up Seattle cuisine in three words, this is it.

Cascina Spinasse (p115) Could be the best Italian food you taste outside Italy.

Bakery Nouveau (p172) Destination bakery that's worth crossing town to West Seattle for – now in Capitol Hill too!

Paseo (p146) Extraordinary Cuban sandwiches and exquisite rice and beans at giveaway prices.

Best by Budget

$

Crumpet Shop (p52) Pike Place phenomenon where thick toppings are lashed on homemade crumpets.

Piroshky Piroshky (p52) Russian buns are rolled in the window of this Pike Place Market hole-in-the-wall.

Top Pot Hand-Forged Doughnuts (p86) The champagne of doughnuts.

Bakery Nouveau (p172) Best bakery this side of...Paris.

$$

Café Campagne (p53) French cuisine that stands an Eiffel Tower above all its competitors.

Serious Pie (p88) Seriously good pizzas with novel toppings.

Wild Ginger (p54) Asian fusion with style and a kick.

Portage Bay Cafe (p134) Astoundingly good brunch.

$$$

Sitka & Spruce (p114) The shrine for all locavores.

Cascina Spinasse (p115) Italian nosh that's worth the extra investment.

Canlis (p101) Queen Anne's oasis of 'posh' with food to boot.

The Whale Wins (p147) A new vegetable-friendly haven of good taste.

Best by Cuisine

Asian

Wild Ginger (p54) All kinds of Asian cuisine under the same downtown roof.

Green Leaf (p72) Vietnamese hole-in-the-wall that's become something of a city legend.

Shiro's Sushi Restaurant (p89) Japanese food as art in the heart of Belltown.

Jade Garden (p72) The best in dim sum in the International District.

Seafood

Walrus & the Carpenter (p162) Ballard oyster bar where they serve 'em raw with white wine.

Steelhead Diner (p54) Located in Pike Place Market, with fresh fish bought yards from your plate.

Ivar's Acres of Clams (p55) Fish-and-chips the old-fashioned way.

Pike Place Chowder (p52) Pike Place institution where there's always 40 people queuing for four tables.

Italian

Cascina Spinasse (p115) Relaxed but classy purveyor of Piedmontese food.

Pink Door Ristorante (p53) Where else can you eat *linguine alle vongole* with a trapeze artist flying over your head?

Vendemmia (p128) New intimate nook lighting up 34th Ave in Madrona.

Tavolàta (p88) Northwest meets Italian cuisine over an open kitchen in Belltown.

Best New Restaurants

Nirmal's (p72) Putting Indian food on the map in Pioneer Square.

The Whale Wins (p147) Plenty of fish but no whales in this rural-kitchen-style place on the Fremont–Wallingford border.

Vendemmia (p128) Refined Italian restaurant with homemade pasta in Madrona.

Simply Soulful (p125) Check out this new purveyor of grits and gumbo in Madison Valley.

Best Restaurants with a View

Canlis (p101) Up on Queen Anne Hill, Canlis overlooks the watery action of Lake Union below.

Ray's Boathouse (p163) Fine dining on Puget Sound where shimmering water views add a sparkle on sunny days.

Salty's on Alki (p172) Top-notch food overlooking Elliott Bay with the Seattle skyline as a backdrop.

Cutter's Crabhouse (p54) Ferries, gulls and snowcapped mountains enhance the food experience at this waterfront crab restaurant.

Drinking & Nightlife

It's hard to complain too much about Seattle's crappy weather when the two best forms of rainy-day solace – coffee and beer – are available in such abundance. No doubt about it, Seattle's an inviting place to enjoy a drink, whatever your poison. Adding fresh flavors to an already complex brew is a new obsession with micro-distilleries and cider houses.

Coffee Culture

When the first Starbucks opened in Pike Place Market in 1971, Seattle was suddenly the center of the coffee universe. It still is, although these days Starbucks is loved and loathed in equal measure.

After Starbucks came the 'third wave': coffee shops that buy fair-trade coffee with traceable origins and concoct it through a micro-managed in-house roasting process that pays attention to everything from the coffee's bean quality to its 'taste notes.' These shops are now as ubiquitous as Starbucks, though they remain independent and adhere strictly to their original manifesto: quality not quantity.

Macro Amounts of Microbrews

The microbrew explosion rocked the Northwest around the same time as the gourmet-coffee craze, but not coincidentally: Seattle's Redhook Brewery was cofounded in 1981 by Gordon Bowker, one of the guys who founded Starbucks.

Most local microbreweries started out as tiny craft breweries that produced European-style ales. Many of these small producers initially lacked the capital to offer their brews for sale anywhere but in the brewery building itself, hence the term brewpub – an informal pub with its own on-site brewery.

Though you can find microbrews at practically every bar in town, brewpubs often feature signature beers and ales not available anywhere else. It's worth asking about specialty brews or seasonal beers on tap. Most of the brewpubs offer a taster's selection of the house brews. Pints range in price from $4 to $6, so a sampler can be good value if you're not sure what you like.

Drinking & Nightlife by Neighborhood

→ **Downtown, Pike Place & Waterfront (p55)** Hotel bars and pleasant old-school drinking nooks tucked away in Pike Place.

→ **Pioneer Square, International District & SoDo (p73)** Gritty saloons in Pioneer Square; bubble tea and restaurant lounges in the ID.

→ **Belltown & Seattle Center (p91)** Belltown's bar-hopping, late-night drinking scene is not as grungy as it once was.

→ **Capitol Hill & First Hill (p115)** *The* place for a night out, with gay bars, dive bars, cocktail lounges and third-wave coffee shops.

→ **U District (p137)** No-frills dives and a plethora of coffee shops designed for the laptop crowd.

→ **Green Lake & Fremont (p148)** Mix of new-ish brewpubs and old-school neighborhood pubs.

→ **Ballard & Discovery Park (p163)** Beer heaven, with old-fashioned pubs sitting alongside boisterous brewpubs and cozy nano-breweries.

→ **Georgetown & West Seattle (p173)** Blue-collar pubs reborn as bohemian Georgetown bars.

NEED TO KNOW

Opening Hours

This is caffeine-addicted Seattle, so some coffee bars open as early as 5am and close at around 11pm, but 7am until 6pm is more standard. Bars usually serve from lunchtime until 2am (when state liquor laws demand they stop selling booze), although some don't open until 5pm and others start as early as 7am.

Ha-Ha-Happy Hours

The term 'happy hour' is a misnomer: most Seattle bars run their happy hours from around 3pm until 6pm. As well as reductions in drink prices, some bars also offer happy-hour deals on bar snacks, appetizers or even full-blown meals.

Lonely Planet's Top Choices

Zeitgeist Coffee (p73) Best coffee in Seattle? Go and find out!

Fremont Brewing Company (p148) The secret's in the hops.

Bookstore Bar (p57) Buy a scotch; snuggle down with a great novel.

Owl & Thistle (p57) No one does pubs like the Irish.

Best Coffee Bars

Zeitgeist Coffee (p73) At Zeitgeist it's all about the coffee – and the gorgeous almond croissants.

Espresso Vivace at Brix (p115) Drink coffee, listen to the Ramones, see the latest in lopsided haircuts.

Milstead & Co (p148) Multiroaster in Fremont choosing the best coffee on the market; menu changes daily.

Victrola Coffee Roasters (p115) When hipsters go to heaven they probably get teleported to Victrola in Capitol Hill.

Best Brewpubs & Tasting Rooms

Fremont Brewing Company (p148) New old-school brewery where you can taste beer at wooden tables on the factory floor.

Pike Pub & Brewery (p55) One of the oldest and most cherished brewpubs in Seattle.

Optimism Brewing Co (p116) At long last, a new industrial-style brewery and tasting room on Capitol Hill.

Machine House Brewery (p173) Small friendly peddler of British-style ales in an old Georgetown beer factory.

Best LGBTIQ Bars

Wildrose (p117) Lesbian pub in Capitol Hill.

R Place (p117) Flamboyant performers and tactile regulars.

Re-Bar (p91) What? A gay club that's not in Capitol Hill?

Outwest Bar (p174) West Seattle, mellow, LGBT outpost.

Best Dive Bars

Blue Moon (p137) Romanticism with a rough edge in poets' haven in the U District.

Shorty's (p91) Pinball, hot dogs, punk rock and beer – a devastating combination in Belltown.

Five Point Café (p92) That stale-beer smell has been there since 1929.

Monkey Pub (p138) A dive by nature not design in the U District.

Café Racer (p138) Improv jazz, eccentric decor and a bad art museum are just three of the flavors in this U District dive.

Best Old-Fashioned Pubs

Owl & Thistle (p57) Genuine Irish pub with good music and cheap fish-and-chips.

Canterbury Ale House (p117) Old-school haven with trivia nights in trendy Capitol Hill.

McGilvra's (p130) Boozy backdrop to Madison Beach with a strong neighborhood feel.

George & Dragon Pub (p150) Seattle's most Anglophile pub, with a high percentage of limeys.

⭐ Entertainment

Quietly aggrieved that it was being bypassed by big-name touring acts in the 1980s, Seattle shut itself away and created its own live-music scene. This explosive grassroots movement is backed up by plenty of other artistic strands, including independent cinema, burlesque theater, bookshop poetry readings and some high-profile opera, classical music and drama.

Live Music

For simplicity's sake, Seattle's music venues can be stacked in a kind of triangular tower. At the summit sits the 17,000-capacity Key Arena (p95). Below this is a trio of medium-sized historic theaters: the 2807-capacity Paramount (p59), the 1800-capacity Moore (p93), dating from 1907, and the 1137-capactiy Showbox (p59), dating from 1939. Next is a handful of more clamorous venues, small enough to foster the close band-audience interaction that was so crucial in the development of Seattle's 1990s music revolution. Some of these '90s bastions still exist, though in a more sanitized form. Still pulling less-mainstream big-name acts are the 560-capacity Crocodile (p93) in Belltown and 650-capacity Neumo's (p117) in Capitol Hill.

Hosting lesser known local talent are various venues such as Ballard's 360-capacity Tractor Tavern (p165) and Fremont's High Dive (p150). At the bottom of the triangle are the ubiquitous pubs, clubs and coffee bars that showcase small-time local talent from Irish fiddlers to Björk-like singers. Seattle has two jazz venues: Tula's (p94) and Dimitriou's Jazz Alley (p93). For a swankier dinner-show scene, hit downtown's Triple Door (p58).

The Arts

Seattle is a book-loving town and there's a literary event practically every night. The film industry also has a national stature. The **Seattle International Film Festival** (SIFF; www. siff.net; ☉May–Jun) is among the most influential festivals in the country, and a thriving independent scene has sprung up in a handful of underground venues. Theater runs the gamut from big productions, such as Ibsen at the Intiman (p94), to staged readings of obscure texts in cobbled-together venues or coffee shops. The Seattle Symphony (p58) has become nationally known and widely respected, primarily through its excellent recordings. For current entertainment listings, scour the *Stranger* (www.thestranger.com) or *Seattle Weekly* (www.seattleweekly.com).

Entertainment by Neighborhood

➡ **Downtown, Pike Place & Waterfront (p58)** Classical music and historic Showbox theater in downtown.

➡ **Pioneer Square, International District & SoDo (p75)** Comedy shows and a few tough pubs peddling punk and metal.

➡ **Belltown & Seattle Center (p93)** Alt-rock and jazz venues in Belltown; opera, ballet and theater in Seattle Center.

➡ **Queen Anne & Lake Union (p104)** Fringe theater and hallowed rock venues such as El Corazon.

➡ **Capitol Hill & First Hill (p117)** Everything outside the mainstream, including alt-rock and electronica.

➡ **U District (p138)** Small pub strummers and stand-up comedy plus name acts at the revived Neptune Theater.

➡ **Green Lake & Fremont (p150)** Intimate High Dive and Nectar Lounge in Fremont book small-name live acts.

➡ **Ballard & Discovery Park (p165)** Pubs and clubs plus the Sunset and Tractor taverns cement a good live-music scene.

NEED TO KNOW

Opening Hours

Typically, live music starts between 9pm and 10pm and goes until 1am or 2am. For most venues you can pay admission at the door; for a small to medium-size venue, the cover charge can be anywhere from $5 to $15.

Tickets & Reservations

Tickets for big events are available through **Ticket-Master** (www.ticketmaster.com). **Brown Paper Tickets** (☎800-838-3006; www.brownpapertickets.com) handles sales for a number of smaller and quirkier venues, from theater to live music. Alternatively, you can often book via the venue website.

Lonely Planet's Top Choices

Crocodile (p93) Even 25 years on, it hasn't lost its ability to rock and roll.

Dimitriou's Jazz Alley (p93) Be-bopping the crowds in Belltown since 1985.

Seattle International Film Festival (p29) One of the best and most multifarious film festivals in the US.

Benaroya Concert Hall (p47) The spectacular HQ for Seattle's prestigious symphony orchestra.

Best Live-Music Venues

Crocodile (p93) Nationally renowned midsize live venue that helped promote grunge.

Neumo's (p117) The other pillar of Seattle's dynamic scene has updated and remains relevant.

McCaw Hall (p93) Go and hear the Seattle Opera raise the roof.

Chop Suey (p118) Diverse selection of live acts, with indie alternating with hip-hop.

Tractor Tavern (p165) The anchor of Ballard's live scene specializes in alt country.

Best Cinemas

Grand Illusion Cinema (p138) Tiny U District nook run by passionate film buffs.

Cinerama (p93) This unique curved screen is the best place to see the latest blockbuster.

Fremont Almost Free Outdoor Cinema (p150) Hedonistic summer cinema with lots of audience participation.

Northwest Film Forum (p118) Arts-club feel lends expertise to this film geek's heaven.

Central Cinema (p130) Only cinema in Seattle that brings in food and drink as you watch the movie.

Best Theaters

A Contemporary Theatre (p58) With its central stage and gilded decor, this is Seattle's best all-round theater.

On the Boards (p104) Cutting-edge contemporary drama in Queen Anne.

Jewel Box Theater (p93) Small gem specializing in burlesque hidden in a Belltown cocktail bar.

Paramount Theater (p59) Touring Broadway shows.

Best Small Live Venues

Espresso Vivace at Brix (p115) Hip coffee bar where local bands play regular laid-back sets.

High Dive (p150) Small Fremont dive for up-and-coming bands.

Nectar Lounge (p150) Early promoter of Seattle's now-famous hip-hop scene.

Owl & Thistle (p57) Downtown Irish pub with fine fiddlers and folk music.

University of Washington Huskies, Husky Stadium (p139)

Sports & Activities

Never mind the rain – that's why Gore-Tex was invented. When you live this close to the mountains, not to mention all that water and an impressive mélange of parks, it's just criminal not to get outdoors, come rain, hail or shine. Seattle is rare for a large city in that many forms of outdoor recreation are available within the city itself.

Spectator Sports

With state-of-the-art stadiums and teams that have recently won with a lot of glory, Seattle is a great town in which to watch the pros play. College games, too, are hugely popular with locals and a fun way to spend an afternoon.

Formed in 1977 and former tenants of the erstwhile Kingdome, the beloved **Seattle Mariners** (Map p234; www.mariners.org; tickets $7-60; Stadium) baseball team play at Safeco Field. They have yet to win a World Series title.

The Northwest's only National Football League (NFL) franchise, the **Seattle Seahawks** (Map p234; www.seahawks.com; tickets $42-95; Stadium) play in 72,000-seat CenturyLink Field. The team has contested the Super Bowl twice in recent years, winning Super Bowl XLVIII in February 2014.

The **University of Washington Huskies** (Map p248; 206-543-2200; www.gohuskies.com; University of Washington) football and basketball teams are another Seattle obsession. The Huskies football team plays at 70,000-capacity Husky Stadium and you'll find the men's and women's basketball

NEED TO KNOW

Buying Tickets

You can buy tickets either in person at the box offices (at CenturyLink Field for soccer and American football, at Safeco Field for baseball), or online through **TicketMaster** (www.ticketmaster.com).

Costs

The following is a price guide for tickets to see Seattle's three main pro sports teams: the Mariners (baseball), the Sounders (soccer) and the Seahawks (American football).

➡ Mariners – from $12 to $75
➡ Sounders – from $28 to $112
➡ Seahawks – from $66 to $300

Planning Ahead

Seattle's pro sports teams enjoy fanatical support and games regularly sell out. It is wise to book weeks, if not months, ahead. For match schedules, check the club websites.

➡ Seattle Sounders (p32)
➡ Seattle Seahawks (p31)
➡ Seattle Mariners (p31)

teams at the Hec Edmundson Pavilion, both of which are on campus. The women's basketball team draws massive crowds.

Reincarnated in 2008, soccer team the **Seattle Sounders** (Map p234; ☑206-622-3415; www.seattlesounders.net; tickets from $37; ⛹Stadium) has fanatical supporters and lots of 'em: 67,000 once attended a friendly against Manchester United. Highly successful, they share digs at CenturyLink Field with the Seahawks. The soccer season runs May to mid-September.

Activities

ON THE WATER

Seeing Seattle from the water is a surefire way to fall in love with the city. A number of places rent kayaks and canoes, or you can arrange a guided tour through the Northwest Outdoor Center (p105), the Agua Verde Paddle Club (p140) or the Moss Bay Rowing & Kayak Center (p105). The Center for Wooden Boats (p99) on Lake Union offers sailing lessons, sailboat rentals and free 45-minute sailboat rides every Sunday morning (first come, first served).

The calmest, safest places to launch are Green Lake, Lake Union or near the water-taxi dock in Seacrest Park in West Seattle. If you're not confident, take a lesson. Several of the rental companies in Green Lake, Westlake (Lake Union) and the U District offer instruction from around $60 per hour.

Seattle's chilly waters are good for diving, with regular sightings of octopus, huge ling cod, cabezon, cathedral-like white anemones and giant sea stars. Most of the area's best dive sites are outside of Seattle, in sheltered coves and bays up and down the coast. Popular spots include Alki Cove, on the eastern side of Alki Point; Saltwater State Park, south of Seattle in Des Moines; and Edmonds Underwater Park near the Edmonds Ferry Dock, north of Seattle.

CYCLING

Despite frequent rain and hilly terrain, cycling is still a major form of both transportation and recreation in the Seattle area. In 2014, the city finally inaugurated a public bike-sharing scheme known as Pronto (p214).

In the city, commuter bike lanes are painted green on many streets, city trails are well maintained, and the friendly and enthusiastic cycling community is happy to share the road. The wildly popular 20-mile **Burke-Gilman Trail** winds from Ballard to Log Boom Park in Kenmore on Seattle's Eastside. There, it connects with the 11-mile long **Sammamish River Trail**, which winds past the Chateau Ste Michelle winery in Woodinville before terminating at Redmond's Marymoor Park.

Other good places to cycle are around Green Lake (congested), at Alki Beach (sublime) or, closer to downtown, through scenic Myrtle Edwards Park. The latter trail continues through Interbay to Ballard, where it links with the Burke-Gilman.

Anyone planning on cycling in Seattle should pick up a copy of the *Seattle Bicycling Guide Map*, published by the City of Seattle's Transportation Bicycle & Pedestrian Program and available online (www.cityofseattle.net/transportation/bikemaps.htm) or at bike shops.

GOLF

Seattle Parks & Recreation (☑206-684-4075; www.cityofseattle.net/parks) operates four public golf courses in Seattle, along with a short (nine-hole) pitch-and-putt course located at Green Lake (p152), a fun spot to go if you're just learning, or lack the patience or experience to go a full round. Green fees for the **Jefferson Park Golf Course** (☎206-762-4513; www.premiergc.com; 4101 Beacon Ave S; 18 holes $35-40; ⊙hours vary; 🖳36) in Beacon Hill and West Seattle Golf Course (p175) start at around $35, more at weekends. When they're not booked, the courses also offer reduced rates in the evenings.

HIKING

In Seattle, it's possible to hike (or run) wilderness trails without ever leaving the city. Seward Park, east of Georgetown, offers several miles of trails in a remnant of the area's old-growth forest, and an even more extensive network of trails is available in 534-acre Discovery Park (p155), northwest of downtown. At the northern edge of Washington Park Arboretum (p124), Foster Island has a 20-minute wetlands trail winding through marshlands created upon the opening of the Lake Washington Ship Canal. This is also a great place for bird-watching, fishing and swimming.

RUNNING

With its many parks, Seattle provides a number of good trails for runners. If you're in the downtown area, the trails along Myrtle Edwards Park (p85) – just north of the waterfront along Elliott Bay – make for a nice run, affording views over the Sound and of the downtown skyline. Green Lake includes two paths: the 2.75-mile paved path immediately surrounding the lake and a less crowded, unpaved path going around the perimeter of the park. The Washington Park Arboretum (p124) is another good choice for running, as the trails lead through some beautiful trees and flower gardens. The trails in the arboretum connect to the Lake Washington Blvd trail system, which extends all the way south to Seward Park, just in case you happen to be training for a marathon.

SWIMMING

When summer temperatures rise, there's no more popular place to be than on one of Seattle's beaches. One of the most visited is Alki Beach (p170) in West Seattle, a real scene with beach volleyball, acres of flesh and teenagers cruising in their cars. Beware: the seawater here is cold! For freshwater, Green Lake Park (p145) has two lakefront swimming and sunbathing beaches, as do several parks along the western shores of Lake Washington, including Madison Park (p124), Madrona Park (p124), Seward Park, Magnuson Park and Mt Baker Park. Lifeguards are on duty at public beaches between 11am and 8pm mid-June to Labor Day (beginning of September).

Some of the larger hotels in downtown have small swimming pools.

Sports & Activities by Neighborhood

➡ **Downtown, Pike Place & Waterfront (p62)** Bike-tour companies and hotel gyms.

➡ **Pioneer Square, International District & SoDo (p77)** Home of Seattle's two pro sports stadiums.

➡ **Belltown & Seattle Center (p95)** Free yoga classes in the Olympic Sculpture Park during summer months.

➡ **Queen Anne & Lake Union (p105)** Multiple water activities available on Lake Union and a multipurpose path that circumnavigates the lake.

➡ **Capitol Hill & First Hill (p119)** Tennis courts and baseball diamonds in Cal Anderson Park; paths for jogging and strolling in Volunteer Park.

➡ **The CD, Madrona & Madison Park (p130)** Parks, beaches and waterside attractions on Lake Washington.

➡ **U District (p140)** Cycling on the Burke-Gilman Trail; boating access on Lake Union; Husky Stadium for college football.

➡ **Green Lake & Fremont (p152)** Jogging, cycling and boating bonanza around Green Lake.

➡ **Ballard & Discovery Park (p166)** Two wild waterside parks and a climbing center.

➡ **Georgetown & West Seattle (p175)** Cycling, kayaking, swimming and in-line skating along Alki Beach.

Shopping

Seattle, like any big US city, has a whole range of big-name stores. You won't have to look for them — they'll find you. More interesting, unique and precious are the quirky, one-of-a-kind shops hidden away in some half-forgotten back alley with a spray-painted sign. The city's tour de force is its bookstores and record stores, surely some of the best in the nation.

Independent Bookstores

Ironically, the city that spawned Amazon guards one of the best collections of indie bookstores in the US. Established local operators include University Book Store (p139), a veritable book emporium founded in 1900 that offers the kind of well-informed personal touches that online shopping can never replicate. Equally revered is Elliott Bay Book Company (p118), where a tranquil cafe, a team of well-read staff and regular author signings provide multiple excuses to linger. Lower down the food chain are more specialist booksellers such as Metsker Maps (p59), for travel-related books, and Fantagraphics (p174), for graphic novels and comic strips. In 2015, Seattle prepared itself for the ultimate oxymoron when Amazon opened its first brick-and-mortar bookstore in the U District. With print book sales on the rise for the first time in over a decade, it was proof that bookstores can and will survive.

Viva Vinyl

Vinyl dead? Think again. Sales have been rising in the US since the mid-2000s. The word on the street is that Seattle has more record stores than any other US city, and with such a weighty musical legacy to call upon, who's arguing? Every neighborhood has its favorite independent dealer; some are encyclopedic, others the size of an average student bedroom. What record stores offer over online deals is atmosphere, expertise and extras.

West Seattle's Easy Street Records (p175) has long been a destination store for collectors and has its own cafe; Ballard's Sonic Boom (p165) hosts live in-house bands, publishes a weekly Top 25 chart and sells gig tickets; while Fremont's Jive Time (p151) is geek heaven, selling bargain secondhand rarities and old, yellowed music magazines.

Shopping by Neighborhood

➡ **Downtown, Pike Place & Waterfront (p59)** Big-name brands in downtown; small-time no-brands in Pike Place; tourist kitsch on the waterfront.

➡ **Pioneer Square, International District & SoDo (p75)** Expensive antiques and carpets in Pioneer Square; cheap Asian supermarkets in the ID.

➡ **Capitol Hill & First Hill (p118)** Huge selection of indie boutiques, esoterica, sex toys, and one of the nation's best bookstores.

➡ **U District (p139)** Cheap vintage clothing for tight student budgets and abundant bookstores for fact-hungry undergraduates.

➡ **Green Lake & Fremont (p151)** Junk stores and vintage-clothing shops being gradually pushed out by fancier boutiques.

➡ **Ballard & Discovery Park (p165)** Card-game emporium, weird T-shirt prints, rare vinyl and artsy Sunday market stalls.

Lonely Planet's Top Choices

Elliott Bay Book Company (p118) Great books, top readings and snug on-site cafe.

Bop Street Records (p165) Every musical genre, overseen by passionate staff.

REI (p104) The original and best of the outdoor outfitters.

Market Magic (p60) Classic Pike Place Market throwback.

Best Vintage Clothes

Fremont Vintage Mall (p151) There's a bit of vintage everything here, including clothes.

Revival (p119) Vintage jewels hand-picked by the owner.

Throwbacks NW (p119) Novel vintage-sportswear shop.

Crossroads Trading Co (p119) Used-clothing store with lower hipster quotient.

Best Markets

Pike Place Market (p42) No intro required – lose yourself for a day, at least!

U District Farmers Market (p136) Produce-only market that's been running since 1993.

Ballard Farmers Market (p166) With food and some crafts, this is *the* place to go on a Sunday.

Melrose Market (p114) Attractive sustainable market plying high-end food products in the Pike–Pine corridor.

Best Bookstores

Elliott Bay Book Company (p118) Best bookstore in the

nation? Add it to the list of contenders.

University Book Store (p139) Everything you need to pass your degree.

Ada's Technical Books & Cafe (p118) New-ish book specialist in Capitol Hill with beautiful decor and fine cafe.

Left Bank Books (p60) Just in case you lost your copy of *Das Kapital.*

Best Esoterica

Market Magic (p60) Everything the young aspiring magician could dream of.

Tenzing Momo (p60) Atmospheric apothecary where you expect to see Professor Snape jump out from behind the counter.

Card Kingdom (p165) Interactive games emporium in Ballard that could delay you for... oh...hours.

Babeland (p119) Classy sex-toy boutique in – where else? – Capitol Hill.

Best Shopping Strips

Pike Place Market (p42) Support your local farmer/craftsperson/third-generation store owner in Seattle's bustling heart.

Downtown (p59) Big-name stores deliver the goods in the city's retail core.

Broadway (p118) Check your hipster rating by going shopping on Capitol Hill's main strip.

'The Ave' (p138) A dearth of designer labels but an abundance of welcome bargains beckon in the U District.

NEED TO KNOW

Opening Hours

Shops are usually open from 9am or 10am to 5pm or 6pm (9pm in shopping malls) Monday to Friday, as well as noon to 5pm or so (later in malls) on weekends. Some places, like record stores and bookstores, may keep later hours, such as from noon to 8pm or 9pm.

Taxes & Refunds

A 9.6% sales tax is added to all purchases except food to be prepared for consumption (ie groceries). Unlike the European VAT or Canadian GST, the sales tax is not refundable to tourists.

Best Record Stores

Bop Street Records (p165) Astounding array of every musical genre known to Homo sapiens.

Easy Street Records & Café (p175) Drink coffee, imbibe beer, eat snacks and...oh...browse excellent records.

Georgetown Records (p174) Rare picture-cover 45s and vintage LPs next door to Fantagraphics comic shop.

Singles Going Steady (p95) If this name means anything to you, this punkish record shop is your nirvana.

PLAN YOUR TRIP SHOPPING

LONNIE GORSLINE / SHUTTERSTOCK ©

Explore Seattle

SEATTLE'S TOP SIGHTS

Neighborhoods at a Glance

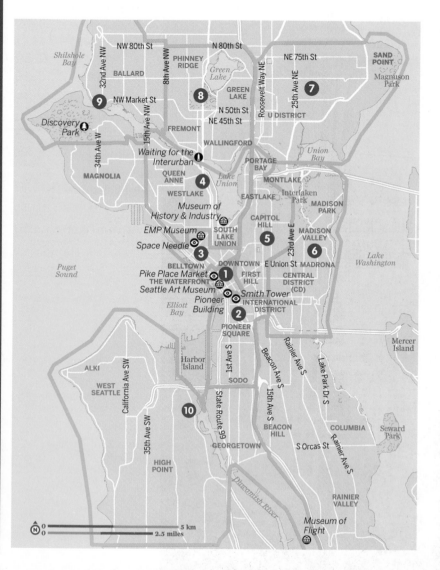

❶ Downtown, Pike Place & Waterfront p40

Downtown is a standard American amalgam of boxy skyscrapers and brand-name shopping opportunities that's given welcome oomph by Pike Place Market, the city's heart, soul and number-one must-see sight. The waterfront, blemished since the 1950s by the soon-to-be-demolished Alaskan Way Viaduct, is undergoing a slow regeneration.

❷ Pioneer Square, International District & SoDo p63

Seattle's birthplace retains the grit of its 'Skid Row' roots with historic architecture and a rambunctious street life tempered by art galleries and locavore restaurants. The International District broadcasts its scruffy cosmopolitanism with dim sum and *pho* restaurants. SoDo is a warehouse district that's attracting new businesses and pot shops.

❸ Belltown & Seattle Center p78

Where industry once fumed, condos now rise in the thin, walkable strip of Belltown. The neighborhood gained a reputation for trendsetting nightlife (read: grunge) in the 1990s, but these days it's renowned for its 100-plus restaurants. The Seattle Center's frequent makeovers have kept it vital and relevant.

❹ Queen Anne & Lake Union p96

Salubrious Queen Anne hoards old money in beautiful fin-de-siècle mansions. Lake Union's southern shores are changing more quickly than the fresh-faced influx of techies can tweet about them, with clean-lined restaurants, a congestion-easing streetcar and the sprawling campus of Amazon.com.

❺ Capitol Hill & First Hill p108

Capitol Hill is Seattle's most unashamedly hip neighborhood where the rich mix with the eccentric. While some of its tattier edges are being gentrified, this is still Seattle's best crash-pad for dive-bar rock-and-roll, LGBTIQ frivolities and easy-on-the-environment lunches. More straitlaced First Hill is home to an art museum and multiple hospitals.

❻ The CD, Madrona & Madison Park p122

Seattle's sometimes gritty Central District (CD) is a traditionally African American neighborhood diversified by an influx of Ethiopian immigrants, which has recently shown signs of gentrification. Madison Park and Madrona are upscale lakeside communities with popular beaches and parks.

❼ U District p131

This neighborhood of young, studious out-of-towners places the beautiful, leafy University of Washington campus next to the shabbier 'Ave,' an eclectic strip of cheap boutiques, dive bars and ethnic restaurants.

❽ Green Lake & Fremont p141

Fremont pitches young hipsters among old hippies, and vies with Capitol Hill as Seattle's most irreverent neighborhood, with junk shops, urban sculpture and a healthy sense of its own ludicrousness. Family-friendly Green Lake is a more affluent suburb centered on a park and favored by fitness devotees.

❾ Ballard & Discovery Park p153

A former seafaring community with Nordic heritage, Ballard still feels like a small town engulfed by a bigger city. Cool, independent and fortified with a sense of its pioneer history, it's slowly being condo-ized but remains a good place to hit a brewpub or see a band.

❿ Georgetown & West Seattle p167

If you think that Belltown has been bleached of its bohemianism, head to Georgetown, a huddle of mildly disheveled redbrick bars where it's still OK to be weird. West Seattle is a suburban neighborhood revered for its municipal beach and fish-and-chips.

NEIGHBOURHOODS AT A GLANCE

Downtown, Pike Place & Waterfront

PIKE PLACE MARKET | DOWNTOWN | WATERFRONT

Neighborhood Top Five

1 Pike Place Market (p42) Seeing, smelling and tasting the unique energy of this Seattle icon, from the charismatic fish throwers to the creative – but disgusting – gum wall.

2 Seattle Art Museum (p46) Experiencing the latest surprise lighting up this constantly evolving museum.

3 Bainbridge Island ferry (p177) Riding on the Bainbridge Island ferry just for the hell of it (and admiring the amazing views).

4 Seattle Great Wheel (p49) Viewing Seattle's ongoing waterfront regeneration from inside an enclosed pod on this giant wheel.

5 Beecher's Handmade Cheese (p50) Joining the line for take-out mac 'n' cheese at Pike Place Market's artisan cheese phenomenon.

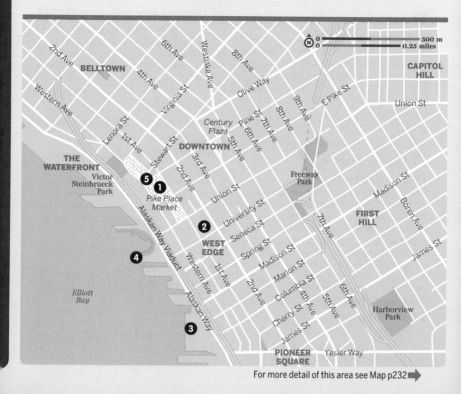

For more detail of this area see Map p232 ➡

Explore: Downtown, Pike Place & Waterfront

You don't have to search long to find Seattle's soul: head directly to Pike Place Market and throw away any map you might have acquired – your nose, eyes and ears are the only compasses you'll need here.

It's particularly important to get to the market early if you want to avoid that cattle-truck feeling (40,000 visitors per day!): weekdays and before 10am on weekends are best. That said, many enjoy the organized chaos of the arcades at Saturday lunchtime. The waterfront is more weather dependent; a sunny weekend afternoon finds it swarming, while on a misty weekday morning you'll have the place pretty much to yourself.

Downtown Seattle, though impressive from a distance, is a bit of an anomaly. Instead of being the beating heart of the city, it's a fairly quiet, functional business district adjacent to Seattle's twin lures: Pike Place Market and Pioneer Sq. What most people mean by 'downtown' is the collection of office buildings, hotels and retail shops between 2nd and 7th Aves. It's best to visit on a weekday, when throngs of people are working and shopping in the area. At night and on weekends it can feel rather desolate.

Downtown is home to much of the city's important architecture. Seattle's retail heaven extends from the corner of 5th Ave and Pike St a few blocks in all directions. A block north, on 5th Ave at Pine St, is the flagship store of Nordstrom, the national clothing retailer that got its start in Seattle. Just to the west is Westlake Center.

Local Life

⇒ **Early-morning market** Get to Pike Place (p42) early and listen to the vendors chitchat as they set up their stalls. Be sure to witness the unique 'market roll call' in the North Arcade, when day-stall vendors are allocated their spaces.

⇒ **Ferry across the Sound** Pretend you're a Puget Sound commuter and stow away on a Bainbridge Island ferry just for the ride.

Getting There & Away

⇒ **Light rail** Sound Transit's Central Link light rail from Sea-Tac Airport has two downtown stations: Westlake, and University St and 3rd Ave.
⇒ **Streetcar** Service to South Lake Union from Westlake.
⇒ **Bus** You can get downtown easily from any part of Seattle by bus.

Lonely Planet's Top Tip

Look down! Seattle's public art extends to its hatch covers (manholes). Nineteen of them have been emblazoned with an imprint of a downtown map with your location marked. It's impossible to get lost.

Best Places to Eat

⇒ Café Campagne (p53)
⇒ Wild Ginger (p54)
⇒ Piroshky Piroshky (p52)
⇒ Pink Door Ristorante (p53)

For reviews, see p50 ⇒

Best Drinking & Nightlife

⇒ Pike Pub & Brewery (p55)
⇒ Storyville Coffee (p56)
⇒ Bookstore Bar (p57)
⇒ Owl & Thistle (p57)
⇒ Zig Zag Café (p56)

For reviews, see p55 ⇒

Best Places to Shop

⇒ Old Seattle Paperworks (p59)
⇒ Pure Food Fish (p60)
⇒ Metsker Maps (p59)
⇒ DeLaurenti's (p52)
⇒ Market Magic (p60)

For reviews, see p59 ⇒

CORIN / SHUTTERSTOCK ©

TOP SIGHT
PIKE PLACE MARKET

A cavalcade of noise, smells, personalities, banter and urban theater sprinkled liberally around a spatially challenged waterside strip, Pike Place Market is Seattle in a bottle. In operation since 1907 and still as soulful today as it was on day one, this wonderfully local experience highlights the city for what it really is: all-embracing, eclectic and proudly unique.

Some History

Pike Place Market is the oldest continuously operating market in the nation. It was established in 1907 to give local farmers a place to sell their fruit and vegetables and bypass the middleman. Soon, the greengrocers made room for fishmongers, bakers, ethnic groceries, butchers, cheese sellers and purveyors of the rest of the Northwest's agricultural bounty. The market wasn't exactly architecturally robust – it's always been a thrown-together warren of sheds and stalls, haphazardly designed for utility – and was by no means an intentional tourist attraction. That came later.

An enthusiastic agricultural community spawned the market's heyday in the 1930s. Many of the first farmers were immigrants, a fact the market celebrates with annual themes acknowledging the contributions of various ethnic groups; past years have featured Japanese Americans, Italian Americans and Sephardic Jewish Americans.

By the 1960s, sales at the market were suffering from suburbanization, the growth of supermarkets and the move away from local, small-scale market gardening. Vast tracts of agricultural land were disappearing, replaced by such ventures as the Northgate Mall and Sea-Tac airport. The internment of Japanese American farmers during WWII had also taken its toll. The entire area became a bowery for the destitute and a center for prostitution and peep shows.

DON'T MISS

➜ Fish throwers
➜ Gum wall
➜ Market roll call
➜ World's oldest Starbucks

PRACTICALITIES

➜ Map p232, C4
➜ www.pikeplace market.org
➜ 85 Pike St
➜ ⊙9am-6pm Mon-Sat, 9am-5pm Sun
➜ ℝWestlake

In the wake of the 1962 World's Fair, plans were drawn up to bulldoze the market and build high-rise office and apartment buildings on this piece of prime downtown real estate. Fortunately, public outcry prompted a voter's initiative to save the market. Subsequently, the space was cleaned up and restructured, and it has become once again the undeniable pulse of downtown; some 10 million people mill through the market each year. Thanks to the unique management of the market, social-services programs and low-income housing mix with commerce, and the market has maintained its gritty edge. These initiatives have prevented the area from ever sliding too far upmarket. A market law prohibits chain stores or franchises from setting up shop and ensures all businesses are locally owned. The one exception is, of course, Starbucks, which gets away with its market location because it is the coffee giant's first outlet (it opened in 1971).

Orientation

If you're coming from downtown, simply walk down Pike St toward the waterfront; you can't miss the huge **Public Market sign** etched against the horizon. Incidentally, the sign and clock, installed in 1927, constituted one of the first pieces of outdoor neon on the West Coast. From the top of Pike St and 1st Ave, stop and survey the bustle and vitality. Walk down the cobblestone street, past perpetually gridlocked cars (don't even think of driving down to Pike Pl) and, before walking into the market, stop and shake the bronze snout of **Rachel the Market Pig**, the de-facto mascot and presiding spirit of the market. This life-size piggy bank, carved by Whidbey Island artist Georgia Gerber and named after a real pig, collects about $10,000 each year. The funds are pumped back into market social services. Nearby is the **information booth** (Map p232; 206-682-7453; cnr Pike St & 1st Ave), which has maps of the market and information about Seattle in general. It also serves as a ticket booth, selling discount tickets to various shows throughout the city.

Main & North Arcades

Rachel the Market Pig marks the main entrance to the **Main & North Arcades** (Map p232; Western Ave), thin shed-like structures that run along the edge of the hill; these are the busiest of the market buildings. With banks of fresh produce carefully arranged in artful displays, and fresh fish, crab and other shellfish piled high on ice, this is the real heart of the market. Here you'll see fishmongers tossing salmon back and forth like basketballs (many of these vendors will pack fish for overnight delivery).

BUSKERS

Anyone can busk in the market as long as they register with the market office, pay a $30 annual fee and perform in one of 13 designated spots. With a guaranteed annual audience of 10 million people passing through, pitches are understandably popular. Well-known market performers include Johnny Hahn, who has been tickling the keys of an upright piano for nearly 30 years, and Emery Carl, who plays guitar while spinning a Hula-Hoop.

In a city as fast-moving as Seattle, not even a historical heirloom like Pike Place Market escapes a makeover. In 2015, ground was broken on the 'Pike Up' project, a 30,000-sq-ft extension of Pike Place. Made possible by the proposed demolition of the Alaskan Way Viaduct, the planned MarketFront complex will create new shops, restaurants and stalls, and link the market to the waterfront via terraces, staircases and green space. It is scheduled to open in 2017.

You'll also find cheese shops, butchers, tiny grocery stalls and almost everything else you need to put together a meal. The end of the North Arcade is dedicated to local artisans and craftspeople – products must be handmade to be sold here. It's also abloom with flower sellers, most of them of Vietnamese Hmong origin. The Main Arcade was built in 1907, the first of Frank Goodwin's market buildings.

Down Under

As if the levels of the market that are above ground aren't labyrinthine enough, below the Main Arcade are three lower levels called the Down Under. Here you'll find a fabulously eclectic mix of pocket-size shops, from Indian spice stalls to magician supply shops and vintage magazines.

Economy Market Building

Once a stable for merchants' horses, the Economy Market Building on the south side of the market entrance has a wonderful Italian grocery store, DeLaurenti's (p52) – a great place for any aficionado of Italian foods to browse and sample. There's also Tenzing Momo (p60), one of the oldest apothecaries on the West Coast, where you can pick up herbal remedies, incense, oils and books. Tarot readings are available here on occasion. Look down at the Economy Market floor and you'll see some of its 46,000 tiles, sold to the public in the 1980s for $35 apiece. If you bought a tile, you'd get your name on it and be proud that you helped save the market floor. Famous tile owners include *Cat in the Hat* creator Dr Seuss and former US president Ronald Reagan.

South Arcade

If you continue past DeLaurenti's, you'll come into the South Arcade, the market's newest wing, home to upscale shops and the lively Pike Pub & Brewery (p55). It's not technically part of the historic market but is with it in spirit and rambunctious energy.

Corner & Sanitary Market Buildings

Across Pike Pl from the Main Arcade are the 1912 **Corner & Sanitary Market Buildings** (Map p232; Pike Place; Westlake), so named because they were the first of the market buildings in which live animals were prohibited. It's now a maze of ethnic groceries and great little eateries, including Three Girls Bakery (p52), which is as old as the building itself; Storyville Coffee (p56), one of the market's newest businesses; and the insanely popular Crumpet Shop (p52). When you've finished digesting your baked goods, you can digest a bit of radical literature in bolshie bookstore, Left Bank Books (p60).

Post Alley

Between the Corner Market and the Triangle Building, narrow Post Alley (named for its hitching posts) is lined with shops and restaurants. Extending north across Stewart St, it offers two of the area's best places for a drink: the Pink Door Ristorante (p53), an Italian hideaway with a cool patio, and Kells (p56), an Irish pub. In Lower Post Alley, beside the market sign, is the **LaSalle Hotel**, which was the first bordello north of Yesler Way. Originally the Outlook Hotel, it was taken over in 1942 by the notorious Nellie Curtis, a woman with 13 aliases and a knack for running suspiciously profitable hotels with thousands of lonely sailors lined up nightly outside the door. The building, rehabbed in 1977, now houses commercial and residential space.

Post Alley continues on the southern side of Pike St where you'll find the beautifully disgusting gum wall (p47).

Market fishmonger

MARKET ROLL CALL

Watching Pike Place's daily market roll call, rung in by an old-fashioned hand bell at 9am (9:30am on Sunday from January to April), is like watching a boisterous rural cattle auction conducted in an indecipherable language. The purpose of roll call is to allocate where the market's temporary craft-sellers will set up on any particular day. As Pike Place has over 200 registered vendors but only 130 available trading spots, each day is a nail-biting lottery. Not everyone gets lucky, but by 9:30am clipboards have been signed, a large whiteboard has been filled out, and people are industriously going about their business. Roll call is held at the north end of the North Arcade and is a great way to imbibe the true spirit of the market and its workings. Anyone can watch. Just don't be late!

Triangle Building

All in a row in the diminutive Triangle Building, sandwiched between Pike Pl, Pine St and Post Alley, are a huddle of cheap food take-outs including **Mee Sum Pastries** (try the steamed pork bun), a juice bar and Cinnamon Works (p52) – all great choices for a stand-up snack.

First Avenue Buildings

These downtown-facing buildings, added mainly in the 1980s, blend seamlessly into the older hive. Here you'll find Pike Place's only two accommodations – Pensione Nichols (p190) and Inn at the Market (p191) – a couple of classic pubs and community resources such as a medical center.

North End

The market's North End stretches along Pike Pl from Pine St to Victor Steinbrueck Park (p47) – a popular meeting point for daily walking tours. The 1918 **Soames-Dunn building**, once occupied by a seed company and a paper company, is now home to the world's oldest Starbucks. Beware of crowds and errant elbows knocking over your mermaid-logo coffee cup.

➡ **If you dislike crowds, visit the market early (before 10am).**

➡ **Wander over to adjacent Victor Steinbrueck Park for clear-weather views of Mt Rainier.**

➡ **Join a Seattle walking tour; plenty of them start in or around the market and all skillfully explain its history.**

JOHN ELK III / GETTY IMAGES ©

◉ TOP SIGHT
SEATTLE ART MUSEUM (SAM)

While not comparable with the big guns in New York and Chicago, Seattle Art Museum (SAM) is no slouch. Always re-curating its collection with new acquisitions and temporary exhibitions, it's known for its extensive Native American artifacts and work from the Northwest school.

Entrance Lobby

SAM is a three-site museum incorporating the Olympic Sculpture Park, the Asian Art Museum and this splendid 150,000-sq-ft downtown facility. The main building is guarded by a 48ft-high sculpture known as *Hammering Man* (p47; pictured above) and contains a cascading stairway inside guarded by Chinese statues called the 'Art Ladder'.

Modern & Contemporary Art

Level 3 is home to Andy Warhol's *Double Elvis* and Jackson Pollock's drippy (and trippy) *Sea Change*. The hallway at the top of the escalators has a collection of exhibits from the Pilchuck Glass School (p83), an excellent appetite whetter if you're heading over to Chihuly Garden & Glass (p82) later.

Native American Art

The Hauberg Gallery on level 3 is dedicated to the museum's collections of items from Northwest coastal peoples, as well as Australian Aboriginal art and American and Native American textiles. Groups such as the Tlingit, Haida and Kwakwaka'wakw are all examined.

Top Floor

Level 4 has a rather scattered collection of world art from Greek pottery to the Italian renaissance. Standout pieces include *Pomponne Il de Bellièvre* by Van Dyck and *Saint Augustine in Ecstasy* by the Spanish baroque painter Esteban Murillo. The 19th century is represented with works by Monet, Matisse and Vuillard.

DON'T MISS

➡ Art Ladder
➡ Native American art
➡ *Double Elvis* by Andy Warhol
➡ Van Dyck's *Pomponne Il de Bellièvre*

PRACTICALITIES

➡ Map p232, D5
➡ 1300 1st Ave
➡ adult/student $19.95/12.95
➡ ⊙10am-5pm Wed & Fri-Sun, 10am-9pm Thu
➡ ⓡUniversity St

◉ SIGHTS

The waterfront is the thin strip of land between Elliott Bay and the soon-to-be-dismantled Alaskan Way Viaduct. Downtown is bounded east–west by I-5 and the Alaskan Way Viaduct along with (by most estimations) Olive Way to the north and Cherry St to the south. Pike Place Market sits to the northwest of the downtown core.

The entire western portion of downtown (including Pike Place Market) between 2nd Ave and the Viaduct is sometimes referred to as the West Edge, although, on the ground, it's hard to differentiate between the two neighborhoods.

◉ Pike Place Market

PIKE PLACE MARKET   MARKET
See p42.

GUM WALL   PUBLIC ART
Map p232 (Post Alley; 🚇University St) Seattle's oddest and most unhygienic sight is the bizarre gum wall situated at the southern end of Post Alley. The once venerable red-brick facade is now covered in used pieces of chewing gum originally stuck there by bored theater-goers standing in line for a nearby ticket office in the 1990s. Despite early attempts by the city council to sanitize the wall, the gum-stickers persevered, becoming ever more creative in their outlandish art arrangements and, in 1999, the wall was declared a tourist attraction.

Feel free to add your own well-chewed morsels to the Jackson Pollock–like display.

VICTOR STEINBRUECK PARK   PARK
Map p232 (cnr Western Ave & Virginia St; 🚇Westlake) When you've had enough of Pike Place Market and its crowds, wander out the end of the North Arcade and cross Western Ave to Victor Steinbrueck Park, a small grassy area designed in 1982 by Steinbrueck and Richard Haag.

A historic armory building once stood on the site, but it was knocked down in 1968, much to the disgust of Steinbrueck, a major preservationist who worked hard to save both Pike Place and Pioneer Sq from the wrecking ball. As consolation, this small breathing space between the waterfront and downtown was created. Perched over

Elliott Bay, it has benches, a couple of totem poles carved by Quinault tribe members James Bender and Marvin Oliver, and great views over the waterfront and bay. Rallies and political demonstrations are often held here.

◉ Downtown

SEATTLE ART MUSEUM   MUSEUM
See p46.

HAMMERING MAN   MONUMENT
Map p232 (🚇University St) Although not unique to Seattle, *Hammering Man,* the 48ft-high metal sculpture that guards the entrance to the Seattle Art Museum on the corner of 1st Ave and University St, has become something of a city icon since it was raised in 1992.

The sculpture, whose moving motor-powered arm silently hammers four times per minute, 364 days a year (he has Labor Day in September off), is supposed to represent the worker in all of us. It was conceived by Jonathan Borofsky, an American artist from Boston, who has designed similar hammering men for various other cities. There are taller and heavier models in Frankfurt, Germany, and Seoul, South Korea.

BENAROYA CONCERT HALL   CONCERT HALL
Map p232 (📞206-215-9494; 200 University St; 🚇University St) With a hefty bill of almost $120 million in construction costs, it's no wonder the Benaroya Concert Hall, primary venue of the Seattle Symphony (p58), oozes luxury. From the minute you step into the glass-enclosed lobby of the performance hall you're overwhelmed by views of Elliott Bay; on clear days you might be lucky enough to see the snowy peaks of the Olympic Range far in the distance.

Even if you're not attending the symphony, you can walk through the foyer and marvel at the 20ft-long chandeliers, specially created by Tacoma glassmaker Dale Chihuly.

SEATTLE CENTRAL LIBRARY   LIBRARY
Map p232 (📞206-386-4636; www.spl.org; 1000 4th Ave; ⊙10am-8pm Mon-Thu, 10am-6pm Fri & Sat, noon-6pm Sun; 🅿🛜; 🚇Pioneer Sq) Rivaling the Space Needle and EMP Museum with its architectural ingenuity, Seattle Central Library looks like a giant diamond

BURYING THE ALASKAN WAY VIADUCT

'Nice bay, shame about the flyover' is a comment you'll sometimes hear yelled above the din of traffic on Seattle's cacophonous waterfront. The flyover in question is the Alaskan Way Viaduct, an ugly elevated section of state Rte 99 built between 1949 and 1953 that carries over 100,000 vehicles a day through downtown Seattle. In the pioneering era of the motorcar, the viaduct served its purpose, redirecting traffic away from Seattle's downtown grid and keeping the peace in Pike Place Market; but by the 1970s many Seattleites had started to view it as a noisy eyesore that was doing untold damage to the city's potentially idyllic waterfront. D-Day came in February 2001, when the viaduct was significantly damaged by the 6.8-magnitude Nisqually earthquake. Although emergency repairs were quickly carried out, the structure was no longer considered safe in such an earthquake-prone city. What would happen if a really big one hit?

Long debates ensued about possible transport alternatives along Seattle's waterfront before it was agreed in 2009 that the viaduct should be dismantled and a 2-mile-long tunnel built in its place (the world's largest bored tunnel by diameter). Such a massive project hasn't been without problems. Digging for the tunnel using a specially designed boring machine began in summer 2013, but, within months, the machine had broken down. It remained 'broken' for two whole years! Originally expected to be finished by 2015, the completion of the $3.1 billion tunnel was put back to 2017, whereupon the Alaskan Way Viaduct will be dismantled and consigned to the history books. In its place, the city has plans for landscaped parks, a waterfront promenade, and a lot less traffic noise and pollution.

Washington State's Department of Transportation has set up a clever, interactive information center in Pioneer Sq about the tunnel project called Milepost 31 (p66).

that's dropped in from outer space. Conceived by Rem Koolhaas and LMN Architects in 2004, the $165.5 million sculpture of glass and steel was designed to serve as a community gathering space, a tech center, a reading room and, of course, a massive storage facility for its one-million-plus books. Come here to enjoy art, architecture, coffee and literary comfort.

The overall style of the library is phenomenal both outside and in. Lemon-yellow escalators, hot-pink chairs and zippy wifi connections make for a modern, tech-friendly experience. There are also 132 research computers available in the **Mixing Chamber**, where librarians in teams help with in-depth research. And the **Book Spiral**, spanning several floors, holds most of the library's nonfiction books. Guests can take self-guided tours using their cell phones (signs display which # you need to enter).

The library is spread over 11 levels with **parking** provided underground. Public art is spread liberally around the facility, but the design pinnacle is undoubtedly the 12,000-sq-ft **reading room** on level 10 with 40ft glass ceilings. It has amazing light, great views of downtown and seating for up to 400 people.

ARCTIC BUILDING LANDMARK

Map p232 (700 3rd Ave, cnr Cherry St; ⓡPioneer Sq) Like the psychedelic Beatles' song, the unique Arctic Building, completed in 1917, is celebrated for its walruses. Their heads (25 of them) surrounded by intricate terracotta ornamentation peek out from the building's exterior.

Though the walruses' tusks were originally authentic ivory, an earthquake in the 1940s managed to shake a few of them loose to the ground. To protect passersby from the unusual urban hazard of being skewered by falling tusks, the ivory was replaced with epoxy.

COLUMBIA CENTER VIEWPOINT

Map p232 (☏206-386-5564; www.skyviewobservatory.com; 701 5th Ave; adult/child $14.25/9; ⓗ10am-8pm; ⓡPioneer Sq) Everyone makes a rush for the iconic Space Needle, but it's not the tallest Seattle viewpoint. That honor goes to the sleek, tinted-windowed Columbia Center at 932ft high with 76 floors. An elevator in the lobby takes you up to the free-access 40th floor, where there's a Starbucks. From here you must take another elevator to the plush Sky View Observatory on the 73rd floor, from where you can look down on ferries, cars, islands, roofs and – ha, ha – the Space Needle!

Built between 1982 and 1985, it's the loftiest building in the Pacific Northwest.

COBB BUILDING   LANDMARK
Map p232 (1301 4th Ave; ☒University St) Look up at the beaux-arts style Cobb Building (1910) and see remnants of an older Seattle. Peering out from the 11-story edifice you'll see several stern-looking terracotta heads of the same Native American chief.

RAINIER TOWER   LANDMARK
Map p232 (1333 5th Ave; ☒University St) With its inverted base that looks like a tree that's been nibbled by a beaver, this urban behemoth was finished in 1977, after which it quickly acquired the nickname 'the Beaver Building'. Taking up an entire block between 4th and 5th Aves and University and Union Sts is Rainier Sq, a shopping center connected to the top-heavy tower.

1201 THIRD AVENUE   LANDMARK
Map p232 (1201 3rd Ave; ☒University St) The beauty of the Seattle skyline is reflected in the 55-story 1201 Third Avenue building at 3rd and Seneca, which changes colors with the clouds and sunsets. This is the second-tallest building in Seattle and dates from 1988. Seattleites have nicknamed it 'the Spark Plug'. Enter off 3rd Ave to explore the building's recently refurbished interior.

WESTLAKE CENTER   MALL
Map p232 (cnr 4th Ave & Pine St; ☒Westlake) Scorned by locals, this cheese-ball shopping mall is useful these days primarily as a landmark. Should you be inclined to part with your money, there's a food court, plenty of underwhelming chain stores and the obligatory Starbucks. More interesting is **Westlake Park** outside, Seattle's diminutive central plaza. The park has recently been cleaned up and equipped with European-style seating, licensed buskers and outdoor games, including table tennis and cornhole.

This is also where the **monorail** stops and starts on its 1.2-mile journey to and from Seattle Center.

SAFECO PLAZA   LANDMARK
Map p232 (1001 4th Ave; ☒University St) Built in 1969 and originally known as 1001 Fourth Avenue Plaza, this was one of the city's first real skyscrapers. At the time, it was a

darling of the architectural world, though nowadays the 50-story bronze block looks dated. Locals nicknamed it 'the box that the Space Needle came in'.

In the plaza outside is the **Three Piece Sculpture: Vertebrae** by Henry Moore – a result of Seattle's '1% for art' clause, under which 1% of the construction cost of the building is invested in public art.

SEATTLE TOWER   LANDMARK
Map p232 (1218 3rd Ave; ☒University St) Formerly the Northern Life Tower, this 26-story art-deco skyscraper, built in 1928, was designed to reflect the mountains of the Pacific Northwest. The brickwork on the exterior blends from dark at the bottom to light on top, the same way mountains appear to do. Check out the 18-karat-gold relief map in the lobby.

WASHINGTON STATE CONVENTION CENTER   CONVENTION CENTER
Map p232 (☏206-447-5000; main entrance cnr 7th Ave & Pike St; ☒Westlake) It's hard to miss this gigantic complex decked out with ballrooms, meeting rooms, space for exhibitions and the Seattle Convention and Visitors Bureau (p219). An arched-glass bridge spans Pike St between 7th and 8th Aves, with what looks like a giant eye in the middle of it.

Freeway Park nearby provides a leafy, fountain-laden downtown oasis.

◉ Waterfront

SEATTLE GREAT WHEEL   FERRIS WHEEL
Map p232 (www.seattlegreatwheel.com; 1301 Alaskan Way; adult/child $13/8.50; ◷11am-10pm Mon-Thu, 11am-midnight Fri, 10am-midnight Sat, 10am-10pm Sun; ☒University St) With the Alaskan Way Viaduct soon to be confined to the 'ugly postwar architecture' chapter of the history books, Seattle has started work on beautifying its often neglected waterfront. Leading the way is this 175ft Ferris wheel that was installed in June 2012 with 42 gondolas, each capable of carrying eight people on a 12-minute ($13!) ride.

The wheel sticks out over the water on Pier 57 and is the tallest of its type on the West Coast, though it pales in comparison with other behemoths such as the London Eye. So far, it has fulfilled its role as a popular Space Needle–like attraction primarily aimed at tourists.

SEATTLE AQUARIUM AQUARIUM

Map p232 (☏206-386-4300; www.seattle aquarium.org; 1483 Alaskan Way, at Pier 59; adult/child 4-12yr $23/16; ◷9:30am-5pm; 🚹; 🚇University St) Though not on a par with Seattle's nationally lauded Woodland Park Zoo, the aquarium – situated on Pier 59 in an attractive wooden building – is probably the most interesting site on the waterfront, and it's a handy distraction for families with itchy-footed kids.

The entry lobby instantly impresses with a giant fish-filled tank called 'Window on Washington Waters' grabbing your attention; background music is sometimes provided by live string quartets. The aquarium houses harbor seals and resident sea and river otters, who float comically on their backs. An underwater dome on the lower level gives a pretty realistic glimpse of the kind of fish that inhabit the waters of Puget Sound, and the daily diver show here is probably the best of the aquarium's live events. For kids there are plenty of hands-on exhibits, including a pool where you can stroke starfish and caress sea urchins.

 EATING

You'll have to dig deep to fill your stomach in the central downtown area: happy hours are your best bet for affordable bar snacks. Plenty of the top-notch hotels in the area have posh dining rooms and bars inside their opulent interiors.

Pike Place is where you go for cheap on-the-go grub, invariably sold to you by the person who picked/made/reared it. Explore the market on an empty stomach and you'll be full by the time you leave, and it won't have cost you much.

The waterfront is where to descend for oysters, clams and fish-and-chips. Watch out for the chip-stealing seagulls.

✕ Pike Place Market

★BEECHER'S HANDMADE CHEESE DELI $
Map p232 (www.beechershandmadecheese. com; 1600 Pike Pl; snacks $3-5; ◷9am-6pm; 🚇Westlake) 🍴 Artisan beer, artisan coffee... next up, Seattle brings you artisan cheese and it's made as you watch in this always-

🚶 Neighborhood Walk
Downtown Architecture

START ARCTIC BUILDING
END WESTLAKE CENTER
LENGTH 2 MILES; ONE HOUR

Downtown Seattle isn't the city's most buzzing or creative neighborhood, but its modern edifices contain some interesting architectural details rarely spared a glance by the suited office workers who hurry from building to building at street level.

Start this walk at the south end of downtown at the ➊**Arctic Building** (p48), built in 1917 as a club for Klondike gold-rush veterans. Crane your neck to get a look at the 25 walrus heads that embellish the building's exterior a couple of floors up. Then walk up Cherry St and take a left onto 4th Ave.

The ➋**Columbia Center** (p48), formerly the Bank of America Tower and the Columbia Seafirst Center, takes up the block between 4th and 5th Aves and Columbia and Cherry Sts. This is the tallest building on the West Coast. If you have time (and $14), check out the observation deck on the 73rd floor.

Follow 4th Ave to Madison St and the ➌**Safeco Plaza** (p49). Built in 1969, this was one of the city's first real skyscrapers, and it ended the Space Needle's short seven-year reign at the top. The building ushered in an era of massive downtown growth – most of it in a vertical direction. It is now Seattle's fifth-tallest skyscraper.

Just across 4th Ave, you certainly won't miss the dramatically post-modern ➍**Seattle Central Library** (p47), spectacular from the outside with its rough-cut diamond shape. It's worth going inside for a quick ride up the lime-green escalators to see how good architecture can combine practicality and beauty. There are wide-ranging views from the top levels.

Continue north on 4th Ave to University St and take a left, walk half a block and look up. Formerly the Northern Life Tower, the ➎**Seattle Tower** (p49), an art-deco skyscraper built in 1928, was designed to reflect the mountains of the Pacific Northwest.

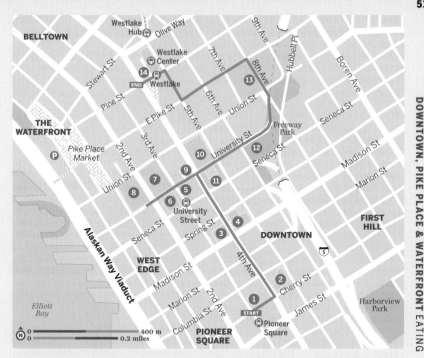

Continue on University St to the **6** **1201 Third Avenue** (p49) building at 3rd Ave and Seneca, which acts like a mirror to the surrounding mountains. Nicknamed 'the Spark Plug,' it is particularly charming at sunset. Enter off 3rd Ave and examine the plush lobby of Seattle's second-tallest building.

Cross University St to **7** **Benaroya Concert Hall** (p47). Walk into the glass-enclosed lobby of the performance hall, where you can take in excellent views of Elliott Bay. For more glassy views look up at the two giant 20ft-long chandeliers sculpted by Tacoma-born glass artist Dale Chihuly.

Since you're this close, continue along University to get an eyeful of the **8** **Seattle Art Museum** (p46). It may not be one of the seven wonders of the architecture world, especially from the outside, but it is a clever solution to the problem of finding more and better gallery space in the crowded downtown core.

Walk back up University St, across 3rd Ave to the corner of 4th Ave. Look up at the **9** **Cobb Building** (p49), built in 1910, one of downtown Seattle's older and more ornate edifices. On a decorative band halfway up, several sculpted heads of an erstwhile Native American chief survey the car chaos below.

Continue on University St across 4th Ave to **10** **Rainier Tower** (p49), which, with its precarious-looking inverted base, has been nicknamed the 'Beaver Building'. A clever piece of engineering, the building takes up an entire block between 4th and 5th Aves and University and Union Sts as Rainier Sq.

Cross University St and enter the domain of the Jazz Age **11** **Fairmont Olympic Hotel** (p190), built in 1924 and undoubtedly one of the classiest remnants of Seattle's early-20th-century heyday. The block-square building looks sober and unrevealing on the outside, but journey through the revolving doors to discover a plush lobby dominated by chandeliers, marble walls and exotic carpets.

Continue northeast on University St past 6th Ave; look ahead to **12** **Freeway Park**. Meander through, then follow the signs to the **13** **Washington State Convention Center** (p49) and the visitor center inside. Leave the convention center through its front doors on Pike St. Follow Pike (you'll see Pike Place Market at the end of the street) to 5th Ave.

Take a right on 5th Ave to Pine St; turn left, toward the **14** **Westlake Center** (p62). Stop for a latte and park yourself in the park opposite, which has recently been refurbished with outdoor tables, games and food trucks.

crowded Pike Place nook, where you can buy all kinds of cheese-related paraphernalia. As for that long, snaking, almost permanent queue – that's people lining up for the wonderful homemade mac 'n' cheese that comes in two different-sized tubs and is simply divine.

★PIROSHKY PIROSHKY   BAKERY $

Map p232 (www.piroshkybakery.com; 1908 Pike Pl; snacks $3-6; ⏰8am-6pm; ⓇWestlake) Piroshky knocks out its delectable sweet and savory Russian pies and pastries in a space about the size of a walk-in closet. Get the savory smoked-salmon pâté or the sauerkraut with cabbage and onion, and follow it with the chocolate-cream hazelnut roll or a fresh rhubarb piroshki.

CRUMPET SHOP   BAKERY $

Map p232 (☑206-682-1598; www.thecrumpetshop.com; 1503 1st Ave; crumpets $3-6; ⏰7am-3pm Mon, Wed & Thu, 7am-4pm Fri-Sun; ⓇWestlake) The treasured British crumpet has been given a distinct American twist with lavish toppings such as pesto, wild salmon or lemon curd at this casual Pike Place Market eatery, family-owned and operated for almost 40 years. Organic ingredients make it very Pacific Northwest, though there's Marmite for homesick Brits.

LOPRIORE BROS. PASTA BAR   ITALIAN $

Map p232 (☑206-621-7545; 1530 Post Alley; sandwiches $10; ⏰10am-5pm; ⓇWestlake) Often hidden behind a queue for the riotously popular Pike Place Chowder, this theatrical sales counter is manned by a couple of wise-cracking Italian Americans who wouldn't look out of place in an early-career Scorcese movie. Oscar-worthy service is backed up by the *cibo,* in particular the open meatball sandwich doused in tomato sauce and Parmesan and spread over a crispy baguette.

THREE GIRLS BAKERY   BAKERY $

Map p232 (☑206-244-1045; 1514 Pike Pl; sandwiches $6-9; ⏰6am-6pm; ⓇWestlake) The 'three girls' in this pioneering business in Pike Place Market first set up shop in 1912, eight years before women in the US got the vote. Times have obviously changed, but the quality of the baking laid down by that trio of ladies hasn't.

There's a take-out window displaying tempting loaves, scones and cookies, or a small space to sit down with soup and sarnies.

CAFFÈ LIETO   BREAKFAST $

Map p232 (☑206-441-7999; www.biscuitbitch.com; 1909 1st Ave; biscuits $6-9.50; ⏰7:30am-3pm Mon-Fri, 8:30am-3pm Sat & Sun; ⓇWestlake) Lieto is famous for one thing – biscuits, those flaky descendants of the British scone that are a cult in the South and usually come (as they do here) smothered in gravy or, should you opt for the 'hot mess bitch,' eggs, grits, cheese and jalapeños. The place goes under the subtitle of 'Biscuit Bitch' and the service is Southern friendly.

CINNAMON WORKS   BAKERY $

Map p232 (☑206-583-0085; 1536 Pike Pl; baked goods from $1; ⏰8am-5pm Mon-Sat; ✍; ⓇWestlake) It's hard to walk past this bakery in Pike Place that has been part of the market's furniture since the early 1980s and not stop. Not surprisingly, the cinnamon buns are warm and delicious (and not too sweet), but the bakery also does other stuff – cookies, for instance – and, this being Seattle, anything comes in gluten-free or vegan versions.

PIKE PLACE CHOWDER   SEAFOOD $

Map p232 (☑206-267-2537; www.pikeplacechowder.com; 1530 Post Alley; medium chowder $7.95; ⏰11am-5pm; ⓇWestlake) Proof that some of the best culinary ideas are almost ridiculously simple, this Pike Place Market hole-in-the-wall takes that old New England favorite (clam chowder) and gives it a dynamic West Coast makeover. You can choose from four traditional chowders in four different sizes accompanied by four different salads. Then you can fight to eat it at one of four indoor tables.

The chowder has been voted the nation's best more than once – in competitions held in New England!

MEE SUM PASTRY   ASIAN $

Map p232 (☑206-682-6780; 1526 Pike Pl; bao $2.95; ⏰9am-6pm; ⓇWestlake) This little storefront window is famed for its giant *hum bao* – eminently portable meat- or vegetable-filled steamed buns that make a great snack or small meal. The steamed pork *bao* is tops. Next door is a smoothie stand, where you can round out your tidy little meat bomb with some fresh fruits and vegetables.

DELAURENTI'S   FOOD $

Map p232 (☑206-622-0141; www.delaurenti.com; 1435 1st Ave; snacks $5-12; ⏰9am-6pm Mon-Sat,

STARBUCKS: IT STARTED HERE (ALMOST)

It's practically impossible to walk through the door of **Starbucks** (Map p232; www.1912pike.com; 1912 Pike Pl; ☺6am-9pm; ⊠Westlake) in Pike Place Market without appearing in someone's Facebook photo, so dense is the tourist traffic. But, while this hallowed business might be the world's oldest surviving Starbucks store, it is not – as many assume – the world's first Starbucks location, nor is it Seattle's oldest espresso bar. The original Starbucks opened in 1971 at 2000 Western Ave (at Western Ave's north end). It moved to its current location, a block away, in 1976. The honor of Seattle's oldest continuously running coffee bar goes to Café Allegro in the U District, which opened in 1975. Until the early 1980s Starbucks operated purely as a retail store that sold coffee beans and equipment (plus the odd taster cup). The company didn't open up its first espresso bar until 1984, after CEO Howard Shultz returned from an epiphanic trip to Italy. The Pike Place cafe is unique in that, in keeping with the traditional unbranded ethos of the market, it doesn't sell food or baked goods – just coffee.

Other interesting Starbucks facilities in Seattle include the cafe on the 40th floor of the **Columbia Center** (p48), Seattle's tallest building; the company's first LEED-certified cafe that opened downtown on the corner of Pike St and 1st Ave in 2009 and sports the original brown logo; and the **Starbucks Reserve Roastery** (p115) in Capitol Hill. The latter is a veritable coffee emporium that opened in 2014 and, ostensibly at least, appears to be the antithesis of everything you normally find in a Starbucks cafe.

10am-5pm Sun; ⊠University St) A Pike Place Market veteran, this Italian grocery store/deli has been run by the same family since 1946. Not needing to roll with the times, it offers a beautifully old-fashioned selection of wine, cheese, sausages, hams and pasta, along with a large range of capers, olive oils and anchovies. The sandwich counter is a great place to order panini, salads and pizza.

PROCOPIO GELATI
GELATERIA $

Map p232 (☎206-622-4280; 1501 Western Ave; gelato $3-5; ☺9am-6pm; ⊠Westlake) If the Pike Place Hill Climb wears you out – or even if it doesn't – stop for an authentic Italian-style gelato. The owner learned his trade from a Milanese gelato maker, and he uses only super-fresh ingredients for completely undiluted flavors.

★CAFÉ CAMPAGNE
FRENCH $$

Map p232 (☎206-728-2233; www.cafecampagne. com; 1600 Post Alley; mains $16-29; ☺11am-10pm Mon-Fri, 8am-11pm Sat, 8am-10pm Sun; ⊠Westlake) Short of teleporting over to Paris, this is about as Gallic as a Seattleite can get. Inside Café Campagne's effortlessly elegant interior you can live vicariously as a French poseur over steamed mussels, hanger steaks, generous portions of *frites* and crispy vegetables. Save room for the crème brûlée dessert. Should you be sufficiently

satisfied, consider coming back for weekend brunch.

LE PICHET
FRENCH $$

Map p232 (☎206-256-1499; www.lepichetseattle. com; 1933 1st Ave; mains $11-22; ☺8am-midnight; ⊠Westlake) Say *bonjour* to Le Pichet, just up from Pike Place Market, a cute and very French bistro with pâtés, cheeses, wine, *chocolat* and a refined Parisian feel. Dinner features delicacies such as wild boar shoulder or foie gras with duck eggs.

LOWELLS
DINER $$

Map p232 (www.eatatlowells.com; 1519 Pike Pl; fish-and-chips $16; ☺7am-9pm; ⊠Westlake) Fish-and-chips is a simple meal often done badly – but not here. Slam down your order for Alaskan cod at the front entry and take your food up to the top floor for delicious views over Puget Sound. Lowells also serves corned-beef hash and an excellent clam chowder.

PINK DOOR RISTORANTE
ITALIAN $$$

Map p232 (☎206-443-3241; www.thepinkdoor.net; 1919 Post Alley; mains $18-29; ☺11:30am-10pm Mon-Thu, 11:30am-11pm Fri & Sat, 4-10pm Sun; ⊠Westlake) A restaurant like no other, the Pink Door is probably the only place in the US (the world?) where you can enjoy fabulous *linguine alle vongole* (pasta with clams and pancetta) and other Italian favorites while watching live jazz, burlesque cabaret, or – we kid you not – a trapeze artist swinging from the 20ft ceiling.

MATT'S IN THE MARKET
NORTHWEST $$$

Map p232 (📞206-467-7909; www.mattsinthe market.com; 94 Pike St, Suite 32; mains lunch $15-18, dinner $30-45; ⏰11:30am-2:30pm & 5:30-10pm Mon-Sat; 🚋Westlake) 🍴 Matt's is perched above the bustle of Pike Place Market with views out over the famous clock, and oversees a menu where most of the ingredients come from down below. Expect plenty of fish, fresh veg and organic meats. For economy, come for the lunchtime sandwiches (the catfish is good). For fruity fish glazes and atmosphere, come for dinner.

For dessert just say the words, 'pecan toffee bread pudding'.

STEELHEAD DINER
SEAFOOD $$$

Map p232 (📞206-625-0129; www.steelheaddiner. com; 95 Pine St; sandwiches $14-18, mains $18-45; ⏰11am-10pm; 🚋Westlake) It's all about the fish at the Steelhead, one of Pike Place Market's posher posts. The fish-and-chips are a given, but you're better off trying the more typically Northwestern smoked salmon cakes, sautéed sole or the multifarious *cioppino* (fish stew) here. The place has a good reputation so it's wise to book ahead.

CUTTER'S CRABHOUSE
SEAFOOD $$$

Map p232 (📞206-448-4884; www.cutterscrab house.com; 2001 Western Ave; mains $25-37; ⏰11am-9pm Mon-Thu, 11am-9:30pm Fri & Sat, 10:30am-9pm Sun; 🚋Westlake) When you're located 70 sailing miles from Dungeness Spit there's no avoiding the crabs. Waterfront-facing Cutter's ain't cheap, but it will deliver the freshest crab catch in Seattle in cakes, gnocchi or just steamed whole. Also recommended are the deep-fried curds from nearby Beecher's Handmade Cheese (p50) and the bread from Macrina bakery.

ETTA'S SEAFOOD
SEAFOOD $$$

Map p232 (📞206-443-6000; www.tomdouglas. com; 2020 Western Ave; brunch $16-23, mains $18-36; ⏰11:30am-9pm Mon-Thu, 11:30am-10pm Fri, 9am-3pm & 4-10pm Sat & Sun; 🚋Westlake) Famous for its gourmet seafood brunch, which includes mouthwatering poached eggs with Dungeness crab and crab-butter hollandaise, Etta's is a reliable and classy place with a fish-focused dinner menu. Look out for 'crabby hour' (weekdays from 3pm to 6pm) when the crustaceans come in all shapes and sizes (and sauces).

🍴 Downtown

⭐ WILD GINGER
ASIAN $$

Map p232 (www.wildginger.net; 1401 3rd Ave; mains $17-33; ⏰11:30am-11pm Mon-Sat, 4-9pm Sun; 🚋University St) All around the Pacific Rim – via China, Indonesia, Malaysia, Vietnam and Seattle, of course – is the wide-ranging theme at this highly popular downtown fusion restaurant. The signature fragrant duck goes down nicely with a glass of Riesling. The restaurant also provides food for the swanky Triple Door (p58) dinner club downstairs.

TASTE RESTAURANT
NORTHWEST $$

Map p232 (📞206-903-5291; www.tastesam.com; 1300 1st Ave; mains $15-25; ⏰11am-close Wed-Sat, 11am-5pm Tue & Sun; 🚋University St) Inside the Seattle Art Museum (p46), Taste has been known to change its menu to honor the gallery's various temporary exhibitions (eg British bangers and mash for Gainsborough). But you don't need to be visiting the museum to drop by. The venue is popular among city workers for its happy hour (3pm to 6pm), when red-eyed bankers wash down oysters with cocktails.

IL FORNAIO
ITALIAN $$

Map p232 (📞206-264-0994; www.ilfornaio.com; 600 Pine St, No 132 Pacific Place Mall; pasta & pizza $15-17; ⏰11:30am-10pm Sun-Thu, 11:30am-11pm Fri & Sat; ♿; 🚋Westlake) Split over two levels (upstairs is more formal), this is the place for quick, hearty, relatively authentic Italian *cucina*. The open kitchen puts on a good show, and the food (fairly standard Italian dishes) comes with ample focaccia and a good kids menu. It abuts the Pacific Place mall. You can enter via the mall or from a separate street-side entrance at ground level.

PURPLE CAFE & WINE BAR
INTERNATIONAL $$$

Map p232 (📞206-829-2280; www.thepurplecafe. com; 1225 4th Ave; mains $23-39; ⏰11am-11pm Mon-Thu, 11am-midnight Fri & Sat, noon-11pm Sun; 🚋University St) Instantly impressive with its high ceiling, lofty mezzanine floor and spectacular tower of wine bottles, the Purple Cafe almost always seems to fill its ostentatious interior, providing an atmosphere not unlike King Street Station five minutes after the Chicago train has pulled in. The multifarious menu reads like *War and Peace.*

To save time, opt for the lobster mac 'n' cheese and a bottle of wine pulled from the collection of 5000 stashed in the tower.

GEORGIAN
AFTERNOON TEA $$$

Map p232 (206-621-7889; 411 University St; afternoon tea $39; 11:30am-2:30pm Mon-Fri, noon-2:30pm Sat & Sun; University St) Once *the* place for Seattle fine dining, the Georgian at the Fairmont Olympic Hotel (p190) discontinued its dinner service in 2016. Its elegantly attired restaurant still serves lunch, but it's probably best reserved for afternoon tea – technically 'high tea' – with its proper British platter of scones, sandwiches and tea in china tea cups. For $10 extra you can add champagne.

✕ Waterfront

IVAR'S ACRES OF CLAMS
SEAFOOD $$

Map p232 (206-624-6852; www.ivars.com; 1001 Alaskan Way, Pier 54; mains $16-27; 11am-9pm Sun-Thu, 11am-10pm Fri & Sat; ; University St) Ivar Haglund was a beloved local character famous for silly promotional slogans ('Keep clam!'), but he sure knew how to fry up fish-and-chips. Ivar's is a Seattle institution that started in 1938, and its founder still stands sentinel at the door (albeit as a statue).

Forgo the dining room for the outdoor lunch counter; the chaotic ordering system involves a lot of yelling, but it seems to work, and then you can enjoy your clam strips or fish-and-chips outdoors on the pier. The tradition at Ivar's is to feed chips to the seagulls, who'll swoop down and take them out of your hand.

ELLIOTT'S OYSTER HOUSE
SEAFOOD $$

Map p232 (206-623-4340; www.elliottsoysterhouse.com; 1201 Alaskan Way, Pier 56; 6 oysters $14; 11am-10pm Sun-Thu, 11am-11pm Fri & Sat; University St) One of the best oyster houses in Seattle overhangs the water on Pier 56. The oyster menu lists over 30 different varieties plucked from practically every inlet and bay in Puget Sound and they're nicely paired with Washington white wines. A progressively happy 'happy hour' kicks off at 3pm with $1.50 per oyster; the price rises 50c an hour until 6pm.

🍷 DRINKING & NIGHTLIFE

Hotel bars are your best bet for drinking here, as there aren't too many watering holes in the downtown commercial core. Some of the finer hotel lounges serve as nice little oases. Coffee shops abound, but those with character are scarce.

There are some extremely romantic and very cozy drinking spots tucked away among the warrenlike market buildings in Pike Pl, and many of them have incredible views across the water. Post Alley has a couple of atmospheric Irish pubs and a wine-tasting room.

🍷 Pike Place Market

★ PIKE PUB & BREWERY
BREWPUB

Map p232 (206-622-6044; www.pikebrewing.com; 1415 1st Ave; 11am-midnight; University St) Leading the way in the US microbrewery revolution, this brewpub was an early starter, opening in 1989 underneath

WINE TASTING

Although it's a long way behind California in terms of annual grape yield, Washington State is the second-largest wine-producing region in the US – and it's growing. Ninety-nine percent of the state's grapes are grown on the eastern side of the Cascade Mountains in 10 different AVAs (American Viticultural Areas) that support over 800 private wineries, many of which are small and family-run. Unlike other wine regions that have become famous for one particular type of grape, Washington is known as a good all-rounder whose youthful wines – in particular the reds – are trumpeted for their fruitiness and fresh acidity. Not surprisingly, Pike Place Market is a good place to sample the wares of some of Washington's best small producers, and there are few better places than the **Tasting Room** (p56), which offers daily tastings from $10 for four 1oz pours. Friendly experts will talk you through the taste notes and tannins of prized vintages from Walla Walla, the Yakima Valley and the Columbia River region.

Pike Place Market. Today it continues to serve good pub food (mains $11 to $20) and hop-heavy, made-on-site beers in a busily decorated but fun multilevel space. Free tours of the brewery are available.

Friendly bar staff will help you pair beer with your food.

ZIG ZAG CAFÉ   COCKTAIL BAR

Map p232 (206-625-1146; www.zigzagseattle.com; 1501 Western Ave; cocktails from $8; ⊗5pm-2am; Ⓡ University St) If you're writing a research project on Seattle's culinary history, you'll need to reserve a chapter for Zig Zag Café. For serious cocktails, this place is a legend – the bar that re-popularized the gin-based Jazz Age cocktail 'The Last Word' in the early 2000s. The drink went viral and the Zig Zag's nattily attired mixers were rightly hailed as the city's finest alchemists.

Times have moved on and Zig Zag does some mean food these days, but the cocktails are still good and remarkably cheap ($7) during happy hour.

The bar is tucked away on the Pike Place Hill Climb.

STORYVILLE COFFEE   CAFE

Map p232 (206-780-5777; www.storyville.com; 94 Pike St; ⊗6:59am-6pm; ☞; Ⓡ Westlake) There are so many coffee bars in Seattle that it's sometimes hard to see the wood from the trees, unless it's the kind of wood that adorns the curved bar of Storyville. Welcome to one of Seattle's newer luxury coffee chains, whose two downtown locations (here and at the corner of 1st and Madison) attract a mixture of tourists and locals who are looking for excellent coffee.

The chocolate-chip cookies with salted centers are exceptional, as is the service; baristas happily chat to punters above the hiss and steam of their machines.

TASTING ROOM   WINE TASTING

Map p232 (206-770-9463; www.winesofwashington.com; 1924 Post Alley; ⊗noon-8pm Sun-Thu, noon-10pm Fri & Sat; Ⓡ Westlake) Pike Place Market is a good spot to sample the wares of some of Washington's best wine producers, and there are few better places than the Tasting Room, which offers four-glass tastings for $10. Friendly experts will talk you through the taste notes and tannins of prized vintages from Walla Walla, the Yakima Valley and the Columbia River region.

ATHENIAN INN   BAR

Map p232 (206-624-7166; www.athenianinn.com; 1517 Pike Place Market; ⊗8am-8pm Mon-Thu, 8am-9pm Fri & Sat, 9am-4:30pm Sun; Ⓡ Westlake) There's nothing fancy about Pike Place Market's Athenian, but it's a landmark and a bastion of unpretentious, frontier-era Seattle. Consider, as you sink that hoppy beer, that this joint has been here since 1909, opening two years after the market itself.

Over time the 'inn' has been a bakery, a lunch counter and a set location in the movie *Sleepless in Seattle*. Today, it seems to have settled in as a diner-bar combination where, especially in the off hours, you can snuggle into a window booth and gaze over Elliott Bay with a plate of fried fish and a frosty mug of Manny's Pale Ale.

KELLS   IRISH PUB

Map p232 (206-728-1916; www.kellsirish.com/seattle; 1916 Post Alley; ⊗11:30am-2am; Ⓡ Westlake) One of three West Coast Kells, this Pike Place Market Irish pub is the most atmospheric and authentic, with its exposed-brick walls, multiple nooks and crannies, and a rosy-cheeked crowd. The perfectly poured Imperial pints of Guinness are divine, there's live Irish-inspired music nightly and you can enjoy a trad Irish fry-up breakfast on Sundays.

ALIBI ROOM   BAR

Map p232 (206-623-3180; www.seattlealibi.com; 85 Pike Pl; ⊗3pm-2am Mon-Thu, noon-2am Fri-Sun, happy hour 3-6pm Mon-Thu, noon-6pm Fri-Sun; Ⓡ University St) Hidden down Post Alley opposite the beautifully disgusting 'gum wall,' the Alibi feels like an old speakeasy or perhaps the perfect place to hide from the perfect crime. Dark and cavernous, it provides surprisingly good entertainment with regular DJ nights, art installations, stand-up performances and experimental-film screenings.

Clientele is a mix of gum wall tourists and starving artists searching for inspiration in their beer.

VIRGINIA INN   PUB

Map p232 (206-728-1937; www.virginiainnseattle.com; 1937 1st Ave; ⊗11:30am-midnight Sun-Thu, 11:30am-2am Fri & Sat; Ⓡ Westlake) Near Pike Place Market (which it predates by four years) is one of Seattle's most likeable bars. Lots of draft beers, a bright brick interior and a recently improved

> **LOCAL KNOWLEDGE**
>
> ## LOCAL COFFEE CHAINS
>
> Unless you fell asleep in 1984 and have just woken up, the word 'Starbucks' needs no elaboration. But Seattle hosts a number of other smaller coffee 'chainlets,' many of which only have branches in the city and its suburbs. Here are a few of the best:
>
> **Uptown Espresso** Some say latte art owes much of its early inspiration to the velvet foam developed at Uptown Espresso, the Seattle coffee veteran that opened its first cafe in Lower Queen Anne in the mid-1980s. It now has eight locations and is known for its generous opening hours.
>
> **Caffe Ladro** Another Queen Anne–founded cafe that saw the light in 1994, Ladro now has 15 branches in and around the city. Not only does it roast its own beans, its also maintains a central bakery that produces delicious fresh snacks daily.
>
> **Zoka Coffee** Opened near Green Lake in 1997, Zoka's cafes (there are now four) are well-equipped with large tables and multiple plug-ins for that quintessential Seattle creature – the laptop camper. The huge U District cafe is typical of the brand and perennially full of students frantically finishing their homework.
>
> **Storyville Coffee Company** One of Seattle's newer cafes, Storyville's busy flagship coffee shop in Pike Place Market (p56) is definitively upmarket with a slick strip-wood counter and a veritable army of staff who'll take their time to pull you the finest cuppa. There are two additional (less-crowded) locations, one in downtown and one – you guessed it – in Queen Anne.
>
> **Caffe Vita** Founded, like so many Seattle coffee chainlets, in Queen Anne in the mid-1990s, Vita has cast its net way beyond Seattle to open cafes in LA, New York and Portland. You'll find its popular micro-roasted coffees served in many of Seattle's restaurants and hotels.
>
> **Victrola Coffee Roasters** So cool that it has located two of its three branches in hip Capitol Hill, unashamedly retro Victrola has put quality over quantity since its grand opening in 2000. Expect to find knowledgeable baristas, home-roasted beans, creative latte art and free public cuppings every Wednesday.
>
> Other chainlets to look out for include Espresso Vivace (three locations), Fuel (three locations), Caffè Fiore (four locations), and Herkimer (three locations).
>
> For great one-off cafes head to **Milstead & Co** (p148), **Zeitgeist** (p73) or **Elm Coffee Roasters** (p74).

menu consisting of 'small plates' make this a good rendezvous point for forays elsewhere.

Downtown

BOOKSTORE BAR
BAR

Map p232 (206-624-4844; www.alexishotel.com; 1007 1st Ave; ⊙7am-midnight Mon-Fri, 8am-midnight Sat & Sun; ⊠Pioneer Sq) Cementing downtown's reputation as a fount of good hotel bars is the Bookstore, encased in the front window of the Alexis Hotel (p191), which mixes books stacked on handsome wooden shelves with whiskey – an excellent combination (ask Dylan Thomas). There are over 100 varieties of Scotch and bourbon available, plus a full gamut of weighty literary tomes from Melville to Twain.

Should you be peckish, the curried crawfish mac 'n' cheese goes down a treat.

SEATTLE COFFEE WORKS
CAFE

Map p232 (www.seattlecoffeeworks.com; 107 Pike St; ⊙7am-7pm Mon-Fri, 8am-7pm Sat, 9am-6pm Sun; ⊗; ⊠Westlake) ⊘ Amid the frenetic action of downtown is a cafe where they truly treat their coffee like wine. Seattle Coffee Works' woody interior is split in two, with a normal walk-up counter and a 'slow bar' where they'll brew your coffee to order and discuss its taste notes like enthusiastic oenologists.

OWL & THISTLE
IRISH PUB

Map p232 (206-621-7777; www.owlnthistle.com; 808 Post Ave; ⊙11am-2am; ⊠Pioneer Sq) One of the best Irish pubs in the city, the dark, multi-roomed Owl & Thistle is located slap-bang downtown but misses most of the tourist traffic (who home in on the more 'themed' Fado) because it's hidden in Post Ave.

Aside from hosting Celtic folk bands or acoustic singer-songwriters who make pleasant noises here most evenings, it serves excellent beer and possibly the cheapest fish-and-chips in the city (around $4 during happy hour). Most importantly, it's run by an Irishman (and his wife).

ELYSIAN BAR   BAR
Map p232 (☎206-467-4458; www.elysianbrew
ing.com; 1516 2nd Ave; ⊙11am-2am; � West-
lake) This new-ish outpost of Elysian Brewing – one of Washington's oldest and largest microbreweries – opened in 2014 and brings the company's legendary Im-mortal IPA to the doorstep of downtown. Great beers aside, this place is also mak-ing a name for itself by slinging inventive cocktails. There's food too, should you need to line your stomach.

☆ ENTERTAINMENT

Not surprisingly, downtown is where to see big-ticket items such as touring Broadway shows and the Seattle Symphony orchestra. There's also at least one good live-music venue and a well-regarded dinner theater that books diverse musical acts.

★A CONTEMPORARY THEATRE   THEATER
Map p232 (ACT; ☎206-292-7676; www.actthea
tre.org; 700 Union St; University St) One of the three big theater companies in the city, the ACT fills its $30 million home at

Kreielsheimer Pl with performances by Seattle's best thespians and occasional big-name actors. Terraced seating surrounds a central stage, and the interior has gorgeous architectural embellishments.

SEATTLE SYMPHONY   CLASSICAL MUSIC
Map p232 (www.seattlesymphony.org; Universi-ty St) A major regional ensemble, the Seattle Symphony orchestra plays at the Benaroya Concert Hall (p47), which you'll find down-town at 2nd Ave and University St.

TRIPLE DOOR   LIVE PERFORMANCE
Map p232 (☎206-838-4333; www.thetripledoor.
net; 216 Union St; University St) This club downstairs from the Wild Ginger (p54) restaurant is a Seattle mainstay with a liberal booking policy that includes coun-try and rock as well as jazz, gospel, R&B, world music and burlesque performances. There's a full menu and a smaller lounge upstairs called the **Musicquarium** with an aquarium and free live music.

5TH AVENUE THEATER   THEATER
Map p232 (☎206-625-1900; www.5thavenue.
org; 1308 5th Ave; ⊙box office 9:30am-5:30pm Mon-Fri; University St) Built in 1926 with an opulent Asian motif, the 5th Avenue opened as a vaudeville house; it was later turned into a movie theater and then closed in 1979. An influx of funding and a heritage award saved it in 1980, and now it's Seattle's premier theater for Broadway musical revivals. It's worth going just for a look at the architecture.

Tickets are available by phone or at the theater box office.

THE TWELFTH MAN

You'll see the number 12 practically everywhere in Seattle these days – fluttering on flagpoles, taped up in shop windows, or emblazoned on the walls of bars – more often than not overlain with the avian insignia of revered NFL football team, the Seahawks.

The number has been a fixture in Seattle ever since the Seahawks retired the num-ber 12 shirt in 1984, a gesture intended to honor the team's loyal fans whose vocifer-ous support is deemed sufficiently fanatical to constitute having an extra player on the field (a so-called 12th man). But the flags and banners really proliferated following the Seahawks first ever Super Bowl victory in February 2014, and local firm Boeing even reproduced it on the tail of one of its 747s.

Although the Seahawks are not the only team to have adopted the 12th-man motif, they have valid claims for being the most passionate. Spectators at CenturyLink Field have twice broken the world record for crowd volume at a sporting event, registering 137 decibels – that's loud enough to drown out rock band AC/DC at their most deafening.

PARAMOUNT THEATER THEATER

Map p232 (⏏206-682-1414; www.stgpresents. org; 911 Pine St; ▣10) A revived multi-use theater hosting music and plays, the Paramount dates from 1928 and was originally conceived as a movie house with back-up from the popular vaudeville acts of the day. It continued as a cinema until 1971 (Bruce Lee was briefly an usher), whereupon it became a rock venue, lost money and degenerated into a tatty shadow of its former self.

Saved from demolition and listed as a historic monument in the mid-1970s, it was restored to its Jazz Age finery in 1995 and has since operated as an esteemed multi-performance venue (rock, comedy, theater), though its forte is touring Broadway shows.

SHOWBOX LIVE MUSIC

Map p232 (⏏206-628-3151; www.showbox presents.com; 1426 1st Ave; ▣University St) This cavernous 1137-capacity showroom – which hosts mostly national touring acts, ranging from indie rock to hip-hop – reinvents itself every few years and successfully rode the grunge bandwagon while it lasted. It first opened in 1939 and its dressing-room walls could probably tell some stories – everyone from Duke Ellington to Ice Cube has played here.

MARKET THEATER THEATER

Map p232 (⏏206-781-9273; www.unexpected-productions.org; 1428 Post Alley; ▣Westlake) The Market Theater is Seattle's bona fide improv comedy theater with shows staged by Unexpected Productions. It was patrons queuing for this theater who started off the famed gum wall (p47) in the 1990s. With the advent of online booking, the queues are more for photos these days. See website for schedule and tickets.

🛍 SHOPPING

The main shopping area in Seattle is downtown between 3rd and 6th Aves and between University and Stewart Sts. If you're anywhere nearby, you can't miss it.

For the compulsive browser, amateur chef, hungry traveler on a budget, or anyone else with their five senses fully intact, Seattle has no greater attraction than Pike Place Market. This is shopping central in Seattle: dozens of market food stalls hawk everything from geoduck clams to fennel root to harissa. Locals shop here just as much as tourists.

For the full gamut of souvenirs, simply stroll up and down the boardwalk along the waterfront.

★ OLD SEATTLE PAPERWORKS POSTERS, MAGAZINES

Map p232 (1501 Pike Place Market, downstairs; ⏱10:30am-5pm; ▣Westlake) If you like decorating your home with old magazine covers from *Life, Time* and *Rolling Stone,* or have a penchant for art-deco tourist posters from the 1930s, or are looking for that rare Hendrix concert flyer from 1969, this is your nirvana. It's in Pike Place Market's Down Under section.

METSKER MAPS MAPS

Map p232 (⏏206-623-8747; www.metskers.com; 1511 1st Ave; ⏱9am-8pm Mon-Fri, 10am-8pm Sat, 10am-6pm Sun; ▣Westlake) In its high-profile location on 1st Ave, this 65-year-old map shop sells all kinds of useful things for the traveler, from maps to guidebooks to various accessories. It also has a good selection of armchair-travel lit and pretty spinning globes for the dreamers.

BARNES & NOBLE BOOKS

Map p232 (600 Pine St; ⏱9am-10pm Mon-Thu, to 11pm Fri-Sun; ▣Westlake) Since the demise of Borders in 2011 and the relocation of Elliott Bay Books to Capitol Hill, Barnes & Noble remains downtown's main book emporium, with generous opening hours and helpful, well-read staff.

ALHAMBRA CLOTHING

Map p232 (www.alhambrastyle.com; 101 Pine St; ⏱10am-6:30pm Mon-Sat, 11:30am-5pm Sun; ▣Westlake) Beautifully laid-out designer boutique showcasing elegant women's clothing for those with fat wallets (or envious window-shoppers).

LA BUONA TAVOLA FOOD

Map p232 (www.trufflecafe.com; 1524 Pike Pl; ⏱10am-6pm; ▣Westlake) If you're struggling to work out which fine Pike Place Market artisan product to take home with you, here's some friendly advice: proceed directly to La Buona Tavola and buy its truffle oil. Made from high-quality Italian truffles, this is a unique and hard-to-procure substance in North America and is well worth the investment. Bonus: there is daily wine tasting ($11).

READ ALL ABOUT IT   MAGAZINES
Map p232 (93 Pike St; ⊙10am-6pm; ⓡUniversity St) Who said magazines are dead? You can read all about it at this Pike Place Market newsstand peddling *Jazz Times, Surfer Journal, Cigar Aficionado,* Spanish tattoo mags, Italian gossip tabloids, Russian comics and the good old *Buddhist Times.*

MARKET MAGIC   MAGIC
Map p232 (☎206-624-4271; www.marketmagicshop.com; 1501 Pike Pl, No 427; ⊙10am-5pm; ⓡWestlake) Selling fake dog turds, stink bombs, water-squirting rings and magic tricks, this Pike Place Market magic shop is heaven for aspiring magicians, pranksters, school kids, and grown-ups who wish they were still school kids.

PURE FOOD FISH   FOOD
Map p232 (☎206-622-5765; www.freshseafood.com; 1511 Pike Pl; ⊙9am-5pm; ⓡWestlake) Perhaps the gift that says 'I heart Seattle' the most is a whole salmon or other fresh seafood from the fish markets. All the markets will prepare fish for transportation on the plane ride home but Pure Food Fish has been around for four generations and has the best reputation for quality and value.

GOLDEN AGE COLLECTABLES   TOYS
Map p232 (☎206-622-9799; www.goldenagecollectables.com; 1501 Pike Place Market; ⊙9:30am-6pm; ⓡWestlake) A haven for geeks, kids and, especially, geeky kids, this shop has comics and comic-book-inspired toys, novelty items (hopping nuns etc), costumes and loads of goth-friendly knickknacks.

MADE IN WASHINGTON   GIFTS & SOUVENIRS
Map p232 (☎206-467-0788; www.madeinwashington.com; 1530 Post Alley; ⊙10am-6pm; ⓡWestlake) If you're looking for something authentically Northwest, head to Made in Washington. One of several locations around the city, this one in Pike Place Market stocks arts and crafts, T-shirts, coffee and chocolate, smoked salmon, regional wines, books and other creative ephemera made in the Evergreen state.

TENZING MOMO   APOTHECARY
Map p232 (☎206-623-9837; www.tenzingmomo.com; Economy Market Bldg, Pike Place Market; ⊙10am-6pm; ⓡUniversity St) Doing a good impersonation of one of the magic shops in Diagon Alley from the *Harry Potter* books, Tenzing Momo is an old-school natural apothecary with shelves of mysterious glass bottles filled with herbs and tinctures to treat any ailment.

BELLA UMBRELLA   FASHION & ACCESSORIES
Map p232 (☎206-297-1540; www.bellaumbrella.com; 1535 1st Ave; ⊙10am-6pm Mon-Sat, 11am-5pm Sun; ⓡWestlake) Highly convenient pit stop on those 150 days of the year when you walk past and it's raining. If it's sunny, Bella Umbrella has a large collection of parasols, vintage umbrellas and wedding props.

NORDSTROM   DEPARTMENT STORE
Map p232 (☎206-628-2111; www.nordstrom.com; Pine St, btwn 5th & 6th Aves; ⊙9:30am-9pm Mon-Sat, 10am-7pm Sun; ⓡWestlake) Born and raised in Seattle by a Klondike gold-rush profiteer, this upmarket department store occupies a giant space in the former Frederick and Nelson Building. In the Westlake Center, the more economical **Nordstrom Rack** (Map p232; ☎206-448-8522; 400 Pine St; ⊙9:30am-9pm Mon-Sat, 10am-8pm Sun; ⓡWestlake) offers close outs and returns from the parent store.

SUR LA TABLE   COOKWARE
Map p232 (☎206-448-2244; www.surlatable.com; 84 Pine St; ⊙9am-6:30pm; ⓡWestlake) It's hard to miss this gigantic cookware store. It's a chain, but a good one, and it started here in Seattle. The rich supply of cookware, books, gear and gadgets is bound to entice any food critic, gourmand or gourmet.

LEFT BANK BOOKS   BOOKS
Map p232 (www.leftbankbooks.com; 92 Pike St; ⊙10am-7pm Mon-Sat, 11am-6pm Sun; ⓡWestlake) This collective of more than 40 years displays zines in *español,* revolutionary pamphlets, essays by Chomsky and an inherent suspicion of authority. You're in Seattle, just in case you forgot.

BROOKS BROTHERS   CLOTHING
Map p232 (☎206-624-4400; 1330 5th Ave; ⊙9:30am-7pm Mon-Fri, 10am-6pm Sat, noon-5pm Sun; ⓡUniversity St) This is the undisputed destination for classy men's clothing in the area. The salespeople are total pros – they greet you at the door, take your measurements and avoid all signs of being pushy.

MACY'S
DEPARTMENT STORE

Map p232 (☎206-344-2121; 1601 3rd Ave; ⊙10am-9pm Mon-Sat, 11am-7pm Sun; ⊠Westlake) Seattle's oldest and largest department store, this hard-to-miss classic – formerly Bon-Marché, but renamed Bon-Macy's in August 2003 when it was bought by Macy's, then shortened for convenience – is a mainstay of clothing and homewares shopping.

THE SOUK
FOOD

Map p232 (☎206-441-1666; 1916 Pike Pl; ⊙10am-6:30pm Mon-Sat, 11am-5pm Sun; ⊠Westlake) Supplies here include Middle Eastern and North African spices and foods. Named after the Arabic word for marketplace, the shop sells everything you'll need to get from cookbook to curry – including cookbooks and curries.

NORTH FACE
SPORTS & OUTDOORS

Map p232 (☎206-622-4111; 1023 1st Ave; ⊙10am-7pm Mon-Sat, 11am-6pm Sun; ⊠Pioneer Sq) For hardcore camping, climbing and hiking clothing and equipment, go to the North Face, downtown toward the waterfront.

YE OLDE CURIOSITY SHOP
GIFTS & SOUVENIRS

Map p232 (☎206-682-5844; Pier 54; ⊙9am-9pm; ⊠University St) This landmark shop on Pier 54 has been around since 1899 – ancient history by Seattle standards. Half the stuff it displays, such as Chief Seattle's hat, a variety of stalagmites and 'tites, and some pretty cool fortune-telling machines, isn't for sale.

The funniest souvenir you can actually buy is a Mt St Helens 'snow globe' – instead of snow, it has little gray particles meant to look like ash from the volcano's eruption.

GUIDED WALKING TOURS

Downtown Seattle, and in particular Pike Place Market, is awash with good, independent walking tours of many types, but with a strong bias towards food and drink. As a rule, the tours are organized by small private individuals or companies who offer professional but highly personal service. All of them will give you a candid view of Seattle, its market and its people. With wet weather rarely off the menu, tours usually go ahead rain or shine.

Seattle Free Walking Tours (Map p232; www.seattlefreewalkingtours.org) FREE A nonprofit set up by a couple of world travelers and Seattle residents in 2012, who were impressed with the free walking tours offered in various European cities, these tours meet daily at 11am on the corner of Western Ave and Virginia St. The intimate two-hour walk takes in Pike Pl, the waterfront and Pioneer Sq. If you have a rip-roaring time (highly likely), there's a suggested $15 donation. Reserve online.

Seattle by Foot (☎206-508-7017; www.seattlebyfoot.com; tours $25-35) This company runs a handful of tours including the practically essential (this being Seattle) Coffee Crawl, which will ply you liberally with caffeine while explaining the nuances of latte art and dishing the inside story on the rise (and rise) of Starbucks. It costs $30 including samples. Registration starts at 9:50am Thursday to Sunday at the *Hammering Man* (p47) outside Seattle Art Museum. The same company also offers a unique Seattle Kids Tour: two hours of educational fun involving art, music and chocolate. Prices are from $100 per family. Reserve ahead.

Savor Seattle (☎206-209-5485; www.savorseattletours.com) These guys lead a handful of gastronomic tours, the standout being the two-hour Booze-n-Bites that runs daily at 4pm from the corner of Western Ave and Virginia St. It costs $65 and visits such culinary bastions as **Von's 1000 Spirits** (Map p232; ☎206-621-8667; www.vons 1000spirits.com; 1225 1st Ave; pizzas $19; ⊙11am-midnight Sun-Thu, 11am-1am Fri & Sat; ⊠University St). Prepare yourself for some sublime cocktails, wine and food.

Seattle Bites (☎425-888-8837; www.seattlebitesfoodtours.com) Try Lummi Island salmon, Nutella crepes, clam chowder, Washington wine and German sausage all in one market tour. This 2½-hour stroll costs $42 and leaves at 10:30am year-round (and 2:30pm May through September), so go easy on breakfast. Participants are given listening devices enabling them to wander off and still hear the guide's words of wisdom.

PACIFIC PLACE   MALL

Map p232 (www.pacificplaceseattle.com; 600 Pine
St; ⊙9:30am-9pm Mon-Sat, 9:30am-7pm Sun;
⍟Westlake) Seattle's best-quality boutique
mall feels a bit like the lobby of an upscale
hotel – it's cylindrical, and the total lack of
that hectic shopping-mall vibe makes it very
pleasant to walk around. Clothiers include **J
Crew** (⌥206-652-9788), **Club Monaco** (⌥20
6-264-8001; www.clubmonaco.com) and **BCBG**
(⌥206-447-3400; www.bcbg.com).

Take a moment to gape in the window at
Tiffany & Co (⌥206-264-1400; www.tiffany.
com) or saunter inside for a special gift.
The mall's top level features a movie theater, a pub and a couple of restaurants. This
is also where you'll find the nicest public
restrooms in downtown Seattle.

WESTLAKE CENTER   MALL

Map p232 (⌥206-467-3044; www.westlakecenter.
com; cnr 4th Ave & Pine St; ⊙10am-8pm Mon-Sat,
11am-6pm Sun; ⍟Westlake) This 'boutique
mall' – also the starting point for the monorail – has an assortment of stores. There
are some well-established chains like Nordstrom Rack (p60), as well as those with
a more local bent like **Made in Washington** (⌥206-623-1063; www.madeinwashington.
com) and an outlet of **Fireworks** (⌥206-682-
6462; www.fireworksgallery.net), which offers
inexpensive arty products by regional
craftspeople – they make great gifts.

🏃 SPORTS & ACTIVITIES

TILLICUM VILLAGE   CULTURAL

Map p232 (⌥206-933-8600; www.tillicumvillage.
com; adult/senior/child $84/75/32; ⊙Apr-Sep;
⍟University St) Present-day Seattle sits on
land once inhabited by the Duwamish tribe
whose venerable leader, Chief Sealth, lent his
name to the city. Little of the Duwamish's
ephemeral settlements remain, but you can
get a candid, if slightly touristy, taste of how
they lived at the purpose-built Tillicum Village on Blake Island where Sealth was born
in 1786.

Argosy Cruises organize all-inclusive
packages to the reconstructed 'village' from
Seattle's waterfront. The four-hour trip
includes a boat ride, salmon bake, storytelling and dance performances from Coast
Salish people.

COPPERWORKS DISTILLING   DISTILLERY

Map p232 (⌥206-504-7604; www.copper-
worksdistilling.com; 1250 Alaskan Way; ⊙noon-
6pm Mon-Thu, noon-7pm Fri & Sat, noon-5pm
Sun; ⍟University St) Smack in the middle of
downtown, this craft distiller is so new its
first batch of whiskey hasn't even finished
ageing yet. Notwithstanding, Copperworks has already made a name for itself
with its vodka and – more emphatically –
its gin made with Washington State barley in Scottish stills before being aged in
Kentucky barrels.

You can spontaneously roll in for tastings (free) at the small waterfront shop, or
take a tour ($10) of the adjacent factory.

SEATTLE CYCLING TOURS   CYCLING

Map p232 (⌥206-356-5803; www.seattle-
cycling-tours.com; 714 Pike St; tours from $55;
⍟10) Perhaps one of the best ways for new
visitors to get oriented with Seattle's burgeoning bicycle culture is with a bike tour.
Seattle Cycling Tours organizes some cork-
ers. Two tours leave daily from its downtown
base, the best going all the way to Ballard
Locks, avoiding Seattle's famous hills.

Another option is the longer weekend
ride to Bainbridge Island. It also rents bikes
($59 per day). Book online.

ARGOSY CRUISES SEATTLE HARBOR TOUR   CRUISE

Map p232 (www.argosycruises.com; Pier 55; adult/
child $25/13; ⍟University St) Argosy's popular
Seattle Harbor Tour is a one-hour narrated
tour of Elliott Bay, the waterfront and the
Port of Seattle. It departs from Pier 55.

Pioneer Square, International District & SoDo

PIONEER SQUARE | INTERNATIONAL DISTRICT | SODO

Neighborhood Top Five

❶ Klondike Gold Rush National Historical Park (p67) Reliving the spirit of the gold rush at this inspiring museum, set in one of the many redbrick Richardsonian Romanesque buildings that sprang up after the 1889 Great Fire.

❷ Zeitgeist Coffee (p73) Plugging into the spirit of the times and enjoying a damn fine cup of coffee.

❸ Jade Garden (p72) Satisfying lunchtime Asian food cravings at this boisterous dim-sum restaurant in the International District.

❹ CenturyLink Field (p75) Warming up in the bars of Pioneer Square before attending a football or soccer game.

❺ Westland Distillery (p77) Getting a taste of the up-and-coming SoDo neighborhood with a throat-warming glass of single malt whiskey.

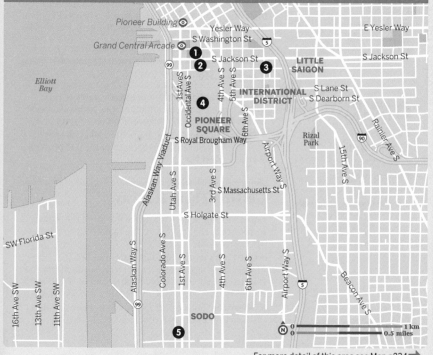

For more detail of this area see Map p234 ➡

Lonely Planet's Top Tip

Pioneer Square social life is heavily affected by the sports events that go on at the two adjacent stadiums. If you like your pubs and restaurants loud and boisterous, come on a game day. If you don't, go elsewhere.

✕ Best Workday Lunches

➡ Salumi Artisan Cured Meats (p70)

➡ Il Corvo Pasta (p70)

➡ Delicatus (p70)

➡ Bakeman's (p71)

For reviews, see p70 ➡

♟ Best Drinking & Nightlife

➡ Zeitgeist Coffee (p73)

➡ 88 Keys Dueling Piano Bar (p74)

➡ Panama Hotel Tea & Coffee House (p74)

➡ Pyramid Ale House (p75)

For reviews, see p73 ➡

🔒 Best Places to Shop

➡ Filson (p76)

➡ Uwajimaya (p76)

➡ Glasshouse Studio (p77)

➡ Flanagan & Lane Antiques (p76)

For reviews, see p75 ➡

Explore: Pioneer Square, International District & SoDo

Browsing the Pioneer Square Historic District is rather like visiting a movie set of early 20th-century Seattle, except that the food and the shopping are better. This is the birthplace of Seattle, and the redbrick district of historical buildings, antique shops and musty bars is still a real crossroads of the modern city.

Some visitors arrive by long-distance bus or train at King Street Station, a good place to get oriented due to its proximity to a trio of local squares. Pioneer Square Park is an architectural showpiece, Occidental Park was recently given a beautiful face-lift, and, just off Occidental Sq, Zeitgeist will brew your first (and possibly best) Seattle coffee. Take time to wander the streets afterwards to admire the handsome architecture.

Next to Pioneer Sq, but nothing like it architecturally, is the International District (ID) – Seattle's de-facto Chinatown. The 'international' moniker has some merit: while predominantly Chinese, there is a strong Vietnamese presence and some interesting Japanese pioneer history.

The ID is perfect hunting ground for cheap food: dim sum and Vietnamese *pho* predominate. You'll also find the Wing Luke Asian Museum and the delectable Panama Hotel Tea & Coffee House. Hidden treasures include everything from sketchy pet shops to a pinball museum.

Access spread-out SoDo by strolling south on 1st Ave S. Beyond its two sports stadiums you'll stumble upon rugged bars, pot shops, a whiskey distillery and a little-known computer museum.

Local Life

➡ **Occidental Park** (p66) You can play table tennis with a homeless person or talk recipes with a food-cart vendor in this recently cleaned-up park.

➡ **Central Saloon** (p74) If the walls could talk they'd have plenty to say in the beery confines of one of Seattle's oldest bars.

Getting There & Away

➡ **Bus** Pioneer Square is a few blocks from downtown, so any of the city buses that stop in downtown will get you pretty close.

➡ **Light rail** Central Link light rail from Sea-Tac Airport stops at Pioneer Square station or International District/Chinatown station. It carries on to Westlake station in downtown and, ultimately, the U District.

➡ **Streetcar** Runs from S Jackson St in Pioneer Square through the ID, CD and First Hill to Capitol Hill.

KEITH LEVIT / GETTY IMAGES ©

TOP SIGHT
PIONEER SQUARE ARCHITECTURE

Many important architectural heirlooms are concentrated in Pioneer Square, the district that sprang up in the wake of the 1889 Great Fire. Instantly recognizable by its handsome redbrick buildings, the neighborhood's predominant architectural style is Richardsonian Romanesque, strongly influenced by America's Chicago School.

Grand Central Arcade
The lovely **Grand Central Arcade** (Map p234; ☎206-623-7417; 214 1st Ave S) was originally Squire's Opera House, erected in 1879. When the Opera House was destroyed in the Great Fire it was rebuilt as the Squire-Latimer Building in 1890 and later became the Grand Central Hotel. The hotel died during the Depression, but it underwent a major restoration in the 1970s and now contains two floors of shops.

Pioneer Building
Built in 1891, the magnificent **Pioneer Building** (Map p234; 606 1st Ave S; pictured above) facing Pioneer Square Park is one of the finest Victorian buildings in Seattle and showcases many of the classic components of Richardsonian Romanesque; look for the Roman arches, a recessed main doorway, curvaceous bay windows and decorative flourishes, most notably the two frontal columns that frame some skillfully embellished bricks.

Smith Tower
A mere dwarf amid Seattle's impressive modern stash of skyscrapers, the 42-story neoclassical **Smith Tower** (Map p234; ☎206-622-4004; www.smithtower.com; 506 2nd Ave) was, for half a century after its construction in 1914, the tallest building west of Chicago. The beaux-arts-inspired lobby is onyx- and marble-paneled, while the brass-and-copper elevator is still manually operated by a uniformed attendant. You can visit the observation deck in the so-called Chinese Room with its ornate wooden ceiling on the 35th floor.

DON'T MISS
➜ Smith Tower
➜ Pioneer Building
➜ Grand Central Arcade

PRACTICALITIES
➜ Map p234, C1
➜ btwn Alaskan Way S, S King St, 5th Ave S, 2nd Ave ext & Columbia St
➜ Ⓡ Pioneer Sq

SIGHTS

Pioneer Square is a veritable outdoor museum of late 19th-century redbrick architecture, with several indoor museums thrown in for good measure.

The International District is more about street bustle. Its reputation for sheltering Asian immigrants is potently summed up in the Wing Luke Museum.

Pioneer Square

PIONEER SQUARE HISTORICAL DISTRICT   AREA
See p65.

PIONEER SQUARE PARK   SQUARE
Map p234 (cnr Cherry St & 1st Ave S; Pioneer Sq) The original Pioneer Square is a cobbled triangular plaza where Henry Yesler's sawmill cut the giant trees that marked Seattle's first industry. Known officially as Pioneer Square Park, the plaza features a bust of **Chief Seattle** (Sealth, in the original language), an ornate pergola and a **totem pole**.

Some wayward early Seattleites, so the story goes, stole the totem pole from the Tlingit native people in southeastern Alaska in 1890. An arsonist lit the pole aflame in 1938, burning it to the ground. When asked if they could carve a replacement pole, the Tlingit took the money offered, thanking the city for payment for the first totem, and said it would cost $5000 to carve another one. The city coughed up the money and the Tlingit obliged with the pole you see today.

PERGOLA   LANDMARK
Map p234 (cnr Yesler Way & James St; Pioneer Sq) This decorative iron pergola in Pioneer Square Park was built in 1909 to serve as an entryway to an underground lavatory and to shelter those waiting for the cable car that went up and down Yesler Way. The reportedly elaborate restroom eventually closed due to serious plumbing problems at high tide. In January 2001, the pergola was leveled by a wayward truck, but it was restored and put back where it belonged the following year, looking as good as new.

YESLER WAY   STREET
Map p234 (Pioneer Sq) Seattle claims its Yesler Way was the coining ground for the term 'skid road' – logs would 'skid' down the steeply sloped road linking a logging area above town to Henry Yesler's mill.

As for Henry Yesler himself, local historians paint him as an ambitious business zealot who clashed frequently with the wild-and-woolly Doc Maynard. These two men, who by all accounts were equally stubborn, both owned part of the land that would eventually become Pioneer Sq. This resulted in a highly symbolic grid clash, in which Yesler's section of the square had streets running parallel to the river, while Maynard's came crashing in at a north–south angle. Yesler maintained, not unreasonably, that Doc was drunk when he submitted his portion of the plans.

MILEPOST 31   MUSEUM
Map p234 (211 1st Ave S; 11am-5pm Tue-Sat; Occidental Mall) FREE A project as comprehensive and long-winded as the Alaskan Viaduct Replacement Program (p48) requires an explanatory museum, and this small but concise exhibit in Pioneer Square does a fine of job of relaying the facts – plus there are some fascinating nuggets of incidental Seattle history thrown in for good measure. Numerous old photos and a scale model of the drilling machine encourage lingering.

The exhibit will remain open as long as the program lasts – until 2018 at least.

ROQ LA RUE   GALLERY
Map p234 (www.roqlarue.com; 532 1st Ave S; noon-5pm Wed-Sat; Occidental Mall) FREE This gallery has secured its reputation by taking risks: the work on view skates along the edge of urban pop-culture. Since opening in 1998, the gallery, which is owned and curated by Kirsten Anderson, has been a significant force in the pop surrealism field and is frequently featured in *Juxtapoz* magazine.

OCCIDENTAL PARK   PARK
Map p234 (btwn S Washington & S Main Sts; Occidental Mall) Once a rather grim place, Occidental Park has undergone a recent renaissance thanks largely to a partnership between the City of Seattle and a couple of nonprofit groups. Following an urban renewal campaign in 2015, the park has been kitted out with attractive seating, outdoor games (including chess and table football), licensed buskers and a regular posse of food carts.

Add this to what was already there (classic redbrick buildings, Native American art and a firefighting sculpture) and you've got an exceptional place to hang out. Friendly 'park ambassadors' (dressed in yellow vests) handle security, clean-ups and tourist information 24/7.

OCCIDENTAL SQUARE   SQUARE

Map p234 (btwn S Main & S Jackson Sts; 🚇 Occidental Mall) Abutting Occidental Park, this rectangular plaza is a cobblestone space flanked by unusually handsome Victorian buildings housing glassblowing studios and specialist galleries.

★KLONDIKE GOLD RUSH
NATIONAL HISTORICAL PARK   MUSEUM

Map p234 (📞206-553-3000; www.nps.gov/klse; 319 2nd Ave S; ⊙10am-5pm; 🚇 Occidental Mall) **FREE** This wonderful museum eloquently run by the US National Park Service has exhibits, photos and news clippings from the 1897 Klondike gold rush, when a Seattle-on-steroids acted as a fueling depot for prospectors bound for the Yukon in Canada. It would cost $20 entry anywhere else; in Seattle it's free!

The best aspect of the museum is its clever use of storytelling. At the outset you are introduced to five local characters who became stampeders (Klondike prospectors) in the 1890s and are then invited to follow their varying fortunes and experiences periodically throughout the rest of the museum. Sound effects and interactive exhibits are used to good effect.

The museum, which opened in 2006, is housed in the old Cadillac Hotel (built in 1889) that was rescued from a grisly fate after nearly being toppled in the 2001 Nisqually earthquake.

WATERFALL PARK   PARK

Map p234 (cnr S Main St & 2nd Ave S; 🚇 Occidental Mall) This unusual park is an urban oasis commemorating workers of the United Parcel Service (UPS), which grew out of a messenger service that began in a basement at this location in 1907. The artificial 22ft waterfall that flows in this tiny open-air courtyard is flanked by tables and flowering plants.

It's the perfect spot to eat a brown-bag lunch as you rest your weary feet.

KING STREET STATION   LANDMARK

Map p234 (303 S Jackson St; 🚇 International District/Chinatown) One of the pillars upon which Seattle built its early fortunes, the old Great Northern Railroad depot was given some much needed Botox in the early 2010s after decades of neglect. Serving as the western terminus of the famous Empire

SODO: A NEIGHBORHOOD ON THE RISE

The baton for Seattle's most ascendant neighborhood has been passed to SoDo, an acronym for the sketchy industrial district SOuth of DOwntown dominated by Seattle's two professional sports stadiums, CenturyLink Field (p75) and Safeco Field (p75).

A tangled confusion of train tracks, warehouses and concrete overpasses regularly rattled by low-flying airplanes, SoDo is not as homogeneous or community-focused as other Seattle neighborhoods, though this hasn't prevented a number of emerging businesses from setting up shop there. Starbucks was an early convert, moving the company's main headquarters into a vintage redbrick building just off 1st Ave S in 1993. In the last few years, it has been joined by an eclectic mix of newer aspirants, including a micro-distillery (p77); a flagship Filson store (p76), the original Klondike outfitters; a computer museum (p70) owned by Microsoft co-founder Paul Allen; and half-a-dozen pot shops. The proliferation of pot shops has led some to facetiously refer to SoDo as SoDope or 'Little Amsterdam.' Current outlets include the city's first recreational cannabis store, Cannabis City (p76), and Ganja Goddess (p76), another early starter that runs a special shuttle to and from downtown. Aside from its fanatically supported sports teams, SoDo has a midsize live-music venue (p75), several downbeat bars and a decent brewpub, the Pyramid Ale House (p75), which is popular with sports fans.

SoDo isn't an obvious walking neighborhood, although many of its sights can be easily accessed from Pioneer Square by strolling south on 1st Ave S. Another entry point is West Seattle, which is linked to SoDo via the 'Duwamish trail' (a designated biking/hiking path) and bus 21.

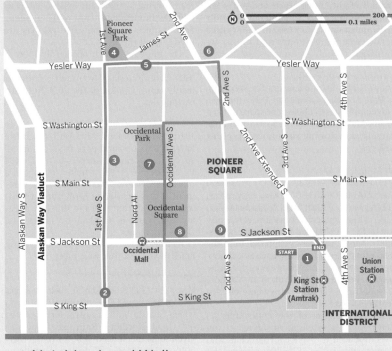

Neighborhood Walk
Historical Pioneer Square Circuit

START KING STREET STATION
END KING STREET STATION
LENGTH 1 MILE; ONE HOUR

Start at **1 King Street Station** (p67), Seattle's main railway terminus, returned to its Gilded Age glory. Before the advent of cars this was most people's first impression of Seattle. Exiting via the side door, walk west along King St in the shadow of CenturyLink Field, home of Seattle's football and soccer teams; the bars and restaurants here are packed with noisy supporters on match days. Turn right onto redbrick **2 1st Ave S**, little altered since it rose in the aftermath of the 1889 fire. Galleries and antique shops will catch your eye, but be sure to descend to the **3 Grand Central Baking Co** (p71) for cakes and sandwiches. **4 Pioneer Square Park** (p66) is usually awash with tourists and homeless people, including local characters selling the newspaper *Real Change*. The small triangular park sports an Eiffel-esque iron pergola and the Richardsonian Romanesque Pioneer Building. Leading east, **5 Yesler**

Way (p66) holds the dubious distinction of being the nation's original 'skid row.' The appearance of the ugly concrete car park on James St convinced the city to introduce greater conservationist measures in the 1960s. You can divert on the corner with 2nd Ave for a glance at the neoclassical **6 Smith Tower** (p65), erected by LC Smith, a man who built his fortune on typewriters (Smith-Corona) and guns (Smith & Wesson). Head south on 2nd Ave S and go right on Washington St S; **7 Occidental Park** (p66), with its ivy-covered edifices and resident food carts and games, opens out on your left. Grab a bite to eat and treat yourself to a game of corn-hole or table football. Cross Main St into Occidental Sq before heading left on **8 S Jackson St**, the western terminus of Seattle's newest streetcar. In the 1890s, S Jackson's stores outfitted prospectors heading for the Klondike, Canada. Fill in your historical gaps at the intellectually stimulating **9 Klondike Gold Rush National Historical Park** (p67) before pacing one block back to King Street Station.

Builder train that runs cross-country be-tween Seattle and Chicago, the station building was designed to imitate St Mark's bell tower in Venice.

It was originally constructed in 1906 by Reed & Stem, who also designed New York City's Grand Central Station, and is nota-ble for many features, not least a fabulous Italianate plasterwork ceiling in the wait-ing room that is rich in period detail. The waiting room was covered up by a horrible suspended ceiling in the 1960s but, as part of a $26 million revamp, the entire interior and exterior of the station was returned to its Gilded Age high watermark in 2012.

FOSTER/WHITE GALLERY   GALLERY
Map p234 (🖉206-622-2833; www.fosterwhite. com; 220 3rd Ave S; ⊙10am-6pm Tue-Sat; 🚇Inter-national District/Chinatown) **FREE** The polished Foster/White Gallery, which opened in 1968, features glassworks, paintings and sculpture by mainstream Northwest artists in a beau-tifully renovated 7000-sq-ft space. Some of the exhibits are for sale (if you're rich), but realistically, this is more a contemporary art gallery – and a fine one too – that deserves half an hour of quiet contemplation.

⊙ International District

UNION STATION   LANDMARK
Map p234 (401 S Jackson St; 🚇International District/Chinatown) A landmark that has benefited from restoration fever is Union Station, the old Union Pacific Railroad depot (1911) that sat unoccupied between 1971 and 1999. The restoration project included the preservation of the original tile floors, clocks and windows. No longer serving as a train station, the building now houses the headquarters for Sound Transit.

Worth a look and usually open for brows-ing is the Great Hall, half the size of a football field.

SEATTLE PINBALL MUSEUM   MUSEUM, GAMES
Map p234 (🖉206-623-0759; www.seattlepinball museum.com; 508 Maynard Ave S; adult/child 7-12yr $13/10; ⊙noon-5pm Mon, Wed & Sun, noon-10pm Thu-Sat; 🚼; 🚇7th & Jackson/Chinatown) Got kids? Got kid-like tendencies? Love the buzzers and bells of good old-fashioned games machines? Lay aside your iPad apps and become a pinball wizard for the day in

REAL CHANGE
....
Pioneer Sq's large population of home-less people can be a shocking sight for the first-time visitor, although they are rarely threatening. In fact, some homeless Seattleites are genuine lo-cal characters. One of the best ways to help these people get back on their feet is to buy the weekly newspaper *Real Change*, sold on the street for $2 by vendors who are often homeless (vendors buy the paper for $0.60 a copy and keep the profit). The paper, founded in 1994, generates nearly $1 million a year for homeless causes and helps to alleviate panhandling.

this fantastic games room in the ID with machines from 1960 retro to 2015 futuristic. Admission buys you unlimited games for the day. Sure plays a mean pinball!

HING HAY PARK   SQUARE
Map p234 (cnr Maynard Ave S & S King St; 🚇7th & Jackson/Chinatown) If you need a tranquil spot to rest while wandering the ID, Hing Hay Park (more of a square than a park) lends a little breathing space to this oth-erwise austere district. The traditional Chinese pavilion was a gift from the people of Taipei. On Saturdays in August you can catch a free outdoor movie here beginning at sunset. Also, look out for Asian dance and licensed buskers.

WING LUKE MUSEUM OF THE ASIAN PACIFIC AMERICAN EXPERIENCE   MUSEUM
Map p234 (🖉206-623-5124; www.wingluke. org; 719 S King St; adult/child $15/10; ⊙10am-5pm Tue-Sun; 🚇7th & Jackson/Chinatown) The beautifully unique Wing Luke examines Asian-Pacific American culture, focusing on prickly issues such as Chinese settle-ment in the 1880s and Japanese intern-ment camps during WWII. There are also art exhibits and a preserved immigrant apartment. Guided tours are available; the first Thursday of the month is free (with extended hours until 8pm).

INTERNATIONAL CHILDREN'S PARK   PARK
Map p234 (cnr S Lane St & 7th Ave; 🚼; 🚇7th & Jack-son/Chinatown) If your offspring aren't up for exploring the Asian markets or sitting still for a dim-sum brunch, then bring them to

GOING UNDERGROUND

It's hard to envisage today, but Pioneer Square's streets were originally 12ft to 30ft lower than their present levels. After the 1889 fire, city planners decided to raise the street level in order to solve long-standing problems with tidal flooding. Hence, the post-fire buildings were constructed with an extra ground floor in anticipation of the impending, but lengthy, regrade. This spooky underground world of abandoned cellars and sidewalks lay forgotten for decades, but was rediscovered and opened to tourists in the 1960s by local historian, Bill Speidel. The tours (p77) are still popular today.

this diminutive coming-up-for-air park with a unique bronze dragon sculpture crying out to be climbed on. It was designed by George Tsutakawa, a Seattle native who spent much of his childhood in Japan, then returned to become an internationally renowned sculptor and painter and a professor at the University of Washington.

⊙ SoDo

LIVING COMPUTER MUSEUM MUSEUM
Map p234 (www.livingcomputermuseum.org; 2245 1st Ave S; adult/child $6/2; ⊙10am-5pm Wed-Sun; 頁SoDo) Owned by unapologetic computer geek and Microsoft co-founder, Paul Allen, this place will evoke heavy nostalgia in anyone who can remember the world pre-internet. Hosted in a nondescript commercial building in industrial SoDo and little known even among locals, it's well worth checking out for its host of antediluvian computers with their blinking green cursors and black, app-free screens. Some of them are large enough to fill an average-sized student bedroom.

Friendly guides give regular tours and you're welcome to 'play' on many of the exhibits.

 EATING

Pioneer Square has changed in recent years with old-school steak and seafood houses being replaced by the kind of chic, rustic restaurants that are more redolent of French kitchens. There's a similar proliferation of gourmet sandwich bars.

The ID can be split into three parts. Japantown which, while light on sushi, is famous for its historic Panama Hotel Tea & Coffee House (p74); Chinatown, notable for its dim-sum restaurants and late-night eating options; and Little Saigon, east of 8th Ave S and I-5, where the flavor becomes decidedly Vietnamese and locals argue fiercely over the best *pho* (noodle soup).

✗ Pioneer Square

★SALUMI ARTISAN
CURED MEATS SANDWICHES $
Map p234 (✆206-621-8772; www.salumicuredmeats.com; 309 3rd Ave S; sandwiches $8.50-11; ⊙11am-1:30pm Mon, 11am-3:30pm Tue-Fri; 頁International District/Chinatown) With a shopfront as wide as a smart car and a following as large as the Seattle Mariners, Salumi is a well-known vortex of queues. But they're worth it for the legendary Italian-quality salami and cured-meat sandwiches (grilled lamb, pork shoulder, meatballs) that await you at the counter. Grab one and go! On Tuesdays, they also ply their homemade gnocchi.

IL CORVO PASTA
ITALIAN $
Map p234 (✆206-538-0999; www.ilcorvopasta.com; 217 James St; pasta $10; ⊙11am-3pm Mon-Fri; 頁Pioneer Sq) A unique hole-in-the-wall, pasta-only place with limited seating and a high turnover of office workers on their lunch breaks. Join the perennial queue, order one of three daily pastas with sauces and grab a seat (if there's one available). You have to bus your own table, Seattle-style, at the end. Wine and bread provide welcome accompaniments.

The only drawback? The frustratingly limited opening hours can invoke weekend withdrawal symptoms in people addicted to their pasta.

DELICATUS
SANDWICHES, DELI $
Map p234 (✆206-623-3780; www.delicatusseattle.com; 103 1st Ave S; sandwiches $9-12; ⊙11am-6pm Mon-Fri, 11am-4pm Sat & Sun; 頁Pioneer Sq) Delicatus is a new-school Pioneer Square sandwich bar/deli where the sarnies are a bit more deluxe than

yesteryear, being both well-stuffed and enlivened with interesting relishes. Go at lunchtime for the best atmosphere.

BAKEMAN'S DINER $

Map p234 (📞206-622-3375; www.bakemans catering.com; 122 Cherry St; sandwiches $3.75-4.75; ⏱10am-3pm Mon-Fri; 🚇Pioneer Sq) A classic Pioneer Square workday lunch place, the subterranean and slightly utilitarian Bakeman's has become practically synonymous with its star take-out – roasted turkey and cranberry sandwich, served as fresh as the day after Thanksgiving. Expect long lines and service that is lean but brisk.

GRAND CENTRAL BAKING CO SOUP, SANDWICHES $

Map p234 (📞206-622-3644; www.grandcentral bakery.com; Grand Central Arcade, 214 1st Ave S; sandwiches $4-10; ⏱7am-5pm Mon-Fri, 8am-4pm Sat; 🚇Occidental Mall) Grand Central (located in the eponymous building) is considered one of the best bakeries in Seattle. Its artisan breads can be bought whole or sliced up for sandwiches in its cafe and enjoyed in the redbrick confines of the Grand Central mall, or at a Euro-chic table in Occidental Park (p66) outside. Beware the lunchtime queues.

There are nine other locations, seven of them in Portland, OR.

CAFE PALOMA TURKISH $

Map p234 (📞206-405-1920; www.cafepaloma. com; 93 Yesler Way; meze $6-8; ⏱10am-6pm Mon, 10am-9pm Tue-Sat, 10am-2pm Sun; 🚇Pioneer Sq) Various words spring to mind when thinking of Cafe Paloma...Bistro. Eggplant. Casual. Friendly. Turkish. Meze. Music. Lemonade. Falafel. If any of this sounds interesting, be sure to drop by this jewel of a restaurant in Pioneer Square where small Turkish miracles are concocted.

★LONDON PLANE CAFE, DELI $$

Map p234 (📞206-624-1374; www.thelondon planeseattle.com; 300 Occidental Ave S; small plates $7-20; ⏱8am-5pm Mon-Tue, 8am-9pm Wed-Fri, 9am-9pm Sat, 9am-5pm Sun; 🚇Occidental Mall) 🍴 Matt Dillon (the Seattle chef, not the Hollywood actor) moved less than a block from his established restaurant, Bar Sajor, to open London Plane, a hybrid cafe, flower shop, deli and breakfast spot that maintains the French country kitchen feel that has become Dillon's trademark.

Sustainability is the overriding theme here. The open prep area is piled high with fresh herbs and myriad foraged plants waiting to be scattered into soups, salads and sandwiches.

BAR SAJOR MEDITERRANEAN $$

Map p234 (📞206-682-1117; www.barsajor.com; 323 Occidental Ave; plates $10-25; ⏱4-9:30pm Tue-Fri, 10am-2pm & 4-9:30pm Sat, 10am-2pm & 5:30-9pm Sun; 🚇Occidental Mall) 🍴 Resembling a bright, open-plan French country kitchen and claiming to serve Portuguese-inspired food created from the raw ingredients of Seattle's hinterland, Bar Sajor is a project from Matt Dillon, who built his reputation at Capitol Hill's hugely popular (and sustainable) Sitka & Spruce (p114).

Both the atmosphere and the food (homemade bread, cheese and salami selections, and genuinely delicious vegetable plates) will have you living vicariously as a European without ever having to abandon your locavore instincts.

DAMN THE WEATHER MODERN AMERICAN $$

Map p234 (📞206-946-1283; www.damnthe weather.com; 116 1st Ave S; small plates $8-12; ⏱4pm-2am Mon-Sat, 4-11pm Sun; 🚇Occidental Mall) Repeating a mantra that flows freely from the lips of many Seattleites, this new-ish venture is perhaps best described as a cocktail bar that also serves damn good food. The interior is typical Pioneer Square – all wooden floors, bare-brick walls and low-lit chandeliers – while the clientele is a blend of hipster meets yuppies on their way home from the office.

Try the octopus risotto or the Caesar salad sandwich. And don't forget the cocktails.

FX MCRORY'S STEAK, CHOP & OYSTER HOUSE STEAK, SEAFOOD $$

Map p234 (📞206-623-4800; www.fxmcrorys. com; 419 Occidental Ave S; mains $12-29; ⏱11am-9pm Mon-Thu, 11:30am-10pm Fri & Sat, noon-10pm Sun; 🚇Occidental Mall) This vast Pioneer Square landmark across from the sports stadiums is a weird blend of class and ass – it's a majestic old space dating from 1906 with a whiskey bar on one side, a dining room on the other and an oyster bar in the middle. Its proximity to the sports stadiums equals a high ballcap-jock quotient on game days.

McRory's has an impressive stash of bourbon – close to 280 labels – at which you can ogle, most of it shaped into a pyramid of booze behind the bar. Food-wise it's good for

HOOVERVILLE

The district known today as SoDo once had a more unsavory sheen. From 1932 to 1941, during the worst years of the Great Depression, a desperate shanty town known as Hooverville took root on the tidal flats south of downtown on land belonging to the Port of Seattle. Covering 9 acres and housing up to 1000 people in roughly 600 homemade shacks fashioned out of discarded junk, Hooverville was not unique to Seattle – there were a number of similarly downbeat slums dotted around the US, all named sarcastically after the US president, Herbert Hoover; notwithstanding, it was the largest and most notorious in the Pacific Northwest.

The 'town' even had its own unofficial mayor, an unemployed lumberjack called Jesse Jackson who liaised with city authorities to win Hooverville a measure of government recognition on the condition that it adhered to basic rules and sanitary standards.

Populated primarily by the unemployed and the transient, the vast majority of Hooverville's inhabitants were male and middle-aged (women and children were officially banned). Most were out of work lumberjacks, sailors, miners or tradesmen who had lost their jobs during the Depression, but stubbornly refused to live off community soup kitchens and flophouses. Those with enough pluck managed to scrape a tenuous living by fishing in and around Elliott Bay or collecting junk and selling it on the streets of Seattle.

Rather than being a dangerous urban ghetto, Seattle's Hooverville evolved into a relatively peaceful, if dilapidated, slum characterized by a backs-to-the-wall neighborly spirit and delicate sense of community. By 1941, with the economy recovering and war in the offing, the township was finally cleared by city authorities concerned about its arthritic buildings and lack of sanitation. Its ghostly foundations were filled by docks, warehouses and light industry in the 1940s and '50s.

prime rib and seafood, particularly Dungeness crab, oysters on the half-shell, smoked salmon, prawns and Penn Cove mussels.

NIRMAL'S   INDIAN $$$

Map p234 (☑206-388-2196; www.nirmalseattle. com; 106 Occidental Ave S; mains $15-30; ◷11am-2pm Mon-Wed, 11am-2pm & 5:30-10pm Thu & Fri, 5:30-10pm Sat; ☐Pioneer Sq) At last...Seattle has filled a massive hole in its culinary resume – good Indian food. Nirmal's is a brave new restaurant that takes a stab at pretty much any flavor under the South Asian umbrella, be it Goan fish curry, Bengali prawns or Kashmiri rack of lamb.

Its minimalist exposed-brick interior is the antithesis of traditional curtains-and-carpet Indian restaurants, but no matter – the multifarious *thalis* (platter of small dishes) and refreshing *kulfis* (frozen desert) are already creating excited lunchtime chatter.

✕ International District

JADE GARDEN   CHINESE $

Map p234 (☑206-622-8181; 424 7th Ave S; dim-sum items $2-3, mains $8-12; ◷10am-2:30am; ☐7th & Jackson/Chinatown) Usually mentioned near

the top of the list of best places for dim sum in the ID, Jade Garden offers a good range of delicacies with everything from standard, newbie-friendly shrimp dumplings and steamed pork buns to more exotic plates such as black cylinders of sesame-paste gel and, of course, chicken's feet. The more things you try, the more fun you'll have.

The Jade Garden's hot pots are also recommended.

GREEN LEAF   VIETNAMESE $

Map p234 (☑206-340-1388; www.greenleaftaste. com; 418 8th Ave S; pho $9, specials $10-12; ◷11am-10pm; ☐7th & Jackson/Chinatown) Popular Green Leaf, located in Chinatown, shoots out rapid-fire dishes from its tiny kitchen that abuts a dining room not much wider than a railway carriage. Choose the traditional *pho* (beef noodle soup) or go for the excellent rice- or vermicelli-noodle dishes – especially the *bún dặc biệt* (with pork, chicken and shrimp). There's also a branch in Belltown at 2800 1st Ave.

PHO BAC   VIETNAMESE $

Map p234 (☑206-568-0882; 1240 S Jackson St; pho from $6.50; ◷8am-9pm; ☐12th & Jackson/ Little Saigon) Pho Bac looks like the sort of place where you can follow last week's crumbs around the table, but hold your judgment: you can get three sizes of excellent *pho* at this boat-shaped Vietnamese food shack with its huge windows gazing onto Little Saigon.

SHANGHAI GARDEN — CHINESE $

Map p234 (📞206-625-1688; www.theshanghai garden.com; 524 6th Ave S; mains $10-16; ⊙11am-9pm Tue-Thu & Sun, 11am-10pm Fri & Sat; 🚇5th & Jackson/Japantown) Hand-shaved barley noodles are the specialty of Shanghai Garden and, frankly, they trounce all expectations you might ordinarily have of a noodle. They're wide and chewy, almost meaty, and just barely dressed with perky spinach and nicely integrated globs of chicken, tofu, beef or shrimp.

It might seem odd to get all rapturous about a plate of noodles, but these deserve it. The sugar-pea vines are also a favorite, and if neither of those options tempts you, there are about 75 other choices.

PURPLE DOT CAFÉ — CHINESE $

Map p234 (📞206-622-0288; www.purpledotseat tle.com; 515 Maynard Ave S; mains $7-14; ⊙9am-1am Sun-Thu, 9am-3:30am Fri & Sat; 🚇7th & Jackson/Chinatown) The Purple Dot looks like the inside of an '80s video game (yes, it's actually purple) and draws a late-night drunken-disco crowd on weekends, but most of the time it's a calm, quiet place to get dim sum and Macao-style specialties (meaning you can feast on baked spaghetti and French toast along with your Hong Kong favorites).

HOUSE OF HONG — CHINESE $

Map p234 (📞206-622-7997; www.houseofhong. info; 408 8th Ave S; dim sum per item $2-3, mains $12-15; ⊙9:30am-11pm; 🚇7th & Jackson/Chinatown) This huge mainstay of the neighborhood serves dim sum from 10am until 4:30pm every day – handy if you're craving Asian snacks around noon.

TAMARIND TREE — VIETNAMESE $$

Map p234 (📞206-860-1414; www.tamarindtree restaurant.com; 1036 S Jackson St; mains $12-17; ⊙10am-10pm Sun-Thu, 10am-midnight Fri & Sat; 🚇Little Saigon) Serving upscale food at low-brow prices in a massively popular dining room, this legendary place has a nuanced menu that includes everything from satays and salad rolls to big bowls of *pho* and rice cakes (squid-, prawn- and pork-filled fried crepes). It also donates some of its profits to the Vietnam Scholarship Foundation. It's hidden at the back of an ugly car park.

✖ SoDo

CAFE CON LECHE — CUBAN $

Map p234 (📞206-682-7557; www.cafeconleche seattle.com; 2901 1st Ave S; mains $10-16; ⊙11am-4pm Mon-Wed, to 7pm Thu & Fri; 🚇SoDo) Cuban food is scant in Seattle but, if you want it, you'll have to trek out to SoDo to this colorful abode, a former food truck that has sprouted foundations. It will be worth it when you dig into the *ropa vieja* (spicy beef stew) or *puerco asado* (roast pork) accompanied by rice and beans and washed down with a *cafecito* (strong sweet espresso).

The adjoining **Club Sur** hosts Cuban music and special dinners on selective nights (see website for dates).

🍷 DRINKING & NIGHTLIFE

Though it lends itself more to frenzied clubbing than casual pint-sipping, Pioneer Square is home to some of the city's oldest and most atmospheric bars. If you prefer a saloon to a salon, this historical part of town is your best bet. Beware: things get particularly lively (and crowded) on sports game days.

The lounges inside many of the restaurants in the ID are good haunts for hiding away with a cocktail any time of day; many of them have afternoon happy-hour food specials, too. The ID is also the place to come for things like bubble tea and unusual herbal-tea concoctions.

🍷 Pioneer Square

★ZEITGEIST COFFEE — CAFE

Map p234 (📞206-583-0497; www.zeitgeist coffee.com; 171 S Jackson St; ⊙6am-7pm Mon-Fri, 7am-7pm Sat, 8am-6pm Sun; 📶; 🚇Occidental Mall) Possibly Seattle's best indie coffee bar, Zeitgeist brews up smooth *doppio macchiatos* to go along with its sweet almond croissants and other luscious baked goods. The atmosphere is trendy industrial, with brick walls and large windows for people-watching. Soups, salads and sandwiches are also on offer.

PIONEER SQUARE, INTERNATIONAL DISTRICT & SODO DRINKING & NIGHTLIFE

88 KEYS DUELING PIANO BAR   BAR

Map p234 (☑206-839-1300; www.ilove88keys.
com; 315 2nd Ave S; ☺5pm-2am; ☐Occidental
Mall) Reviving the almost lost art of dueling
pianos, this sports bar–jazz haunt has two
grands set up facing each other on a raised
stage (so, strictly speaking, it's 176 keys).
The time to come is Friday or Saturday
night, when two talented musicians belt
out piano classics in unison (everything
from Fats Domino to Billy Joel) with plenty
of audience interaction.

There's food and drink, of course. But this
place is all about the music – and the electric
atmosphere.

ELM COFFEE ROASTERS   COFFEE

Map p234 (☑206-445-7808; www.elmcoffee
roasters.com; 240 2nd Ave S; ☺7am-7pm Mon-Fri,
8am-4pm Sat, 9am-5pm Sun; ☎; ☐Occidental
Mall) Currently one of Seattle's freshest coffee
'freshmen,' Elm opened in December 2014 in
a spacious cafe-cum-roasting room in Pioneer Sq. It's a good indie option if you're after
a quick sweet snack and a cup of something
home-roasted. The entrance is on Main St.

CAFFÈ UMBRIA   CAFE

Map p234 (☑206-624-5847; www.caffeumbria.
com; 320 Occidental Ave S; ☺6am-6pm Mon-Fri,
7am-6pm Sat, 8am-5pm Sun; ☐Occidental Mall)
Started by an immigrant from Perugia in
Italy, Umbria has a true Italian flavor with its
8oz cappuccinos, chatty clientele, pretty Italianate tiles and baguettes so fresh they must
have been teleported over from Milan. Ideal
for Italophiles and Starbucks-phobes.

FUEL   SPORTS BAR

Map p234 (☑206-405-3835; www.fuelseattle.
com; 164 S Washington St; ☺11:30am-close;
☐Pioneer Sq) This TV-filled sports bar is the
favored meet-up for Seattle Sounders 'Emerald City Supporters' soccer fans on match
days, and also Seahawks fans. Tuck your elbows in and inhale deeply as you enter.

CENTRAL SALOON   PUB

Map p234 (☑206-622-0209; 207 1st Ave S;
☺11am-2am; ☐Occidental Mall) It may be two
years younger than the official 'Oldest Bar
in Seattle' (Georgetown's Jules Maes), but
the Central isn't exactly new and shiny.
More of a locals' hangout than an object
of historical interest, this long, narrow
joint makes grotty bathrooms and blah
food seem charming, by virtue of cheap
suds, friendly barkeeps and a comfortable,
unfussy vibe.

Nirvana, Soundgarden and most of the
grunge nobility have played here, and live
music still happens regularly.

J&M CAFÉ   BAR

Map p234 (☑206-292-0663; www.jandmcafe.
com; 201 1st Ave S; ☺11am-2am; ☐Occidental
Mall) In one of Seattle's oldest buildings
(1889) sits one of Seattle's oldest bars, trading as J&M's since around 1902. Most of the
original furnishings were sold off in 2009
when the owners went out of business, but
the bar was back a year later – albeit in a
less classic and authentic form – knocking
out its no-frills beer and burgers.

🍷 International District

PANAMA HOTEL
TEA & COFFEE HOUSE   CAFE

Map p234 (☑206-515-4000; www.panamahotel.
net; 607 S Main St; ☺8am-9pm; ☐5th & Jack-
son/Japantown) The Panama, a historic 1910

THE SOUND OF THE SOUNDERS

If you think soccer is a niche sport in the US inspiring little of the passion and noise of
football and baseball, you obviously haven't been to Seattle. The Seattle Sounders
(p32), the third incarnation of Seattle's main soccer club who launched in 2008, are
the best supported Major League Soccer (MLS) team, garnering more than twice as
many home supporters as local baseball team the Mariners. Indeed, their average
home gates currently top out at 43,000, higher than many high-ranking British Premier
League teams.

Sounders fans, who are organized into half a dozen supporters groups, are famous for
their highly musical 'March to the Match' which kicks off from Occidental Park (p66) in
Pioneer Square a couple of hours before the real kickoff. There's plenty to shout about.
Since 2009, the team have won an unprecedented four US Open Cups and – perhaps,
more importantly – the Supporter's Shield (the MLS championship) in 2014.

building containing the only remaining Japanese bathhouse in the US, doubles as a memorial to the neighborhood's Japanese residents forced into internment camps during WWII. The beautifully relaxed cafe has a wide selection of teas, serves Lavazza Italian coffee and holds a National Treasure designation.

🔊 SoDo

PYRAMID ALE HOUSE   BREWPUB
Map p234 (☎206-682-3377; www.pyramidbrew. com; 1201 1st Ave S; ⊘11am-10pm Mon-Thu, 11am-11pm Fri & Sat, 11am-9pm Sun; 🚇Stadium) In SoDo by Safeco Field, this brewpub has the cleaned-up-industrial feel – all bricks and brass and designer lighting – that defines the Pacific Northwest brewpub. It's a nice mainstream (but still appreciably Seattle-ish) place to take your parents or tenderfoot visitors. But don't even try on a game day, unless you want to squeeze into the standing-room-only beer tent outdoors.

☆ ENTERTAINMENT

Entertainment primarily means sport in this neck of the woods: Seattle's two main stadiums overshadow Pioneer Sq.

CENTURYLINK FIELD   STADIUM
Map p234 (800 Occidental Ave S; 🚇Stadium) The late, mostly unlamented Kingdome, long Seattle's biggest eyesore, was once the home field for the city's professional baseball and football franchises. Then it was imploded spectacularly in 2000 and replaced by this 72,000-seat stadium, home of the NFL Seattle Seahawks (p31) and Seattle's soccer team, the Sounders (p32).

SAFECO FIELD   STADIUM
Map p234 (☎206-346-4241; 1250 1st Ave S; tours adult/child $12/10; ⊘1¼hr tours 10:30am, 12:30pm & 2:30pm non-game days Apr-Oct; 🚇Stadium) Home of Seattle's pro baseball team, the Mariners (p31), the $517 million Safeco Field opened in July 1999. With its retractable roof, 47,000 seats and real grass, the stadium was funded by taxpayers and tourists with the Mariners coughing up the difference. The stadium's unique design means it commands fantastic views of the surrounding mountains, downtown and Puget Sound.

NORDO'S CULINARIUM   THEATER
Map p234 (www.cafenordo.com; 109 S Main St; 🚇Occidental Mall) A theatrical group with culinary inclinations, Cafe Nordo marries two themes in one – food and theater – putting on inspired plays-cum-dinner shows where the performers double as the waitstaff. It's a unique formula first hatched in 2009 when the then homeless group put on occasional plays in Fremont's Theo Chocolate factory.

Finding a permanent home in 2015 in Pioneer Sq, the newly christened Nordo's Culinarium guarantees a wonderfully surreal night out – with plenty of good food too. Follow link on website for tickets.

COMEDY UNDERGROUND   COMEDY
Map p234 (☎206-628-0303; www.comedyun derground.com; 109 S Washington St; tickets $6-55; 🚇Occidental Mall) The best comedy club in Seattle has an 8:30pm show most nights and a second 10:30pm show on Friday and Saturday. Talent is mainly local and there's a full bar, plus a pizza-and-burger-style food menu. Under-21s are welcome Sunday to Thursday. Monday is open mike, a crapshoot of the surprisingly good or the skincrawlingly bad.

Buy tickets through **TicketWeb** (☎866-468-3399; www.ticketweb.com), preferably in advance.

SHOWBOX SODO   LIVE MUSIC
Map p234 (www.showboxpresents.com; 1700 1st Ave S; 🚇Stadium) The newer sister-club of downtown's Showbox, this SoDo version is actually bigger with a capacity for 1800 in an old warehouse. Touring rock bands play here.

STUDIO SEVEN   LIVE MUSIC
Map p234 (☎206-286-1312; www.studioseven.us; 110 S Horton St; free or cover; 🚇Stadium) This all-ages club is south of the sports stadiums in SoDo, just off 1st Ave S one block north of Spokane St. It books local and touring punk and metal shows.

🛍 SHOPPING

Not surprisingly, given its historical importance to the city, Pioneer Square is the place to shop for antiques. It's also a good place to find reasonably priced artwork and crafts by local artists, particularly blown glass and traditional art by coastal Native American artists.

In addition to the behemoth Uwajimaya, it's worth exploring the nooks and crannies of the ID for odd shopfronts and imported Asian wares.

★ FILSON   SPORTS & OUTDOORS

Map p234 (✆206-622-3147; www.filson.com; 1741 1st Ave S; ☉10am-6pm Mon-Sat, noon-5pm Sun; ⊞Stadium) Founded in 1897 as the original outfitters for prospectors heading for the Klondike, Filson is a long-standing Seattle legend that, in 2015, opened up this hugely impressive flagship store in SoDo. Wall-mounted bison heads and sepia-toned photos evoke the Klondike spirit while flop-down sofas and literary tomes encourage lingering.

Then there's the gear: top-quality bags, outdoor jackets and clothing durable enough to survive another gold rush or two. Even better, much of the stuff is designed and made on-site (you can view people working through a glass screen).

GLOBE BOOKSTORE   BOOKS

Map p234 (✆206-682-6882; 218 1st Ave S; ☉10:30am-6pm; ⊞Occidental Mall) This small but comfortably cramped shop is an erudite emporium of new and secondhand books, not all of which make it on to the shelves. Thumbing through its piles and racks is so much more serendipitous than an online 'search.'

UWAJIMAYA   MALL

Map p234 (✆206-624-6248; www.uwajimaya. com; 600 5th Ave S; ☉8am-10pm Mon-Sat, 9am-9pm Sun; ⊞5th & Jackson/Japantown) Founded by Fujimatsu Moriguchi, one of the few Japanese to return here from the WWII internment camps, this large department and grocery store – a cornerstone of Seattle's Asian community – has everything from fresh fish and exotic fruits and vegetables to cooking utensils, and you'll come face-to-face with those dim sum ingredients you've always wondered about.

The current location is a self-styled community that includes living quarters and occupies a whole block. There's a food court in addition to the grocery store. It's a great place to browse.

GANJA GODDESS   POT SHOP

Map p234 (✆206-682-7220; www.ganjagod-dessseattle.com; 3207 1st Ave S; ☉10am-9pm Mon-Wed, 10am-10pm Thu-Sat, 10am-8pm Sun; ⊞SoDo) A long way from the street-side dope-scoring of yore, this clean, welcoming, 100% legal pot shop in SoDo is redolent of a jewellery store with its collection of marijuana edibles, vaporizers and concentrates laid out in polished glass cabinets.

It's overseen by group of very helpful and unpretentious staff and offers a free shuttle service picking and dropping off clients in and around Seattle's downtown core.

CANNABIS CITY   POT SHOP

Map p234 (✆206-682-1332; www.cannabiscity. us; 2733 4th Ave S; ☉8am-9pm Mon-Thu, 8am-10pm Fri, 9am-10pm Sat, 9am-8pm Sun; ⊞SoDo) Seattle's first licensed 'recreational' pot shop opened in July 2014 to long queues. Its first sale was apparently to a 65-year-old grandmother. While it doesn't look much from the outside, the interior is rather plush with plenty of assistants to take you through the basics. You'll need to show your ID at the door.

FLANAGAN & LANE ANTIQUES   ANTIQUES

Map p234 (✆206-682-0098; www.flanagan-laneantiques.com; 165 S Jackson St; ☉11am-5pm Mon-Sat, noon-5pm Sun; ⊞Occidental Mall) This plush antiques shop is devoted to American, English and Continental furniture and

---

FIRST THURSDAY ART WALK

Art walks are two a penny in US cities these days, but they were pretty much an unknown quantity when the pioneering artists of Pioneer Square instituted their first amble around the local galleries in 1981. The neighborhood's **First Thursday Art Walk** (www. firstthursdayseattle.com) claims to be the oldest in the nation and a creative pathfinder for all that followed (and there have been many). Aside from gluing together Pioneer Sq's network of 50-plus galleries, the walk is a good excuse to admire creative public sculpture, sip decent coffee (many cafes serve as de-facto galleries), browse an array of stalls set up in Occidental Park, and get to know the neighborhood and its people. The Art Walk is self-guided, but you can pick up a map from the information booth in Occidental Park. Free parking is also offered from 5pm to 10pm. Check details on the website.

myriad decorative pieces. It's good if you're in the market for grandfather clocks, or chairs and tables that look as if they once accommodated French royalty.

SILVER PLATTERS MUSIC
Map p234 (206-283-3472; www.silverplatters.com; 2930 1st Ave S; 10am-10pm Mon-Sat, 11am-7pm Sun; SoDo) Something of a record supermarket bivouacked out in SoDo offering CDs and vinyl with an expansive side trade in DVDs (movies mainly). The selection is extremely broad and the staff is pretty knowledgeable.

GLASSHOUSE STUDIO ARTS & CRAFTS
Map p234 (206-682-9939; 311 Occidental Ave S; demonstrations 10-11:30am & 1-5pm Mon-Sat; Occidental Mall) The Seattle area is known for its Pilchuck School of glassblowing art, and this is the city's oldest glassblowing studio. Stop by to watch the artists in action and pick up a memento right at the source.

SEATTLE MYSTERY BOOKSHOP BOOKS
Map p234 (206-587-5737; www.seattlemystery.com; 117 Cherry St; 10am-6pm Mon-Sat, noon-5pm Sun; Pioneer Sq) The name gives it away – Seattle Mystery Bookshop is a specialty store for page-turners and whodunits.

HAU HAU MARKET MARKET
Map p234 (206-329-1688; 412 12th Ave S; 9am-8:30pm; 12th & Jackson/Little Saigon) Hau Hau is an agreeably disheveled Chinese and Vietnamese food market where you can get cheap produce (outside), specialty meats such as pig's ears and chicken's feet, fireworks, and Asian gifts and knickknacks.

KINOKUNIYA BOOKS
Map p234 (206-587-2477; 525 S Weller St; 10am-9pm Mon-Sat, 10am-8pm Sun; 5th & Jackson/Japantown) A great source for hard-to-find imported books and magazines in Asian languages (and in English about Asian culture), this bookstore inside Uwajimaya (p76) is also one of the few shops in the country where you can buy the lesser-known films of Kinji Fukasaku and other masters of Asian cinema on DVD.

PACIFIC HERB & GROCERY FOOD, HERBS
Map p234 (206-340-6411; 610 S Weller St; 9:30am-6:30pm; 7th & Jackson/Chinatown) A good place to get a sense of Chinatown

is along S Weller St. Apart from the many restaurants, there's Pacific Herb & Grocery, where the herbal-medicine specialists can tell you all about the uses of different roots, flowers and teas. The shop next door is a great place to buy tofu at low prices – you can even watch them make it on the premises.

SPORTS & ACTIVITIES

★**WESTLAND DISTILLERY** DISTILLERY
Map p234 (206-767-7250; www.westlanddistillery.com; 2931 1st Ave S; 11am-6pm Tue-Thu, 11am-8pm Fri & Sat; SoDo) On a drizzly day in Puget Sound, the damp essence of Seattle isn't a million miles from the Western Isles of Scotland, a comparison that hasn't been lost on the precocious young whiskey-makers of Westland, arguably one of Seattle's finest nascent distilleries. From its plush new tasting room and factory in SoDo, this company is breaking seals on some already legendary barrels of micro-distilled single malt.

You can taste it in a number of Seattle's burgeoning whiskey bars, or – better still – visit Westland's SoDo headquarters for an informal but informative distillery tour followed by a throat-warming tipple of the 'water of life.'

BILL SPEIDEL'S UNDERGROUND TOUR WALKING
Map p234 (206-682-4646; www.undergroundtour.com; 608 1st Ave; adult/senior/child $19/16/9; departs every 30min 10am-6pm Oct-Mar, 9am-7pm Apr-Sep; Pioneer Sq) This cleverly conceived tour of Seattle's historic 'underground' – the part of the city that got buried by landfill in the 1890s (p70) – benefits from its guides, who are excellent, using wit and animation to relate Seattle's unusual early history.

The tour starts at Doc Maynard's Public House with a lighthearted preamble and progresses through a series of subterranean walkways whose shabbiness adds to their authenticity. It is massively popular, especially in prime tourist season and no reservations are accepted, so try to arrive half an hour early if you want to be sure you get in.

Belltown & Seattle Center

BELLTOWN | SEATTLE CENTER

Neighborhood Top Five

❶ Chihuly Garden & Glass (p82) Pondering the shimmering glass art that sprang from the creative mind of Dale Chihuly in Chihuly Garden & Glass underneath the Space Needle.

❷ Olympic Sculpture Park (p85) Watching the sun slip behind faraway mountains from the grassy slopes of the Olympic Sculpture Park.

❸ Space Needle (p80) Going to the top of the Space Needle in the footsteps of millions of others – just because it's there.

❹ Bars of 2nd Ave (p91) Stringing together an elongated bar crawl in the dive-y and not-so-dive-y bars of 2nd Ave.

❺ Museum of Pop Culture (p84) Plugging in a guitar at the Sound Lab and pretending you're Jimi Hendrix.

For more detail of this area see Map p238 ➡

Explore: Belltown & Seattle Center

Belltown's compact, walkable core is long on dining and entertainment but relatively short on daytime attractions. The exception is the Olympic Sculpture Park, an art garden that anchors the neighborhood and snares visitors strolling between Pike Place Market and the Seattle Center.

Capitol Hillers might disagree, but Belltown's main nightlife zone (1st and 2nd Aves between Blanchard and Battery Sts) is the best place in the city to string together a bar-hopping evening out. A few of the grunge-era landmarks are still in business, but these days distorted guitars compete with the chatter of the cocktail crowd. Whatever your fashion affiliations, Belltown's after-dark scene is hip and noisy and rarely stands still. Watch out for drunken hipsters and sidewalk vomit.

The Seattle Center, site of the highly successful 1962 World's Fair, is Belltown in reverse; sights and museums abound, but you'll struggle to find any memorable food. The solution: spend most of your sightseeing time in the Seattle Center (Museum of Pop Culture, Chihuly Garden and Glass, and the Space Needle merit a day between them) and escape to adjacent Belltown for food and drinks.

Entertainment-wise, the Seattle Center offers plenty of sit-down plays, concerts and films. The McCaw Hall is home of the Seattle Opera and the Pacific Northwest Ballet, plus there's a cinema, a children's theater and a regional theater in the complex. It's also a fun place to just hang out, especially in summer when alfresco events and street performers take over.

Local Life

➡ **Serious Pie** (p88) It's all communal tables at Tom Douglas' riotously popular pizza restaurant, where you can discuss weird pizza toppings, microbrews and where Seattle's culinary maestro might open up next.

➡ **2nd Ave bars** The tight cluster of bars and clubs on the stretch of 2nd Ave between Battery and Blanchard Sts is about all that's left of un-gentrified Belltown. Jump into the nocturnal melee before it's too late.

Getting There & Away

➡ **Bus** Nearly all Belltown buses go up and down 3rd Ave and originate in downtown.

➡ **Monorail** The famous train in the sky runs every 10 minutes between downtown's Westlake Center, at Pine St and 4th Ave, and the Seattle Center. Tickets cost $2.25/1 per adult/child. The journey takes two minutes.

➡ **Walking** Lacking busy arterial roads, Belltown is a highly walkable neighborhood and easily reachable on foot from downtown, Pike Place Market, the Seattle Center and Lower Queen Anne.

Lonely Planet's Top Tip

Many people – including a lot of locals – consider the Space Needle to be an expensive tourist trap. If you're on a budget, you might be better off investing your money in tickets for the Museum of Pop Culture (p84) or Chihuly Garden and Glass (p82). You can get a *free* nearly-as-good view of Seattle from nearby Kerry Park (p99).

Best Places to Eat

➡ Top Pot Hand-Forged Doughnuts (p86)
➡ Tavolàta (p88)
➡ Serious Pie (p88)
➡ Macrina (p86)

For reviews, see p86 ➡

Best Drinking & Nightlife

➡ Rendezvous (p91)
➡ Shorty's (p91)
➡ Five Point Café (p92)
➡ Bedlam (p91)

For reviews, see p91 ➡

Best Live Music

➡ Crocodile (p93)
➡ Dimitriou's Jazz Alley (p93)
➡ McCaw Hall (p93)
➡ Cinerama (p93)

For reviews, see p93 ➡

SONGQUAN DENG / SHUTTERSTOCK ©

TOP SIGHT
SPACE NEEDLE

Whether you're from Alabama or Timbuktu, your abiding image of Seattle will probably be of the Space Needle, a modern-before-its-time tower built for the 1962 World's Fair that has been the city's defining symbol for over 50 years. The needle anchors the Seattle Center and persuades over a million annual visitors to ascend to its flying-saucer-like observation deck.

Some History

The Space Needle (originally called 'the Space Cage') was designed by Victor Steinbrueck and John Graham Jr, reportedly based on the napkin scribblings of World's Fair organizer Eddie Carlson. Looking like a cross between a flying saucer and an hourglass, and belonging to an architectural subgenre commonly referred to as Googie (futuristic, space age and curvaceous), the Needle was constructed in less than a year and proved to be an instant hit; 2.3 million people paid $1 to ascend it during the World's Fair, which ran for six months between April and October 1962. The lofty revolving dome originally housed two restaurants (they were amalgamated in 2000) and its roof was initially painted a brilliant 'Galaxy Gold' (read: orange). After many color changes, it was repainted in the same shade for its 50th anniversary in 2012. The structure has had two major refurbishments since the '60s: the first in 1982 when the Skyline level was added, and the second in 2000 in a project that cost as much as the original construction. The tradition of holding fantastical New Year's Eve firework displays at the Needle began in 1992.

DON'T MISS

→ Observation deck
→ Lunch in the SkyCity Restaurant
→ Joint-ticket offers

PRACTICALITIES

→ Map p238, C3
→ ☎206-905-2100
→ www.spaceneedle.com
→ 400 Broad St
→ adult/child $22/13
→ ⊙10am-9:30pm
→ ⑤Seattle Center

Vital Statistics

Standing apart from the rest of Seattle's skyscrapers, the Needle often looks taller than it actually is. On its completion in 1962, it was the highest structure west of the Mississippi River, topping 605ft, though it has since been easily surpassed (it's currently the seventh-tallest structure in Seattle). The part of the Needle that's visible above ground weighs an astounding 3700 tons. Most visitors head for the 520ft-high observation deck on zippy elevators that ascend to the top in a mere 41 seconds. The 360-degree views of Seattle and its surrounding water and mountains are suitably fabulous.

Visiting

To avoid the queues, purchase your ticket from one of the self-service machines outside the Space Base (tourist shop) and proceed up the ramp. You'll undergo a friendly bag search and then enter the gold capsule elevators, where an attendant will give you a quick-fire 41-second précis of the Needle (the time it takes to ascend). The elevators dock at the **observation deck**. To get to the **SkyCity Restaurant** you have to descend one level by stairs (or another lift). The observation deck has a reasonable cafe (with drinks and sandwiches), plenty of wall-mounted facts, free telescopes and some interesting touch screens. One takes you on a 'virtual' walk through Pike Place Market, Seattle Aquarium and some of Lake Union's houseboats. Another is a high-powered telescope that you can move around and zoom in and out to see close-up images of the street below flashed up on a screen. It's all a little nosy and voyeuristic!

The alfresco part of the observation deck (open the same hours, weather permitting) is guarded by a Perspex screen and an enclosed wire fence. The view is broad: on clear days, you can see three Cascade volcanoes (Mts Rainier, Baker and St Helen's), the Olympic range, the jagged coastline of Puget Sound and the sparkling surfaces of Lakes Union and Washington fanning out in the haze. Equally interesting is the complex topography of Seattle and its splayed neighborhoods that lie beneath you.

VIRTUAL REALITY SPACE NEEDLE

If, while standing on the Space Needle's observation deck, you ever wondered what it was like to balance on the structure's outer rim or, perhaps, climb its pointed spire, wonder no more. You can now enjoy these vertiginous views by purchasing a free mobile app and watching it on your cell phone through a special virtual reality box. See www.spaceneedle.com/vr for details.

If you decide to ascend the Space Needle, it's more economical to tie it in with lunch. Standard Space Needle tickets cost $22 (just for the view). However, if you go up for lunch in the rotating SkyCity Restaurant, the standard entry will be waived as long as your order costs at least $25. The restaurant rotates fully every 47 minutes, ideal for a leisurely view-enhanced lunch. The menu is true to Seattle's locavore tradition with a strong emphasis on fish.

COURTESY OF CHIHULY GARDEN AND GLASS ©

CHIHULY GARDEN & GLASS

Opened in 2012 and reinforcing Seattle's position as the Venice of North America, this exquisite exposition of the life and work of dynamic local sculptor Dale Chihuly is possibly the finest collection of curated glass art you'll ever see. It shows off Chihuly's creative designs in a suite of interconnected rooms and an adjacent garden in the shadow of the Space Needle.

Dale Chihuly

With his Long John Silver eye patch and shock of electric hair, Dale Chihuly looks every part the eccentric artist. Born in Tacoma, WA, in 1941, the world's best-known glass sculptor majored in interior design at the University of Washington before moving to Venice, where he enthusiastically immersed himself in the delicate art of glassblowing. Returning to the Seattle area in 1971, Chihuly founded a glass art school and gradually began to establish a reputation before two successive accidents in the 1970s left him with permanent injuries to his eye and shoulder and no longer able to contribute directly to the glassblowing process. Undeterred by the setback, Chihuly channeled his energies 100% into design, hiring vast teams of glassblowers to enact his lucid artistic visions. It was a highly successful formula. With Chihuly acting as both composer and conductor to a large orchestra of employees, the size and scale of his exhibits soared. Before long, his provocative glass art leaped onto the world stage. By the 1980s, Chihuly's opulent creations were being exhibited all over the globe, inspiring a mixture of awe and controversy in all who saw them but never failing to get a reaction.

DON'T MISS

→ Sealife Tower
→ Chandeliers
→ The Sun
→ Glasshouse

PRACTICALITIES

→ Map p238, C3
→ ☎206-753-4940
→ www.chihulygarden andglass.com
→ 305 Harrison St
→ adult/child $27/16
→ ⊙9am-9pm Mon-Thu, 9am-10pm Fri-Sun
→ ⑤Seattle Center

Layout

The masterpieces are split between an eight-room exhibition center, a glasshouse filled with natural light, and a garden. Between them they showcase the full gamut of Chihuly's Pacific Northwest influences, most notably Native American art, Puget Sound sea life, and wooden canoe-like boats.

Exhibition Hall

The first standout exhibit is **Sealife Tower**, a huge azure structure of intricately blown glass that looks as if it has sprung straight out of Poseidon's lair. Look out for the small octopuses and starfish melded into the swirling waves and examine Chihuly's early sketches for the work that adorn the surrounding walls. The next exhibit, **Persian Ceilings**, creates a reflective rainbow of light in an otherwise unfurnished room, while the ambitious **Mille Fiori** presents glass as vegetation with multiple pieces arranged in an ethereal *Wizard of Oz*–like 'garden.' The **Ikebana & Float Boat** consists of several boats overflowing with round glass balls and was inspired by Chihuly's time in Venice: he casually threw luminous glass spheres into the canals and watched as local children enthusiastically collected them in boats. In the adjoining room lie the main objects of the *Chihuly over Venice* project: rich, ornate **chandeliers** of varying sizes and colors that were hung artistically around the city in 1996.

The Glasshouse

Sitting like a giant greenhouse under the Space Needle, the Glasshouse offers a nod to London's erstwhile Crystal Palace, one of Chihuly's most important historical inspirations. You'll notice that the floor space of the glasshouse has been left empty (the area can be hired for wedding receptions), drawing your eye up to the ceiling where a huge medley of flower-shaped glass pieces imitate the reds, oranges and yellows of a perfect sunset. Adjacent to the glasshouse is the **Collections Café**, where numerous collected objects (accordions, bottle openers, toy cars) adorn the ceiling, tables and toilets. Nearby, a **theater** shows several revolving short films including *Chihuly over Venice*.

The Garden

Seattle's relatively benign climate means glass can safely be displayed outside year-round. Chihuly uses the garden to demonstrate the seamless melding of glass art and natural vegetation. Many of the alfresco pieces are simple pointed shards of glass redolent of luminescent reeds, but the real eye-catcher is **The Sun**, a riot of twisted yellow 'flames' whose swirling brilliance erases the heaviness of the most overcast Seattle sky.

LEARN GLASSBLOWING

In the summer of 1971, Dale Chihuly co-founded **Pilchuck Glass School** (www. pilchuck.com) at a campus in Stanwood, WA, 50 miles north of Seattle on an old tree farm. Inhabiting rustic buildings constructed in typical Northwestern style, the school remains popular 45 years on, especially in the summer, when it offers intensive two-week courses in glassblowing.

If you really fall in love with Chihuly Garden and Glass (warning: it isn't difficult), it's possible to go back and enjoy the art in some novel new ways. Yoga Under Glass is an atmospheric one-hour yoga class held in Chihuly's spectacular glasshouse. Through the Lens is a chance for photographers to make art out of art without a bevy of tourists blocking every frame. Walk with the Gardener is a one-hour walk and talk that reveals how the museum's green team have tried to frame Chihuly's dramatic designs with nature. All three activities take place pre-opening (usually between 8am and 10am) and cost $22. Check the website for times and dates.

MUSEUM OF POP CULTURE

The **Museum of Pop Culture** is an inspired marriage between super-modern architecture and rock-and-roll history that sprang from the imagination of Microsoft co-creator Paul Allen. Inside its avant-garde frame, you can tune into the famous sounds of Seattle, including Jimi Hendrix and grunge, or attempt to imitate the rock masters in an Interactive 'Sound Lab.'

Architecture

The highly unusual building with its crinkled folds colored in metallic blues and purples was designed by renowned Canadian architect Frank Gehry, a strong proponent of deconstructivism. Gehry – who designed the equally outlandish Guggenheim Museum in Bilbao, Spain – supposedly used one of Hendrix's smashed-up guitars as his inspiration.

Main Exhibits

The main exhibit hall is anchored by *If VI Was IX,* a tower of 700 instruments designed by German-born artist Trimpin. Many of the permanent exhibits center on Hendrix, including the Fender Stratocaster guitar that he played at Woodstock in 1969. Dominating proceedings on level 2 is the **Sky Church**, a huge screen displaying musical and sci-fi films.

Sound Lab

On the 3rd floor is the interactive **Sound Lab**, where you can lay down vocal tracks, play instruments, fiddle with effects pedals and – best of all – jam in several mini studios. **On Stage** gives you the opportunity to belt out numbers under stage lights with a virtual audience.

Icons of Science Fiction

A separate Science Fiction Museum opened on the site in 2004 and, in 2012, was incorporated into the museum in a permanent 2nd-floor mini-museum, 'Icons of Science Fiction. ' Expect to come face to face with a *Doctor Who* Dalek, a *Terminator 2* skull and more.

DON'T MISS

→ Sound Lab
→ *Nirvana: Taking Punk to the Masses*
→ On Stage
→ Icons of Science Fiction

PRACTICALITIES

→ Map p238, D2
→ 325 5th Ave N
→ adult/child $25/16
→ ⏰10am-7pm Jun-Aug, to 5pm Sep-May
→ Ⓢ Seattle Center

NAN728 / SHUTTERSTOCK ©

◉ SIGHTS

The Seattle Center hosts three of Seattle's big-hitter sights within spitting distance of each other. Belltown is more about bars and restaurants, although the Olympic Sculpture Park is a worthy diversion.

◉ Belltown

TIMES SQUARE BUILDING   LANDMARK

Map p238 (cnr Olive Way & Stewart St; ☒West-lake) This terracotta and granite structure, guarded by eagles perched on the roof, was designed by the Paris-trained architect Carl Gould (who also designed the Seattle Asian Art Museum and the University of Washington's Suzzallo Library). It housed the *Seattle Times* from 1916 to 1931.

AMAZON TOWER I   LANDMARK

Map p238 (cnr Westlake & 7th Aves; ☒Westlake & 7th) The new Seattle HQ of online retail behemoth Amazon opened in December 2015. Called Amazon Tower I, but known colloquially as 'the Doppler,' it will soon be joined by two further towers and an innovative sphere-shaped 'bio-dome'. The project is due for completion by the end of 2017.

MYRTLE EDWARDS PARK   PARK

Map p238 (☒13) Your best bet for an uninterrupted walk or jog if you're staying downtown is this fringe of lawn and trees along Elliott Bay that starts next to the Olympic Sculpture Park and continues as far as the Interbay area between Queen Anne and Magnolia.

The park (sometimes erroneously called Elliott Bay Park) was named after a Seattle councillor and environmental campaigner in the 1960s, and the path that runs through it is a favorite of joggers and power-walkers pursuing lunchtime fitness. In warm weather, the linked paths, with stupendous views over the Sound to the Olympic Mountains, make a good place for a picnic (eagles are sometimes spotted). Halfway through the park a large, distinctive grain terminal bridges the walkway.

BELLTOWN & SEATTLE CENTER SIGHTS

◉ TOP SIGHT
OLYMPIC SCULPTURE PARK

The Olympic Sculpture Park, a clever urban renewal project and outpost of the Seattle Art Museum, was inaugurated in 2007 to widespread local approval. The terraced park, which cost $85 million and covers 8.5 acres, is landscaped over railway tracks and overlooks Puget Sound with the distant Olympic Mountains winking on the horizon. Joggers and dog-walkers meander daily through its zigzagging paths, enjoying over 20 pieces of modern sculpture that sprout dramatically from the surrounding plants and foliage.

Hard to miss on the shoreline, *Echo* (2011), by Catalan artist Jaume Plensa, is a huge white head that appears to contort depending on which angle you look at it from. Another head-turner is Alexander Calder's *The Eagle* (1971), whose curvaceous red arches frame the nearby Space Needle. Many miss Roxy Paine's *Split* (2003), a stainless-steel tree that draws attention to the sometimes blurry split between art and nature and underlines one of the park's central themes. Much more conspicuous is Claes Oldenburg and Coosje van Bruggen's *Typewriter Eraser, Scale X*, with its blue sprouts bristling over Elliott Ave.

The pavilion building at the top of the park contains a small cafe, restrooms, a gift shop, wi-fi and visitor information (limited hours).

DON'T MISS

➡ *Echo* by Jaume Plensa

➡ *The Eagle* by Alexander Calder

➡ *Typewriter Eraser, Scale X* by Claes Oldenburg and Coosje van Bruggen

➡ Pavilion building

PRACTICALITIES

➡ Map p238, B4

➡ 2901 Western Ave

➡ admission free

➡ ☉sunrise-sunset

➡ ☒13

◉ Seattle Center

CHIHULY GARDEN AND GLASS   MUSEUM
See p82.

MUSEUM OF POP CULTURE   MUSEUM
See p84.

SPACE NEEDLE   LANDMARK
See p80.

BILL & MELINDA GATES FOUNDATION
VISITOR CENTER   VISITOR CENTER
Map p238 (www.gatesfoundation.org; 440 5th
Ave N; ⊙10am-5pm Tue-Sat; ⑤Seattle Center)
🖋 FREE The world's most unselfish bil-
lionaire's generous actions are eloquently
displayed at this suitably high-tech visitor
center, part of a larger foundation building
located opposite the Space Needle. Spread
over five rooms with highly interactive exhibits, the center lays out the Gates' bios
and shows examples of their work around
the world including fighting malaria in
Africa and notable philanthropic activities
inside the US.

It also offers plenty of scope for visitor
involvement. Various screens and note-
pads invite visitors to jot down ideas, help
solve tricky problems and lend their own
brainpower to the foundation's 'intellectual
bank.'

INTERNATIONAL FOUNTAIN   FOUNTAIN
Map p238 (🖵light-show schedule 206-684-7200;
⑤Seattle Center) A remnant of the 1962
World's Fair, the International Fountain
was completely rebuilt in 1995. With 272
jets of water (recycled, of course) pumping
in time to a computer-driven music system
at the heart of the Seattle Center, it's a great
place to rest your feet, eat lunch, or have
a cold shower on a warm day. On summer
nights there's a free light-and-music show.

PACIFIC SCIENCE CENTER   MUSEUM
Map p238 (☑206-443-2001; www.pacificscience
center.org; 200 2nd Ave N; adult/child exhibits only $19.75/14.75, with IMAX $25.75/18.75;
⊙10am-5pm Mon-Fri, 10am-6pm Sat & Sun; 🖈;
⑤Seattle Center) This interactive museum
of science and industry once housed the
science pavilion of the 1962 World's Fair.
Today the center features virtual-reality
exhibits, a tropical butterfly house, laser
shows, holograms and other wonders of science, many with hands-on demonstrations.

Also on the premises is the vaulted-screen
IMAX Theater, a saltwater tide pool and a
planetarium.

CHILDREN'S MUSEUM   MUSEUM
Map p238 (☑206-441-1768; www.thechildrens
museum.org; 305 W Harrison St; $9.25; ⊙10am-
5pm Mon-Fri, 10am-6pm Sat & Sun; 🖈; ⑤Seattle Center) In the basement of the Seattle
Center Armory near the monorail stop, the
Children's Museum is old-school entertainment and a good bet if you want to tear
your offspring away from iPads and redirect
them towards Lego (remember that?), fort-
building and pretending to be a check-out
assistant. For some it's a little dated; others
find it charming and endearing. Best for
kids under seven.

🍴 EATING

**Belltown has a UN of eclectic restaurants
catering to all budgets. Among its rows
of bars and cocktail lounges – where
condo-clean and dive-dirty often sit
right next to each other – are a great
variety of cafes, delis, top-of-the-line
restaurants and low-budget burger
dives frequented by arty musicians and
starving students. The other advantage
of Belltown is that you're more likely
to be able to find late-night dining,
thanks to an active cocktail scene that
encourages many restaurants to serve
at least a bar menu until 2am.**

★TOP POT HAND-FORGED
DOUGHNUTS   CAFE $
Map p238 (www.toppotdoughnuts.com; 2124 5th
Ave; doughnuts from $1.50; ⊙6am-7pm Mon-
Fri, 7am-7pm Sat & Sun; 🖵13) Sitting pretty
in a glass-fronted former car showroom
with art-deco signage and immense book-
shelves, Top Pot's flagship cafe produces
the Ferraris of the doughnut world. It might
have morphed into a 20-outlet chain in recent years, but its hand-molded collection
of sweet rings are still – arguably – worth
visiting Seattle for alone. The coffee's pretty
potent too.

MACRINA   BAKERY $
Map p238 (☑206-448-4032; www.macrina
bakery.com; 2408 1st Ave; sandwiches $5-8.75;
⊙7am-6pm; 🖵13) That snaking queue's
there for a reason: damned good artisan

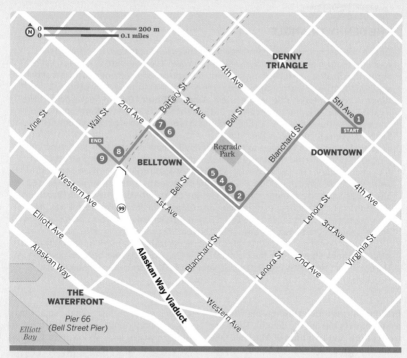

Neighborhood Walk
The Belltown Hustle

START TOP POT DOUGHNUTS
END CYCLOPS
LENGTH 1 MILE; A FULL EVENING

Start the tour by filling up with coffee and sugar at ❶ **Top Pot Hand-Forged Doughnuts** (p86), whose book-lined cafe in a former car showroom sits under the concrete pillars of the monorail on 5th Ave. Imbibe their rocket fuel and be on your merry way!

Wander down Blanchard St to 2nd Ave where, on the corner, you'll spot the snakeskin-green sign of the ❷ **Crocodile** (p93), a key venue in the rise of grunge. Check its windows for upcoming shows. The Crocodile marks the start of one of Seattle's best nightlife strips that stretches west along 2nd Ave. ❸ **Tula's** (p94) is a great jazz venue and home to some of Seattle's best improvisers. If you're after more active pursuits and are thirsty, pace a few doors down to ❹ **Shorty's** (p91), otherwise known as pinball heaven. Grab a cheap beer or a slushy blue cocktail and head straight to the back room to test your reflexes.

When the pinball wears you out or simply beats you into submission, hop next door to the ❺ **Lava Lounge** (p91), another groovy nightspot with comfy wooden booths. Continue on past hipsters and city slickers to ❻ **Rendezvous** (p91), a classy Prohibition-era venue with a curvilinear bar and the adorable, recently gussied-up ❼ **Jewel Box Theater** (p93) in the back.

Turn left on Battery St toward the water, then right on 1st Ave: halfway down the block you'll see ❽ **Macrina** (p86), one of Seattle's best bakeries. If it's past 6pm and it's shut, make menu notes for tomorrow's hangover cure.

Hungry? What – already?! Head toward the corner of 1st Ave and Wall St, where you can procure a substantial snack in ❾ **Cyclops** (p88), a prime location for observing the street's late-night dramas. If you're lucky enough to be staying at the Ace Hotel, you can chill at the Cyclops until your eyes match the bleary, bloodshot one hanging over the door, then stumble upstairs and fall into bed.

WORTH A DETOUR

THE DENNY TRIANGLE

Once a nondescript no-man's land shoehorned between South Lake Union and Belltown, the triangle of streets bordered by Denny Way, Olive Way and 6th Ave is positioning itself as Seattle's next big thing with ambitious plans for offices, condo towers and super-modern multi-use buildings. The surge is being led by online retail behemoth Amazon, whose new Seattle headquarters, **Amazon Tower I** (p85) – known colloquially as 'the Doppler' – opened in December 2015. With two more Amazon towers due to be completed by the end of 2017, the neighborhood is on the cusp of becoming one of the fastest-growing tech zones in the nation.

Though it's hard to envisage today, the Denny Triangle sits on some important pioneer history. Seattle's first land claim was staked here by the Denny Party in 1852, though the weary, rain-lashed pioneers probably wouldn't recognize their fledgling settlement now. Until the 1890s, the area was occupied by a steep hill that covered 62 city blocks and had a summit at the intersection of modern-day 4th Ave and Blanchard St. Seen as an impediment to the continued expansion of downtown, the hill was gradually 'demolished' and sluiced into Elliott Bay in a massive public-works project known as the Denny Regrade that began in 1898 and took 32 years to complete.

Devoid of sights per se, the triangle's most recognizable landmark is the gaudy neon **pink elephant sign** outside the Elephant Super Car Wash that has been revolving on the corner of Denny Way and Battery St since 1956. To locals it is as quintessentially Seattle as the Space Needle – and six years older!

bread (you can watch through the window as the experts roll out the dough). There are two options and two lines at Macrina. One is for the fantastic take-out bakery (possibly the best in Seattle); the other's for the sit-down cafe with its so-good-it-could-be-Paris sandwiches, soups and other such snacks. Join the pilgrimage.

ASSEMBLY HALL   PAN-ASIAN, CAFE $
Map p238 (206-812-8413; www.assembly hallseattle.com; 2121 6th Ave; sandwiches $8-9; 6am-6pm Mon-Fri, 7am-6pm Sat & Sun; Westlake & 7th) Top Seattle chef Tom Douglas owns half a dozen eating places in Belltown these days. His secret: they're all (gastronomically speaking) excellent, but none of them are remotely alike. Assembly Hall is a veritable food emporium. Its ground floor hosts a Pan-Asian restaurant called TanakaSan, along with a chili bar, a coffee shop and a European-style produce market with great take-out pizza.

The mezzanine floor is reserved for relaxation and free games. Pool, shuffle board and computer games are all up for grabs.

CYCLOPS   AMERICAN $
Map p238 (www.cyclopsseattle.com; 2421 1st Ave; mains from $8; 5pm-2am daily, 9am-2pm Sat & Sun; 13) Sometimes when you're tramping the streets in search of food and drink (and a restroom) after a day of arduous

sightseeing, you just want somewhere cheap, unpretentious and comfortable to rest your weary legs. Welcome to Cyclops, where a pint of Boundary Bay IPA and a good ole burger can be consumed amid the to-ing and fro-ing of Belltown life.

It has some rather eclectic decor (a swordfish, bullfighting portraits and a collection of metal crosses) – lap it up.

★TAVOLÀTA   ITALIAN $$
Map p238 (206-838-8008; 2323 2nd Ave; pasta dishes $18-22; 5-11pm; 13) Owned by top Seattle chef Ethan Stowell, Tavolàta is a dinner-only Italian-inspired eatery emphasizing homemade pasta dishes. Keeping things simple with venison-stuffed ravioli and linguine nero (clams with black pasta), the results are as good as those found in Italy – and there's no praise finer than that!

Another highlight is the theater of the cooking. Get a seat in the mezzanine and you can look down on the chefs spinning their magic in the open kitchen below.

SERIOUS PIE   PIZZA $$
Map p238 (206-838-7388; www.tomdouglas.com; 316 Virginia St; pizzas $16-18; 11am-11pm; Westlake) In the crowded confines of Serious Pie you can enjoy beautifully blistered pizza bases topped with such unconventional ingredients as clams, potatoes, nettles, soft eggs, truffle cheese

and more. Be prepared to share a table and meet a few Seattleites.

The pizzas have proved so popular that Serious Pie has spawned several new outlets, including one in the Starbucks Reserve Roastery.

TILIKUM PLACE CAFE
BISTRO, BRUNCH **$$**

Map p238 (☑206-282-4830; www.tilikumplace cafe.com; 407 Cedar St; brunch mains $9-14; ⏰11am-10pm Mon-Fri, 8am-10pm Sat & Sun; ☐3) Sometimes old Belltown and new Belltown sit bumper to bumper, and the juxtaposition is never more marked than on Cedar St, where the suave, pseudo-Parisian Tilikum Place lies next door to 90-year-old dive bar, the Five Point Café (p92). The former has the words 'European bistro' written all over it and is particularly popular for lunch (quiche, sardine sandwiches) and brunch (baked pancakes).

SHIRO'S SUSHI RESTAURANT
JAPANESE **$$**

Map p238 (☑206-443-9844; www.shiros.com; 2401 2nd Ave; 5-piece sashimi $14-20; ⏰5-10pm; ☐13) A little pricey, but with over 20 years of glowing testimonies about its black cod and deep-fried prawn-heads, Shiro's is Belltown's best Japanese option. Although founder Shiro Kashiba no longer runs the restaurant, it has kept its name and reputation for cool, sophisticated food and service.

VITTLES
EUROPEAN **$$**

Map p238 (☑206-448-3348; www.vittlesseattle. com; 2330 2nd Ave; mains $13-19; ⏰4-11pm Mon-Thu, 4pm-2am Fri, 9am-2am Sat, 9am-11pm Sun; ☐13) Pitching itself as a 'neighborhood bistro,' Vittles entered the Belltown restaurant inferno in 2014. Not aping any particular trend, it concentrates on the important stuff: attentive but informal service, a good mix of people and a menu where almost everything is a standout dish.

Candlelit in the evening and inflected with a definitive Europhile feel, you can't go wrong with the shepherd's pie, beautifully cooked lamb chops and vegetable-laden flatbreads.

360 LOCAL
NORTHWEST **$$**

Map p238 (☑206-441-9360; www.local360.org; cnr 1st Ave & Bell St; mains $14-28; ⏰11am-late Mon-Fri, 9am-late Sat & Sun; ☐13) 🍴 Snaring 90% of its ingredients from within a 360-mile radius, this restaurant follows its ambitious 'locavore' manifesto pretty rigidly. The farms where your meat was reared are

displayed on the daily blackboard menu and the restaurant's wood-finish interior looks like a rustic barn. With such a fertile hinterland to draw upon, the food is pretty special; try the rabbit, the clams or the chickpea cake.

Fresh vegetables supplement most meals, and even the whiskey is local.

BELLINI ITALIAN BISTRO
ITALIAN **$$**

Map p238 (☑206-441-4480; 2302 1st Ave; mains $11-27; ⏰5-10pm Tue-Fri, 3-10pm Sat & Sun; ☐13) Bellini is relatively new, but there's something comfortingly old-fashioned about its laid-back service and Italian bistro feel. One gets the sense that it's not trying to be unnecessarily fancy or retro – just good. The food is Italian with a southern nod. Try the *vongole* (clams), bruschetta, homemade gnocchi or the sweet cannoli for desert. It also has its own pizza oven.

PINTXO
TAPAS **$$**

Map p238 (☑206-441-4042; www.pintxoseattle. com; 2207 2nd Ave; tapas $6-10; ⏰5pm-midnight Tue-Sun; ☐13) Say the word Basque and you might as well be saying 'gourmet' – the Spanish autonomous region has collected a constellation of Michelin stars. *Pintxos* are the Basque version of tapas, and they are served authentically in this ice-cool bar that could have you planning your next vacation to San Sebastián.

Honorable mentions should go to the lamb kefta sliders with yogurt dip, and the *choricitos a la miel* (chorizo with cider and honey reduction).

LA VITA É BELLA
ITALIAN **$$**

Map p238 (☑206-441-5322; www.lavitaebella. us; 2411 2nd Ave; pasta $14-18; ⏰11:30am-10pm Mon-Sat, 5-10pm Sun; ☐13) As any Italian food snob will tell you, it's very hard to find authentic home-spun Italian cuisine this side of Sicily. Thus extra kudos must go to La Vita é Bella for trying and largely succeeding in a difficult field. The pizza margherita is a good yardstick, though the *vongole* (clams), desserts and coffee are also spot on.

As in all good Italian restaurants, the owners mingle seamlessly with the clientele with plenty of handshakes and good humor.

QUEEN CITY GRILL
SEAFOOD **$$**

Map p238 (☑206-443-0975; www.queencity grill.com; 2201 1st Ave; mains $16-28; ⏰4:30-11pm Sun-Thu, 4:30pm-midnight Fri & Sat; ☐13)

This longtime Belltown favorite in an old redbrick building is known for its grilled seafood and expertly mixed cocktails. The clams are always good, either as a starter or served Italian-style with linguine. There's also ahi tuna, rainbow trout and – for avowed carnivores – New York steak. Warm lighting and starched white tablecloths make the room feel cozy yet sophisticated.

Reservations are recommended.

FARESTART RESTAURANT   NORTHWESTERN **$$**

Map p238 (☑206-443-1233; www.farestart.org; 700 Virginia St; 3-course dinner $29.95; ◷11am-2pm Mon-Fri, 5:30-8pm Thu; 圓Westlake & 7th) 🖉 FareStart serves substantial meals that benefit the community. All proceeds from lunch and the popular Thursday-night Guest Chef dinners – when FareStart students work with a famous local chef to produce outstanding meals – go to support the FareStart program, which provides intensive job training, housing assistance and job placement for disadvantaged and homeless people.

The constantly changing lunch menu is pretty gourmet for the price – try the hot sandwiches or seafood pasta. Reservations are strongly recommended for dinner.

CANTINA LEÑA   MEXICAN **$$**

Map p238 (☑206-519-5723; www.cantinalena. com; 2105 5th Ave; mains $14-18; ◷8am-10pm Mon-Fri, 9am-10pm Sat & Sun; 圓13) Filling a hole in Seattle's sometimes lackluster Mexican *comida* offerings, Tom Douglas' latest Belltown fiefdom is casual and reasonably priced. Small-town Mexican soul food it isn't, but if you fancy hot, smoky chicken tacos and a cooling guacamole dip before a movie at the adjacent Cinerama (p93), this could hit the spot.

And, if that doesn't swing it, come back in the morning for breakfast *churros* (deep-fried doughnut strips).

BAROLO RISTORANTE   ITALIAN **$$$**

Map p238 (☑206-770-9000; www.baroloseattle. com; 1940 Westlake Ave; pasta $16-24, mains $20-44; ◷11:30am-10:30pm Sun-Thu, to 11pm Fri & Sat; 圓Westlake & 7th) An upscale Italian place named after one of Italy's finest vinos, Barolo provides a good excuse to taste the deep, powerful 'king of wines' or – if your budget won't stretch that far – a supporting cast of half a dozen under-appreciated Barberas or Dolcettos (there's a generous and popular 'happy hour' that kicks off daily at 3pm).

If you're sitting down to eat, the rigatoni with lamb and Parmesan, followed by a *secondo* of lemony veal, is as good as anything you'll find in Piedmont. The restaurant is located in the Denny Triangle, a five-minute walk from the Westlake Center.

LOLA   GREEK, MEDITERRANEAN **$$$**

Map p238 (☑206-441-1430; www.tomdouglas. com; 2000 4th Ave; mains $26-34; ◷6am-11pm Mon-Thu, 6am-2am Fri, 7am-3pm & 4pm-1am Sat & Sun; 圓Westlake) Seattle's ubiquitous cooking maestro Tom Douglas goes Greek in this ambitious Belltown adventure and delivers once again with gusto. Stick in trendy clientele, some juicy kebabs, heavy portions of veg, shared meze dishes, and pita with dips, and you'll be singing Socratic verse all the way back to your hotel.

PALACE KITCHEN   NORTHWESTERN **$$$**

Map p238 (☑206-448-2001; www.tomdouglas. com; 2030 5th Ave; mains $25-38; ◷4:30pm-1am; 圓Westlake) One of Tom Douglas' harder to classify restaurants, the Palace is known for its upscale 'New American' cuisine, late-night happy hour and cool cocktail scene. Food-wise, it's especially good for its Applewood grill items, including trout and rotisserie chicken, although the menu also nurtures some fine Italianate features; try the *plin*, a Piedmontese-style ravioli.

This is an ideal place to come if you want to eat late. Late-night happy hour starts at 11pm (Sunday to Thursday) and includes small plates such as chicken wings ($6), plus drink specials.

DAHLIA LOUNGE   NORTHWESTERN **$$$**

Map p238 (☑206-682-4142; www.tomdouglas. com; 2001 4th Ave; mains $26-38; ◷11:30am-2:30pm & 5-10pm Mon-Fri, 9am-2pm & 5-11pm Sat & Sun; 圓Westlake) 🖉 Seattle's most well-known and decorated chef, Tom Douglas, established his rapidly growing restaurant empire here in 1989. Some say it has single-handedly made Seattleites more sophisticated with its now familiar Douglas hallmarks: locally-grown produce, organic ethos and fusion flavors that lean heavily toward Pacific Northwestern favorites. The seasonal spot prawns and Dungeness crab cakes are standout dishes.

There's a bakery next door where you can pick up one of the Dahlia's fabulous desserts to go. Reservations are recommended.

BUENOS AIRES GRILL STEAK $$$

Map p238 (206-441-7076; www.buenosaires
cuisine.com; 2000 2nd Ave; steaks $29-42; 5-
10:30pm Tue-Thu, 5pm-12:30am Fri-Sun; 13)
You don't need a culinary PhD to know
that Argentinians like their steak. Tucked
into a Belltown side street, the BA Grill
fits the stereotype in the best possible way
with minty-fresh cocktails, unusual salads
and huge portions of well-prepared meat.
Adding entertainment value is the staff's
tendency to tango on request.

🍷 DRINKING &
🍸 NIGHTLIFE

**For many people, Belltown remains
the pinnacle of Seattle nightlife.
Others dream nostalgically of the
days when stage-diving was still an
acceptable form of social interaction
and commoners could bump into
A-list grunge-musicians in the bars
of 2nd Ave. Whichever view you hold,
Belltown has the advantage of having
numerous bars lined up in tidy rows, an
arrangement that facilitates plenty of
all-night bar-hopping.**

⭐ **RENDEZVOUS** BAR

Map p238 (206-441-5823; www.rendezvous.
rocks; 2320 2nd Ave; 3pm-2am; 13) Like
the last tree standing after a hurricane,
the Rendezvous is one of Belltown's old-
est heirlooms that started life in 1927 as a
speakeasy and a screening room for early
Hollywood talkies.

Now on its umpteenth incarnation, the
subterranean speakeasy has morphed into
'the Grotto' (with weekly comedy), the
screening room has become the diminu-
tive Jewel Box Theater (p93) and the clam-
orous space upstairs a chic-ish bar and
restaurant.

SHORTY'S BAR

Map p238 (206-441-5449; www.shorty
dog.com; 2222 2nd Ave; noon-2am; 13)
Shorty's is all about beer, arcade games
and music (mostly punk and metal). A
remnant of Belltown's grungier days that
refuses to become an anachronism, it
keeps the lights low and the music loud.
Pinball machines are built into some of the
tables, and basic snacks (hot dogs, nachos)
soak up the booze.

THE WHISKY BAR BAR

Map p238 (206-443-4490; www.thewhisky
bar.com; 2122 2nd Ave; 2pm-2am Mon-Fri,
noon-2am Sat & Sun; 13) This recently re-
opened bar, relocated a block or so from
its old haunt, is about more than just the
whiskey, though that, of course is good. If
you're sticking to home turf, try the locally-
made Westland single malt. There are gen-
uine British food treats as well. Where else
in Seattle can you get Welsh rarebit – or
Scotch eggs for that matter?

And if that doesn't have you pining for
ole Blighty, the weekly bagpipe perfor-
mances probably will.

STREET BEAN ESPRESSO COFFEE

Map p238 (www.streetbeanespresso.org; 2711
3rd Ave; 6am-5pm Mon-Fri, 8am-3pm Sat,
8am-noon Sun; 3) A commendable com-
munity resource and a fine perch to imbibe
your morning coffee, Street Bean provides
opportunities for disadvantaged youths to
find work as baristas. The coffee (roasted
on-site) is pretty good too.

BEDLAM CAFE

Map p238 (www.bedlamite.com; 2231 2nd Ave;
6am-10pm Mon-Fri, 7am-10pm Sat & Sun; 13)
There's nothing mad about Bedlam, unless
you count the wall-mounted bicycle and the
Space Needle sculpture – made out of old
junk – that guards the door. Welcome to a
one-off coffee bar with no pretensions and
a low geek count that specializes in decent
lattes and ultra-thick slices of wholemeal
toast loaded with peanut butter and jam.

RE-BAR GAY

Map p240 (206-233-9873; www.rebarseattle.
com; 1114 Howell St; 70) This storied indie
dance club, where many of Seattle's de-
fining cultural events happened (such as
Nirvana album releases), welcomes gay,
straight, bi or undecided revelers to its
lively dance floor. Also come for its offbeat
theater, burlesque shows and poetry slams
– among other wacky offerings.

LAVA LOUNGE COCKTAIL BAR

Map p238 (206-441-5660; 2226 2nd Ave;
3pm-2am; 13) This well-worn, tiki-
themed dive has games of all kinds and
over-the-top art on the walls. It's more old-
school Belltown than new and sits on the
agreeably disheveled block on 2nd Ave also
inhabited by a handful of other much-loved
dives.

BELLTOWN RELICS

Belltown was a featureless amalgam of dull warehouses and low-rise office blocks in the mid-1980s, and well off the radar of the city's condo-dwelling yuppies. Offering cheap rents and ample studio space, it became an escape hatch for underground musicians and hard-up artists whose arrival heralded a creative awakening and led, in part, to the spark that ignited grunge. But, while the grit and grime of '80s Belltown were crucial components in the rise of the Seattle sound, the music's runaway international success had a catalytic effect: Belltown – much to the chagrin of the hard-up rockers who created it – became cool.

So followed a familiar story: seedy inner-city neighborhood attracts artists, gets creative, becomes cool, attracts hipsters, gentrifies, and loses its edge. Belltown's rise, brief honeymoon and rapid decline largely mirrored that of grunge, which, in the eyes of many purists, died the day Nirvana's *Nervermind* hit No 1. By the 2000s, many locals thought the neighborhood was over. Condos were rising, wine bars were replacing exciting music venues, and the martini-and-cocktail set had suddenly decided it was the ideal place to live. But all was not lost. A handful of Belltown's more tenacious older businesses – despite frequent threats of closure – have put up a brave rearguard action. Bars such as Shorty's continue to attract a loyal clientele, old record shops have benefited from a resurgent interest in vinyl, and the neighborhood's most iconic club, the Crocodile (despite a 2009 clean-up), is still an important part of Seattle's alt-music scene. Add in the general air of excitement among the people that crowd the streets, restaurants and clubs every night (even if half of them now wear stilettos), and reports of Belltown's death have clearly been exaggerated. Sure, the bars no longer place cardboard boxes on their toilet floors to soak up the urine, but look hard and you'll see there's life in the old beast yet.

For a taste of the grittier Belltown of yore, check out the following survivors:

➜ **Shorty's** (p91) No-compromise dive bar with pinball machines and potty mouths.

➜ **Moore Theatre** (p93) The oldest theater in Seattle (dating from 1907) retains its gritty authenticity despite a 2013 makeover.

➜ **Crocodile** (p93) The live-music venue that opened at the height of grunge was reincarnated in the late 2000s in slightly less grungy form.

➜ **Rendezvous** (p91) Velvety bar with good burgers and an adjoining burlesque theater that's been around since 1927.

➜ **Singles Going Steady** (p95) Memories of punk rock in a vinyl/CD store.

➜ **Five Point Café** A bar that's older than your grandad (unless your grandad's 90) and all the better for it.

FIVE POINT CAFÉ
BAR

Map p238 (206-448-9993; www.the5pointcafe.com; 415 Cedar St; 24hr; 3) There are Belltown relics and then there's the Five Point whose seedy neon sign and cantankerous advertising blurb ('cheating tourists and drunks since 1929') is practically as iconic as the Space Needle – and 33 years older! Half diner, half bar and too worn-in to be mistaken for hip, it's where seasoned Charles Bukowski look-a-likes go to get wasted, any time of day.

ROB ROY
COCKTAIL BAR

Map p238 (206-956-8423; www.robroyseattle.com; 2332 2nd Ave; 4pm-2am; 13) A proper cocktail lounge, Rob Roy is dignified yet comfortable – there's a long, dark bar and sophisticated touches such as cologne in the restroom, but there's also puffy wallpaper, squishy leather couches and a boar's head and antlers on the wall.

NITELITE LOUNGE
BAR

Map p238 (206-443-0899; 1926 2nd Ave; 4pm-2am; Westlake) A classic Belltown dive that has somehow managed to hang on and resuscitate its soul despite recent attempts at a face-lift. Drinks are stiff and the action's boisterous when there's a concert at the adjacent Moore Theatre. It's attached to the old-school Moore Hotel (p192).

⭐ ENTERTAINMENT

The Seattle Center acts as a huge entertainment nexus with opera, ballet, theater, cinema and live music all concentrated on one campus.

Belltown is the preserve of smaller clubs plying local acts.

⭐CROCODILE   LIVE MUSIC
Map p238 (📞206-441-4618; www.thecrocodile.com; 2200 2nd Ave; 🚌13) Nearly old enough to be called a Seattle institution, the Crocodile is a clamorous 560-capacity music venue that first opened in 1991, just in time to grab the coattails of the grunge explosion. Everyone who's anyone in Seattle's alt-music scene has since played here, including a famous occasion in 1992 when Nirvana appeared unannounced supporting Mudhoney.

Despite changing ownership in 2009 and undergoing a grunge-cleansing refurbishment, the Croc remains plugged into the Seattle scene, though these days aspiring stage-divers are more likely to get kicked out than crowd-surfed on the arms of an adoring audience. There's a full bar, a mezzanine floor and a no-frills pizza restaurant on-site.

⭐MCCAW HALL   OPERA
Map p238 (📞206-684-7200; 321 Mercer St; 🚈Seattle Center) Home of the Seattle Opera and Pacific Northwest Ballet, this magnificent structure in the Seattle Center was given a massive overhaul in 2003.

CINERAMA   CINEMA
Map p238 (www.cinerama.com; 2100 4th Ave; tickets $15; 🚌13) Possibly Seattle's most popular cinema, Cinerama, famous for its giant curved three-panel screen, is one of only three of its type left in the world and has a cool, sci-fi feel. Sparkling after a 2014 renovation, it has recently acquired a space-age mural, wider seats and a raft of additional extras, including microbrews on tap and Tom Douglas nosh.

It is *the* place to go for big new releases *and* old classics, preferably enjoyed with a bag of its legendary chocolate popcorn.

DIMITRIOU'S JAZZ ALLEY   JAZZ
Map p238 (📞206-441-9729; www.jazzalley.com; 2033 6th Ave; ⏰shows 7:30pm & 9:30pm; 🚈Westlake & 7th) Hidden in an unlikely spot behind a boring-looking office building is Seattle's most sophisticated and prestigious jazz club. Dimitriou's hosts the best of the locals as well as many national and international acts passing through.

KEXP   LIVE PERFORMANCE
Map p238 (📞206-520-5800; www.kexp.org; 472 1st Ave N; 🚈Rapid Ride D-Line) The new KEXP radio headquarters opened in the Seattle Center in December 2015 and provides a central gathering space for live music and parties, a see-through DJ booth and a live recording studio with room for audiences of up to 75 people.

PACIFIC NORTHWEST BALLET   DANCE
Map p238 (www.pnb.org; 🚈Seattle Center) The foremost dance company in the Northwest and one of the most popular in the US puts on more than 100 shows a season from September through June at Seattle Center's McCaw Hall.

SEATTLE OPERA   OPERA
Map p238 (www.seattleopera.org; 🚈Seattle Center) Seattle Opera is distinguished and diverse. Based at the McCaw Hall, it has hosted everything from Verdi's *La Traviata* to Pete Townshend's *Tommy*. It's particularly known for its performances of Wagner's *Ring* cycle, first staged in 1973.

JEWEL BOX THEATER   THEATER
Map p238 (2320 2nd Ave) The restored Jewel Box Theater, tucked away behind the sleek Rendezvous (p91) cocktail bar, has live music and independent theater events including burlesque. It dates from 1927 and was once a screening room for Hollywood movies.

MOORE THEATRE   LIVE MUSIC
Map p238 (📞206-443-1744; www.stgpresents.org/moore; 1932 2nd Ave; 🚈Westlake) Attached to a stately old hotel, the Moore is the city's oldest surviving theater (from 1907) and a piece of Seattle history. Its 1800-seater auditorium was the recent recipient of a refurbishment and exudes a battered grace and sophistication, whether the act is a singer-songwriter, a jazz phenomenon or a rock band. It mainly hosts music and dance.

Look out for the free theater tours on the second Saturday of each month at 10am.

TULA'S JAZZ
JAZZ

Map p238 (📞206-443-4221; www.tulas.com; 2214 2nd Ave; ⏰4pm-midnight; 🚌13) Tula's is an intimate jazz club with live music seven nights a week, from big bands and Latin jazz to up-and-coming names on tour. It focuses mainly on local talent and acts as a non-indie-rock oasis in the booze alley that is Belltown.

INTIMAN THEATRE FESTIVAL
THEATER

Map p238 (📞206-441-7178; www.intiman.org; 201 Mercer St; 🚇Seattle Center) Beloved theater company based at the Cornish Playhouse in the Seattle Center. Artistic director Andrew Russell curates magnificent stagings of Shakespeare and Ibsen, among others. Productions run from July to October.

SEATTLE CHILDREN'S THEATER
THEATER

Map p238 (📞206-441-3322; www.sct.org; 201 Thomas St; tickets $27-40; ⏰Thu-Sun Sep-Jun; 🚇Seattle Center) This highly esteemed theater group has two auditoriums in its Seattle Center campus. Friday and Saturday matinees and evening performances run September to June. There's also a Drama School summer season.

SIFF FILM CENTER
CINEMA

Map p238 (📞206-324-9996; www.siff.net; Northwest Rooms, Seattle Center; 🚇Seattle Center) The digs of the famous Seattle International Film Festival since 2011 runs movies in a small auditorium year-round.

SEATTLE REPERTORY THEATRE
THEATER

Map p238 (📞206-443-2222; www.seattlerep.org; 155 Mercer St; tickets from $15; ⏰box office 10am-6pm Tue-Fri; 🚇Seattle Center) The Seattle Repertory Theatre (the Rep) won a Tony Award in 1990 for Outstanding Regional Theater. The largest nonprofit resident theater outfit in the Pacific Northwest, it's known for elaborate productions of big-name dramas and second-run Broadway hits.

Its facility in the Seattle Center has three auditoriums, the largest of which is the 842-seat **Bagley Wright Theatre**.

VERA PROJECT
THEATER

Map p238 (📞206-956-8372; www.theveraproject.org; cnr Republican St & Warren Ave N; 🚇Seattle Center) An excellent nonprofit community center run by and for teenagers and young adults, the Vera Project books exclusively all-ages shows in a smoke-free and alcohol-free environment. It's also dedicated to giving youth a place to learn skills, make art and get involved in the community. Get involved or check out a concert.

🛍 SHOPPING

Belltown's shopping is patchy. Look hard and you'll find a punk-rock record store and the polar-fleece-happy Patagonia. But, never fear, downtown is near.

KEXP – THE SOUND OF SEATTLE

Arguably, one of the most unique and envied public radio stations in the nation, nonprofit KEXP is perhaps the primary reason why Seattle has been able to maintain such a robust independent music scene since the 1980s. Home-grown and proud of it, the station's antecedents go back to the hippy era in the early 1970s, when four University of Washington students put on their DIY hats and dreamed up KCMU, a quietly revolutionary radio station that became known for its innovative 'volunteer' DJs, some of whom went on to form the seminal grunge bands, Soundgarden and Mudhoney.

As the '70s became the '80s, KCMU morphed into something bigger, hiring full-time DJs and moving frequencies to 90.3FM. Notwithstanding, the station never fully abandoned its underground roots. In 1988, it was the first radio station to play Nirvana and trend-anticipating DJs became deftly instrumental in pushing local talent onto a bigger stage: recent examples include rappers Macklemore and Ryan Lewis. It was also the first station to stream over the internet.

What has always kept KEXP (the name changed in 2001) interesting is its music-obsessed DJs and the fabulous shows they curate. Worth singling out are the station's 10-part documentary series on musical genres. Highlights have included 'Blues for Hard Times,' 'Hip Hop: The New Seattle Sound' and, inevitably, 'Grunge.'

In December 2015, KEXP logged another landmark when it opened a new **headquarters** (p93) in the Seattle Center next to the Key Arena. As well as hosting a broadcasting space, the venue has accessible areas for live music concerts and band appearances.

ZANADU COMICS

Map p238 (www.zanaducomics.com; 1923 3rd Ave; ⊙10am-6pm Mon-Sat, noon-5pm Sun; ⓡWestlake) Awash with superheroes and sci-fi geekdom, Zanadu specializes in comics (hundreds of them) and comic-related toys.

SINGLES GOING STEADY MUSIC

Map p238 (☑206-441-7396; 2219 2nd Ave; ⊙noon-7pm Tue-Thu, noon-8pm Fri & Sat, noon-6pm Sun; ⓺13) Singles Going Steady – named after an album by those British punk pioneers the Buzzcocks – is a niche record store specializing in punk, oi, reggae and ska, mostly in the form of 7in vinyl singles, as well as posters, patches and other accessories. There's a good little magazine selection, too.

EXOFFICIO SPORTS & OUTDOORS

Map p238 (☑206-283-4746; www.exofficio.com; 114 Vine St; ⊙10am-6pm Mon-Fri, 10am-5pm Sat, 11am-5pm Sun; ⓺13) Kit yourself out for the Sahara or – closer to home – Mt Rainier National Park at this handy travel-gear shop.

PETER MILLER ARCHITECTURE & DESIGN BOOKS BOOKS

Map p238 (www.petermiller.com; 2326 2nd Ave; ⊙10am-6pm Mon-Sat; ⓺13) This distinctly 'New-Belltown' store, whose window arrangements will make a bibliophile or a design fiend drool, specializes in luxurious architecture books, stationery and art supplies.

🏃 SPORTS & ACTIVITIES

VELO BIKE SHOP CYCLING

Map p238 (☑206-325-3292; wwwvelobikeshop.com; 2151 6th Ave; ⊙10am-7pm Mon-Thu, 10am-6pm Fri & Sat, noon-5pm Sun; ⓡWestlake & 7th) Formerly resident in Capitol Hill, Velo moved into this new space in Belltown adjoining Tom Douglas' Assembly Hall in 2013. If you need a bike with more flexibility than those offered by Seattle's Pronto bike-sharing scheme, this place can help out. Sturdy 'city bikes' with handy covered back-racks go for $35 a day.

SEATTLE GLASSBLOWING STUDIO COURSE

Map p238 (www.seattleglassblowing.com; 2227 5th Ave; ⊙9am-6pm Mon-Sat, 10am-6pm Sun; ⓺13) If Dale Chihuly's decadent chandeliers have inspired you, try creating your own modest glass art at this blow-your-own glass studio a few blocks from the master's museum. One-off sessions cost $55 to $150, or there are four-hour group workshops on Saturdays for $150. Alternatively, you can just watch the fascinating process from the on-site cafe, which has a viewing window overlooking the workshop.

RIDE THE DUCKS OF SEATTLE TOURS

Map p238 (☑206-441-4687; www.ridetheducksofseattle.com; 516 Broad St; adult/child $29/18; ⓭; ⓢSeattle Center) These hugely popular tours in amphibious vehicles are partly on land and partly in the water. From their start point near the Space Needle the 90-minute tours encompass the waterfront, Pioneer Square and Fremont before pitching (quite literally) into Lake Union for half an hour. The guides are renowned for their humor and the tours are very popular with families.

KEY ARENA STADIUM

Map p238 (www.keyarena.com; 305 Harrison St; ⓢSeattle Center) Looking a little like a concrete tent, the Key Arena in the Seattle Center is primarily a basketball venue (home to women's team, Seattle Storm), but it also serves as one of the city's larger music venues used by big-name touring bands.

It began life at the 1962 World's Fair when it accommodated the *Bubbleator,* a hydraulic elevator that took visitors on a journey through the near future. As a music venue it has hosted Elvis, the Beatles (in one of their last-ever live performances), Jimi Hendrix (in a triumphant 1969 homecoming) and Macklemore.

Queen Anne & Lake Union

QUEEN ANNE | LAKE UNION

Neighborhood Top Five

① **Museum of History & Industry** (p98) Riding the streetcar to this fabulous museum for a first-class exposition of Seattle's grunge-playing, aircraft-building, computer-designing history.

② **Cheshiahud Loop** (p105) Circumnavigating Lake Union on foot (or bike) on this well-signposted 6-mile route.

③ **Opulent Mansions** Admiring the wealthy array of fin-de-siècle architecture atop Queen Anne Hill.

④ **Center for Wooden Boats** (p99) Sallying forth on Lake Union on a free public sailboat ride from this one-of-a-kind museum and boating enthusiasts' center.

⑤ **Kerry Park** (p99) Viewing lakes, islands, skyscrapers and the even more sky-scraping Mt Rainier from this spectacular lookout at sunset, amid Beverly Hills–like mansions.

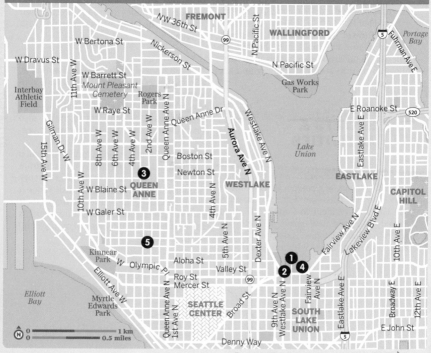

For more detail of this area see Map p240 ➜

Explore: Queen Anne & Lake Union

At some point during your Seattle sightseeing sojourn, you'll exit the tourist-heavy Seattle Center and be deposited on one of the busy thoroughfares of Lower Queen Anne, a lived-in urban locale good for a cheap meal or an eye-widening dose of Seattle coffee culture. To get a view of a posher side of the neighborhood, take a steep hike (or jump on a bus) up Queen Anne Ave N, aka 'the Counterbalance' to a markedly different neck of the woods.

Sitting on a 456ft hill above the Seattle Center, Queen Anne proper is an elegant collection of majestic redbrick houses and apartment buildings, sweeping lawns manicured to perfection, and gorgeous views of the city and Elliott Bay. Vistas aside (and, yes, they're worth the energy expenditure), the favorite pastime here is 'mansion-viewing,' ie wandering at will along the traffic-lite streets spying on an opulent array of fin-de-siècle architecture.

To the east, Lake Union – Seattle's watery playground – covers a large area that encompasses several neighborhoods including Fremont and the U District. To get an overview of its famous houseboats and various water-based activities, start in Lake Union Park and circumnavigate the lake on the Cheshiahud Loop, a 6-mile walking circuit. If you have less time, head straight for the Museum of History & Industry, one of Seattle's headline sights. Across Mercer St there are enough restaurants and coffee bars in the burgeoning South Lake Union neighborhood to keep you fueled until dinner time. The handy streetcar will zap you back from lakeside to downtown in 10 minutes.

Local Life

➺ **Coffee culture** Examine the velvet foam on your latte at Uptown Espresso Bar (p103) while eavesdropping on cell-phone conversations, yoga enthusiasts comparing breathing techniques, and 20-somethings bragging about how many Twitter followers they have.

➺ **Brunch hangout** Find out about the party you missed last night while standing in line for a hangover-curing brunch at 5 Spot (p100).

Getting There & Away

➺ **Bus** Metro buses 2 and 13 run frequently to Queen Anne from downtown and Seattle Center. Buses 62 and 70 serve the Westlake and Eastlake neighborhoods of Lake Union from downtown.

➺ **Streetcar** One of Seattle's two main streetcar lines runs between South Lake Union and the Westlake Center in downtown every 10 minutes.

Lonely Planet's Top Tip

Hit a Queen Anne supermarket or sandwich bar and take a picnic over to Kerry Park (p99), weather permitting, to enjoy what many locals claim is Seattle's finest view.

Best Places to Eat

➺ Toulouse Petit (p101)
➺ How to Cook a Wolf (p101)
➺ Canlis (p101)
➺ Serafina (p102)

For reviews, see p100 ➺

Best Drinking & Nightlife

➺ El Diablo Coffee Co (p103)
➺ Uptown Espresso Bar (p103)
➺ Mecca Café (p103)
➺ Hilltop Ale House (p103)

For reviews, see p102 ➺

Best Places to Shop

➺ REI (p104)
➺ Feathered Friends (p105)
➺ Queen Anne Book Company (p105)

For reviews, see p104 ➺

QUEEN ANNE & LAKE UNION

RICHARD CUMMINS / GETTY IMAGES ©

MUSEUM OF HISTORY & INDUSTRY

Almost everything you need to know about Seattle is crammed into the fabulous Museum of History & Industry, located in plush digs on the southern shore of Lake Union. In operation since the 1950s, and with an archive of over four million objects, MOHAI displays its stash of historical booty in an impressively repurposed naval armory building.

DON'T MISS

➡ Film and TV exhibit
➡ Main atrium
➡ Periscope

PRACTICALITIES

➡ Map p240, F5
➡ 860 Terry Ave N
➡ adult/child under 14yr $19.95/free
➡ ⊙10am-5pm, 10am-8pm 1st Thu of month
➡ 👪
➡ 🚇Lake Union Park

Interactive Exhibits

The big eye-catcher as you walk into the hangar-sized space is a 1919 **Boeing airplane** hanging from the roof (the first commercial Boeing ever made). Indeed, the name 'Boeing' looms large over the whole museum, along with numerous other Seattle icons (Starbucks, Rainier beer, grunge). In the city that produced Microsoft, there is no shortage of interactive exhibits to enjoy (kids will have a ball), including a photo and comment booth, touchscreen TVs and an opportunity to explore railroad history by banging large mallets on railway sleepers. With so many artifacts to call upon, exhibits can change regularly, although the museum's overriding sentiment remains constant: an unashamed celebration of Seattle's short but action-packed history.

The Upper Floors

On the upper floors, rooms are arranged around a mezzanine with the exhibits unfolding chronologically using various themes to paint a multi-layered portrait of the city room by room. Highlights include the early Native American settlers, the 1889 Great Fire, the 1962 World's Fair, a focus on film and TV (covering everything from *Twin Peaks* to *Grey's Anatomy*), and an interesting dip into Seattle's counterculture – including a self-critical look at the 1999 WTO conference riots.

On the top floor there's an ingenious **periscope** that offers visitors a 360-degree view of the world outside, dominated by the glistening waters of Lake Union.

⊙ SIGHTS

Queen Anne and Lake Union host a good selection of small parks beautified with fine city and water views.

Lake Union's southern shore harbors the wonderfully unique Center for Wooden Boats along with the recently relocated Museum of History & Industry – one of Seattle's big-hitter sights.

⊙ Queen Anne

QUEEN ANNE COUNTERBALANCE   AREA
Map p240 (Queen Anne Ave N, north of W Roy St; 🚋2) The streetcar that chugged up and down the steep grade along Queen Anne Ave started operating on overhead-wire electricity in 1900, but it still needed some help to manage the hill. So engineers designed a system of counterweights – a 16-ton train that ran in a tunnel beneath the street would go up when the cable car went down and vice versa. The cable cars were retired in 1943, but the underground tunnels are still there (although they're not currently open to the public).

TREAT HOUSE   LANDMARK
Map p240 (1 W Highland Dr, at Queen Anne Ave N; 🚋2) This 14-gabled house near the top of Queen Anne Hill was built in 1905 by Harry Whitney Treat, a friend of William F 'Buffalo Bill' Cody. Treat also created Golden Gardens Park (p157) in northwest Ballard. After Treat's death in the 1920s, the building was converted into 15 apartments. Built in English arts-and-crafts style, it's worth admiring from the outside.

KERRY PARK   PARK, VIEWPOINT
Map p240 (211 W Highland Dr; 🚻; 🚋2) Amid the glittering Beverly Hills–like mansions of Highland Dr, mere commoners can enjoy eagle's-eye views of downtown Seattle and Elliott Bay (and Mt Rainier, should it take its cloudy hat off) from this spectacular lookout.

Binoculars (50¢) are provided, so you can look back at the people at the top of the Space Needle looking over at you. The park is set on a steep incline of Queen Anne Hill (looking south) and is split in two, with a stairway linking to a popular children's playground below. This is a favorite spot to end a romantic date night – or make a proposal!

MARSHALL PARK   PARK
Map p240 (🚋2) Atop Queen Anne Hill at the west end of W Highland Dr this tiny but loftily positioned park has expansive views stretching west across Puget Sound to the Olympic Mountains.

⊙ Lake Union

MUSEUM OF HISTORY & INDUSTRY   MUSEUM
See p98.

LAKE UNION PARK   PARK
Map p240 (🚻; 🚌Lake Union Park) Opened in 2010, this welcome green patch occupies ex-navy land on the southern tip of Lake Union and has a wading pond (with model sailboats you can use), an attractive bridge and a boat launch. It hosts the Museum of History & Industry in the old naval armory building and the Center for Wooden Boats.

Various interpretive panels chronicle Seattle's maritime connections. The South Lake Union streetcar stops outside.

CENTER FOR WOODEN BOATS   MUSEUM
Map p240 (📞206-382-2628; www.cwb.org; 1010 Valley St; sailboat/rowboat rental per hour $38/35, beginner sailing course $420; ⊙10am-6pm Tue-Sun; 🚻; 🚌Lake Union Park) Honoring Seattle's historical, aquatic and Native American antecedents, this one-of-a-kind museum and enthusiasts' center features vintage and replica boats and offers sailing lessons, including an excellent beginner course that gives you eight to 12 lessons over a four-month period. Best of all, however, are its free Sunday public sailboat rides on Lake Union (first come, first served; sign-ups start 10am).

Seasoned sailors who are a little rusty can take a one-on-one lesson for around $50 per hour, and there are also classes on sail repair and boat building. You can rent kayaks, canoes, rowboats and sailboats (the latter requires a 30-minute boat-handling test, which costs $10).

The museum will open a new **Education Center** in Lake Union Park in 2017 to help further showcase Seattle's maritime heritage and provide more space for its boat restorers to work in.

DENNY PARK   PARK
Map p240 (🚌Westlake & Denny) Seattle's oldest park was originally designated a cemetery – but that status ended up being rather

temporary, and the land was rededicated as parkland. Formerly part of Denny Hill, the park was later flattened in the Denny Regrade of 1910, over protests by preservationists. Today it attracts homeless people and tentative tourists from the nearby Space Needle.

EATING

Many of the dining options in Lower Queen Anne, just west of Seattle Center (p78), are geared toward the pre- or post-event attending functions at Key Arena (p95). If you head up the hill to Upper Queen Anne, you'll find the restaurants have more of the neighborhood's quiet, grown-up, family-friendly atmosphere.

The area around Lake Union used to be a bit of a culinary wasteland, but things have changed, especially in South Lake Union, with big-name chefs such as Tom Douglas moving in to cater for the new affluent businesses and residents. Places get busy during weekday lunchtimes and after-work happy hours.

✖ Queen Anne

5 SPOT   BREAKFAST $
Map p240 (www.chowfoods.com; 1502 Queen Anne Ave N; brunch $8-14; ☺8am-11pm Mon-Fri, 8am-3pm & 5pm-midnight Sat & Sun; ♠; ▣2)
Top of the hill, top of the morning and top of the brunch charts: the queues outside 5 Spot at 10am on a Sunday testify to a formidable late breakfast. The crowds inspire a great atmosphere, and the hearty menu, which has perfected French toast, huevos rancheros and plenty more American standards, will shift the stubbornest of hangovers.

DICK'S DRIVE-IN   BURGERS $
Map p240 (✆206-285-5155; www.ddir.com; 500 Queen Anne Ave N; burgers from $1.40;

◉ TOP SIGHT
LAKE UNION

Unifying Seattle's various bodies of water, the appropriately named Lake Union is a freshwater lake carved by glacial erosion 12,000 years ago. Native American Duwamish tribes once subsisted on its then isolated shores, but they wouldn't recognize the place today. Twenty-first-century Lake Union is backed by half a dozen densely packed urban neighborhoods and is linked to both Lake Washington and Puget Sound by the Washington Ship Canal, built as part of a huge engineering project in the 1910s. Not surprisingly, the lake is a nexus for water-sports enthusiasts – you'll regularly see kayakers, rowers, sailboats and paddle boarders negotiating its calm-ish teal waters.

It also acts as a runway for seaplanes. **Kenmore Air** (www.kenmoreair.com; 950 Westlake Ave N) operates services to Victoria (Canada) and the San Juan Islands from here. Houseboats have punctuated the lake since the 1890s, and it still hosts one of the largest houseboat populations in the US (around 500). The most famous houseboat is that of Sam, the fictional character played by Tom Hanks in the movie *Sleepless in Seattle*.

Surrounding the lake on its eastern, western and southern shores respectively are the neighborhoods of **Eastlake** (dominated by the decommissioned City Light Steam Plant – now occupied by a biotech company), **Westlake** and **South Lake Union**, the city's fastest developing neighborhood-in-the-making.

DON'T MISS
→ Houseboats
→ Kayaking
→ South Lake Union

PRACTICALITIES
→ Map p240, F5
→ ▣Lake Union Park

10:30am-2am; 13) If you're down to your last few dollars and dying for something to eat, don't panic! Dick's is calling you. Welcome to the only fast-food joint in Seattle where you can still buy a burger for $1.40, along with $1.75 fries (hand cut, no less) and $2.50 milkshakes (made with 100% ice cream, of course).

Gourmet it isn't, but as quintessential only-in-Seattle experiences go, it's up there with the Space Needle (and a lot cheaper).

QUEEN ANNE CAFÉ AMERICAN, BREAKFAST $

Map p240 (206-285-2060; 2121 Queen Anne Ave N; breakfast $9-11; 7:30am-8pm Mon-Fri, 8am-9pm Sat, 8am-2:30pm Sun; ; 13) Locals flock to this light-filled neighborhood spot for traditional comfort food, including broiled pork chops and various sandwiches, but the place really shines at breakfast. Expect a bit of a wait for weekend brunch.

★TOULOUSE PETIT CAJUN, CREOLE $$

Map p240 (206-432-9069; www.toulousepetit. com; 601 Queen Anne Ave N; mains $19-26; 8am-2am; 13) Hailed for its generous happy hours, cheap brunches and rollicking atmosphere, this perennially busy Queen Anne eatery has the common touch. The menu is large and varied, offering choices such as blackened rib-eye steak, freshwater gulf prawns and housemade gnocchi with artichoke hearts.

HOW TO COOK A WOLF ITALIAN $$

Map p240 (206-838-8090; www.ethanstowell-restaurants.com; 2208 Queen Anne Ave N; pasta $16-19; 5-11pm; 13) Despite its scary name, the Ethan Stowell-run HTCAW has nothing to do with roasting wild fauna over your campfire. Rather the name is poached from a book written by MFK Fisher during wartime rationing about how to make the most of limited ingredients. Though times have changed, Stowell embraces the same philosophy.

The food is simple but creative Italian nosh listed on a single sheet of paper and served in a small den-like restaurant. If they ever invent a culinary genre called 'Pacific Northwest Italian,' HTCAW will be its archetype.

PESO'S KITCHEN & LOUNGE MEXICAN, BREAKFAST $$

Map p240 (206-283-9353; www.pesoskitchen-andlounge.com; 605 Queen Anne Ave N; brunch $9-15, dinner $12-17; 4pm-midnight Mon & Tue,

11am-2am Wed & Thu, 9am-2am Fri-Sun; 13) A place that wears many sombreros, Peso's serves fine Mexican food in the evenings amid a cool, trendy scene that is anything but Mexican. But the trump card comes the next morning, after the beautiful people have gone home, with an acclaimed egg-biased breakfast.

PARAGON BAR & GRILL AMERICAN $$

Map p240 (206-283-4548; 2125 Queen Anne Ave N; mains $12-22; 11:30am-2am Mon-Sat, 10am-2am Sun; 13) The Paragon is a bastion of American regional cooking, specializing in grilled fish and updated classics. Try the baby back ribs or a plate of fried green tomatoes. There's an open fireplace and a lively bar scene (the bar's open until 2am). Bonus! Most nights there's live music or DJs playing everything from indie rock to jazz.

CANLIS AMERICAN $$$

Map p240 (206-283-3313; 2576 Aurora Ave N; 3-/4-course dinner $85/100; 5:30pm-late Mon-Sat; 5) One of Seattle's most celebrated restaurants, Canlis is old-school posh and one of the few places in the city where people regularly get dressed up for dinner. The menu is Pacific Northwest traditional (halibut, pork, fresh veg and Grand Marnier soufflé) and the decor's like something out of a 1950s-era Hitchcock movie – all angled glass and sweeping views.

Prices are hefty, ties and jackets ubiquitous and reservations are pretty much essential. A special-occasion dinner.

✖ Lake Union

CAFFÈ TORINO ITALIAN, SANDWICHES $

Map p240 (206-682-2099; www.caffetorino-seattle.com; 422 Yale Ave N; sandwiches $7-8.50; 6:30am-6pm Mon-Fri, 8am-5pm Sat & Sun; ; Terry & Mercer) If you're up on the nuances of regional Italian food culture, you'll know that Turin (Torino) is a temple of good food and coffee, which is why you may want to decamp here for a Lavazza cappuccino, a Nutella cookie and a Caprese sandwich. Best of all is Caffè Torino's honoring of the *aperitivo* tradition, the late-afternoon *'pausa'* for cheap bites and prosecco.

SERIOUS BISCUIT AMERICAN $

Map p240 (206-436-0050; www.seriouspie-seattle.com/westlake; 401 Westlake Ave N; biscuits $7-13; 7am-3pm Mon-Fri, 9am-3pm Sat &

LOCAL KNOWLEDGE

LOWER QUEEN ANNE

Hungry tourists from the Seattle Center bump into affluent young techies on their lunch breaks in Lower Queen Anne, the thin strip at the bottom of 'the Counterbalance' (p99) that strikes a less haughty (and more economical) pose than its eponymous neighbor up on the hill. A northern extension of Belltown, Lower Queen Anne – or 'Up-town' as it's sometimes known – is locally renowned for its eclectic mix of restaurants, most of which are quick, casual and, above all, easy on the wallet. Concert-goers and sports fans from the nearby McCaw Hall (p93) and Key Arena (p95) naturally gravitate here after performances and games (Queen Anne Ave N and Roy St are the main drags), while downtown is only two minutes away on the monorail. As a neighborhood, Lower Queen Anne has more in common with Belltown than Queen Anne, with new condos slowly snuffing out remnants of its erstwhile seediness.

Sun; 🚌Westlake & Thomas) After Serious Pie (p88) comes Serious Biscuit, Tom Douglas' first bite at the South Lake Union cookie that has lured so many new restaurants into the neighborhood in the last couple of years. The buttery biscuits (the savory American rather than sweet British variety) serve as flaky bases to a variety of brunch-worthy toppings – the 'zach' (fried chicken, gravy, bacon and egg) is a perennial favorite.

Bear in mind that this is a typical Douglas domain with shared tables and limited seating. Upstairs, he operates another of his Serious Pie pizza joints in the evenings.

CITIZEN COFFEE   SANDWICHES, BREAKFAST $
Map p240 (📞206-284-1015; www.citizencoffee. com; 706 Taylor Ave N; breakfast & sandwiches $5-10; ⏰6am-9pm Mon-Thu, 7am-10pm Fri & Sat, 7am-9pm Sun; 🚌3) Citizen serves all-day breakfast and it's a good one. There are plenty of options at this popular redbrick joint near the Space Needle, where you can opt for Greek yogurt and fruit, biscuits and gravy, or huevos rancheros. The slightly tucked-away location means it's less tourist-heavy and more local.

BLUE MOON BURGERS   BURGERS $
Map p240 (📞206-652-0400; www.bluemoon burgers.com; 920 Republican St; burgers $6-10; ⏰11am-8pm Mon-Fri, noon-8pm Sat; 🍴; 🚌Westlake & Mercer) 🌱 One in a quartet of local burger joints (the others are in Fremont, Capitol Hill and West Seattle), Blue Moon has brought locavore ethics to fast food, sourcing its brioche buns from Pioneer Square's Grand Central Baking Co (p71) and its grass-fed beef from local farms. It also offers 100% vegan burger options.

SERAFINA   ITALIAN $$
Map p240 (📞206-323-0807; www.serafinase attle.com; 2043 Eastlake Ave E; starters $5-12, pastas $16-18, mains $23-42; ⏰11:30am-2:30pm & 5-10pm Mon-Fri, 5-11pm Sat, 10am-2:30pm & 5-11pm Sun; 🚌70) This lovely neighborhood Italian restaurant in Eastlake specializes in regional Tuscan-style cooking, with simply prepared meat and fish, as well as pastas that can be ordered as a first or main course. A gorgeous leafy deck area behind the restaurant doubles as the entryway to **Cicchetti**, Serafina's sister restaurant, which serves Mediterranean snacks. Reservations are recommended.

RE:PUBLIC   MODERN AMERICAN $$
Map p240 (📞206-467-5300; www.republicse attle.com; 429 Westlake Ave N; mains $15-28; ⏰11am-2:30pm & 5-11pm Mon-Thu, 10am-2am Fri & Sat, 5-11pm Sun; 🚌Westlake & Mercer) 🌱 Although the name might read like the sobriquet of a rap artist, Re:public (don't forget the colon), situated on the corner of Republican St, is filled with a distinctly South Lake Union type of public – ie young, tech-ish and affluent. As a kind of microcosm of the new neighborhood, it serves modern farm-to-table food – artisanal cheese plates, wild-boar Bolognese – in a neat, minimalist space.

🍷 DRINKING & NIGHTLIFE

When it comes to drinking, this neighborhood is all over the map. Pleasantly sleepy Queen Anne has everything from traditional beer halls and dives to swanky jazz bars. South

Lake Union is full of new corporate bars where the password is Amazon.

Queen Anne is a breeding ground for coffee shops and many of Seattle's popular coffee chainlets opened their first branches here.

🍷 Queen Anne

★EL DIABLO COFFEE CO   CAFE

Map p240 (www.eldiablocoffee.com; 1811 Queen Anne Ave N; ⊘5:30am-8pm Mon-Fri, 6:30am-8pm Sat, 6:30am-6pm Sun; 🛜; 🚍13) Anyone for a *café cubano*? While the US trade embargo against Cuba prevents the sale of Cuban coffee beans, you can at least enjoy your coffee Cuban-style – ie strong, short, black and loaded with sugar – in this colorful little cafe on Queen Anne Hill. If you're hungry try the *ropa vieja* (spicy stewed beef) sandwich.

CAFFE LADRO   CAFE

Map p240 (www.caffeladro.com; 2205 Queen Anne Ave N; ⊘5:30am-8pm Sun-Thu, 5:30am-9pm Fri & Sat; 🛜; 🚍13) 🍴 With an Italian name that translates as 'coffee thief,' apparently because it set out to pinch business from Starbucks, Ladro has subsequently established its own small Seattle-only chain (15 branches and counting). This one in Lower Queen Anne is the original, dating from 1994. Not only does it roast its own beans, it does its own baking.

UPTOWN ESPRESSO BAR   CAFE

Map p240 (☏206-285-3757; 525 Queen Anne N; ⊘5am-10pm Mon-Thu, 5am-11pm Fri, 6am-11pm Sat, 6am-10pm Sun; 🛜; 🚍13) Competing with Starbucks for generous opening hours, Uptown has been around since the early 1980s and is famous for the 'velvet foam' that embellishes its lattes. The original and best cafe – there are now eight locations – is this neighborhood nexus in Lower Queen Anne (aka 'Uptown'), an oasis of casual elegance.

HILLTOP ALE HOUSE   PUB

Map p240 (☏206-285-3877; www.seattleale houses.com; 2129 Queen Anne Ave N; ⊘11am-11pm Sun-Thu, 11am-midnight Fri & Sat; 🚍13) Hilltop is a comfy neighborhood hangout on Queen Anne Hill, sister to the 74th Street Ale House (p150) in Green Lake. It has a friendly vibe and a large selection of microbrews, served in proper 20oz pints,

and the menu is well above your standard pub fare.

MECCA CAFÉ   BAR

Map p240 (☏206-285-9728; 526 Queen Anne Ave N; burgers $8.75; ⊘7am-2am; 🚍13) A kind of sister-dive to the nearby Five Point Café (p92), the Mecca was founded at the tail end of Prohibition (1930) and has been hailed at many points in its history as the best bar in Seattle. Half of the long, skinny room is a ketchup-on-the-table diner, but all the fun happens on the other side, where decades worth of beer mat scribbles line the walls and the bartenders know the jukebox songs better than you do.

MCMENAMINS QUEEN ANNE   MICROBREWERY

Map p240 (www.mcmenamins.com; 200 Roy St; ⊘11am-1am; 🚍13) The McMenamin brothers' microbrewing empire is a product of Portland, OR, but you can enjoy a comforting out-of-state taste of the brand's ever-successful blend of psychedelia meets art nouveau meets wood-paneled gentleman's club at this Lower Queen Anne perch. The real draw, of course, is the beer, including the classic Hammerhead pale ale, loaded with Oregon hops. It's kid-friendly.

CAFFÈ FIORE   COFFEE

Map p240 (☏206-282-1441; www.caffefiore.com; 224 W Galer St; ⊘6am-6pm Mon-Sat, 7am-6pm Sun; 🛜; 🚍2) 🍴 Queen Anne hosts an abundance of coffee shops and most of them are good, but Fiore, which is part of a small four-cafe Seattle chain, has the advantage of being near Kerry Park (p99) up on the hill and retains a cozy Queen Anne neighborhood feel. People rave about its 'Sevilla' (mocha with orange zest), but its espressos are pretty potent too.

🍷 Lake Union

BRAVE HORSE TAVERN   PUB

Map p240 (www.bravehorsetavern.com; 310 Terry Ave N; ⊘11am-midnight Mon-Fri, 10am-midnight Sat & Sun; 🚍Terry & Thomas) With this place, posing as a kind of German beer hall meets Wild West saloon, Tom Douglas has made his (inevitable) lunge into the world of pubs. Brave Horse sports two dozen draft beers (local amber ales are well represented) and the place even bakes its own pretzels in a special oven.

QUEEN ANNE WHO?

Observant students of history might wonder why the Seattle neighborhood of Queen Anne is named after an undistinguished British queen who reigned between the years 1702 and 1714, 150 years before the city was even founded. The answer is rooted in architecture. The hill on which the Queen Anne neighborhood sits is embellished by a rather nebulous style of revivalist architecture first concocted in the UK in the 1860s and brought to North America in the early 1880s, where it remained in vogue until around 1910 (when the neighborhood was being laid out).

Queen Anne architecture supposedly harked back to the English baroque buildings of the early 18th century (during the reign of Queen Anne), but the name quickly became something of a misnomer, as the revivalist Queen Anne style took on a life of its own, particularly in the US. Typical Queen Anne features in North America include large bay windows, wraparound porches, steep gabled roofs, polygonal towers, shingles and lavish gardens. To see some of the more whimsical examples, wander at will among the large private houses on top of Queen Anne Hill. The mansions along Highland Dr are particularly opulent.

With the Amazon HQ around the corner, the crowds are predictably Amazonian, though there's plenty of intermingling at the shuffleboard tables.

⭐ ENTERTAINMENT

TEATRO ZINZANNI   LIVE PERFORMANCE

Map p240 (www.zinzanni.com; 222 Mercer St; tickets incl dinner $99-173; ☐13) Welcome to the zany world of the 'circus dinner show,' a sort of vaudeville meets Vegas meets Cirque du Soleil. Sit back in an improvised big top for a night of jugglers, jokers, trapeze artists, music and food. The Teatro has been running since 1998 and became a permanent fixture in 2002.

The menu varies but is often topical to the performance and includes five courses.

ON THE BOARDS   DANCE, THEATER

Map p240 (📞206-217-9888; www.ontheboards. org; 100 W Roy St; ☐13) *The* place for avant-garde performance art, the nonprofit On the Boards makes its home at the intimate Behnke Center for Contemporary Performance, and showcases some innovative and occasionally weird dance and music.

EL CORAZON   LIVE MUSIC

Map p240 (📞206-381-3094; www.elcorazon seattle.com; 109 Eastlake Ave E; ☐70) Formerly the Off-Ramp, then Graceland, El Corazon has lots of history echoing around its walls – and lots of sweaty, beer-drenched bodies bouncing off them. Save your clean shirt for another night, and don't expect perfect

sound quality at every show. The gutsy bands play loud, presumably to drown out the traffic noise from I-5 just outside the door.

The venue is etched in grunge-era mythology. Pearl Jam, then going under the name of Mookie Blaylock, played their first ever gig here in October 1990.

SIFF CINEMA UPTOWN   CINEMA

Map p240 (📞206-285-1022; 511 Queen Anne Ave N; ☐13) The Uptown is joint HQ for the Seattle International Film Festival (p29) (SIFF), meaning its three screens get an intelligent and varied turnaround of movies.

🛍 SHOPPING

Lake Union, home of the state-of-the-art REI megastore, is good for outdoor equipment shops. Queen Anne specializes in library-quiet bookshops and small boutiques.

⭐REI   OUTDOOR EQUIPMENT, CLOTHING

Map p240 (📞206-323-8333; www.rei.com; 222 Yale Ave N; ☺9am-9pm Mon-Sat, 10am-7pm Sun; ☐70) As much an adventure as a shopping experience, the state-of-the-art megastore of America's largest consumer co-op has its own climbing wall – a 65ft rock pinnacle to the side of the store's entryway. The wall offers various climbing options from open climbs to private instruction. Check the website for details.

REI is also the be-all and end-all of outdoor clothing and equipment, and is equipped with some additional perks like an outdoor mountain-bike test track. The store also rents various ski packages, climbing gear and camping equipment, and organizes a ton of courses from map-reading to bike maintenance.

QUEEN ANNE BOOK COMPANY   BOOKS
Map p240 (☏206-283-5624; 1811 Queen Anne Ave N; ⊙10am-7pm Mon-Fri, 10am-5pm Sat & Sun; 🚌13) This charming little nook is everything a neighborhood bookstore should be with frequent poetry readings and book signings. The adjoining El Diablo (p103) coffee shop has a lovely little patio where you can sip a coffee and pore over your latest book purchase.

FEATHERED FRIENDS   SPORTS & OUTDOORS
Map p240 (☏206-292-2210; www.feathered friends.com; 119 Yale Ave N; ⊙10am-7pm Mon-Fri, 10am-6pm Sat, 11am-5pm Sun; 🚌70) Feathered Friends stocks high-end climbing equipment, made-to-order sleeping bags and backcountry ski gear. Products made with down are the specialty.

PATRICK'S FLY SHOP   SPORTS & OUTDOORS
Map p240 (☏206-325-8988; www.patricksfly shop.com; 2237 Eastlake Ave E; ⊙10am-6pm Mon-Sat, 10am-3pm Sun; 🚌70) Located near Lake Union, this shop has been around as long as anyone can remember. It offers workshops on fly-fishing, sells equipment and gives advice.

ONCE UPON A TIME   CHILDREN
Map p240 (☏206-284-7260; www.onceupona timetoys.net; 1622 Queen Anne Ave N; ⊙10am-6pm Mon-Sat, 11am-5pm Sun; 🚻; 🚌13) This children's store stocks top international brands like BabyBjörn for savvy parents who like to dress their renaissance tots in labels from around the world. You'll find everything from the practical to the simply adorable: strollers, knit toys, train sets, books, games, little socks and hats, and more.

🏃 SPORTS & ACTIVITIES

Lake Union is one of the main access points to Seattle's many kayak-friendly bodies of water.

CHESHIAHUD LOOP   WALKING, RUNNING
Map p240 Inaugurated several years ago to tie in with the landscaping of Lake Union Park (p99), this well-signposted 6-mile route circumnavigates Lake Union by gelling together an amalgam of existing trails, sidewalks and paths. Named for a Duwamish chief who once headed a lakeside village, it's a good way to keep away from busy roads while walking/jogging/cycling through at least five Seattle neighborhoods.

NORTHWEST OUTDOOR CENTER   KAYAKING
Map p240 (☏206-281-9694; www.nwoc.com; 2100 Westlake Ave N; rental per hour from $16; 🚌62) Located on the west side of Lake Union, this place rents kayaks and stand-up paddle boards, and offers tours and instruction in sea and white-water kayaking.

MOSS BAY ROWING & KAYAK CENTER   KAYAKING
Map p240 (☏206-682-2031; www.mossbay.net; 1001 Fairview Ave N; kayak/paddle board rental per hour $15/16; ⊙9am-8pm summer, 10am-5pm Thu-Mon winter; ⛴Fairview & Campus Dr) Moss Bay offers rentals, extensive lessons and tours (from $45 per person) on Lake Union.

Music & Nightlife

Detroit, New Orleans, Nashville...Seattle! There aren't many cities in the US that can claim to have redirected the path of modern music. But, while the angry firmament of grunge may have faded since the demise of Nirvana et al, the city's rambunctious nightlife scene remains varied and vital.

OSCAR C. WILLIAMS / SHUTTERSTOCK ©

1. Neumo's (p117)
This mid-sized venue is a pillar of Seattle's music scene.

2. & 3. Outdoor live music (p93)
Al fresco events and street performers abound in summer, particularly around the Seattle Center (p93).

4. Museum of Pop Culture (p84)
This super-modern museum is a paean to rock-and-roll and pop culture history.

5. Stage-diver at Key Arena (p95)
This Seattle Center venue has played host to a legendary list of performers, including the Beatles and Jimi Hendrix.

PETER CARROLL / GETTY IMAGES ©

LAWRENCE WORCESTER / GETTY IMAGES ©

Capitol Hill & First Hill

Neighborhood Top Five

1 **Victrola Coffee Roasters** (p115) Testing the water on the Pike–Pine corridor while imbibing strong coffee behind the large glass windows of this fine coffee purveyor.

2 **Neumo's** (p117) Seeing a name band at this legendary live-music venue, one of Seattle's most revered.

3 **Water Tower Observation Deck** (p110) Climbing the water tower in Volunteer Park to admire dazzling vistas of Seattle and Mt Rainier.

4 **Lost Lake Cafe & Lounge** (p112) Enjoying a very late beer or a very early breakfast at the 24-hour *Twin Peaks*–themed Lost Lake Cafe.

5 **Elliott Bay Book Company** (p118) Coming up for air after an afternoon of lazy literary immersion at Seattle's most beloved bookstore.

For more detail of this area see Map p244

Explore: Capitol Hill & First Hill

To decipher Seattle's most diverse, fashionable and consciously cool neighborhood it's useful to understand a little of its geography. There are three main commercial strips worth exploring in Capitol Hill – Broadway (the main drag), 15th Ave and the ultra-cultural Pike–Pine corridor – all of which are refreshingly walkable. Geographically the strips are gelled together by Capitol Hill's residential grid, a mixture of cheap apartment buildings, large grandiose houses and the green expanse of Volunteer Park. This weird but never caustic juxtaposition of rich/budget and chic/scruffy is one of the neighborhood's biggest allures. Herein lives Seattle's wildest assortment of people.

If you're walking up from downtown crossing I-5 on E Pine St, you'll enter the neighborhood close to Melrose Market at the western end of the Pike–Pine corridor. This stretch of aging brick warehouses and former 1950s car dealerships made over into gay bars, live-music clubs, coffeehouses, record stores and fashionable restaurants is Seattle's nightlife central. Explore it by night on foot.

Perpendicular to Pike–Pine is Capitol Hill's main commercial street, Broadway, while several blocks east is the quieter business district of 15th Ave E. This is where some of the city's wealthiest residents live in the grand old mansions that embellish tree-lined streets such as 14th Ave (aka Millionaires Row). Gawp at the opulence as you make your way up to Capitol Hill's peak, Volunteer Park, home to the Asian Art Museum, a conservatory and a water tower.

More genteel First Hill is best accessed from the bottom of Pike–Pine or by Seattle's newest streetcar.

Local Life

→ **Park play** On warm summer evenings, Cal Anderson Park is the place to come to watch bike polo, office baseball games and tattooed bodies picking up a tan.

→ **Silent reading party** Only in Seattle can you invite yourself to a 'party (p118)' where nobody talks, but everybody reads books.

Getting There & Away

→ **Bus** Metro bus 10 links Capitol Hill with downtown (Pine and 5th); bus 8 goes to the Seattle Center. To reach First Hill, catch bus 2 on the western side of 3rd Ave downtown and get off at the Swedish Medical Center.

→ **Streetcar** The First Hill streetcar links Capitol Hill and First Hill with the ID and Pioneer Square.

→ **Light rail** The new light-rail line heads north to the U District and southwest to downtown (and, ultimately, Sea-Tac airport) from Capitol Hill station.

→ **Walk** Capitol Hill can be reached from downtown by walking up E Pine St (10 to 15 minutes).

Lonely Planet's Top Tip

In Capitol Hill, restaurants, bars and cafes usually put quality over quantity. Thus the neighborhood abounds with specialist micro- or (even smaller) nano-businesses. Look out for microbreweries (beer), micro-roasteries (coffee), micro-distilleries (spirits) and micro-creameries (ice cream).

Best Places to Eat

→ Sitka & Spruce (p114)
→ Cascina Spinasse (p115)
→ Poppy (p115)
→ Coastal Kitchen (p113)

For reviews, see p112 ➡

Best Drinking & Nightlife

→ Espresso Vivace at Brix (p115)
→ Victrola Coffee Roasters (p115)
→ Optimism Brewing Co (p116)
→ Capitol Cider (p116)

For reviews, see p115 ➡

Best Places to Shop

→ Elliott Bay Book Company (p118)
→ Ada's Technical Books & Cafe (p118)
→ Wall of Sound (p119)
→ Revival (p119)

For reviews, see p118 ➡

⊙ SIGHTS

Parks, churches and a couple of excellent art museums make up the sights on Seattle's two most famous hills.

⊙ Capitol Hill

JIMI HENDRIX STATUE   MONUMENT
Map p244 (1600 Broadway E; 🚊Broadway & Pine) Psychedelic guitar genius of the late 1960s and Seattle's favorite son, Jimi Hendrix is captured sunk to his knees in eternal rock-star pose in this bronze sculpture by local artist Daryl Smith, created in 1997 and located close to the intersection of Broadway and E Pine St.

Hendrix fans often leave flowers and candles at the statue's base, and it's not unusual to find a half-burnt spliff stuck between his lips.

GAY CITY LIBRARY   LIBRARY
Map p244 (📞206-860-6969; www.gaycity.org; 517 E Pike St; ⊙11am-8pm Mon-Fri, 11am-5pm Sat; 🚊10) This library was set up in 2009 by Gay City, a community organization, and has already collected 6000 volumes on LGBTIQ topics. There are regular readings, meditation classes, a lesbian book club and free HIV testing.

SEATTLE ASIAN ART MUSEUM   MUSEUM
Map p244 (www.seattleartmuseum.org; 1400 E Prospect St; adult/child $9/5, 1st Thu of month free; ⊙10am-5pm Wed & Fri-Sun, 10am-9pm Thu; 🚊10) In stately Volunteer Park, this outpost of the Seattle Art Museum houses the extensive art collection of Dr Richard Fuller, who donated this late art-deco gallery (a fine example of Streamline Moderne architecture) to the city in 1932. Spread over one floor and beautifully presented in uncluttered, minimalist rooms, the collection is notable for its **Japanese hanging scrolls**, some of which date from the 1300s and have been skilfully restored (the restoration process is detailed along with the art).

Also of interest are the **Indian stone sculptures** in the foyer and some remarkably intricate **Chinese bronzes** dating from around 1600 BC.

VOLUNTEER PARK   PARK
Map p244 (🚊10) Seattle's most manicured park sits atop Capitol Hill and is named for US volunteers in the 1898 Spanish-American War. While wandering among its leafy glades, check out the glass-sided Victorian conservatory, filled with palms, cacti and tropical plants; climb the water tower; visit the Asian Art Museum; and don't depart before you've taken in the opulent mansions that embellish the streets immediately to the south.

VOLUNTEER PARK
CONSERVATORY   CONSERVATORY
Map p244 (📞206-684-4743; 1400 E Galer St; day pass adult/reduced $4/2; ⊙10am-4pm Tue-Sun; 🚊10) The conservatory is a classic Victorian greenhouse built in 1912. Filled with palms, cacti and tropical plants, it features five galleries representing different world environments. Check out the creepy corpse flower.

WATER TOWER
OBSERVATION DECK   LANDMARK
Map p244 (1400 E Prospect St; 🚊10) **FREE** It's practically obligatory to climb the 107 steep steps to the top of the 75ft water tower in Volunteer Park. Built in 1907, it provides wonderful vistas of the Space Needle, Elliott Bay and – should it be in the mood – Mt Rainier. Explanatory boards in the covered lookout detail the history and development of Seattle's park system.

ST MARK'S CATHEDRAL   CHURCH
Map p244 (📞206-323-0300; 1245 10th Ave E; ⊙performances 9:30pm Sun; 🚊49) Go north on Broadway (as the dandyish boutiques turn to well-maintained houses with manicured lawns) until it turns into 10th Ave E and you're within a block of Volunteer Park. At the neo-Byzantine St Mark's Cathedral, the Compline Choir performs for free on Sunday, accompanied by a 3944-pipe Flentrop organ.

LAKEVIEW CEMETERY   CEMETERY
Map p244 (🚊10) One of Seattle's oldest cemeteries and the final resting place of many early settlers, Lakeview Cemetery borders Volunteer Park to the north. Arthur Denny and his family, Doc and Catherine Maynard, Thomas Mercer and Henry Yesler are all interred here. This is also the grave site of Princess Angeline, the daughter of Duwamish Chief Sealth, after whom Seattle was named. Most people, however, stop by to see the graves of martial-arts film legends **Bruce and Brandon Lee**.

ℹ PUBLIC TRANSPORTATION REVOLUTION

Two new public transportation projects were completed in 2016 opening up Capitol Hill and First Hill to the rest of the city. The **First Hill streetcar** marked the second stage of Seattle's ambitious streetcar project (complementing the existing South Lake Union streetcar). The new line stretches 2.5 miles from Pioneer Square, up through First Hill and its medical facilities, to the intersection of Broadway and Denny Way in Capitol Hill. The streetcar, which has 10 stops, became operational after many delays in February 2016.

The vastly more expensive **University Link light-rail** line, which opened in March 2016, cost $1.9 billion and links Capitol Hill station on Broadway via an underground tunnel with Westlake Station in downtown and – in the opposite direction – with the U District. It is an extension of the Sea-Tac Airport–Downtown line that opened in 2009.

Flowers from fans are usually scattered around Brandon's red and Bruce's black tombstones, which stand side by side in a tiny part of the cemetery. The graves are not easy to find: enter the cemetery at 15th Ave E and E Garfield St; follow the road in and turn left at the Terrace Hill Mausoleum. At the crest of the hill you'll see the large Denny family plot on your left. Look a little further along the road, and you'll find the Lees. Even if you're not usually into graveyards, you'll at least enjoy the beautiful views at this one.

LOUISA BOREN LOOKOUT VIEWPOINT
(15th Ave E, at E Garfield St; 🚌10) Outside the Volunteer Park boundaries, the Louisa Boren Lookout provides one of the best views over the university and Union Bay. The small park is named after the longest-surviving member of the party that founded Seattle in 1851.

◉ First Hill

First Hill, just south of the Pike–Pine corridor, is scattered with traces of Seattle's pioneer-era glory, including a few magnificent old mansions and some excellent examples of early Seattle architecture. If you're going to break a leg, do it here: First Hill is nicknamed 'Pill Hill' because it's home to three major hospitals. There's also a good museum and a historic hotel worth visiting.

FRYE ART MUSEUM MUSEUM
Map p244 (🕿206-622-9250; www.fryemuseum. org; 704 Terry Ave; ⊙11am-5pm Tue, Wed & Fri-Sun, 11am-7pm Thu; 🅿; 🚌Broadway & Terrace) FREE
This small museum on First Hill preserves

the collection of Charles and Emma Frye. The Fryes collected more than 1000 paintings, mostly 19th- and early 20th-century European and American pieces, and a few Alaskan and Russian artworks. Most of the permanent collection is stuffed into a rather small gallery and comes across as a little 'busy'; however, the Frye's tour de force is its sensitively curated temporary shows, which usually have a much more modern bent.

STIMSON-GREEN MANSION HISTORIC BUILDING
Map p244 (🕿206-624-0474; www.stimsongreen. com; 1204 Minor Ave; tours $10, registration required; ⊙1-2:30pm 2nd Tue each month; 🚌64) One of the first homes on First Hill, the baronial Stimson-Green Mansion is an English Tudor–style mansion completed in 1901 by lumber baron and real-estate developer CD Stimson. Built from brick, stucco and wood, this stately home is now owned by Stimson's granddaughter and used for private catered events such as weddings and themed dinners.

The interior rooms are decorated to reflect the different design styles popular at the turn of the 20th century. To register for a tour, call the **Washington Trust for Historic Preservation** (🕿206-624-9449; www.preservewa.org).

ST JAMES CATHEDRAL CHURCH
Map p244 (www.stjames-cathedral.org; 804 9th Ave; ⊙7:30am-6pm; 🚌64) Seattle's beautiful Italian Renaissance–style Catholic cathedral was built in 1907. The original dome collapsed in 1916, the victim of a rare Seattle snowstorm, but the two impressive towers remain. Inside, the altar is located unusually in the church's center.

Tours are offered at 1pm on Wednesday in the summer only.

CAPITOL HILL & FIRST HILL SIGHTS

SORRENTO HOTEL HISTORIC BUILDING

Map p244 (900 Madison St; 🚌64) This grand working hotel located on First Hill is a fine example of Italian Renaissance architecture. Built in 1909 by a Seattle clothing merchant, the Sorrento was one of the first hotels designed to absorb the crowds arriving in Seattle for the Alaska-Yukon-Pacific Exposition (the 1909 World's Fair held in Seattle). Don't miss a chance to nose around the interior opulence, including the wood-paneled **Fireside Room**.

✖ EATING

Ninety-five percent of the best eating choices in this area are in Capitol Hill, one of Seattle's finest culinary neighborhoods. The scene on Capitol Hill is almost as much about style as food: it's no use enjoying a fabulous dinner if no one can see how chic you look while you're eating it. The restaurants along Broadway and 15th Ave and the Pike–Pine corridor offer the full range of Seattle dining options.

Full up with health-care facilities and educational establishments, First Hill doesn't offer much in the way of restaurants, unless you like hospital food...

⭐**LOST LAKE CAFE & LOUNGE** AMERICAN $

Map p244 (📞206-323-5678; www.lostlake cafe.com; 1505 10th Ave; mains $9-15; ⏰24hr; 🚌Broadway & Pine) Ever feel like you've strolled inadvertently into a 1990s David Lynch TV series full of eerie atmospherics and zany characters? If the answer is a resounding 'no,' grab a bar-side pew at Lost Lake Cafe, order a piece of pie (preferably cherry) and a damn fine cup o' coffee, and then go home and look up *Twin Peaks* on YouTube.

For those in the know, the Lost Lake is a retro *Twin Peaks*–inspired diner with two curved bars, cozy orange-hued booths and wooden fish mounted on the wall. Big bonus: it's open 24/7.

RUMBA CARIBBEAN $

Map p244 (📞206-583-7177; www.rumbaonpike. com; 1112 Pike St; small plates $6-13; ⏰5pm-1am Sun-Thu, 5pm-2am Fri & Sat; 🚌10) With its bright turquoise seating booths and sunny interior, Rumba exhibits a palpable Caribbean vibe. Indeed, you might just think

---

PIKE–PINE CORRIDOR: A VILLAGE WITHIN A VILLAGE

The Pike–Pine corridor, a sinuous urban strip on the eastern edge of Capitol Hill, is Seattle's factory of hip, a village within a village where the city's most fashionable offspring come to party like bright young things in a latter-day F Scott Fitzgerald novel.

Once a huddle of auto showrooms (only a couple remain), the area underwent a metamorphosis in the early 21st century when an influx of artists and young entrepreneurs snapped up the vacant car lots and transformed them into unique community-run boutiques, cafes, restaurants, clubs and bars.

A fast-evolving scene was quickly established as Pike–Pine garnered a reputation as the best place in Seattle to buy back your grandma's sweaters, bar crawl with Kurt Cobain's ghost, get your hair cut like Phil Oakey from the Human League or merely pull up a street-side chair and watch life go by.

And what a colorful life it is. Style in Pike–Pine is edgy and ephemeral. Typical interior design juxtaposes old high-school desks and sofas rescued from junkyards with chandeliers, ethnic antiques and post-Pollock art. Even more voguish is the neighborhood's retro-cool fashion scene, which marries beatnik beards and 1980s indie-pop hairstyles with ironic tattoos, natty headgear and Simone de Beauvoir's old dress collection. Tolerance is widespread. This is the epicenter of Seattle's gay life and a haven for every alternative philosophy this side of San Francisco. In the space of half a dozen blocks you'll find a lesbian pub, a *Twin Peaks*–themed restaurant, an apothecary, a shop selling sex toys, countless indie coffee shops and Seattle's finest bookstore.

To experience Pike–Pine in all its glamorous glory, start at Melrose Market (p114) near I-5 in the early afternoon, then walk up E Pike St to Madison Ave and come back down E Pine St. There are enough interesting distractions to keep you occupied until at least midnight – the next day!

you've died and gone to Jamaica when you taste its plump coconut prawns and rum cocktails. Come for an aperitif and share a plate of something small and tasty as you contemplate a night out in Capitol Hill.

BLUEBIRD MICROCREAMERY ICE CREAM $

Map p244 (1205 E Pike St; ice cream from $3; ⊙3-10pm Mon-Fri, noon-10pm Sat & Sun; 🚌Broadway & Pine) We've already witnessed the birth of the microbrewery, the micro-roastery and the micro-distillery, so it was only a matter of time before someone came up with the micro-creamery. Bluebird has gone further than other small-scale ice-cream makers by serving its own microbrewed beer in the same space, either separately (ie in a cup or glass) or mixed in as an ice-cream flavor.

Ask for a tasting spoon and get your head (and tongue) around stout-flavored ice cream made using the beer from Elysian brewery next door.

ELTANA WOOD-FIRED BAGEL CAFE CAFE $

Map p244 (www.eltana.com; 1538 12th Ave; bagels $5-10; ⊙7am-4pm; 🚌Broadway & Pine) Bagels and crosswords tax brains and palates at Eltana (this location in Capitol Hill is one of a Seattle quartet). The bagels are baked in a wood-fired oven on-site and smeared with heavenly toppings including cream cheese and lox. The crosswords are mounted on the wall and reproduced on paper for the bagel-eating clientele. Clues change regularly.

BIMBO'S CANTINA MEXICAN $

Map p244 (☎206-329-9978; www.bimboscantina.com; 1013 E Pike St; burritos $7.50-9.50; ⊙noon-2am; 🚌Broadway & Pine) Bimbo's slings fat tacos, giant burritos and juicy quesadillas until late. The space is bordello kitsch with velvet matador portraits, oil paintings with neon elements and a hut-style thatched awning. The best feature of the restaurant is its subterranean bar, the Cha-Cha Lounge.

ANNAPURNA CAFE NEPALESE $

Map p244 (☎206-320-7770; www.annapurnacafe.com; 1833 Broadway E; mains $9-16; ⊙noon-9:30pm Mon-Thu, noon-10pm Fri & Sat, noon-9pm Sun; ☏; 🚌Capitol Hill) One of the hill's best ethnic places is this subterranean Nepalese restaurant on Broadway whose extensive menu mixes in a few Indian and Tibetan varietals as well. There are soups, *thalis* (platters of small dishes), curries, breads and

plenty of vegetarian options. It's busy (good sign), but service is quick and efficient.

HONEYHOLE SANDWICHES $

Map p244 (☎206-709-1399; www.thehoneyhole.com; 703 E Pike St; sandwiches $8-10; ⊙11am-midnight Mon-Fri, 11am-1am Sat & Sun; 🚌Broadway & Pine) Cozy by day, irresistible at night, the Honeyhole has a lot to recommend it: big, stuffed sandwiches with funny names (Emilio Pestovez, the Texas Tease), greasy fries, a full bar, DJs and a cool cubbyhole atmosphere after sunset.

COASTAL KITCHEN MODERN AMERICAN $$

Map p244 (☎206-322-1145; www.coastalkitchenseattle.com; 429 15th Ave E; mains $18-34; ⊙8am-11pm; 🚌10) Coastal Kitchen has become a Capitol Hill legend since its inception in 2012 with its culinary theme (fish) and variations (a different geographical influence is introduced quarterly). Weekend 'Blunch' is mega, as is the recently added oyster bar that complements the favorites: namely, Dungeness crab cakes, Alaskan cod, Taylor shellfish and an epic sardine-doused pasta.

The decor's kind of interesting Euro-cafe meets sleek Pacific Northwest lounge and there's piped language lessons in the toilets (seriously!).

ERNEST LOVES AGNES ITALIAN $$

Map p244 (☎206-535-8723; www.ernestlovesagnes.com; 600-602 19th Ave E; pizzas $15-18, pasta $13-22, mains $20-24; ⊙4-11pm Mon-Fri, 9am-midnight Sat, 9am-11pm Sun; 🚌10) The Ernest in question is Hemingway, while Agnes is the nurse he supposedly fell in love with in Italy during WWI. A plaque outside this new place on 19th Ave recounts the story. The food, no surprises, is Italian of the type so beloved in Seattle these days – homemade pasta, traditional Italian toppings and a few Northwestern spins.

Crème de la crème: it also serves the classic Hemingway Daiquiri cocktail (with lime and grapefruit).

RIONE XIII ITALIAN $$

Map p244 (☎206-838-2878; www.ethanstowellrestaurants.com; 401 15th Ave E; mains $15-38; ⊙5-11pm; 🚌10) 🍴 The secret of Roman food lies in two words: 'simple' and 'effective.' That's its inherent beauty. Local legend Ethan Stowell probably guessed as much when he opened Rione XIII on cool 15th Ave in 2012. Come here for epic *caccio e pepe*

MELROSE MARKET

Melrose Market (Map p244; ☑206-568-2666; www.melrosemarketseattle.com; 1501–1535 Melrose Ave; ⊙11am-7pm; ⊒10) 🖉, at the base of the trendy Pike–Pine corridor in Capitol Hill, is a kind of modern antidote to Pike Place: small, free of tourist elbows and consciously curated. The two places do, however, share one thing in common: they're both fastidiously locavore.

Popular Melrose vendors, all of whom are permanent, include **Homegrown** the sustainable sandwich shop; **Taylor Shellfish**, which runs a sustainable shellfish farm near Bellingham; a couple of specialist cheese and meat sellers; a cocktail bar; and the peerless Sitka & Spruce, arguably the purist of Seattle's 'Northwestern' restaurants.

The indoor market is encased in an old 1920s car showroom embellished with plenty of wood and given a clean-lined neo-industrial finish. An attractive mezzanine overlooks the action.

(spaghetti with four ingredients), Roman street pizzas, fried artichokes and the popular four-cheese taster plate (spoiler: they're all mozzarella).

Otherwise, Rione exhibits the usual Stowell hallmarks: modern-rustic decor, evening-only opening, and a single-page, ever-changing menu.

MAMNOON
MIDDLE EASTERN **$$**

Map p244 (☑206-906-9606; www.mamnoon restaurant.com; 1508 Melrose Ave; takeout $6-9, mains $17-35; ⊙11:30am-9:30pm Sun-Thu, 11:30am-10:30pm Fri & Sat; ⊒10) If you're working your way around the world in one neighborhood, Mamnoon is Capitol Hill's token Middle Eastern stop – with strong Syrian and Lebanese inflections. Slink inside for an unusual and wonderfully memorable voyage to the culinary Levant where you'll quickly be immersed in fragrant flatbreads and perfumed dips that are complemented by some fine meat kebabs.

Prices are reasonable and there's a handy takeout window upfront offering crispy falafels.

The chic perch is in the 'Melrose Triangle,' which has also been sequestered by the slavishly locavore Melrose Market.

ODDFELLOWS CAFE
MODERN AMERICAN **$$**

Map p244 (☑206-325-0807; www.oddfellowscafe. com; 1525 10th Ave; mains $16-28; ⊙8am-late; ⊒Broadway & Pine) 🖉 A trendy dude dressed in '70s retro gear welcomes you at the door and puts your name on the list. The wait's 10 minutes, and the food, when it comes, is just what your taste buds were craving, especially the brunch, a smorgasbord of flaky biscuits, fluffy eggs and well-dressed salads.

Waiting for your table gives you the perfect opportunity to take in the decor (historic meeting hall reborn as rustic-meets-urban restaurant) and the clientele (dressed mostly like the guy at the door).

OSTERIA LA SPIGA
ITALIAN **$$**

Map p244 (☑206-323-8881; www.laspiga.com; 1429 12th Ave; pastas $18; ⊙11:30am-2:30pm & 5-10pm Mon-Fri, 5-10pm Sat & Sun; ⊒Pine & Broadway) Italian restaurants in Pike–Pine aren't labeled 'Italian' anymore; instead, their names are regionalized. Hence, La Spiga describes itself as 'Emilia-Romagna,' specializing in the food of the Bologna and Parma region – arguably Italy's finest.

The *'osteria'* moniker doesn't really fit (the restaurant is large and contemporary), but the food – *tagliatelle al ragú* and the authentic Romagna bread called *piadina* – shouldn't disappoint Italians or recent visitors to Italy. All pasta is homemade.

★SITKA & SPRUCE
MODERN AMERICAN **$$$**

Map p244 (☑206-324-0662; www.sitkaand spruce.com; 1531 Melrose Ave; plates $12-33; ⊙11:30am-2pm & 5-10pm Mon-Fri, 10am-2pm & 5-11pm Sat, 10am-2pm & 5-9pm Sun; 🖉; ⊒10) The king of all locavore restaurants, Sitka & Spruce was the pilot project of celebrated Seattle chef Matt Dillon. It's since become something of an institution and a trendsetter with its small country-kitchen decor and constantly changing menu concocted with ingredients from Dillon's own Vashon Island farm. Sample items include the housemade charcuterie, conica morels or roasted asparagus and liver parfait.

Vegetarians will have a field day.

The restaurant is located in Capitol Hill's gorgeous Melrose Market (p114), an oasis of sustainability.

CASCINA SPINASSE
ITALIAN $$$

Map p244 (☏206-251-7673; www.spinasse. com; 1531 14th Ave; mains $25-35; ⊘5-10pm Sun-Thu, to 11pm Fri & Sat; ☐11) Successfully re-creating the feel of an Italian trattoria, Spinasse specializes in cuisine of the Piedmont region of northern Italy. This means dishes like *agnolotti* (veal-stuffed pasta pockets) in beef broth, veal in tuna sauce, and top-notch risotto (from the region famous for its arborio rice). The finely curated wine list includes the kings and queens of Piedmontese reds: Barolo and Barbaresco.

POPPY
FUSION $$$

Map p244 (☏206-324-1108; www.poppyseattle. com; 622 Broadway E; thalis $27-29; ⊘5:30-11pm; ☐60) A *thali* is an Indian culinary tradition whereby numerous small taster dishes are served on one large plate. At Poppy they've cleverly applied the same principle to a broader list of Seattle/Northwest specialties, meaning that instead of chicken korma you get small portions of halibut, black-eyed peas and orange pickle. It's as good as it sounds.

🍷⚓ DRINKING & NIGHTLIFE

Capitol Hill is *the* place to go out for drinks, whether you want a fancy cocktail, a cappuccino, a beer or – if recent trends are anything to go by – a gin or a cider. It's also where 90% of the city's gay bars are located.

★VICTROLA COFFEE ROASTERS
CAFE

Map p244 (www.victrolacoffee.com; 310 E Pike St; ⊘6:30am-8pm Mon-Fri, 7:30am-8pm Sat & Sun; ☐10) Purveyors of a damned fine cup o' coffee since 2000, Victrola, to its credit, has clung to its grassroots, maintaining only three cafes. You can ponder how small is beautiful while watching the action in the roasting room staffed by bearded boffins who walk around like Q in a James Bond film brandishing earmuffs and clipboards.

Come for the free 'cuppings' with a coffee expert on Wednesday at 11am.

★ESPRESSO VIVACE AT BRIX
CAFE

Map p244 (www.espressovivace.com; 532 Broadway E; ⊘6am-11pm; 🛜; ☐Capitol Hill) Loved in equal measure for its no-nonsense walk-up stand on Broadway and this newer cafe (a large retro place with a beautiful Streamline Moderne counter), Vivace is known to have produced some of the Picassos of latte art. But it doesn't just offer pretty toppings: many of Seattle's coffee experts rate its espresso shots as the best in the city.

SUN LIQUOR DISTILLERY
BAR

Map p244 (www.sunliquor.com; 514 E Pike St; ⊘11am-2am; ☐10) More trendsetting on the Hill. Sun is a micro-distillery that makes its own gin and vodka behind the same bar where they're served (in cocktails, mainly). Even better, the place also offers a full food menu, making it pretty unique in the US; could this be the first in a long line of gastro-distilleries?

Opened in 2011, the distillery is the brainchild of the same guy who co-founded Top Pot Hand-Forged Doughnuts (p86).

STARBUCKS RESERVE ROASTERY & TASTING ROOM
COFFEE

Map p244 (www.starbucks.com/roastery; 1124 Pike St; coffees $3-12; ⊘7am-11pm) Pinch yourself before you enter the new-ish and (so far) unique Starbucks Reserve Roastery. Even the most cynical Starbucks-phobe will probably find something to like here – be it the tasting menu (three 8oz brews for $15), the coffee library, the huge copper casks, the micro- and small-batch roasters, or the custom-made retro furniture.

This huge, hip high church to the joys of coffee-drinking is the antithesis of everything Starbucks-y that has gone before. It is Starbucks going back to its roots and attempting to emulate its newer and hipper competition, and the results are encouraging. Both coffee and service are excellent too.

ELYSIAN BREWING COMPANY
MICROBREWERY

Map p244 (☏206-860-1920; www.elysianbrew ing.com; 1221 E Pike St; ⊘11:30am-2am Mon-Fri, noon-2am Sat & Sun; ☐Broadway & Pine) Elysian Brewing's Immortal IPA personifies the strong, bitter 'hop-forward' beers that have become part of craft beer folklore in the Pacific Northwest, although at 6.3% alcohol per volume, it won't take many to liberally loosen your tongue. Despite being bought out by Anheuser-Busch in January 2015, Elysian maintains several popular Seattle pubs, including this one (its 1996 original) in Capitol Hill.

OPTIMISM BREWING CO   MICROBREWERY

Map p244 (📞206-651-5429; www.optimism brewing.com; 1158 Broadway; ⊙4-11pm Wed & Thu, 4pm-midnight Fri, noon-midnight Sat, noon-9pm Sun; 🚼; 🚇Broadway & Pine) Capitol Hill has lagged behind Fremont and Ballard in beer terms recently, but this optimistically named brewery put froth back on the local pints when it opened in 2015. In the fine style of similarly orientated Fremont Brewing (p148), Optimism offers a tasting room where you can sit at picnic benches on the factory floor and order pretty much straight from the beer vat.

The brewery, located in a spacious former car showroom, has several huge pros (aside from the beer): large windows, kid- and pet-friendly policies, bring-your-own food and no TVs (you have to talk!).

CAPITOL CIDER   PUB

Map p244 (📞206-397-3564; www.capitolcider. com; 818 E Pike St; ⊙4pm-2am Mon-Fri, 10am-2am Sat & Sun; 🚇Broadway & Pine) The best cider pub in Seattle is far more than a taproom for apple-infused alcoholic beverages – although the 20-item cider menu is, of course, a big bonus. There's decent food, live music, game nights, craft beer, cocktails and a wonderful 'pub' feel set off by its cozy booths and portrait-bedecked walls.

TAVERN LAW   COCKTAIL BAR

Map p244 (📞206-322-9734; www.tavernlaw. com; 1406 12th Ave; ⊙5pm-2am; 🚍12) Named for the 1832 law that legalized drinking in public bars and saloons, Tavern Law is one of Seattle's most sought-after high-end cocktail bars (they call them 'libations' here). It's themed like a speakeasy – or, at least, a romanticized version of a speakeasy, as such establishments were never this plush.

Expect bar staff with styled hair and wearing waistcoats shaking and stirring up a storm. The small food plates have a large fan base, especially the seared pork belly.

FUEL COFFEE   COFFEE

Map p244 (📞206-329-4700; www.fuelcoffee seattle.com; 610 19th Ave E; ⊙6am-8pm Mon-Fri, 7am-8pm Sat & Sun; 🚍10) For once a cafe that

doesn't try too hard to be cool. Fuel has a tangible community feel, retro gas-station motifs and great coffee.

STUMPTOWN ON 12TH   COFFEE

Map p244 (📞206-323-1544; www.stumptown coffee.com; 1115 12th Ave; ⊙6am-8pm Mon-Fri, 7am-8pm Sat & Sun; 🚍12) 🎔 There's a tug of loyalties with Stumptown, Portland's coffee pioneers founded in 1999 by Duane Sorenson, who originally hails from Puyallup near Seattle. Stumptown practically defined the new third-wave coffee movement when it opened its first cafe in downtown Portland, selling fair-trade, single-origin, home-roasted coffee with an emphasis on taste rather than cup size.

The ethics served to inspire just about every other indie coffee roaster in the US, so it's hardly surprising you'll still find a sizable contingent of Stumptown loyalists, especially among the Seattleites who congregate in this busy nook, one of two Stumptowns in Capitol Hill.

COMET TAVERN   BAR

Map p244 (📞206-323-9853; www.thecomettav ern.com; 922 E Pike St; ⊙noon-2am; 🚇Broadway & Pine) The Comet 2.0 replaced the dirty, dive-y, older version in 2014 after a brief closure. While not as endearingly disheveled as its predecessor, the place still occupies the grungier end of the Pike–Pine ladder and now serves food (shock horror!). Sporadic live bands rock the rafters.

CAFFÉ VITA   CAFE

Map p244 (www.caffevita.com; 1005 E Pike St; ⊙6am-11pm Mon-Fri, 7am-11pm Sat & Sun; 🚇Broadway & Pine) The laptop camper, the first-daters, the radical student, the homeless person, the philosopher, the business dude heading to work: the whole neighborhood passes through this Capitol Hill institution (one of six in Seattle), whose on-site roasting room is visible through a glass partition.

LINDA'S TAVERN   BAR

Map p244 (📞206-325-1220; www.lindastavern. com; 707 E Pine St; ⊙4pm-2am Mon-Fri, 10am-2am Sat & Sun; 🚇Broadway & Pine) The back patio here is an excellent place to observe the nocturnal habits of *Hipsterus Northwesticus*. Linda's is one of the few joints in town where you can recover from your hangover with an Emergen-C cocktail and a vegetarian brunch while taxidermied moose heads stare at you from the walls.

MICRO-DISTILLERIES

Not content with helping to shape North America's microbrewing revolution in the 1980s and '90s, Seattle has recently embraced further alcohol-inspired craftsmanship in the shape of micro-distilled spirits. Though the trend is evident all over the US, Washington State is – as ever – at the vanguard, harboring a fifth of the nation's micro-distilleries, all of them churning out meticulously produced small-batch tipples of gin, vodka, whiskey, brandy and even limoncello.

Thanks to state laws that, until 2008, discouraged small businesses from obtaining distilling licenses, craft distilling was pretty much off the menu until the 2010s. As restrictions gradually loosened, a raft of new spirit-makers hit the Seattle drinking landscape. Many offer tours of their nascent businesses and most have tasting rooms. At least one, Sun Liquor Distillery (p115), has an on-site cocktail bar with a small eating outlet (selling burgers and sandwiches mainly), where it uses its own gin and vodka to fortify the drinks. Other excellent new distilleries include Copperworks Distilling (p62) in downtown, a passionate purveyor of gin and vodka, and Westland Distillery (p77) in SoDo, known for its single malt Scottish-style whiskey made using locally grown barley.

Linda's was grunge central in the 1990s (band members galore piled in here) and it's still a pretty cool place to hang out.

WILDROSE LESBIAN
Map p244 (206-324-9210; 1021 E Pike St; 5pm-midnight Mon, 3pm-1am Tue-Thu, 3pm-2am Fri & Sat, 3pm-midnight Sun; Broadway & Pine) This small, comfortable lesbian bar has theme nights (dykes on bikes, drag-king shows) as well as a light menu, pool, karaoke and DJs. On weekends it gets packed, so figure on a bit of a wait to get in.

NEIGHBOURS GAY
Map p244 (www.neighboursnightclub.com; 1509 Broadway E; 9am-2am Mon, Tue & Sat, 9am-4am Thu & Fri, 10am-midnight Sun; Broadway & Pine) Check out the always-packed dance factory for the gay club scene and its attendant glittery straight girls.

R PLACE GAY
Map p244 (206-322-8828; www.rplaceseattle.com; 619 E Pine St; 4pm-2am Mon-Fri, 2pm-2am Sat & Sun; Broadway & Pine) Weekend cabaret performances, amateur strip shows, go-go boys and DJs – there's something entertaining going on pretty much every night at this three-floor gay entertainment complex. Relax with a beer on the deck or dance your ass off. The ground floor is the lowest key; the top floor is where the dancing gets unashamedly flamboyant.

CANTERBURY ALE HOUSE PUB
Map p244 (206-322-3130; www.thecanterburyalehouse.com; 534 15th Ave E; 11am-2am Mon-Fri, 10am-2am Sat & Sun; 10) Capitol

Hill's default old-world pub was the recipient of a recent makeover, which got rid of dark booths and the suit of armor that once guarded the door. These have been replaced with a more open, gastropub feel, which has its good points (better food and a fine rendering of Chaucer's *Canterbury Tales* on the wall), and bad (too many TVs).

The trivia nights are a local legend.

HIGH LINE BAR
Map p244 (206-328-7837; www.highlineseattle.com; 210 Broadway E; 11am-2am Mon-Fri, 9am-2am Sat & Sun; Capitol Hill) Bar, meat-free restaurant, live-music venue, people-watching perch – call it what you will. The High Line is best suited to vegan punk rockers who like playing Foosball and arcade games, although all types are welcome.

BALTIC ROOM CLUB
Map p244 (206-625-4444; www.thebalticroom.net; 1207 Pine St; cover varies; 9pm-2am; 10) Classy with high ceilings, wood-paneled walls, paper lanterns and an elegant balcony, this Capitol Hill club hosts an excellent mix of local and touring DJs in a range of genres, from reggae and house to drum-and-bass. There's occasional live music.

⭐ ENTERTAINMENT

NEUMO'S LIVE MUSIC
Map p244 (206-709-9442; www.neumos.com; 925 E Pike St; Broadway & Pine) This punk, hip-hop and alternative-music joint

is, along with the Crocodile (p93) in Belltown, one of Seattle's most revered small music venues. Its storied list of former performers is too long to include, but, if they're cool and passing through Seattle, they've probably played here. The audience space can get hot and sweaty, and even smelly, but that's rock and roll.

NORTHWEST FILM FORUM CINEMA

Map p244 (www.nwfilmforum.org; 1515 12th Ave; ⬚Broadway & Pine) A film arts organization whose two-screen cinema offers impeccable programming, from restored classics to cutting-edge independent and international films. It's in Capitol Hill, of course!

CHOP SUEY LIVE MUSIC

Map p244 (www.chopsuey.com; 1325 E Madison St; ⊘4pm-2am Mon-Fri, 9pm-2am Sat & Sun; ⬚12) Chop Suey is a small dark space with high ceilings and a ramshackle faux-Chinese motif. Reborn under new ownership in 2015, it now serves burger-biased food as well as booze and music. The bookings are as mixed as the dish it's named after – electronica, hip-hop, alt-rock and other creative rumblings from Seattle's music underground.

ANNEX THEATRE THEATER

Map p244 (☎206-728-0933; www.annextheater. org; 1100 E Pike St; ⬚Broadway & Pine) Seattle's main experimental-fringe theater group is the Annex whose 99-seat theater (with bar) inhabits the Pike–Pine corridor. The highlight for many is the 'Spin the Bottle' nights on the first Friday of every month (11pm), a riot of comedy, music and variety.

RICHARD HUGO HOUSE PERFORMING ARTS

Map p244 (☎206-322-7030; www.hugohouse. org; 704 Terry Ave; ⊘office 10am-6pm Mon-Fri; ⬚Broadway & Terrace) Established in honor of famed Northwest poet Richard Hugo, and the nexus of Seattle's literary community, the Hugo House hosts readings, classes and workshops, as well as offering various events around town. Writers-in-residence keep office hours during which they're available for free consultations about writing projects.

The community will be temporarily housed in the Frye Art Museum (p111) from 2016 to 2018 while its Capitol Hill HQ is redeveloped.

LOCAL KNOWLEDGE

SILENT READING PARTY

Seattle is a famously literate city with a high quotient of bibliophiles. It is also the inventor of a rather peculiar 'party' that people attend purely to read books.

The Silent Reading Party is held at 6pm on the first Wednesday of every month in the wood-paneled Fireside Room at the Sorrento Hotel (p112). But, this is no conventional book club. Rather it's an excuse to just sit down and read silently, the only distractions being the discreet drinks service, some tinkling background piano music, and perhaps the chance to eavesdrop on other people's whispered book recommendations. It's curiously popular.

🛍 SHOPPING

Shopping on Capitol Hill makes you instantly hipper; even just window-shopping is an education in cutting-edge popular culture. This is the place to find great record shops, unusual bookstores, vintage clothing and risqué sex toys.

⭐ELLIOTT BAY BOOK COMPANY BOOKS

Map p244 (☎206-624-6600; www.elliottbaybook.com; 1521 10th Ave; ⊘10am-10pm Mon-Fri, 10am-11pm Sat, 10am-9pm Sun; ⬚Broadway & Pine) Seattle's most beloved bookstore offers over 150,000 titles in a large, airy, wood-beamed space with cozy nooks that can inspire hours of serendipitous browsing. Bibliophiles will be further satisfied with regular book readings and signings.

ADA'S TECHNICAL BOOKS & CAFE BOOKS

Map p244 (☎206-322-1058; www.seattletechnicalbooks.com; 425 15th Ave E; ⊘8am-9pm Sun-Thu, 8am-10pm Fri & Sat; ⬚10) Bookstores dead? Not if Ada's is anything to go by. Indeed this place – a hugely inviting bookshop-cafe combo that opened in 2013 – might just prove that online book sales have peaked and the joy of browsing and lingering (with a coffee and sweet snack to boot) is back in fashion.

Ada's plush interior is done out in clean white wood with royal blue accents. There's a cafe on one side and a small but well-curated collection of books on the other (it specializes in tech books). You can relax at the cafe tables or on a comfy chair in front of an old-fashioned fireplace. It also sells breakfast and sandwiches.

REVIVAL
VINTAGE

Map p244 (☑206-395-6414; www.revivalshop-seattle.com; 233 Broadway E; ⊙11am-7pm Tue-Sat, noon-6pm Sun; ⊠Capitol Hill) Imagine a brick-and-mortar version of eBay with gear chosen by your ultimate personal shopper. This new vintage/used clothes shop is far from being a dumping ground for someone else's unwanted clothes. Rather it is a collection of little gems uncovered by skilled and resourceful treasure hunters.

WALL OF SOUND
MUSIC

Map p244 (☑206-441-9880; 1205 E Pike St; ⊙11am-7pm Mon-Sat, noon-6pm Sun; ⊠10) Bedroom-sized Wall of Sound has a civilized, studious air and a penchant for avant-garde sounds. If you're into esoterica or weird musical sub-genres such as 'Japanoise,' this could be heaven.

CROSSROADS TRADING CO
CLOTHING

Map p244 (www.crossroadstrading.com; 325 Broadway E; ⊙11am-8pm Mon-Sat, 11am-7pm Sun; ⊠Capitol Hill) This used-clothing store is less expensive than others in the area but also generally less hipster-chic, which is nice if you just want to shop for basics without having some too-cool clerk stare down their nose at your khaki slacks. There's another branch in the U District (p139).

TWICE SOLD TALES
BOOKS

Map p244 (☑206-324-2421; 1833 Harvard Ave; ⊙10am-9pm; ⊠Capitol Hill) Twice Sold Tales is a cozy den full of very-well-priced used books, stacked haphazardly along narrow aisles. A book 'happy hour' discount kicks in after 6pm. A bunch of aloof cats roam the shop, actively ignoring everybody.

BABELAND
ADULT

Map p244 (www.babeland.com; 707 E Pike St; ⊙11am-10pm Mon-Sat, noon-7pm Sun; ⊠Broadway & Pine) Remember those pink furry handcuffs and that glass dildo you needed? Well, look no further.

DILETTANTE CHOCOLATES
CHOCOLATE

Map p244 (☑206-329-6463; www.dilettante.com; 538 Broadway E; ⊙11am-11pm Sun-Thu, 11am-1am Fri & Sat; ⊠Capitol Hill) If you have a sweet tooth to satisfy, try the confection truffles here. There's a great selection of desserts, too. You can taste chocolates in the shop, along with good coffee and other snacks, or pick up a box to take home. The European-style chocolates are made in-house.

URBAN OUTFITTERS
CLOTHING

Map p244 (☑206-322-1800; 401 Broadway E; ⊙11am-9pm Mon-Wed, 10am-9pm Thu-Sat, 11am-8pm Sun; ⊠Capitol Hill) Urban Outfitters in the Broadway Market sells clothing geared toward young folks looking to score points on the hip scale without having to think too hard about putting together a look.

THROWBACKS NW
CLOTHING

Map p244 (www.throwbacksnw.com; 1205 E Pike St; ⊙11am-7pm Mon-Sat; ⊠Broadway & Pine) A niche vintage shop that focuses on sport-line clothing that not only evokes nostalgia for sports teams, but revisits the hip-hop street fashions of the 1980s and '90s.

ZION'S GATE RECORDS
MUSIC

Map p244 (☑206-568-5446; 1100 E Pike St; ⊙noon-8pm Sun-Thu, noon-10pm Fri & Sat; ⊠Broadway & Pine) A dusty, slightly unkempt record store where some rummaging will uncover dog-eared heavy metal, second- and third-hand Bowie and rare reggae 45s.

🏃 SPORTS & ACTIVITIES

CENTURY BALLROOM
COURSE

Map p244 (☑206-324-7263; www.centuryballroom.com; 915 E Pine St; ⊠Broadway & Pine) Dance lessons ($15 to $20 for drop-ins) followed by an everyone-out-on-the-floor dance free-for-all makes a night at the Century the perfect combination of spectating and participating. Dance nights include everything from the lindy hop to salsa. Check the website for a schedule of events.

There's also a restaurant on-site.

Art & Culture

You don't have to go to a gallery to see Seattle's art. Creativity is everywhere: on walls, under bridges, in parks and on hatch covers. Join an art walk, organize an 'art attack' or just wait around in neighborhoods like Fremont and Capitol Hill for the local Picassos to show up.

COURTESY OF CHIHULY GARDEN AND GLASS ©

CDRIN/SHUTTERSTOCK ©

JIMI HENDRIX, BY ARTIST DARYL SMITH. COMMISSIONED BY MICHAEL MALONE. IMAGE: MAX HERMAN / SHUTTERSTOCK ©

1. Chihuly Garden & Glass (p82)
This attraction provides a spectacular homage to Dale Chihuly, the master of glass art.

2. Seattle Asian Art Museum (p110)
A late-art-deco gallery that's home to a beautifully presented collection of Asian art.

3. Fremont Rocket (p144)
Created for the Cold War, this zany-looking rocket was adopted by Fremont as a community totem.

4. Jimi Hendrix statue (p110)
This 1997 statue immortalizes the guitar god and is something of a shrine for fans.

LONELY PLANET / GETTY IMAGES ©

The CD, Madrona & Madison Park

MADISON PARK | MADRONA | THE CD

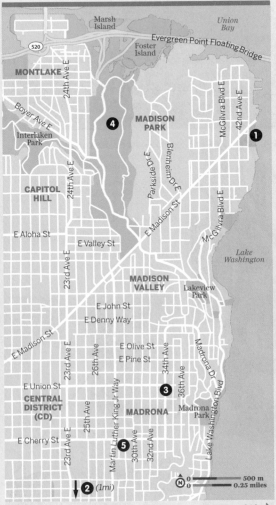

Neighborhood Top Five

❶ Madison Park Beach (p124) Following the old trolley route down E Madison St to original Seattle seaside resort Madison Park Beach for a game of Frisbee, a brave dip in the lake and some wholesome restaurant food.

❷ Northwest African American Museum (p124) Learning about Seattle's little-known African American heritage in this Central District museum.

❸ European Food (p125) Finding French, Italian and other European flavors on the taste-heavy commercial strip of 34th Ave in Madrona.

❹ Washington Park Arboretum (p124) Tree-spotting and bird-watching in this wild and lovely park.

❺ Little Ethiopia (p125) Seeking out great African food in the CD's 'Little Ethiopia,' especially along E Cherry St.

For more detail of this area see Map p246

Explore: The CD, Madrona & Madison Park

The three neighborhoods sandwiched between Capitol Hill and Lake Washington are somewhat spread out and, while individually distinct, don't really form a coherent whole. Although they can be explored together, most non-residents come here for a specific reason: eg the beach at Madison Park, brunch in Madrona, or French food in Madison Valley.

Running down the east slope of First Hill, the Central District (CD) represents the heart of Seattle's African American community and is relatively easy to reach from downtown. The neighborhood's sometimes scruffy, but rejuvenated arteries are 23rd Ave and Martin Luther King Jnr Way, but it lacks any real nexus and can feel semi-abandoned after Capitol Hill. You can take a stroll of its streets starting from the top of the Pike–Pine corridor.

Keep walking east through the CD and you'll hit Madrona, one of Seattle's more ethnically diverse neighborhoods that is being quickly gentrified with some positively opulent mansions overlooking Lake Washington. Madrona is worth a trip to indulge in some imaginative Europhile food along its unofficial 'main street,' 34th Ave, followed by a walk along the lakefront.

If the weather's good, Madison Park merits a separate visit for its cute beach and short strip of glass-fronted cafes and restaurants. It is best reached on bus 11 along E Madison St, following an old trolley line that once bussed in knackered lumber workers for some weekend R and R. About a mile before you reach the beach it's worth stopping in tree-lined Madison Valley, aka 'Little France,' for buttery croissants and a quiet stroll in the Washington Park Arboretum.

Local Life

→ **Beach play** Some say Madison Park Beach (p124), aka 'the Park,' is snooty, but it ain't true, at least not on sunny days, when the whole neighborhood hits the small lakeside beach.

→ **Community coffee** Tougo Coffee (p130) is the ultimate CD coffee bar, which locals once rallied to save.

Getting There & Away

→ **Bus** Metro bus 11 runs from downtown along Pike and E Pine Sts to Capitol Hill and then along E Madison St all the way to Madison Park. Bus 8 goes from the Seattle Center via Capitol Hill to the CD, where it runs north–south through the neighborhood along Martin Luther King Jr Way. Buses 2 and 3 connect downtown with Madrona Beach via Capitol Hill.

Lonely Planet's Top Tip

Madison Valley, the 'other' (fourth) neighborhood in this rather disparate grouping, is worth a visit in its own right. Enjoy some fine French, vegetarian or Southern soul food from one of several eating places before taking a peek at the tree collection in the Washington Park Arboretum (p124).

Best Places to Eat

→ Vendemmia (p128)
→ Simply Soulful (p125)
→ Voila! (p125)
→ Cafe Soleil (p128)

For reviews, see p125 ➡

Best Drinking & Nightlife

→ Tougo Coffee (p130)
→ Madrona Arms (p130)
→ Attic Alehouse & Eatery (p129)
→ McGilvra's (p130)

For reviews, see p129 ➡

👁 SIGHTS

👁 Madison Park

WASHINGTON PARK ARBORETUM   PARK
Map p246 (🚌11) This wild and lovely park stretching from Madison Valley up to Union Bay offers a wide variety of gardens, a wetlands nature trail and 200 acres of mature forest threaded by paths. More than 5500 plant species grow within the arboretum's boundaries. In the spring **Azalea Way**, a meandering trail that winds through the arboretum, is lined with a giddy array of pink- and orange-flowered azaleas and rhododendrons.

Trail guides to the plant collections are available at the **Graham Visitors Center** (Map p246; 2300 Arboretum Dr E; ⊙9am-5pm). Free tours of the grounds take place at 1pm on Sundays from January to November.

JAPANESE GARDEN   GARDENS
Map p246 (📞206-684-4725; adult/senior & student $6/4; ⊙10am-7pm Apr-Sep, to dusk Oct-Mar; 🚌11) At the southern edge of Washington Park Arboretum, this 3.5-acre garden has koi pools, waterfalls, a teahouse and manicured plantings. Granite for the garden's sculptures was laboriously dragged in from the Cascades. Tea-ceremony demonstrations are frequently available. Call for a schedule.

MADISON PARK BEACH   BEACH
Map p246 (🚻; 🚌11) A riotously popular place in the summer with a grassy slope for lounging and sunbathing, two tennis courts, a swimming raft floating in the lake, and lifeguards on duty from late June to Labor Day. The park has been a lure for townies since the early 20th century, when a trolley route was built from downtown to bus everyone in.

VIRETTA PARK   PARK
Map p246 (🚌2) Amid a lakeside nirvana of posh mansions, you'll find two-tiered Viretta Park, from which you can see the large house once owned by Nirvana's Kurt Cobain and Courtney Love – it's the house on the north side of the benches. Cobain took his life with a shotgun in the mansion's greenhouse in April 1994.

The greenhouse is long gone and Love no longer owns the house, but Nirvana fans still make the pilgrimage to this small park to pay tribute and scribble messages on the two benches that overlook Lake Washington.

DENNY BLAINE PARK   PARK
Map p246 (200 Lake Washington Blvd E; 🚌2) South of Madison Park toward the tail of Lake Washington Blvd is Denny Blaine Park, found at the end of a looping tree-lined lane. This predominantly lesbian beach is surrounded by an old stone wall, which marked the shoreline before the lake level was dropped 9ft during construction of the shipping canal.

👁 Madrona

MADRONA PARK & BEACH   PARK, BEACH
Map p246 (🚻; 🚌2) Madrona Park Beach, down a steep hill from the business district in Madrona Park, is one of the nicest along the lake. In clear weather the views of Mt Rainier are fantastic. Swimming is only for hardy souls, however, as the water's icy cold, even in summer. Further south, past the yacht moorage, is **Leschi Park**, a grassy green space with a children's play area.

👁 The CD

NORTHWEST AFRICAN AMERICAN MUSEUM   MUSEUM
(NAAM; 📞206-518-6000; www.naamnw.org; 2300 S Massachusetts St; adult/reduced $7/5; ⊙11am-5pm Wed & Fri-Sun, 11am-7pm Thu; 🚌7) Small, concise and culturally valuable, NAAM opened in 2008 after more than 30 years of planning. It occupies the space of an old school, which, until the 1980s, educated a large number of African American children in the Central District. After the school closed, it was occupied for a while by community activists who prevented it from being demolished. Inside, the museum's main exhibits map the story of black immigration to the Pacific Northwest, especially after WWII.

Details are given of some of the leading African American personalities, including George Washington Bush (the first black settler in Washington state), Manuel Lopes (Seattle's first black resident), Quincy Jones (the record producer who grew up in Seattle) and Jimi Hendrix (no introduction required). One of the prize exhibits is a hat Hendrix wore at a 1968 concert in LA. A separate room is given over to temporary exhibitions. The building famously featured in Macklemore & Ryan Lewis' 'Thrift Shop' music video.

LITTLE ETHIOPIA

The Central District has a history of reinventing itself to incorporate successive waves of immigrants. In the 1910s it was a primarily Jewish neighborhood, pre-WWII it welcomed Japanese settlers, and postwar it became Seattle's main African American enclave, a characteristic it partly retains. However, since the 1970s the neighborhood has seen an increasing number of African immigrants moving in, particularly from Ethiopia.

The first Ethiopians arrived in 1974 after the country's Derg takeover provoked a massive exodus. In 1970 there were no more than 20 Ethiopians in Seattle; today the region counts approximately 25,000, one of the biggest communities in the US. The East African flavor is most prevalent along E Cherry St, where you'll see taxi businesses, grocery stores selling local Amharic-language newspapers, and a slew of Ethiopian restaurants (five alone color the crossroads of E Cherry St and Martin Luther King Jr Way). Not surprisingly, the name 'Little Ethiopia' is sometimes used to describe the area. In 2013, Joseph W Scott and Solomon A Getahun published a book about the diaspora called *Little Ethiopia of the Pacific Northwest*.

JIMI HENDRIX PARK
PARK

(www.jimihendrixparkfoundation.org; 2400 S Massachusetts St; 🚍7) Dedicated to Hendrix in 2006, the park abuts the Northwest African American Museum (p124) just north of the Beacon Hill neighborhood. Phase 1 finally opened in August 2016 after a decade-long push to raise funds for its refurbishment. Expect the completed park to include a performance space, song lyrics etched on pathways, a butterfly garden and a 'shadow wave wall' with Hendrix silhouettes.

EATING

Ethiopian restaurants enliven the CD (especially along E Cherry St), which has also been a bastion of the African American community, clinging onto a handful of Deep South–worthy 'Southern' restaurants offering grits, biscuits and gravy, catfish and fried chicken.

Madison Valley has established itself as a gourmet Gallic quarter with several French-run establishments. Other small restaurant huddles punctuate Madison Park and the increasingly upmarket business strip on 34th Ave in Madrona. The brunches in the latter neighborhood are legendary.

✗ Madison Park

SIMPLY SOULFUL
SOUTHERN $

Map p246 (☏206-474-9841; www.simply-soulful.com; 2909b E Madison St; mains $10-17; ⊗8am-7pm Tue-Fri, 8am-4pm Sat, 10am-3pm Sun; 🚍11)

This new-ish, African American–owned, soul-food restaurant in Madison Valley is close enough to the CD to counter some of the gentrification fears. Welcome back to good old-fashioned throw-your-diet-out-the-window grub of the Southern tradition.

Inside the diminutive cafe, the decor is largely forgettable, but the food certainly isn't, especially the all-day breakfast, a riot of catfish and grits, chicken and waffles, and biscuits and gravy. You can stodge it up further with belt-loosening desserts such as pecan pie and banana pudding.

VOILA!
FRENCH $$

Map p246 (☏206-322-5460; www.voilabistrot.com; 2805 E Madison St; mains $14-23; ⊗11:30am-2:30pm & 5pm-late Tue-Sat; 🚍11) A cozy Gallic bistro with an old French flag in the window that looks like it got left behind by some romantic revolutionaries. Half the deal here is in creating an exotic Euro-flavored atmosphere that is as fine honed as the food. The menu's *plats* consist of well-known French standards from pâté to pork chops to escargot. Velvet curtains enhance the vibe.

CACTUS
TAPAS, MEXICAN $$

Map p246 (☏206-324-4140; www.cactusrestaurants.com; 4220 E Madison St; dinner $14-20; ⊗11am-10pm Mon-Fri, 10am-11pm Sat, 10am-10pm Sun; 🚍11) Instantly cheery, this Mexican-Southwest restaurant – with branches in Kirkland and Alki Beach – is a fun place to go and pretend you're on a sunny vacation even if it's pouring with rain. A margarita and a king-salmon torta or butternut squash enchilada will scare off the grayest clouds, and the jaunty staff and fun music do the rest.

Only in Seattle

Turn your chewing gum into communal art, sneer back at a grimacing statue of Vladimir Ilyich Ulyanov (aka Lenin), watch fishmongers play catch with giant halibut, and meet *Star Trek* nerds in a futuristic museum that's all about sci-fi...and rock and roll. And you thought Seattle was normal?

1. Monorail & Seattle Center (p78)
The monorail runs by the Museum of Pop Culture on its journey between the Westlake Center and Seattle Center.

2. Gum wall (p47)
A bright, unsanitary Seattle icon in Pike Place Market.

3. Lenin statue (p143)
This bronze Bolshevik resides among the public art of Fremont.

4. Pike Place Market fishmongers (p43)
The piscine purveyors of Pike Place are at the heart of the market.

CAFÉ FLORA — VEGETARIAN, VEGAN $$

Map p246 (206-325-9100; www.cafeflora.com; 2901 E Madison St; starters & mains $12-19; 9am-9pm Sun-Thu, 9am-10pm Fri & Sat; ; 11) A longtime favorite for vegan and vegetarian food, Flora has a garden-like feel and a creative menu, with dinner treats like artichoke croquettes, breaded coconut tofu dipped in chili sauce, a grilled asparagus pizza and black-bean burgers. Or go for the hoppin' John fritters or tomato asparagus scrambles at brunch.

✗ Madrona

CAFE SOLEIL — AMERICAN, ETHIOPIAN $

Map p246 (206-325-1126; 1400 34th Ave; mains $9-13; 5:30-9pm Wed-Fri, 8:30am-2pm & 5:30-9pm Sat, 8:30am-2pm Sun; 2) Surprise! It looks like an American diner and serves a hearty American brunch (and is less crowded than Hi Spot Café around the corner), but Cafe Soleil's real specialty is Ethiopian food – it's like a becalmed offshoot of 'Little Ethiopia' in the CD. The bright, light-filled room is an excellent place to dip your *injera* (flatbread) in spicy African stews.

HI SPOT CAFÉ — BREAKFAST $

Map p246 (206-325-7905; www.hispotcafe.com; 1410 34th Ave; mains $10-14; 7am-4pm Mon-Fri, 8am-4pm Sat & Sun; 2) The cinnamon rolls here are bigger than your head, and that's no exaggeration. It's a comfy little space in an old craftsman-style house where you can either get a sit-down meal (brunch is best) or a quick espresso and pastry to go.

VENDEMMIA — ITALIAN $$$

Map p246 (206-466-2533; www.vendemmiaseattle.com; 1126 34th Ave; pasta $14-21, mains $26-43; 5-10pm; 2) Sometimes it feels as if Seattle has got as many upscale Italian restaurants as Turin, all of them peddling the same modern Italian American staples: handmade pasta, one-page menus and heavily plugged local greens that often include foraged nettles. Newly opened Vendemmia doesn't stray too far from this genre.

What makes it different is its location – in Madrona, a neighborhood that's long lacked this kind of Mediterranean quality.

RED COW — FRENCH $$$

Map p246 (206-454-7932; www.ethanstowellrestaurants.com; 1423 34th Ave; mains $23-47; 5-10pm Sun-Thu, 5-11pm Fri & Sat; 2) Welcome to a new endeavor from lauded Seattle chef Ethan Stowell who normally specializes in Italian fare, but for this venture has crossed the Alps into France. The decor is typical Stowell – open kitchen, intimate interior and clean-lined minimalist design – while the menu star is steak (seven different cuts), *frites* and garlic aioli.

On other plates, the food doesn't stray too far from France. Bank on lamb terrine, vol-au-vents and *moules-frites* (mussels and fries).

It's located on the recently gentrified strip of 34th Ave in Madrona.

✗ The CD

FAT'S CHICKEN & WAFFLES — SOUTHERN $

Map p246 (206-602-6863; www.fatschickenandwaffles.com; 2726 E Cherry St; mains $12-14; 11am-9pm Tue-Fri, 9am-3pm & 5-10pm Sat, 9am-3pm & 5-9pm Sun; 3) Occupying the intersection once inhabited by old-school CD institution Catfish Corner, Fat's is considered by most to be a credible replacement. Wisely, it's chosen to continue the long-standing CD tradition for Southern food in an area that has otherwise lost a lot of its old-school grit (and grits).

Menu highlights include the obvious chicken and waffles, along with prawns and grits and – in a nostalgic nod – catfish.

EZELL'S FAMOUS CHICKEN — SOUTHERN $

Map p246 (206-324-4141; www.ezellschicken.com; 501 23rd Ave; meals $7-11; 10am-9pm Mon-Fri, 10am-10pm Sat & Sun; 3) There's fast food and then there's fast food. This is the good kind. Ezell's was started by a transplanted Texan in 1984 right here in the CD. Its crispy, spicy, Southern-style chicken and equally scrumptious side dishes like coleslaw and sweet-potato pie have since spread nationwide and, in 2015, went international when Ezell's opened a restaurant in Dubai.

CAFE SELAM — ETHIOPIAN $

Map p246 (206-328-0404; www.cafeselam.com; 2715 E Cherry St; mains $12-14; 10am-9pm; 3) The windows could do with a scrub and the tables are a bit wobbly, but you don't come to Selam in the CD's proverbial 'Little Ethiopia' for interior design. Ethiopia is home to Africa's spiciest cuisine, with dishes such as *foul* (a fava-bean concoction that's not at all foul) and *fir fir* (*injera* flatbread, yogurt and lamb) – all done to perfection here.

MARIJUANA IN SEATTLE: THE NITTY-GRITTY

In November 2012, Washington State – along with Colorado – made history when it approved Initiative 502 by popular ballot, permitting limited marijuana use for people over the age of 21.

While the measure might have changed perceptions of marijuana in the Pacific Northwest, it hasn't created the bong-happy US version of Amsterdam that some were dreaming of – yet. Instead, Initiative 502's small print is a little more cautious. Adults aged 21 and over may now buy up to 1oz of pure weed (or 16oz of solid edibles, or 72oz of liquid product) for private consumption in Seattle from a licensed seller. Most of the so-called 'recreational' pot shops are in the outlying districts of SoDo, Fremont and Ballard, but none allow customers to imbibe their products in-house. Thus, the first dilemma for travelers buying vape pens, concentrates or edibles is: where can they enjoy them? To date, only a handful of accommodations permit joint-smoking or vaporizer use on their premises; Bacon Mansion B&B (p194) allows discreet use of marijuana products on-site. Furthermore, blazing a joint in public can land you a $27 fine. Early attempts to provide marijuana 'clubs' where people could imbibe hassle-free came up against legal red tape. One pioneering club, Zero, opened in SoDo in September 2015, but it was forced to close less than a month later. As of mid-2016, nothing had replaced it.

For travelers interested in marijuana, it is important to use discretion, especially when choosing where to smoke, vape or ingest. To wise up on the nitty-gritty of cannabis culture it might be useful to attend a festival or go on a guided tour first. Seattle's **Hempfest** (www.hempfest.org; ☉Aug) is a large annual festival that began as a kind of stoner's convention in 1991, but has since morphed into a full-on celebration of marijuana culture attended by over 100,000 people. It's held in Myrtle Edwards Park on the Seattle waterfront on the third weekend in August. Another option for curious novices is to join a legal cannabis tour with **Kush Tourism** (Map p234; www.kushtourism.com; 1300 S Dearborn St; ☐Jackson & 12th/Little Saigon), a company that runs educational trips to marijuana-growing facilities and pot shops. Extra Kush activities include glassblowing and painting.

For more information about weed in Washington, pick up the *Green Guide,* a free magazine available in most pot shops, or peruse the special 'Weed' section of the *Stranger* newspaper (available in print or online; www.thestranger.com). The Kush Tourism website also has a good stash of pot-related information.

When leaving Seattle, it is important to note that it is illegal to transport any marijuana you have (legally) bought in Washington out of the state.

As marijuana is still federally illegal, the industry remains in flux, thus the information here might be subject to change.

The only catch is the lack of knives and forks. In true local style you must scoop up your beans, lamb, okra etc using torn-off bits of bread. Selam even roasts its own coffee, the product so beloved by Seattleites, which was first 'discovered,' legend has it, by an Ethiopian goat herder.

🍷 DRINKING & NIGHTLIFE

Wave goodbye to franchises! Search around in the CD, Madrona and Madison Park, and you'll find some of Seattle's most understated neighborhood pubs and coffee bars.

Although it lacks a solid scene these days, the CD has a legacy of nurturing strong musical talent, most notably in the jazz and hip-hop genres.

📍 Madison Park

ATTIC ALEHOUSE & EATERY   PUB
Map p246 (☏206-323-3131; 4226 E Madison St; ☉11am-2am Mon-Fri, 8:30am-2am Sat & Sun; ☐11) Decades ago, according to legend, the Attic was a shooting-gallery/bowling-alley combo. It first became a restaurant in the mid-'30s, then a tavern in the 1950s. The current 1960s-vintage building has morphed into a friendly neighborhood pub that has no inclinations to be hip (phew). Slide in to watch the footie on

the telly while enjoying a beer and a hand-made burger ($7 to $9).

MCGILVRA'S   IRISH PUB

Map p246 (☑206-325-0834; www.mcgilvras.com; 4234 E Madison St; ⊙11am-midnight Mon-Fri, 9am-2am Sat & Sun; ☐11) This backdrop to Madison Beach is definitely more pub than bar and has a loyal local following of drinkers slapping on the after-sun lotion. You can get your Guinness in a glass or poured over your beef stew. The Jameson Irish whiskey, meanwhile, often ends up in the crab soup. Dozens of soccer jerseys are hung from the ceiling.

🍺 Madrona

MADRONA ARMS   PUB

Map p246 (☑206-739-5104; www.madronaarms. com; 1138 34th Ave; ⊙11am-midnight Mon-Fri, 9am-2am Sat & Sun; ☐2) New neighborhood pub in Madrona fashioned in the old British tradition with obvious nods to Seattle (local draft ales). It's run by an Irishman so there's Guinness on tap and some old-country food standards, including bangers and mash, and shepherd's pie.

🍺 The CD

TOUGO COFFEE   CAFE

Map p246 (www.tougocoffee.com; 1410 18th Ave; ⊙6am-6pm Mon-Fri, 7am-6pm Sat & Sun; ☐2) Community cafe par excellence where the skilled barista doubles as an excellent DJ. And it's not part of a chain!

☆ ENTERTAINMENT

Don't be fooled by the quiet exterior; there's precious history in these neighborhoods. The CD once bebopped with segregated jazz bars, while a decade later Jimi Hendrix played his first gig at the Temple de Hirsch Sinai on the corner of E Pike St and 15th Ave. These days the area's entertainment – with a couple of exceptions – is noticeably thin on the ground. The streetwise head to adjacent Capitol Hill instead.

CENTRAL CINEMA   CINEMA

Map p246 (☑206-686-6684; www.central-cinema.com; 1411 21st Ave; ☐2) Welcome to a bona fide dine-in cinema. What might be par for the course in Portland, OR, is a rare sight in Seattle, which makes this small neighborhood movie house in the CD all the more precious. The food consists of relatively simple pizzas, but it's backed up by some decent local microbrews. Movies range from screwball comedies to British 1960s classics.

🛍 SHOPPING

UNCLE IKE'S POT SHOP   POT SHOP

Map p246 (www.uncleikespotshop.com; 2310 E Union St; ⊙8am-11:45pm; ☐2) On a corner where you used to be able to score marijuana illegally, you can now buy it legally. With a big sign and a highly visible location, Ike's is possibly Seattle's busiest and best-stocked pot shop.

It courted a bit of controversy soon after its 2014 opening when it was dragged reluctantly into the CD's ongoing gentrification debate. Notwithstanding, the budtenders here are courteous and the interior, with its well-displayed stock and old-school posters, retains a bit more character than other marijuana businesses.

ORIGINAL CHILDREN'S SHOP   CLOTHING

Map p246 (www.theoriginalchildrensshop.com; 4216 E Madison St; ⊙10am-5:30pm Mon-Sat; ♿; ☐11) A piece of the Madison Park furniture, this family-run business has been operating since 1952 selling children's apparel and also functioning as a kids' hair salon.

🏃 SPORTS & ACTIVITIES

FOSTER ISLAND

WETLANDS TRAIL   WALKING, BIRDWATCHING

Map p246 (☐43) The northern edge of Washington Park Arboretum (p124) includes this wonderful woodchip-paved trail around Foster Island in Lake Washington's Union Bay, a picnic spot that was once a burial ground for Union Bay Native Americans. The waterfront trail winds through marshlands and over a series of floating bridges to smaller islands and reedy shoals.

Bird-watching is popular here, as are swimming, fishing and kayaking. It's just too bad that the busy, elevated Hwy 520 roars above the island.

U District

Neighborhood Top Five

❶ University of Washington (p133) Reliving (or living) your cerebral undergraduate years on the leafy, architecturally attractive campus of the University of Washington with its art galleries, neo-Gothic library and tree-studded quad.

❷ The Ave (p138) Reliving the non-cerebral part of your undergraduate days in the pubs and bars of the so-called 'Ave.'

❸ Blue Moon (p137) Reading the graffiti and listening to the latest street poet at this legendary counterculture dive.

❹ Burke Museum (p134) Deciphering the indigenous cultures of the Pacific at this hybrid museum, which also covers natural history.

❺ University Book Store (p139) Spending a bibliophilic afternoon in Seattle's oldest bookstore, founded in 1900.

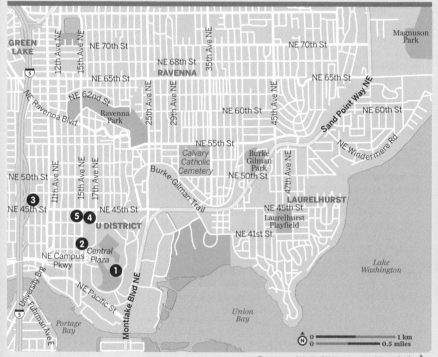

For more detail of this area see Map p248 ➡

Lonely Planet's Top Tip

A great way to explore the university is on a bicycle: the Burke-Gilman Trail (p140) follows the south side of campus, providing easy access. Further exercise can be procured on water: the campus abuts the shores of Lake Union and is one of the best places in Seattle to hire a kayak.

✕ Best Places to Eat

➡ Portage Bay Cafe (p134)
➡ Ristorante Doria (p137)
➡ Schultzy's Bar & Grill (p136)
➡ Morsel (p134)

For reviews, see p134 ➡

◉ Best Places to Study

➡ Suzzallo Library (p134)
➡ Zoka Coffee (p137)
➡ Cafe Solstice (p136)
➡ Café Allegro (p137)

For reviews, see p133 ➡

🔒 Best Bookstores

➡ University Book Store (p139)
➡ Magus Books (p139)
➡ Half Price Books (p139)

For reviews, see p139 ➡

Explore: U District

Head east off I-5 north of Lake Union and suddenly you'll feel as if you're no longer in Seattle. The U District, named for 'U Dub' (what locals call the University of Washington, or UW), feels like its own little college town. Just like you, most of the people here are visitors – they're merely staying a bit longer (several semesters or more).

Nearly everyone gets oriented in the U District on 'the Ave' (University Way, roughly between 40th and 50th Sts), an atmospheric main drag full of tiny cheap eateries, thrift stores, record stores, secondhand bookstores, tattoo parlors, bars and coffee shops full of deadline-chasing, laptop-gazing students. Everyone on the sidewalks around here seems to be between the ages of 18 and 24, but these kids know where it's at. Read fly-posters on lampposts, eavesdrop on conversations in coffee bars and follow the action on the Ave and you'll soon feel 23 again (if you aren't already).

The number of cheap places to eat, especially Indian and Asian, makes the Ave the best place to find an inexpensive meal. Another place to lose your youth is the cavernous University Book Store, which takes up an entire city block.

Reserve a sunny day to explore the adjacent UW campus, a veritable arboretum/architectural showcase with a couple of top-notch museums focusing on art and natural history. The campus is made for people-watching (or, more specifically, student-watching) and you can enter many of the buildings unannounced, including the Suzzallo Library and the Hub (student union).

Local Life

➡ **The Ave** Hang around on University Way, aka 'the Ave (p138),' anywhere between 40th and 50th Sts and follow the crowds.

➡ **Bohemian bar** Bump into U Dub's more bohemian demographic at colorful Café Racer (p138).

➡ **Local library** Watch other people doing their homework or just admire the ornate church-like interior of the Suzzallo Library (p134).

Getting There & Away

➡ **Bus** Several Metro buses, including buses 70 and 74, run frequently to the U District from downtown Seattle. Bus 32 links the U District with the Seattle Center via Fremont.

➡ **Light rail** A new train line links the University of Washington to Capitol Hill, downtown and, ultimately, Sea-Tac International Airport.

⊙ SIGHTS

The University of Washington campus, originally laid out as the Alaska-Yukon-Pacific Exposition site in 1909, is a beautiful place to explore, especially when the weather cooperates. Among its regal buildings are two notable museums, the Burke Museum (p134) and the Henry Art Gallery (p134).

UNIVERSITY OF WASHINGTON   UNIVERSITY
Map p248 (www.washington.edu; ⊞University of Washington) Founded in 1861, Seattle's university is almost as old as the city itself and is highly ranked worldwide (the prestigious *Times Higher Education* magazine listed it 32nd in the world in 2016). The college was originally located in downtown on a 10-acre site now occupied by the Fifth Avenue Theater (the university still owns the land), but with both university and city outgrowing their initial confines, a new site was sought in 1895.

The present-day 700-acre campus that sits at the edge of Lake Union about 3 miles northeast of downtown is flecked with stately trees and beautiful architecture, and affords wondrous views of Mt Rainier framed by fountains and foliage. Roughly 34,000 students and 13,000 staff enjoy the noble setting, making 'U Dub' easily the largest university in the state. The core of the campus is Central Plaza, known as **Red Sq** (Map p248;) because of its terracotta-brick base rather than its Marxist-Leninist inclinations. Close by you can pick up information and a campus map at the visitor center (p219).

The university is ideal for gentle strolls, people-watching and lung-stretching exercise on the Burke-Gilman Trail (p140). The campus also hosts two decent museums, fine sports facilities, a theater, a library, and a student-union building where leaflet-filled noticeboards advertise the kinds of outré, spontaneous events that typically color student life.

RAINIER VISTA   VIEWPOINT
Map p248 (⊞University of Washington) What other US university campus has a perfectly framed view of a glacier-drizzled, 14,410ft stratovolcano? This beautiful green corridor of lawns and walkways emanates from the steps of UW's Red Sq and was designed by John Olmsted as the centerpiece for the 1909 Alaska-Yukon-Pacific Expo.

QUAD   LANDMARK
Map p248 (⊞University of Washington) The lovely Quad is home to some of the original campus buildings, many of them built in a Collegiate

U DISTRICT SIGHTS

THE ALASKA-YUKON-PACIFIC EXPOSITION

Seattle's 1962 World's Fair wasn't the only time the city has hosted an international 'expo.' Along with five other US cities, Seattle has been bequeathed the honor twice – the first time in 1909 with the so-called Alaska-Yukon-Pacific Exposition (the AYPE).

The AYPE helped transform Seattle from a boom-bust Northwestern backwater into a city of national prestige. Initially inspired by the Klondike gold rush of 1896–7, an event that Seattle both supported and supplied, the expo quickly morphed into a wider celebration of Pacific Rim trade and the nascent vitality of the Pacific Northwest region.

Built on what was then the relatively new campus of the University of Washington, the expo site was designed by influential American landscapers, the Olmsted brothers, who covered 250 acres of formerly virgin forest with a regal cluster of temporary buildings.

While the 1962 World's Fair left behind the Space Needle (p80) and the Seattle Center (p78), the AYPE's legacy was more general. Only two original buildings remain (the university's **Architecture Hall** and **Cunningham Hall**). However, the expo's landscaped gardens with their trickling fountains and tree-lined Mt Rainier vistas, later became the grand stencil upon which the modern University of Washington developed. The campus today owes much to the Olmsted brothers' inspired vision.

Approximately 3.7 million people attended the AYPE, which was considered a success for the time. Driven by new technologies, the event instigated a car race from New York to Seattle (the winner completed it in 23 days), and was the first time that many Seattleites saw an airplane. Among those impressed by the flying display was a 27-year-old local timber merchant named William Boeing...

Gothic style reminiscent of New England. On sunny days, you can relax on the grass amid Frisbee throwers, sunbathers dodging seminars, earnest politics undergraduates discussing Obamacare, and young love blossoming under the cherry trees.

SUZZALLO LIBRARY   LANDMARK

Map p248 (麗University of Washington) The architecturally minded will be interested in the University of Washington's Suzzallo Library. Designed by Carl Gould in 1926, this bibliophile's dream was inspired by Henry Suzzallo, UW's president at the time. Suzzallo wanted it to look like a cathedral, because 'the library is the soul of the university.' Unfortunately for him, his bosses disagreed; on reviewing the building, they deemed it too expensive and fired Suzzallo for his extravagance.

However, the dream was partially realized in the grand neo-Gothic entrance lobby and the truly beguiling **reading room** with its massive cathedral-like windows that, on fine days, cast filtered sunlight onto the long reading pews.

BURKE MUSEUM   MUSEUM

Map p248 (✆206-543-5590; www.burkemuseum. org; cnr 17th Ave NE & NE 45th St; adult/child $10/7.50, 1st Thu of month free; ⊙10am-5pm, to 8pm 1st Thu of month; ☐70) An interesting hybrid museum covering both natural history and indigenous cultures of the Pacific Rim. On the entry level floor is, arguably, Washington's best natural-history collection focusing on the geology and evolution of the state. It guards an impressive stash of fossils, including a 20,000-year-old sabre-toothed cat. Downstairs is the 'Pacific Voices' exhibition with cultural artifacts amassed from around the Pacific Rim from Hawaii to Japan to Micronesia. The centerpiece is an excellent Pacific Northwest collection with some dramatic Kwakwaka'wakw masks from BC.

HENRY ART GALLERY   MUSEUM

Map p248 (www.henryart.org; cnr 15th Ave NE & NE 41st St; adult/senior $10/6, Thu free; ⊙11am-4pm Wed & Fri-Sun, 11am-9pm Thu; ☐70) Approaching 90 years of age, the Henry is Seattle's modern-art masterpiece. Set in a sophisticated space on the University of Washington campus, it revolves around a remarkable permanent exhibit created in 2003 by light-manipulating sculptor James Turrell. Backing it up is a full revolving

program of high-quality temporary and touring collections. Expos here are modern, provocative and occasionally head-scratching. There are also regular artist talks, discussion groups and workshops.

DRUMHELLER FOUNTAIN   FOUNTAIN

Map p248 (麗University of Washington) Drumheller Fountain sits inside what was originally known as Geyser Basin (now 'Frosh Pond'), one of the few remaining pieces left over from the 1909 expo that beefed up the university.

RAVENNA PARK   PARK

Map p248 (🚹; ☐74) Just north of the U District is Ravenna, a residential neighborhood that's home to a lot of professors and university staff. At its heart is Ravenna Park, a lush and wild park with two playgrounds on either side of the foliage-drenched ravine carved by Ravenna Creek. Escape the clamor of the city – briefly.

✖ EATING

This is one of the best districts in Seattle for cheap and authentic ethnic food. Vegan and vegetarian haunts also abound.

When you're browsing for lunch or dinner, don't be put off by unappetizing-looking storefronts; some of the most interesting food comes from places that have the outward appearance of rundown five-and-dime stores. The adventurous will be rewarded.

⭐PORTAGE BAY CAFE   BREAKFAST $

Map p248 (✆206-547-8230; www.portagebay cafe.com; 4130 Roosevelt Way NE; brunch $10-15; ⊙7:30am-2:30pm; ☐74) 🍴 Hugely popular brunch spot and for good reason. Aside from the usual suspects (eggs, bacon, pancakes), there's a help-yourself breakfast bar loaded with fresh fruit, cream, syrup, nuts and the like (all local, of course), waiting to be spread on your doorstep-thick slices of French toast. Arrive early or after 1pm at weekends to avoid the rush.

MORSEL   CAFE $

Map p248 (✆206-268-0154; www.morselseattle. com; 4754 University Way NE; biscuits $3-7; ⊙8am-3pm; ☐70) A diminutive cafe that specializes in biscuits (the US kind) – and they're not morsels! Choices include the classic (with

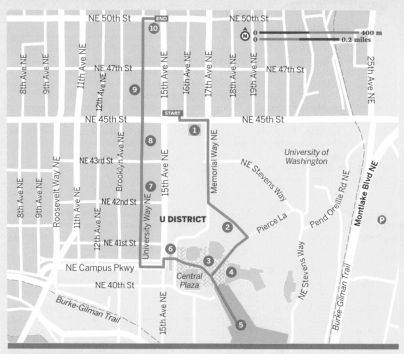

🏃 Neighborhood Walk
U District

START BURKE MUSEUM
END THE AVE, OR GRAND ILLUSION CINEMA
LENGTH 2 MILES; ONE HOUR

Start this tour at the ① **Burke Museum** (p134), which you may choose to visit now (this will add at least an hour to the tour time) or simply note to check out later. Its collection of indigenous art from around the Pacific is not to be missed. From here, walk along NE 45th St to Memorial Way NE – take a right and amble into campus through the university's north gate.

Cut behind the Department of Anthropology, cross Denny Yard and enter the ② **Quad** (p133), the campus's prettiest nook. From here a straight path cuts southwest to central ③ **Red Square** (p133), full of crisscrossing students rushing to lectures.

Red Sq is dominated by the gorgeous, cathedral-like ④ **Suzzallo Library** (p134). Admire it from the inside and out, then take a sharp left when you exit. Descend the stairs and walk straight ahead toward ⑤ **Drumheller Fountain** (p134), which

spews out of the circular pool known as 'Frosh Pond.' Along the pathway leading to the fountain, you'll be stunned (if it's a clear day) by the views from what is appropriately named the Rainier Vista.

Head back toward Red Sq, and bear left at the library. This will lead you to the ⑥ **Henry Art Gallery** (p134), one of the best contemporary galleries in Seattle. After being blinded by modern art, head over to bustling University Way NE, aka 'the Ave.' If you're harboring caffeine-withdrawal symptoms duck into ⑦ **Café Allegro** (p137), accessed via an alley behind Magus Books. Opened in 1975, this (not Starbucks) is Seattle's oldest surviving espresso bar. Continue wandering up the Ave, peeking into shops and cafes along the way. Put your hunger on hold while you investigate the ⑧ **University Book Store** (p139), then cross the road and squeeze into ⑨ **Thai Tom** (p136) for Bangkok street food. The tour concludes at the intersection with NE 50th St, where you may want to check out what's showing at the arthouse **Grand Illusion Cinema** (p138).

LOCAL KNOWLEDGE

FARMERS MARKET

In a city that produced Pike Place Market, it's not surprising that there is a rich stash of other weekly farmers markets where you can sniff out the freshest veg. The largest and oldest (and best in the eyes of many) is the **U District Farmers Market** (Map p248; cnr NE 50th St & University Way NE; ⊙9am-2pm Sat; 🚌70) 🍃, which has been held every Saturday in the vicinity of the university year-round since 1993. Faithful to the spirit of farmers markets, the U District is a food-only affair – all of its displayed produce comes from an alliance of 60-plus stall-holding farmers and is grown 100% in Washington state. Products of note include spot prawns (May and June), cheeses, Washington wines and apples (over 30 varieties). **Market Bites** is a collection of small take-out stalls designed for hungry shoppers on the go. In August look out for **Ready, Set, Go...Cook!**, a popular cooking competition where chefs are permitted to use only market ingredients.

gravy), or a formidable leaning tower of bacon, egg and cheese. Enjoy them while making friends at the shared tables.

FLOWERS
CAFE **$**

Map p248 (☎206-633-1903; 4247 University Way NE; lunch buffet $8, mains $7-15; ⊙noon-midnight; 🗷; 🚌70) Popular with a certain type of hip, vegetarian under- or post-grad, Flowers serves vegetarian-biased food (including plenty of sandwiches) in a funky space known for its mirrored ceiling. There's usually a vegan lunch buffet. Later in the evening, a more bohemian atmosphere takes over with cocktails and local draft brews.

THAI TOM
THAI **$**

Map p248 (☎206-548-9548; 4543 University Way NE; mains $7-10; ⊙11:30am-9:30pm; 🚌70) About as wide as a train carriage with permanently steamed-up windows, an open-kitchen lunch counter, and flames leaping up from beneath the constantly busy pans on the stoves, Thai Tom feels like some backstreet Bangkok hole-in-the-wall. Yet, many hail its simple Thai food as the best in the city.

Push in among the elephant heads, dark-brown walls and elbow-to-elbow crowds to find out. Cash only.

CAFE SOLSTICE
CAFE **$**

Map p248 (☎206-675-0850; 4116 University Way NE; mac & cheese $5; ⊙6:30am-11pm Mon-Fri, 7am-9pm Sat, 7am-11pm Sun; 🛜🗷; 🚌70) This coffee shop on 'the Ave' is large. It needs to be in order to accommodate the armies of laptop campers who seemingly descend here to churn out their own inferior versions of *War and Peace*. There's a nice wooden outdoor patio and a comfy organic vibe with lots of vegan and bran-heavy snacks.

Indeed, the atmosphere can feel so laid-back you wonder if anyone is actually drinking the coffee. There are also panini, salads, beers and wines.

AGUA VERDE CAFÉ
MEXICAN **$**

Map p248 (☎206-545-8570; 1303 NE Boat St; 3 tacos $9-11; ⊙7:30am-9pm Mon-Fri, 9am-9pm Sat, 9am-8pm Sun; 🚌70) On the shores of Portage Bay at the southern base of University Ave, Agua Verde Café is a little gem that overlooks the bay and serves fat tacos full of lemony cod, catfish or portobello mushrooms, plus other Mexican favorites.

There's usually a wait for a table, but you can have a drink and linger on the deck, or order from the walk-up window. Kayaks (p140) can be rented in the same building, in case you want to work off your dinner.

SCHULTZY'S BAR & GRILL
GERMAN **$**

Map p248 (☎206-548-9461; 4142 University Way NE; brats $8-10; ⊙10am-2am Mon-Fri, 11:30am-2am Sat, 11:30am-10pm Sun; 🚌70) There are really only two words you need to know about Schultzy's – beer and sausages. The most obvious common denominator between the two is 'German' and it's true, there are good German beers and bratwurst here; but this is also the kind of place you can get a Cajun sausage burger and even sausage gumbo.

Rotating draft beers embellish the menu and there's chicken and veggie burgers for those not overly enamored with sausages.

CHACO CANYON CAFÉ
VEGAN **$**

Map p248 (☎206-522-6966; www.chacocanyon cafe.com; 4757 12th Ave NE; sandwiches $9-16; ⊙7am-9pm Mon-Fri, 9am-9pm Sat & Sun; 🗷; 🚌74) 🍃 Possibly Seattle's most ethical restaurant,

Chaco Canyon (there are now three outposts) serves vegan food from a revolving cache of partner farms (all in Washington state). It's also big on raw food. If you're a first-timer try the grilled pineapple lentil burger. For those going raw, there's a raw enchilada plate with mango, cashew and avocado adding to the taste.

Other highlights are the Thai peanut bowl and the Elvis smoothie (banana and peanut butter). Chaco is serious about recycling and composting too, and would rather lend you a real fork than hand you a plastic one.

CEDARS RESTAURANT INDIAN, MIDDLE EASTERN $
Map p248 (206-527-4000; www.cedars seattle.com; 4759 Brooklyn Ave NE; mains $8-15; 11:30am-10pm Mon-Sat, 1-9pm Sun; ; 70) Seattle isn't exactly London or Mumbai when it comes to Indian restaurants, but there's some relief for curry lovers at Cedars, a family run 'Indian' with a few eastern Mediterranean cameos (falafel and gyros mainly). The measuring stick for many is the chicken tikka masala or the creamy butter chicken. Lentils, *aloo gobi* and *paneer* provide comfort for vegetarians.

The covered wooden patio is a cool hangout in nice weather.

ORANGE KING BURGERS $
Map p248 (206-632-1331; 1411 NE 42nd St; burgers $3-6; 10:30am-9:30pm Mon-Fri, 3-9pm Sat; 70) At this tiny, old-fashioned greasy spoon just off 'the Ave,' you can still get an unholy mix of burgers, fries and chicken teriyaki on a starving student budget. It's not gourmet, but it's fast, cheap and, in its own way, charming.

ALADDIN GYRO-CERY MIDDLE EASTERN $
Map p248 (206-632-5253; 4143 University Way NE; gyros $5-7.50; 10am-2:30am; ; 70) Handy late-night beer soaker-upper or emergency day-after hangover 'cure' on 'the Ave.' What student hasn't craved it at least once? There are plenty of vegetarian options.

RISTORANTE DORIA ITALIAN $$
Map p248 (206-466-2380; www.ristorantedoria. com; 4759 Roosevelt Way NE; pasta & mains $16-24; 4-9:30pm Tue-Sun; 74) Doria applies the U District stencil of non-budget-breaking, plentiful, salt-of-the-earth food to Italian cuisine. There is nothing nouveau about the food or service. Instead, the owner, who is from Milan, regularly works the tables just

as they do in the old country, checking that you like your gnocchi, calamari or chicken parmigiana.

DRINKING & NIGHTLIFE

No surprise. The U District has some of the city's best and most eccentric dive bars, as well as its most student-friendly coffee shops: bank on strong wi-fi, lots of plug-ins and no 'tut-tuts' if you sit around for more than two hours. 'The Ave' (University Way NE) is a jolly fine place to string together a cheap bar crawl with plenty of late-night greasy-spoon holes-in-the-wall available to soak up the beer afterward.

★BLUE MOON BAR
Map p248 (206-675-9116; www.bluemoon seattle.wordpress.com; 712 NE 45th St; 2pm-2am Mon-Fri, noon-2am Sat & Sun; 74) A legendary counterculture dive near the university that first opened in 1934 to celebrate the repeal of the Prohibition laws, Blue Moon makes much of its former literary patrons – Dylan Thomas and Allen Ginsberg among them. The place is still agreeably tatty with graffiti carved into the seats and punk poets likely to stand up and start pontificating at any moment.

ZOKA COFFEE CAFE
Map p248 (www.zokacoffee.com; 2901 NE Blakeley St; 6am-9pm Mon-Fri, 7am-9pm Sat & Sun; ; 74) Aside from its desirable coffee (home-roasted, of course), Zoka is *the* place to go for a marathon laptop session. Don't feel guilty about lingering: the staff actively encourage you to stay with plenty of plug-in points scattered around a vast wooden interior full of students all seemingly on the same deadline.

CAFÉ ALLEGRO CAFE
Map p248 (206-633-3030; www.seattlealle gro.com; 4214 University Way NE; drinks from $2; 6:30am-10pm Mon-Fri, 7:30am-10pm Sat, 8am-10pm Sun; 70) You can dispel a few urban myths in Café Allegro. It is this place, not Starbucks, that is the oldest functioning coffee bar in Seattle. Founded in 1975, it was a bona fide espresso bar when Starbucks was still just a store that sold coffee beans and machinery.

LOCAL KNOWLEDGE

'THE AVE'

University Way NE, the sometimes seedy, sometimes studious strip that runs north–south through the U District is known to anyone with even the sketchiest knowledge of Seattle as 'the Ave.' Pretty much anything a penny-counting, beer-guzzling, fashion-craving student might desire can be found on or close to this hallowed urban artery. Tick off Seattle's oldest still-functioning espresso bar, one of the city's earliest brewpubs, its weirdest cinema, its oldest bookstore and copious consignment shops. And all this before you've even tasted the food – a veritable UN of choices hidden, more often than not, behind smudged-glass windows decorated with taped-up, handwritten notices.

Panhandlers, frat parties and seminar-dodging undergraduates all stalk the Ave, though it's not an overly unsavory place. Some deride sporadic attempts to clean it up; others celebrate its eclecticism. University of Washington hip-hop band the Blue Scholars once wrote a song about the Ave, describing its social scene as an essential part of a U-Dub education.

Stuffed into a back alley between NE 42nd and NE 43rd Sts, the cafe hasn't changed much since its pioneer days. Bevies of industrious students still drop by to scribble over papers, or moon over professors, although nowadays they're frequently distracted by their iPhones.

CAFÉ RACER   BAR
(206-523-5282; 5828 Roosevelt Way NE; 9am-2am; 67 from UW station) A bohemian beauty tucked away in the northern part of the U District, the Racer is an eclectic headspinner full of crazy little details. It's known for its hearty brunches (the corn-beef hash hits the spot), fine coffee, on-site **Obama room** (Official Bad Art Museum of Art) and Sunday 'Racer Sessions' (improv jazz). Ah, if only all Seattle bars were like this.

BIG TIME MICROBREW & MUSIC   BREWERY
Map p248 (206-545-4509; www.bigtimebrewery.com; 4133 University Way NE; 11:30am-2am; 70) A fun hangout, this expansive brewpub is quiet and casual in the daytime but gets hopping at night. During the school year, it can be crowded with students still testing out their resistance (or not) to alcohol. It's been around since 1988 – ancient history by brewpub standards.

MONKEY PUB   BAR
Map p248 (206-523-6457; www.monkeypub.com; 5305 Roosevelt Way NE; 5pm-1:45am; 74) This unironic U District dive is one of the few places in town where you can slug pitchers of cheap beer, shoot free pool and sing drunken karaoke on a weekend night without having to do any planning whatsoever. If the karaoke sucks, there's always the jukebox alleged to be the best in town. And did we mention the beer's cheap?

UGLY MUG   CAFE
Map p248 (206-547-3219; www.uglymugseattle.com; 1309 NE 43rd St; snacks $2-8; 8am-11pm Mon-Fri, 10am-10pm Sat; 70) Good soups, sandwiches and the atmosphere of a cozy living room make this coffee shop just off 'the Ave' worth a peek. It also serves excellent home-roasted coffee, as is standard for any Seattle coffee shop.

⭐ ENTERTAINMENT

★ GRAND ILLUSION CINEMA   CINEMA
Map p248 (206-523-3935; www.grandillusioncinema.org; 1403 NE 50th St; 70) Totally unique! Far from being a reincarnated Gilded Age movie house, the Grand Illusion sits in an old dentist's office. Run by volunteers and passionately not-for-profit, it has a cherished national reputation among independent movie guerrillas for its director retrospectives and other cool, under-the-radar series. It helps organize and host the facetiously named STIFF (Seattle's True Independent Film Festival).

NEPTUNE THEATER   LIVE MUSIC
Map p248 (www.stgpresents.org; 1303 NE 45th St; 70) Providing an ideal pulpit for young indie bands and smirking comedians sharpening their teeth on the university-gig circuit, the Neptune, a historic theater originally dating from the silent-movie era, reopened its doors in 2011 as a performing arts venue (it formerly functioned purely as a cinema).

Run by the not-for-profit Seattle Theater Group, the 800-capacity venue offers a welcome midsize (but relatively intimate) live venue. Alt-rock, hip-hop and alt-comedy predominate.

HUSKY STADIUM
STADIUM
Map p248 (University of Washington) With room for 70,000, the Husky is a scenic giant with splendid water and mountain views. Once Seattle's largest sports stadium, it has undergone four remodels since its inception in 1920; the most recent in 2013 cost a whopping $280 million. It is home to the successful Washington Huskies (p31) college football team, which you'll quickly ascertain wears the colors purple and gold.

Games are well known for being noisier than a Nirvana gig.

VARSITY THEATRE
CINEMA
Map p248 (206-632-3131; 4329 University Way NE; 70) Independent and international arthouse films are shown at this 1940 cinema, the scene of many an undergraduate date night.

🛍 SHOPPING

Bookstores and thrift shops are the main thing here and bargains abound. 'The Ave' is the main shopping drag.

★ UNIVERSITY BOOK STORE
BOOKS
Map p248 (206-634-3400; www.ubookstore.com; 4326 University Way NE; 9am-8pm Mon-Fri, 10am-7pm Sat, noon-5pm Sun; 70) University Book Store is a vast all-purpose book emporium founded in 1900, making it Seattle's oldest. Its huge catalog of tomes is a browser's dream, and helpful staff, a regular program of events and a cozy cafe mean you could quite easily spend a whole afternoon here.

There's also a gift shop and free parking on-site.

SCARECROW VIDEO
DVD/VIDEO
Map p248 (206-524-8554; www.scarecrow.com; 5030 Roosevelt Way NE; 11am-10pm Sun-Thu, 11am-11pm Fri & Sat; 74) In an era when video stores appear to have befallen the same fate as the *Tyrannosaurus rex*, Scarecrow soldiers on. It's the largest video store in the country, with over 100,000 films in stock, many of them rare. A true community resource.

MAGUS BOOKS
BOOKS
Map p248 (206-633-1800; www.magusbooksseattle.com; 1408 NE 42nd St; 10am-8pm Sun-Thu, 10am-10pm Fri & Sat; 70) Magus is a great used-book store, the kind of place where you can literally spend hours getting lost in the crooked, narrow aisles on the hunt for that obscure out-of-print title you're not sure you can even remember any more.

HALF PRICE BOOKS
BOOKS
Map p248 (206-547-7859; 4709 Roosevelt Way NE; 9am-10pm; 74) If the encyclopedic University Book Store wasn't good (or cheap) enough for you, try the second-, third- or fourth-hand tomes here.

AMAZON BOOKS
BOOKS
Map p248 (206-524-0715; 4601 26th Ave NE; 9:30am-9pm Mon-Sat, 11am-6pm Sun; 32 to Seattle Center) Amazon's first brick-and-mortar bookstore opened in University Village, an outdoor shopping mall, in November 2015. Though heavy on gloss and technical gadgetry, the business lacks the cozy informality characteristic of traditional bookstores. A fairly limited selection of books is displayed with printed customer reviews.

CROSSROADS TRADING CO
CLOTHING
Map p248 (206-632-3111; www.crossroadstrading.com; 4300 University Way NE; 11am-8pm Mon-Sat, 11am-7pm Sun; 70) Consignment store buying and selling 'gently used' clothing (it's what they call 'secondhand' these days). Go and pop some tags and see if Macklemore was right. There's another branch (p119) in Capitol Hill.

BUFFALO EXCHANGE
CLOTHING
Map p248 (206-545-0175; www.buffaloexchange.com; 4530 University Way NE; 10am-9pm Mon-Sat, 11am-8pm Sun; 70) This secondhand-clothing store is comfortable to browse in but can be hit-and-miss in terms of good finds. Some of its merchandise is on the square side – which doesn't, ironically, make it any easier to sell your old clothes here: staff are notoriously picky.

RED LIGHT
CLOTHING
Map p248 (206-545-4044; www.redlightvintage.com; 4560 University Way NE; 11am-8pm Mon-Sat, 11am-7pm Sun; 70) The U District

WORTH A DETOUR

THE BURKE-GILMAN TRAIL

Cutting a leafy, vehicle-free path through multiple north Seattle neighborhoods, including a large segment of the U District, the Burke-Gilman Trail gets busy with human-powered traffic on sunny days at weekends, when cyclists overtake joggers, and skaters weave in and out of walkers and strollers. The asphalt trail was first laid out in 1978 along the path of a former railroad pioneered by two Seattle attorneys, Thomas Burke and Daniel Gilman, in 1885 (the railway ceased operation in 1971). Initially extending for 12 miles, the route has since been lengthened and now runs almost 20 miles from Kenmore on the northeast shore of Lake Washington to Golden Gardens Park in northwest Ballard.

There is a 'missing link' in Ballard between 11th Ave NW and Hiram M Chittenden Locks, though it's easy to navigate through the relatively quiet streets and reconnect. The Burke-Gilman has plenty of pretty sections, many of them surrounded by foliage and close to water, but to get a real taste for the neighborhoods through which it passes (U District, Wallingford, Fremont and Ballard), you need to wander off and explore a little.

Zoka Coffee (p137) in the U District and Fremont Coffee Company (p150) and Milstead & Co (p148) in Fremont make for great coffee pit stops, while for a picnic, try Gas Works Park (p145) in Wallingford, Hiram M Chittenden Locks (p156) or Golden Gardens Park (p157) in Ballard. The best spots to dine in include Agua Verde Café (p136) in the U District, Pie (p146) in Fremont and Geo (p158) in Ballard.

For bike hire look no further than Ballard Bike Co (p166) in Ballard or Recycled Cycles in the U District.

branch of Red Light carries stylish, painstakingly selected vintage clothing essential for any U-Dub hipster's wardrobe.

HARDWICK'S HARDWARE STORE HARDWARE
Map p248 (206-632-1203; 4214 Roosevelt Way NE; 8am-6pm Mon-Fri, 9am-6pm Sat; 74) Locals in the know come to Hardwick's to explore the rows and rows of buckets filled with bizarre little gadgets and gizmos. Some people probably know what these objects are for, but most shoppers are looking for things to use in their art projects. It's a hive of a place that's fun just to explore.

🏃 SPORTS & ACTIVITIES

The U District's access to freshwater and the Burke-Gilman cycling trail mean that it's ideal for outdoor activities of the biking/boating variety.

RECYCLED CYCLES CYCLING
Map p248 (206-547-4491; www.recycled cycles.com; 1007 NE Boat St; rental per day $40-60; 10am-8pm Mon-Fri, 10am-6pm Sat & Sun; 70) Rent bikes here and hit the nearby Burke-Gilman Trail to explore out as far as Fremont, Ballard and Discovery Park without touching road. Kids' chariots and trail-a-bikes are also available; reserve in summer.

AGUA VERDE PADDLE CLUB KAYAKING
Map p248 (206-545-8570; www.aquaverde. com; 1303 NE Boat St; single/double kayaks per hour $18/24; 10am-dusk Mon-Sat, to 6pm Sun Mar-Oct; 70) On Portage Bay, near the university, you can rent kayaks from this friendly place right at the edge of the water. Stand-up paddle boards are also available ($23 per hour). When you get back from your paddle, be sure to visit the cafe (p136) upstairs to eat fish tacos on the covered deck.

Green Lake & Fremont

Neighborhood Top Five

1 **Sculpture** (p143) Walking around Seattle's most irreverent neighborhood in search of its peculiar public art, as well as keeping an eye out for any spontaneous 'art attacks.'

2 **Woodland Park Zoo** (p145) Exploring one of the better animal projects in the US.

3 **Green Lake Park** (p145) Joining the walking, running, skating, cycling mass of humanity powering around beautiful Green Lake Park.

4 **Fremont Brewing Company** (p148) Biking in for a fruity beer at the positively jubilant Fremont Brewing Company.

5 **Fremont Almost Free Outdoor Cinema** (p150) Watching the wackily attired audience (while keeping half an eye on the film) at the outdoor cinema.

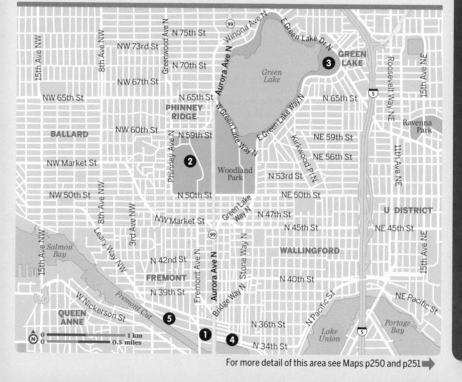

For more detail of this area see Maps p250 and p251

Lonely Planet's Top Tip

If you've had your fill of police sirens, panhandlers and the frenetic pace of downtown Seattle, consider staying over in Fremont – the affordable Hotel Hotel Hostel (p196) is a dependable bet – for a more laid-back, under-the-radar look at one of the city's most interesting neighborhoods.

🍷 Best Drinking & Nightlife

➧ Fremont Brewing Company (p148)

➧ Milstead & Co (p148)

➧ Outlander Brewery & Pub (p149)

➧ Schilling Cider House (p149)

For reviews, see p148➧

☆ Best Entertainment

➧ Fremont Almost Free Outdoor Cinema (p150)

➧ High Dive (p150)

➧ Atlas Theater (p150)

➧ Nectar Lounge (p150)

For reviews, see p150➧

🛍 Best Places to Shop

➧ Fremont Vintage Mall (p151)

➧ Wide World Books & Maps (p151)

➧ Jive Time Records (p151)

➧ Brooks Sports Inc (p152)

For reviews, see p151➧

Explore: Green Lake & Fremont

Set your watch back five minutes, turn your brain setting to 'ironic' and cross the Fremont Bridge into the self-proclaimed 'People's Republic of Fremont.'

Weirder than Ballard and more self-deprecating than Capitol Hill, Fremont's essential business is its public sculpture. Most of its outlandish statues and monuments lie clustered around a few square blocks on the southern edge of the neighborhood close to the bridge, making viewing easy. Here you'll also find the bulk of the cheap eating places and Fremont's only hotel.

Fremont's a great neighborhood for getting a taste for local life, especially in summer, when festivals and regular outdoor movies send the locals positively delirious. With good bus connections and a bike-friendly intraurban trail, it can easily be incorporated with visits to the adjacent neighborhoods of Ballard and Wallingford.

Just north of Fremont lies Green Lake, a small natural lake that's the hub of a large park complex and a pleasant low-key neighborhood punctuated by detached craftsman-style houses. The lake is packed with crowds in summer, but it's even better in fall, when the leaves are changing, or on a rare rain-free day in winter. Any time of the year, it's a picturesque spot for a walk or a run, or just to sit back on a bench and watch the rowers on the water.

Below Green Lake, Woodland Park Zoo is eternally popular. And don't neglect to head further up to Phinney Ridge, the hilltop neighborhood north of the zoo along Phinney Ave N, for some quiet everyone-knows-everyone-else pubs and restaurants.

Local Life

➧ **Green Lake Park exercisers** Meet the 75-year-old marathon runner, the hyperventilating weight watcher, the in-line skater on his cell phone, and the lawyer from Phinney Ridge getting bullied by his personal trainer at this well-kept park (p145).

➧ **Wallingford** (p151) Take a good book and spend a Sunday afternoon working through the bars and cafes of this underrated Seattle neighborhood chapter by chapter.

Getting There & Away

➧ **Bus** Three different metro buses link Fremont to central Seattle. Bus 62 runs from downtown to Fremont and then onto Green Lake Park. Bus 5 runs from downtown via Fremont to Phinney Ridge and Woodland Park Zoo. Bus 40 originates in downtown and makes stops along Fremont's N 36th St before breezing off to Ballard. For cross-town connections, buses 31 and 32 link Fremont with the U District.

WOLFGANG KAEHLER / GETTY IMAGES ©

Long known for its wry contrarianism, Fremont does bizarre like the rest of the world does normal. For proof, look no further than its public sculpture, an eclectic amalgamation of the scary, the politically incorrect and the downright weird. The five most famous pieces are scattered around four square blocks in the southern part of the neighborhood abutting the Lake Washington Ship Canal, between N 34th St, N 36th St, Aurora Ave N and Evanston Ave N.

DON'T MISS

➡ Fremont Troll
➡ Statue of Lenin
➡ Fremont Rocket
➡ *Waiting for the Interurban*

PRACTICALITIES

➡ Map p250, C3
➡ btwn N 34th St, N 36th St, Aurora Ave N & Evanston Ave N
➡ 🚌5

Statue of Lenin

Fremont's provocative bronze **statue of Lenin** (Map p250; cnr N 36th St & Fremont Pl N; 🚌40) was salvaged from the people of Poprad, Czechoslovakia, in 1993 who, having suffered for 40 years under communism, were probably glad to see the back of the bearded curmudgeon. It was unearthed by a resident of Issaquah, WA, named Lewis Carpenter, who found it unloved and abandoned in a junkyard while working in Czechoslovakia as an English teacher soon after the Velvet Revolution. Carpenter forked out $13,000 to purchase the fierce 16ft-tall re-creation of the wily Bolshevik leader and then put up another $41,000 (by remortgaging his home) to ship it to the US. After Carpenter's death in 1994, the statue turned up – where else? – in Fremont. It still belongs to the Carpenter family and is allegedly 'for sale' for around $300,000.

Fremont Troll

Just when you thought you had returned to planet earth, up sprouts the **Fremont Troll** (Map p250; cnr N 36th St & Troll Ave; 🚌62; pictured above), a 13,000lb steel and concrete sculpture of a troll crushing a Volkswagen Beetle in its hand that resides under the Aurora Bridge and does a good job of scaring off skateboarders, drug dealers and any passing billy goats. The sculpture was the winner of a 1989 Fremont Arts Council competition to design some thought-provoking public art. It took seven weeks to make.

ART ATTACKS

There are two types of art attack in Fremont. The first targets existing monuments: decorating the *Interurban* is one example; sticking drag on the Lenin statue is another. The second type of attack is to concoct brand-new urban art exhibits. Most of these pieces are temporary and appear anonymously overnight. There have been many classics over the years, including papier-mâché cows, an 8ft-long steel pig, and an enormous spider suspended over a parking lot. The bulk of these inspired creations are quickly removed, though some have entered local folklore and been allowed to stay.

Dedicated in 2008, the life-sized statue on N 34th St of two clowns, arms interlinked, striding off in opposite directions, honors the characters JP Patches and Gertrude, who appeared daily on the children's JP Patches Show on Seattle TV during the 1960s and '70s. Located a mere 250yd east of Waiting for the Interurban, it has been humorously christened Late for the Interurban.

Fremont Rocket

Fremont has adopted the phallic and zany-looking **Fremont Rocket** (Map p250; cnr Evanston Ave & N 35th St; 🖳40), grafted onto the corner of a shoe shop, as its community totem. Constructed in the 1950s for use in the Cold War, the rocket was plagued with engineering difficulties and never went anywhere, leaving its constructors with the unfortunate problem of not being able to get it up. Before coming to Fremont, it was temporarily affixed to an army surplus store in Belltown. When the store went out of business in 1993, the Fremont Business Association snapped it up.

On the building opposite sits Fremont's newest art piece, a giant fiberglass model of the planet **Saturn** and its rings seemingly floating 65ft above the street.

Waiting for the Interurban

Seattle's most popular piece of public art, **Waiting for the Interurban** (Map p250; cnr N 34th St & Fremont Ave N; 🖳62), sculpted in recycled aluminum, depicts six people waiting for a train that never comes. The train that once passed through Fremont stopped running in the 1930s, and the people of Seattle have been waiting for a new train – the Interurban – ever since (a new train connecting Seattle with Everett opened in 2003 but doesn't stop in Fremont). The sculpture is prone to regular art attacks, when locals lovingly decorate the people in outfits corresponding to a special event, the weather, someone's birthday, a Mariners win – whatever. Rarely do you see the sculpture undressed. Take a look at the human-faced dog peeking out between the legs of the people. That face belongs to Armen Stepanian, one of the founders of today's Fremont and its excellent recycling system. Sculptor Richard Beyer and Stepanian had a disagreement about the design of the piece, which resulted in Beyer's spiteful yet humorous design of the dog's face.

The Guidepost

The whimsical **guidepost** (Map p250; cnr Fremont Ave N & Fremont Pl N; 🖳5) that points in 16 different directions – including towards the Troll, the Lenin statue and the Milky Way – appeared anonymously on Fremont Ave in 1995, the result of one of the neighborhood's periodic art attacks. Unlike other ephemeral sculptures, the guidepost stayed put and quickly became a neighborhood symbol. Originally made out of cedar wood, the rotting signpost was replaced in 2009 by a better-quality one made out of pressure-treated wood. At the same time, the artist revealed himself to be Maque DaVis, a resident of nearby Ballard, but a Fremonter in spirit. The signpost advertises itself as 'the center of the known universe,' a phrase that has since been adopted as a popular Fremont slogan.

◉ SIGHTS

◉ Fremont

FREMONT PUBLIC SCULPTURE MONUMENT
See p143.

FREMONT BRIDGE BRIDGE
Map p250 (🚻5) Built in 1916 and since dwarfed by the far taller George Washington Memorial Bridge (colloquially known as the Aurora Bridge), the distinctive orange-and-blue Fremont Bridge became necessary after the construction of the Lake Washington Ship Canal linked Lake Union with Puget Sound. It is the busiest drawbridge in the US, opening numerous times a day to let boat traffic pass through.

APATOSAURS SCULPTURE
Map p250 (🚻40) Along the banks of the ship canal and abutting the Burke-Gilman Trail at the bottom of Phinney Ave N, you'll see two life-size 'apatosaurs' fashioned out of ivy. The adult dino measures 66ft long, making it the world's largest known topiary (ornamental shrub). The apatosaurs were originally displayed in the Pacific Science Center, but were picked up by the Fremonters in 1999.

GAS WORKS PARK PARK
Map p240 (Meridian Ave, at N Northlake Way; 🚻; 🚻62) Urban reclamation has no greater monument in Seattle than Gas Works Park. The former power station here produced gas for heating and lighting from 1906 to 1956. The gas works was thereafter understandably considered an eyesore and an environmental menace. But the beautiful location of the works, with stellar views of downtown over Lake Union, sailboats and yachts sliding to and from the shipping canal, induced the city government to convert the former industrial site into a public park in 1975.

However, rather than tear down the factory, landscape architects preserved it. Painted black and now highlighted with rather joyful graffiti, it looks like some odd remnant from a former civilization. It also makes a great location for shooting rock album covers and music videos. The park's small hill with its sundial is a favorite spot for flying kites.

◉ Green Lake

WOODLAND PARK ZOO ZOO
Map p251 (📞206-548-2500; www.zoo.org; 5500 Phinney Ave N; adult/child 3-12yr May-Sep $19.95/12.25, Oct-Apr $13.75/9.25; ⏱9:30am-6pm May-Sep, 9:30am-4pm Oct-Apr; 🚻; 🚻5) In Woodland Park, up the hill from Green Lake Park, the Woodland Park Zoo is one of Seattle's most popular tourist attractions, consistently rated as one of the top 10 zoos in the country. It was one of the first in the nation to free animals from their restrictive cages in favor of ecosystem enclosures, where animals from similar environments share large spaces designed to replicate their natural surroundings.

Feature exhibits include a tropical rainforest, two gorilla exhibits, an African savanna and an Asian elephant forest.

SEATTLE ROSE GARDEN GARDENS
Map p251 (⏱7am-dusk; 🚻5) The 2.5-acre Seattle Rose Garden, near the entrance road to the zoo off N 50th St, was started in 1924 and contains 5000 plants, including heirloom roses and a test garden for All-America Rose Selections.

★GREEN LAKE PARK PARK
Map p251 (🚻62) A favorite hunting ground for runners, personal trainers and artistically tattooed sunbathers, scenic Green Lake Park surrounds a small natural lake created by a glacier during the last ice age. Two paths wind around the lake, but these aren't enough to fill the needs of the hundreds of joggers, power-walkers, cyclists and in-line skaters who throng here daily; the city government now regulates traffic on the paths.

In the early 1900s, city planners lowered the lake's water level by 7ft, increasing the shoreline to preserve parkland around the lake. After the lowering, however, Ravenna Creek, which once fed the lake, no longer flowed through. Green Lake became stagnant and filled with stinky green algae. Massive dredging efforts to keep it navigable continue, although the lake remains prone to algae blooms.

GREEN LAKE AQUA THEATER LANDMARK
Map p251 (🚻Rapid Ride E-Line) The lonely-looking grandstand at the southern end of Green Lake is all that remains of the former

FREEDOM TO BE PECULIAR

Coined the 'Artistic Republic of Fremont' by irreverent locals who once symbolically voted to secede from the rest of Seattle, the neighborhood of Fremont has always marched eccentrically to its own bongo – albeit with its tongue stuck firmly in its cheek. Where else in the US can you find an un-desecrated statue of Vladimir Lenin, an antediluvian Cold War rocket, an annual nude cyclists parade, and a sculpted troll crushing a Volkswagen Beetle under a bridge? Even Fremont's vandals are creative. The neighborhood's famous statue *Waiting for the Interurban*, a study of six commuters waiting for a train that never comes, is regularly decorated by audacious art guerrillas who dress the figures up in clothes, hats and ties, or cover them with amusing placards.

Some of Fremont's countercultural spirit comes from its history: it was a separate city until 1891, and still is in the minds of many of its residents. 'Set your watch back five minutes' reads a sign on Fremont Bridge as you cross over from the stiffer, less self-deprecating neighborhood of Queen Anne. Fremont's idiosyncratic personality resurfaced in the 1970s, when community activism attempted to offset years of economic decline. The Fremont Public Association, today the envy of every neighborhood association in Seattle, was created in 1974 to provide shelter, food and help to disadvantaged residents. Its formation spawned a number of other thriving community associations, including the Fremont Arts Council, and, in 1994, irked by bureaucratic planning and boundary laws, the neighborhood made its token and somewhat humorous secession.

These days, Fremont is showing signs of creeping gentrification. Various software companies including Google have opened up offices since the mid-2000s, and trendy boutiques are starting to compete with the area's legendary junk shops. But the spirit of ludicrousness still resounds, enshrined in the neighborhood's libertine motto: *De Libertas Quirkas* (Freedom to be Peculiar). Enough said.

5500-capacity Green Lake Aqua Theater, an outdoor auditorium overlooking the lake (where the stage once was) that stood here from 1950 to 1970.

Back in the day, the theater's big crowd-puller was its annual summer *Aqua Follies* show, a kind of kitschy water ballet, but it also staged opera, jazz and, towards the end of its tenure, a couple of legendary rock performances by Led Zeppelin and the Grateful Dead. Newer, drier venues built for the World's Fair in 1962 eventually put the theater out of business and it closed in 1970. History panels explain the story.

✕ EATING

Fremont's restaurant scene is a regularly shuffled pack of cards with a few jokers thrown in. There have been some welcome new faces recently and a few relocations. Locavore food is a big deal, waitstaff are chatty and informality rules.

Green Lake has an everybody-knows-each-other neighborhood feel to it, and the cafes and restaurants consequently tend to be welcoming and casual.

✕ Fremont

★PASEO   CARIBBEAN $
Map p251 (☎206-545-7440; www.paseorestau rants.com; 4225 Fremont Ave N; sandwiches $8.50-11.50; ⊙11am-9pm Tue-Fri, 11am-8pm Sat, 11am-6pm Sun; ☐5) A glorified food shack whose overflowing Cuban sandwiches (which are a lot more generously stuffed than they are in Cuba) have long prompted plenty of Seattleites to re-route their daily commute in order to savor them. If you've driven this far, you shouldn't overlook the exquisitely simple rice and beans either.

Be prepared to queue, lick your fingers a lot and perch at a wobbly table on an equally wobbly chair.

PIE   PIES $
Map p250 (☎206-436-8590; www.sweetand savorypie.com; 3515 Fremont Ave N; pies $5.95; ⊙9am-9pm Mon-Thu, to 2am Fri & Sat, 10am-6pm Sun; ☐5) ✐ It's as simple as P-I-E. Bake

fresh pies daily on-site, stuff them with homemade fillings (sweet and savory), and serve them in a cool, bold-colored Fremont cafe. The pies are ideal for a snack lunch or you can double up and get a sweet one for dessert too. Broccoli cheddar and peanut-butter cream are crowd-pleasers.

MIGHTY-O DONUTS   CAFE **$**

Map p251 (☑206-547-5431; www.mightyo.com; 2110 N 55th St; doughnuts from $1.50; ⊙6am-5pm Mon-Fri, 7am-5pm Sat & Sun; 🛜🚗♿; 🚌62) 🏴 Going up against Top Pot Hand-Forged Doughnuts is a tall order, but Mighty-O isn't so bothered about the competition, knocking out its vegan doughnuts from this light-filled cafe in 'Tangletown' on the cusp of Green Lake and Wallingford. Forget any preconceived ideas you might have about veganism. The sweet creations are sugary and decadent; they just happen to be devoid of animal fat too.

HOMEGROWN   SANDWICHES **$**

Map p250 (☑206-453-5232; www.eathome grown.com; 3416 Fremont Ave N; half/full sandwiches $7/12; ⊙8am-8pm; 🚌5) 🏴 Slavishly sustainable, this locavore sandwich bar proves that green doesn't have to be tasteless. Bread is baked daily in-house and filled with unique ingredients such as split-pea pesto and pork loin rubbed in Stumptown coffee that's been laced with cayenne. Now that's what you call creative.

REVEL   KOREAN, AMERICAN **$$**

Map p250 (☑206-547-2040; www.revelseattle. com; 403 N 36th St; small plates $12-16; ⊙11am-2pm & 5-10pm Mon-Fri, 10am-2pm & 5-10pm Sat & Sun; 🚌40) This slick, modern, Korean-American crossover restaurant (with a bit of French influence thrown in) has quickly established itself as a big name on the Seattle eating scene thanks, in part, to its simple, shareable plates. Of note are the pork-belly pancakes, the short-rib dumplings and the massive duck dumpling hot pot, all of which go down well with a cocktail or two

POMEROL RESTAURANT FRENCH, AMERICAN **$$**

Map p250 (☑206-632-0135; www.pomerol restaurant.com; 127 N 36th St; mains $19-26; ⊙5-10pm Sun-Thu, 5-11pm Fri & Sat; 🚌40) Experienced Vietnamese American restaurant owner serves French-influenced, contemporary American food in small but perfectly proportioned sizes in Fremont: if this concept sounds interesting, then you should probably book a table at Pomerol, one of the newer additions to Fremont's rapidly expanding restaurant universe, where seared foie gras and grilled steelhead trout share top menu credits.

ROUX   CAJUN **$$**

Map p251 (☑206-547-5420; www.restaurantroux. com; 4201 Fremont Ave N; mains $14-32; ⊙4pm-10pm Mon-Fri, 9am-2pm & 5pm-10pm Sat & Sun; 🚌5) Many of Fremont's newer restaurants inhabit the fine end of the dining spectrum. But Roux, which morphed out of a po'boy-selling food truck in 2013, keeps it relatively down-to-earth with a French Creole–themed menu knocking out fine renditions of catfish, jambalaya, grits, oysters and the like.

The atmosphere is loud and cheerful, while the decor has plenty of trendy hallmarks.

⭐**THE WHALE WINS**   EUROPEAN **$$$**

(☑206-632-9425; www.thewhalewins.com; 3506 Stone Way N; mains $25-29; ⊙5-10pm Mon-Sat, 5-9pm Sun; 🚗; 🚌62) 🏴 Forget the whale, it's the sardines that are the main winners at this eccentrically named fish-biased restaurant that shares trendy Euro-style digs with the equally hip Joule restaurant next door. The said sardines arrive on thick crispy bread spread with a heavenly mayo concoction and adorned with zesty veg. Indeed, the 'Whale' excels in veg. Have carrots and fennel ever tasted this good?

AGRODOLCE   ITALIAN **$$$**

Map p250 (☑206-547-9707; www.agrodolce restaurant.net; 709 N 35th St; pasta $17-20, mains $18-30; ⊙11:30am-2:30pm & 4:30-10pm Mon-Fri, from 10am Sat & Sun; 🚌5) 🏴 Agrodolce feels more like a restaurant with a southern Italian bent than a southern Italian restaurant per se, though all the basic premises of Puglian/Silician cuisine are there: durum pasta, spring greens, lots of veg and, of course, fish. The spaghetti and clams merits a mention, as does the stinging-nettle pesto. The minimalist decor is warmed up by congenial neighborhood atmospherics.

✖ Green Lake

BETH'S CAFÉ   BREAKFAST **$**

Map p251 (☑206-782-5588; www.bethscafe. com; 7311 Aurora Ave N; omelets $6-12; ⊙24hr; 🚌Rapid Ride E-Line) The best – or at least biggest – hangover breakfast in the world is at Beth's, and you can get it all day long in an agreeably greasy space decorated with the amateur scribblings of former diners. You can't smoke in here any more, which, depending on your view, either ruins everything or makes it possible to enjoy Beth's infamous 12-egg omelet while breathing.

The cafe is on down-at-heel Aurora Ave which sits in ironic juxtaposition between the salubrious suburbs of Green Lake and Phinney Ridge.

RED MILL BURGERS
BURGERS $

Map p251 (📞206-783-6362; www.redmillburg ers.com; 312 N 67th St; burgers $4-10; ⊙11am-9pm Tue-Sat, noon-8pm Sun; 🚌5) You can find what is possibly Seattle's most popular burger in this urban legend in Phinney Ridge, the second incarnation of a restaurant that originally opened in 1937. The key is in the burger's simplicity...plus the crispy onion rings, which act as the de rigueur side dish. There's usually a line out the door, but it moves along quickly.

PETE'S EGG NEST
BREAKFAST $

Map p251 (📞206-784-5348; 7717 Greenwood Ave N; breakfast $8-10; ⊙7am-2:30pm Tue-Fri, 7am-3pm Sat & Sun; 🚌5) This Greek-leaning breakfast joint up on Phinney Ridge is famous for humongous portions of the satisfying standards – omelets, biscuits and gravy, and mountainous hash browns. Seasonal specials are recommended.

TANGLETOWN PUB
NORTHWEST $$

Map p251 (📞206-547-5929; www.elysianbrew ing.com; 2106 N 55th St; mains $10-18; ⊙11am-midnight Mon-Fri, 10am-midnight Sat & Sun; 🚻; 🚌62) This northern outpost of the Elysian Brewing Company has become a darling feature of the Tangletown neighborhood, where it established a child-friendly, laid-back space in the old 1910-vintage Keystone Building, which it shares with Mighty-O Donuts (p147). Supporting the locally lauded Elysian ales – headed up by the Immortal IPA – is glorified pub food such as chicken wings and eggplant panini.

NELL'S
CONTINENTAL $$$

Map p251 (📞206-524-4044; www.nellsrestau rant.com; 6804 E Green Lake Way N; mains $26-34, tasting menu $48; ⊙5:30-10pm Sun-Wed, 5:30-10:30pm Thu-Sat; 🚌62) For fine dining opposite Green Lake, Nell's serves up classic European items with Northwestern flair.

Beloved dishes include the sweet onion tart and the calamari with fried capers, parsley and aioli. Opt for seafood dishes, and don't skip dessert (or the cheeseboard).

🍷 DRINKING & NIGHTLIFE

Fremont is home to an excellent array of bars, taverns and brewpubs, and is a good place to uncover Seattle's latest trends and zeitgeist. The less bohemian Green Lake area specializes in relaxing family-orientated neighborhood pubs.

🍸 Fremont

★FREMONT BREWING COMPANY
BREWPUB

(📞206-420-2407; www.fremontbrewing.com; 3409 Woodland Park Ave N; ⊙11am-9pm; 🚌62) This relatively new microbrewery, in keeping with current trends, sells its wares via an attached tasting room rather than a full-blown pub. Not only is the beer divine (try the seasonal bourbon barrel-aged Abominable beer), the industrial-chic tasting room and 'urban beer garden' are highly inclusive spaces, where pretty much everyone in the hood comes to hang out at communal tables.

A liberal policy on pets and minors keeps things congenial, meaning you'll see more dogs and kids than hardened drinkers as you work your way through trays of small samplers. Although there's no food service, bowls of free pretzels help soak up any light-headedness.

★MILSTEAD & CO
CAFE

Map p250 (📞206-659-4814; www.milstead andco.com; 900 N 34th St; ⊙6am-6pm Mon-Fri, 7am-6pm Sat & Sun; 🚻; 🚌62) A relatively new multi-roaster business, this fabulous neighborhood coffee bar in Fremont prefers to carefully select other people's beans rather than roast their own, but chooses them with the skill and precision of a French sommelier. The 'bean menu' changes daily, but, thanks to the expertise of owner Andrew Milstead, it rarely disappoints.

Equally attractive are the beautifully concocted sweet snacks and the everybody-knows-everyone-else neighborhood vibe inside.

CIDER IS THE NEW BEER

Legend has it that the puritanical Pilgrim Fathers furtively smuggled a barrel of cider aboard the *Mayflower* back in 1620. A couple of years later, with several budding colonies established on dry land, America's first apple orchard inauspiciously took root in Boston, courtesy of a dissident Anglican priest.

Considering its early appearance in popular American culture, it is perhaps a little surprising that the US' appetite for cider has only recently taken off, with hard cider consumption having jumped a purported 400% since the turn of the decade. These days, the bulk of the nation's apple crop (over 60%) is grown in Washington State and – not coincidentally – some of the best new craft cider is being produced in the state's largest city, Seattle, where a strong locavore culture, a penchant for culinary experimentation and a flair for technical ingenuity encourage nascent micro-businesses.

The craft cider industry has been particularly active since the early 2010s, shadowing and, no doubt, learning a little from Seattle's well-established microbrewers. Small operators press and ferment their carefully chosen Washington State apples before making them into small-batch experimental ciders, which they then line up for tastings in various pubs and taprooms. Leader in the field so far is Schilling Cider House in – where else? – Fremont, where you can get a tray of six small tasting samples or grab take-out bottles and cans from a fridge. Also worth visiting is Capitol Cider (p116) in Capitol Hill, which offers a full food menu and numerous ciders (including some English classics) in a pub-like atmosphere that retains a decidedly Anglo feel.

GREEN LAKE & FREMONT DRINKING & NIGHTLIFE

OUTLANDER BREWERY & PUB MICROBREWERY
Map p250 (206-486-4088; www.outlander brewing.com; 225 N 36th St; 4-10pm Tue & Wed, 4pm-midnight Thu, 4pm-1am Fri & Sat, 2-10pm Sun; 40) A tiny microbrewery not quite small enough to be classed as a nano-brewery, Outlander occupies the downstairs rooms of a creaky wooden house dating from the early 1900s and provides a cozy antidote to the crowded ebullience of Fremont's other bars. It looks like someone's front room... and probably was once.

SCHILLING CIDER HOUSE BAR
Map p250 (206-420-7088; www.schillingcider. com; 708 N 34th St; noon-11pm; 62) Continuing a tradition that apparently began with the Pilgrim Fathers (who allegedly smuggled a barrel of cider onto the *Mayflower*), Schilling is at the forefront of Seattle's craft cider boom, offering 32 of its fruity concoctions on draft at this woody Fremont taproom. The modus operandi: get six small taster glasses for $12 and wet your palate.

Take-out cans are also available.

BROUWER'S CAFE BAR
Map p250 (206-267-2437; 400 N 35th St; 11am-2am; 40) Rather than producing its own beer, Brouwer's stocks the brews of others – lots of them. Indeed, it, arguably, offers the finest beer selection in the city:

an astounding 64 brews on tap along with over 300 bottled varieties.

Rarely short of a bevy of drinkers propping up its bar, the establishment is revered by beer aficionados and neophytes alike for its warm, non-pretentious pub atmosphere and simple Belgian-influenced food, including pretzels, *frites,* steamed mussels and sausages.

BAD JIMMY'S MICROBREWERY
(206-789-1548; www.badjimmysbrewingco. com; 4358b Leary Way NW; 3pm-midnight Mon-Thu, noon-2am Fri & Sat, noon-midnight Sun; 40) Follow the happy noises to this small taproom in a garage in the boxy warehouse district of West Fremont (or is it East Ballard?). Feeling more nano- than microbrewery, it specializes in strongly flavored ales – be they citrus, chocolate or even coconut – with high ABVs (ie your head will be swimming after one pint).

It's pet- and kid-friendly and you can bring your own food.

HALE'S ALES BREWERY BREWPUB
(www.halesbrewery.com; 4301 Leary Way NW; 11am-10pm; 40) A relative old-timer, Hale's was only the third microbrewery in Washington State when it opened in 1983. Its large, contemporary brewery and pub on the cusp of the Ballard and Fremont neighborhoods mixes seasonal brews with old

favorites including its flagship tipple, Hale's Pale Ale, a good entry-point beer for beginners keen to learn how to differentiate their malt from their hops.

GEORGE & DRAGON PUB   PUB

Map p250 (www.georgeanddragonpub.com; 206 N 36th St; ☺11am-2am; 🚍40) Attracting every Brit within a 10-mile radius, the George & Dragon is a definitive English boozer where the 'football' on TV is that 11-a-side game you play with your feet; 'chips' are rectangular, fried and not remotely French; and Tetley's is a dark, warm beer as opposed to a brand of tea.

FREMONT COFFEE COMPANY   CAFE

Map p250 (www.fremontcoffee.net; 459 N 36th St; ☺6am-8pm Mon-Fri, 7am-8pm Sat & Sun; 🖥; 🚍40) One-of-a-kind coffee shop in an old craftsman-style house with art-adorned rooms and wicker chairs on a wraparound porch. The clientele are hip-meets-hippie, and the coffee is refreshingly strong.

🍴 Green Lake

74TH STREET ALE HOUSE   PUB

Map p251 (📞206-784-2955; 7401 Greenwood Ave N; ☺11am-11pm Sun-Thu, 11am-midnight Fri & Sat; 🚍5) A sibling to the Hilltop Ale House (p103) in Queen Anne, this is the kind of place that, if you lived nearby, you'd find yourself in several times a week. It's as comfortable as a British country pub, with an ambience that will make you feel like an instant regular – plus there are dozens of outstanding beers on tap (including plenty of British favorites).

HERKIMER COFFEE   COFFEE

Map p251 (📞206-784-0202; www.herkimercoffee.com; 7320 Greenwood Ave N; ☺6am-6pm Mon-Fri, 7am-6pm Sat & Sun; 🖥; 🚍5) One of Seattle's smaller coffee chains (with three cafes only), this place is a good rest stop if you're up in Phinney Ridge and in need of a caffeine boost. It also doubles as their roasting room.

EL CHUPACABRA   BAR

Map p251 (📞206-706-4889; www.elchupacabra.com; 6711 Greenwood Ave N; ☺11:30am-midnight Sun-Thu, 11am-2am Fri & Sat; 🚍5) This Phinney Ridge bar is known for its front patio (great for sipping margaritas), kitschy decor (let's call it punky Mexican) and San Francisco–style burritos. Be warned: service can be slow when the place is crowded.

⭐ ENTERTAINMENT

HIGH DIVE   LIVE MUSIC

Map p250 (www.highdiveseattle.com; 513 N 36th St; ☺7pm-2am; 🚍40) A bit of a dive – but not an unpleasant one – this is one of two local live-music stalwarts in Fremont. It hosts rock primarily for small-name bands on their way up. Strong drinks and BBQ food provide the accompaniment.

FREMONT ALMOST FREE
OUTDOOR CINEMA   CINEMA

Map p250 (www.fremontoutdoormovies.com; 3501 Phinney Ave N; ☺Jul & Aug; 🚍40) Some come dragging sofas, others arrive dressed as cowboys or zombies from *Shaun of the Dead*. Every summer, Fremonters take over this small parking lot for evening movies that quickly turn into frivolous community events with food carts, fancy dress and harmless high jinks. Movies are projected onto a large wall flanked by iconic murals of Bogart and Bergman.

NECTAR LOUNGE   LIVE MUSIC

Map p250 (📞206-632-2020; www.nectarlounge.com; 412 N 36th St; ☺8pm-2am; 🚍40) A small and comfortable live-music venue in Fremont that has grown out of its humble beginnings to become a well-established club that includes a covered patio with stage views. It prides itself on hosting any genre of music and was an early refuge for hip-hop acts. Macklemore has played here.

ATLAS THEATER   COMEDY

Map p250 (📞425-954-5618; www.seattlecomedygroup.com; 3509 Fremont Ave N; tickets from $14; ☺shows 8pm & 10pm Fri & Sat; 🚍5) Spend more than five minutes in Fremont and you'll quickly glean that it's got a healthy sense of humor. So it'll come as no bombshell to discover this tiny theater specializing in improv comedy with the odd adult-only 'blue' show thrown in for good measure. Check the calendar and reserve tickets online.

BATHHOUSE THEATER   THEATER

Map p251 (📞206-524-1300; www.seattlepublictheater.org; 7312 W Green Lake Dr; 🚍Rapid Ride E-Line) The Bathhouse Theater on the western side of Green Lake was a 1928 bathing pavilion that was converted into a live-

WALLINGFORD

The best reason to visit sleepy, residential Wallingford, sandwiched like a tangy relish in between Fremont and the U District, is that no one else does – apart from the several thousand people who call it home. Welcome to a neighborhood bereft of any real tourist 'sights,' where you can while away an afternoon slumped in an unpretentious cafe and quietly imbibe a side of Seattle that one million annual visitors to the Space Needle never get to see. Wallingford's arterial road, NE 45th St, supports an eclectic parade of local businesses ranging from the homespun to the bizarre, with dedicated bookstores, one-off tearooms, an enlightening Afghan restaurant and a handful of small Seattle 'chains' including an Uptown Espresso and the original Dick's Drive-In. About a mile to the south, the car-free Burke-Gilman Trail (p140) bisects the neighborhood east–west along the northern shores of Lake Union. Stop, if you have time, amid the post-industrial landscape of Gas Works Park (p145), where a rusting disused power plant contrasts sharply with the surrounding greenery. It remains a favorite spot for lakeside kite-flyers and rock album cover shoots.

A wander along NE 45th St rewards with lots of interesting places to eat, drink and browse. Don't miss the following:

➡ **Wide World Books & Maps** (Map p251; ☑888-534-3453; www.worldwidetravelstore. com; 4411 Wallingford Ave N; ☉10am-7pm Mon-Sat, 10am-6pm Sun; ☐62) If you thought guidebooks were dead, visit this multifarious travel emporium staffed by a team of seasoned globetrotters just off N 45th St.

➡ **Pam's Kitchen** (Map p251; ☑206-696-7010; www.pams-kitchen.com; 1715 N 45th St; mains $9-20; ☉5-10pm Sun-Thu, 5-11pm Fri & Sat; ☐62) Discover the spices hidden in the wonderful Trinidadian flavors of this Caribbean restaurant, recently relocated from the nearby U District.

➡ **Kabul** (Map p251; ☑206-545-9000; www.kabulrestaurant.com; 2301 N 45th St; mains $9-21; ☉5-9:30pm Wed-Mon; ☐62) Fine-tune your international tasting palate with Afghan food, including stewed eggplant, lamb kebabs, yogurt, and mild, creamy curry.

➡ **Teahouse Kuan Yin** (Map p251; ☑206-632-2055; www.teahousekuanyin.com; 1911 N 45th St; ☉9am-10pm; ☎; ☐62) In Seattle's burgeoning tea scene, Kuan Yin is a leading light. It's usually stuffed with laptop campers until late evening.

GREEN LAKE & FREMONT SHOPPING

performance venue in 1970. It's currently home to Seattle Public Theater who stage mainly contemporary plays.

LITTLE RED HEN   LIVE MUSIC
Map p251 (☑206-522-1168; www.littleredhen. com; 7115 Woodlawn Ave NE; ☉9am-2am; ☐62) This is Seattle's only real venue for pure live country music. Nightly entertainment includes country karaoke and good-time honky-tonk bands – or you can don a cowboy hat for the free line-dancing lessons held on Mondays at 8pm. There's a small food menu touting cheap Tex-Mex.

🛍 SHOPPING

★**FREMONT VINTAGE MALL**   ANTIQUES
Map p250 (☑206-548-9140; www.fremontvintage mall.com; 3419 Fremont Pl N; ☉11am-7pm Mon-Sat, 11am-6pm Sun; ☐5) Descending into this subterranean antique mall is like diving down to a sunken Spanish galleon full of plundered treasure. Who knows what you might bring to the surface? An old 1950s vending machine? A clownish unicycle? An Afghan coat that looks exactly like something Hendrix once wore?

JIVE TIME RECORDS   MUSIC
Map p250 (www.jivetimerecords.com; 3506 Fremont Ave N; ☉11am-9pm Mon-Sat, 10am-7pm Sun; ☐5) A vinyl collector's dream come true full of rarities and secondhand bargains stuffed into a diminutive interior.

FREMONT SUNDAY MARKET   MARKET
Map p250 (www.fremontmarket.com; N 34th St, btwn Phinney Ave N & Fremont Ave; ☉10am-5pm Sun; ☐5) 🅿 People come from all over town for this market. It features fresh fruit and vegetables, arts and crafts, and all kinds of people getting rid of junk.

BROOKS SPORTS INC SPORTS & OUTDOORS

(✆425-488-3131; www.brooksrunning.com; 3400 Stone Way N, Wallingford; ⊙10am-7pm Mon-Sat, 10am-6pm Sun; ◻62) One of the greenest buildings in Seattle (LEED platinum status), super-modern Stone 34 was finished in 2014 and sits beside the Burke-Gilman running-cycling trail in Fremont. Appropriately, its first tenants are running-shoe company Brooks Sports Inc, who have made Fremont their new global headquarters.

Their ground-floor shop is as much a place for runners to seek advice as a place to buy shoes, although there's slick footwear on offer if you're tempted. The friendly staff are real pros.

HAVE A HEART POT SHOP

Map p250 (✆206-632-7126; 316 N 36th St; ⊙9am-10pm Sun-Wed, 9am-11:45pm Thu-Sat; ◻40) One of several pot shops in Fremont, this place has recently switched from selling medicinal to recreational marijuana and is doing good business in a neighborhood that has long boasted about its 'freedom to be peculiar.' Like pot shops elsewhere in the city, it is clean, well laid out and very friendly.

OPHELIA'S BOOKS BOOKS

Map p250 (www.opheliasbooks.com; 3504 Fremont Ave N; ⊙11am-7pm Mon-Sat, 11am-6pm Sun; ◻5) Like an indie record store for bibliophiles, Ophelia's is full of rare, yellowing, story-filled ex-trees that possess bags more character than electronic readers.

FROCK BOUTIQUE CLOTHING

Map p251 (✆206-297-1638; www.frockboutique. com; 6500 Phinney Ave N; ⊙10am-6pm Tue-Sat, 10am-5pm Sun & Mon; ◻5) This recent reincarnation of the former Frock Shop was taken over by Portland's similarly orientated Frock Boutique in 2015. It offers an elegant blend of unique dresses with vintage influences.

PICNIC FOOD & DRINK

Map p251 (www.picnicseattle.com; 6801 Greenwood Ave N; ⊙11am-6pm Wed-Sat, noon-5pm Sun; ◻5) Like a Euro deli crossed with a California wine store, Picnic provides ample justification to put together a gourmet outdoor

meal (Green Lake Park beckons). It specializes in locally produced, hard-to-find products (cheese, cured meat, honey, chocolate) and also has a small cafe with wine tastings.

🏃 SPORTS & ACTIVITIES

THEO CHOCOLATE FACTORY FOOD & DRINK

Map p250 (✆206-632-5100; www.theochocolate. com; 3400 Phinney Ave N; tours $10; ⊙10am-6pm, tours every half hour 10.30am-4pm; ◻40) Adding a bit of Willy Wonka to Fremont's atypical street life is this chocolate factory on the site of the old Redhook Brewery (now moved to Woodinville, WA). The chocolate microproducer makes organic chocolate and the detailed tour is both witty and interesting (if you don't mind donning the obligatory hairnet). And, yes, there are tastings!

FREMONT TOUR WALKING

Map p250 (www.thefremonttour.com; adult/child $20/free; ⊙Jun-Sep; ◻62) To help outsiders infiltrate Fremont's wacky underbelly, a group of enterprising locals have instituted the Fremont Tour, a 90-minute neighborhood stroll accompanied by outlandishly costumed guides with names such as Rocket Man and Crazy Cat Lady.

Tours meet at the Waiting for the Interurban statue (p144), on the corner of N 34th St and Fremont Ave N.

GREEN LAKE BOAT RENTAL BOATING

Map p251 (✆206-527-0171; rentals per hour $18; ⊙9am-7pm May-Sep; ♿; ◻62) You can rent kayaks, canoes, paddleboats and stand-up paddleboards from March to October from the kiosk on the eastern shore of the Green Lake (where there's also a cafe). In March and April it opens weekends only.

GREEN LAKE PITCH & PUTT GOLF

Map p251 (✆206-632-2280; 5701 W Green Lake Way N; adult/child $8/6; ⊙9am-6:45pm Mar-Oct; ♿; ◻62) This nine-hole pitch-and-putt course is a fun spot for short golf if you're just learning or lack the patience or experience to go a full round. It's also kid-friendly.

Ballard & Discovery Park

Neighborhood Top Five

1 **Hiram M Chittenden Locks** (p156) Watching birds, fishing boats, motor yachts, kayaks and salmon negotiating the locks on a sunny summer's evening from the grassy banks of Carl English Jr Botanical Gardens.

2 **Nordic Heritage Museum** (p157) Perusing Ballard's Nordic antecedents in this enlightening museum.

3 **Discovery Park** (p155) Feeling like you've left the city far, far behind in the verdant ocean-side oasis of Discovery Park.

4 **Nano-breweries** (p164) Coming to Ballard on a beer pilgrimage and discovering the neighborhood's remarkable collection of micro- and nano-breweries.

5 **Ballard Farmers Market** (p166) Enjoying Sunday brunch in Ballard Ave NW followed by a visit to the farmers market.

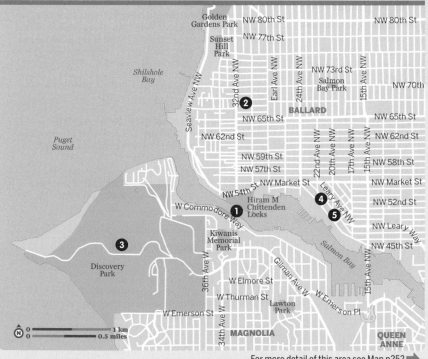

For more detail of this area see Map p252 ➡

Lonely Planet's Top Tip

Don't miss the unconnected western section of the recreational Burke-Gilman Trail that stretches from Hiram M Chittenden Locks out to Golden Gardens Park (1.75 miles) and takes in a different, quieter side of Ballard that faces the open Sound.

⊙ Best Waterside Attractions

➡ Hiram M Chittenden Locks (p156)

➡ Fishermen's Terminal (p156)

➡ Discovery Park (p155)

➡ Golden Gardens Park (p157)

For reviews, see p156 ➡

🍷 Best Drinking & Nightlife

➡ Populuxe Brewing (p163)

➡ Noble Fir (p163)

➡ Hattie's Hat (p164)

➡ Sunset Tavern (p165)

For reviews, see p163 ➡

🍴 Best Places to Eat

➡ Bastille Cafe & Bar (p162)

➡ Walrus & the Carpenter (p162)

➡ Stoneburner (p162)

➡ Geo (p158)

For reviews, see p158 ➡

BALLARD & DISCOVERY PARK

Explore: Ballard & Discovery Park

Though just a bridge away from its big metro brother, Ballard is probably the most distinct and independent of Seattle's neighborhoods, whatever libertine Fremonters or Capitol Hillers might say. There's a self-contained music and drinking scene here and a tangible neighborhood identity, forged out of Ballard's history as a separate city. Founded by hard-working Swedish, Norwegian and Danish fishermen, it was incorporated in 1890 and annexed by Seattle in 1907.

Although the neighborhood's quite spread out, the heart of old Ballard is contained within Ballard Ave NW. This is where you'll find Ballard's notable live-music venues – the Tractor and Sunset Taverns – and some eclectic bars and pubs where you can warm up first. Seven redbrick blocks have been named a Historic Landmark District, but fortunately the buildings have not been thoughtlessly glamorized: the structures in this district are old, not 'olde.'

NW Ave is the other main drag, with a good stash of boutique shops and one-off restaurants, but you've really only seen half of Ballard unless you head west to the Hiram M Chittenden Locks, a beautiful melding of fine engineering and watery Pacific Northwest beauty. Continue on the Burke-Gilman Trail to Golden Gardens Park for more expansive Elliott Bay views.

Discovery Park is 534 acres of urban wilderness northwest of downtown Seattle and just southwest of the mouth of Chittenden Locks. Locals love to come here to escape the ever-present manicure of city gardens and get windswept along the park's many trails. Though it's easy to reach, it feels utterly remote.

Local Life

➡ **Fishermen's Terminal** (p156) Pampering little to the tourist dollar, the home of Seattle's fishing fleet is all about hard work, fresh catch, sea air, and age-old working practices. Drink it in.

➡ **Nano-breweries** You'll feel like you've stumbled into someone's backyard barbecue on a fine summer's evening in the cheery confines of Populuxe Brewing (p163).

Getting There & Away

➡ **Bus** Rapid Ride D-Line is the fastest direct bus into downtown. Metro bus 40 travels from downtown via Fremont to Ballard stopping at multiple places in the neighborhood. For Golden Gardens Park and the Shilshole Marina, take bus 44 from the U District, or express bus 17X from downtown (weekdays only).

CHECUBUS / SHUTTERSTOCK ©

DISCOVERY PARK

A former military installation ingeniously transformed into a wild coastal park, Discovery Park is a relatively recent addition to the city landscape; it wasn't officially inaugurated until 1973. The largest green space in Seattle at 534 acres, its compact cornucopia of cliffs, meadows, dunes, forest and beaches stands as a healthy microcosm of the surrounding Pacific Northwest ecosystems.

Fort Lawton

The peninsula occupied by the park was originally Fort Lawton, an army base established in 1897 to protect Seattle from unnamed enemies. Fort Lawton didn't see much action until WWII, when it was used as barracks for troops bound for the Pacific theater. Over the course of the war it held up to 1400 German and Italian prisoners. When the fort was declared surplus property in the 1960s, the City of Seattle decided to turn it into a park, but various historic buildings from the fort remain.

Orientation & Trails

For a map of the park's trail and road system, stop by the **Discovery Park Environmental Learning Center** (Map p252; ☎206-386-4236; 3801 W Government Way; ◷8:30am-5pm) near the Government Way entrance. Here you can organize educational programs including Saturday nature walks, day camps for children and bird-watching tours. The main walking trail is the 3-mile-long **Loop Trail**, part of a 12-mile network of marked paths. Branch off onto the South Beach trail descending down a steep bluff if you want to view the still-functioning **West Point Lighthouse** (pictured above), a great spot for panoramic views of the Sound and mountains to the west. You can circumnavigate back round to the Loop Trail via North Beach.

Seventeen acres in the north of the park are Native American land and home to the **Daybreak Star Indian Cultural Center**, a community center for the United Indians of All Tribes Foundation (UIATF), a confederation of the many Native American tribes in the Seattle area.

DON'T MISS

➡ Loop Trail

➡ West Point Lighthouse

➡ South Beach

PRACTICALITIES

➡ Map p252, E4

➡ www.seattle.gov/parks/environment/discovery.htm

➡ 🚌33

◉ SIGHTS

Ballard protects a ring of shoreline-hogging marvels – parks, fishing terminals, locks and marinas. Hidden in its suburban grid is one of Seattle's most serendipitous secrets – the fact-packed and wonderfully curated Nordic Heritage Museum.

Discovery Park is technically in the Magnolia neighborhood, but is easily accessible from Ballard via Hiram M Chittenden Locks (by foot or bicycle).

DISCOVERY PARK   PARK
See p155.

FISHERMEN'S TERMINAL   DOCKS
Map p252 (cnr 18th Ave & W Nickerson St; ⬛Rapid Ride D-Line) Seattle's fishing fleet resides at Fishermen's Terminal, in a wide recess in the ship canal called Salmon Bay on the south side of the Ballard Bridge. Fishermen's Terminal is a popular mooring spot because the facility is in freshwater, above the Chittenden Locks; freshwater is much less corrosive to boats than salt water.

It's great fun to wander the piers, watching crews unload their catch, clean their boats and repair nets. Many of these fishing boats journey to Alaska in summer and return to dry dock while they wait out the winter. Outdoor interpretive displays explain the history of Seattle's fishing fleet, starting with the native inhabitants who first fished these waters in canoes. A statue, the bronze Seattle Fishermen's Memorial at the base of the piers, commemorates Seattle fishers lost at sea. This memorial is also the site of the ceremonial blessing of the fleet, held annually on the first Sunday in May.

In the two terminal buildings are some good restaurants specializing in the freshest seafood in Seattle, a general store, a ship chandler and a charts and nautical gifts store. Stop at the Wild Salmon Seafood Market (Map p252; ☎206-283-3366; www.wildsalmonseafood.com; 1900 W Nickerson St; ⊙8:30am-6pm) to buy the freshest pick of the day's catch.

BERGEN PLACE PARK   LANDMARK
Map p252 (cnr NW Market St & Leary Ave NW; ⬛40) In case you forget where you are or the origin of the people to whom Ballard owes its existence, a quintet of flags fly over diminutive Bergen Place Park: those of Norway, Sweden, Denmark, Iceland and Finland, the five so-called Nordic countries. The park was inaugurated by King Olaf V of Norway in 1975 and sports five 'Witness Tree' sculptures.

The community noticeboard gives details of the latest Nordic-themed events – Mrs Lundqvist's meatball cook-off and the like.

★HIRAM M CHITTENDEN LOCKS   LOCK
Map p252 (3015 NW 54th St; ⬛40) Seattle shimmers like an impressionist painting on sunny days at the Hiram M Chittenden Locks. Here, the fresh waters of Lake Washington and Lake Union drop 22ft into saltwater Puget Sound. Construction of the canal and locks began in 1911; today 100,000 boats pass through them annually. You can view fish-ladder activity through underwater glass panels, stroll through botanical gardens and visit a small museum.

Located on the southern side of the locks, the fish ladder was built in 1976 to allow salmon to fight their way to spawning grounds in the Cascade headwaters of the Sammamish River, which feeds Lake Washington. Keep an eye out for the migrating salmon; nets keep them from over-leaping and stranding themselves on the pavement. Meanwhile, sea lions chase the fish as they attempt to negotiate the ladder. The best time to visit is during spawning season, from mid-June to September.

On the northern entrance to the lock area is the Carl English Jr Botanical Gardens, a charming arboretum and specimen garden. Trails wind through beds filled with flowers and mature trees, each labeled. Flanking the gardens is a visitor center (Map p252; ⊙10am-4pm Thu-Mon Oct-Apr, 10am-6pm May-Sep) FREE containing a small museum documenting the history of the locks.

SHILSHOLE BAY MARINA   MARINA
Map p252 (Seaview Ave NW; ⬛44 from U District) The Shilshole Bay Marina, about 2 miles northwest of the Hiram M Chittenden Locks along Seaview Ave NW, offers pleasant views across Puget Sound framed by multiple masts. As Seattle's primary sailboat moorage it also has a glittery collection of boats – millions of dollars worth. Inside the marina, you can

rent sailboats or take classes at **Wind-works** (Map p252; ☏206-784-9386; www.windworkssailing.com).

LEIF ERIKSON STATUE   STATUE
Map p252 (☐44 from U District) Looking out over the modern yachts in the Shilshole Bay Marina is this magnificent statue of the Icelandic explorer and 'discoverer' of America, Leif Erikson, surrounded by a stone circle. The statue is an important reminder of Seattle's (and Ballard's) Nordic heritage: the city claims more Icelandic Americans than anywhere else in the US.

GOLDEN GARDENS PARK   PARK
(8498 Seaview Pl NW; ☐45 from U District) Golden Gardens Park, established in 1904 by Harry W Treat, is a lovely 95-acre beach park with sandy beaches north of Shilshole

Bay Marina. There are picnic facilities, restrooms, basketball hoops, volleyball nets, gangs of Canadian geese, lots of parking and plenty of space to get away from all the activity. The Burke-Gilman Trail (p140) effectively ends here.

Rising above Golden Gardens is **Sunset Hill Park** (NW 77th St & 34th Ave), a prime perch for dramatic sunsets and long views.

★NORDIC HERITAGE MUSEUM   MUSEUM
Map p252 (☏206-789-5707; www.nordicmuseum.org; 3014 NW 67th St; adult/child $8/6; ☉10am-4pm Tue-Sat, noon-4pm Sun; ☐40) Reason alone to come to Ballard – if the beer, fine food and waterside parks weren't enough – is this little gem of a museum dedicated to the brave Nordic pioneers who helped found the neighborhood (then a separate city) in the late

SEATTLE'S NORDIC HERITAGE

Seattle, like many US cities, is ethnically diverse, its population concocted from a complex melange of natives and immigrants, from the original Duwamish tribe to the Hmong flower-sellers of Pike Place Market. In common with the US' Upper Midwest, much of the city's early history was forged by Nordic immigrants from the countries of Norway, Sweden, Finland, Denmark and Iceland. Their arrival in such large numbers wasn't coincidental. The rain-sodden fjords, forests and mountains of Puget Sound coupled with the dominant industries of fishing and logging reminded 19th-century Scandinavian settlers of home; and home it quickly became.

The bulk of Seattle's Nordic immigrants arrived in the late 19th and early 20th centuries, pushed out of their native lands by a lack of good farmland and lured to America by cheap homesteads, higher wages and religious tolerance. Nordics were instrumental in rebuilding Seattle after the 1889 Great Fire and were equally important in the early evolution of Ballard, then a separate city, but eerily redolent of a Norwegian fishing settlement with its burgeoning salmon industry.

Famous Seattle Nordics during this era included John Nordstrom, a Swede, who struck it rich in the Klondike gold rush before turning his nascent Seattle shoe shop into a chain of high-end department stores; Nils Johanson, who founded Seattle's famous nonprofit Swedish Medical Center; and Ivar Haglund, the son of Norwegian-Swedish immigrants who made his name with a still popular fish-and-chip shop called Ivar's Acres of Clams (p55).

Generational cultural assimilation has blunted some of Seattle's Nordic identity in recent years, but thanks to Ballard's fine Nordic Heritage Museum and its affiliated events and festivals, the culture can still be tasted, if you know where to look.

If you're a real Nordic aficionado visit Bergen Place Park (p156), with its five national flags in Ballard, or park your suitcase at Hotel Ändra (p193), a boutique Scandinavian-themed hotel in Belltown with woody minimalist decor and Finnish-designed furniture. Pure Nordic-themed restaurants are thin on the ground, but excellent treats emerge out of Ballard's Larsen's Danish Bakery (p162), known for its Danish pastries, especially its kringles (pretzel-shaped sweet puff-pastry snacks). Seattle also retains a Swedish Club (by Lake Union) and marks Viking Days (p21) in Ballard in August, a celebratory combo of aquavit, music and warriors in horned helmets.

19th century. It brings together a hugely accomplished collection of stories, artifacts and other assorted treasures from Norwegian, Swedish, Finnish, Danish and Icelandic immigrants.

Each country gets their own dedicated room, plus there's a broad trajectory on the ground floor filled with life-size exhibits of the whole immigrant experience from home country via Ellis Island to the Pacific Northwest.

The museum also acts as a heritage center and has regular readings, events and temporary exhibitions from Nordic Americans in the Ballard/Seattle community.

In early 2018, the museum is scheduled to move to a brand-new purpose-built campus on NW Market St closer to the center of Ballard.

EATING

Ballard offers a growing number of reputable places to eat and drink, reflected in its recent penchant for gastropubs and cocktail bars offering shareable 'small plates.' Among its restaurants, Latino cuisine and fresh fish are well represented.

GEO   CUBAN $

Map p252 (☏206-706-3117; www.geoscuban.com; 6301 Seaview Ave NW; sandwiches $9-12; ⊘11am-8pm; 🚌44 from U District) Tucked in between a couple of upmarket fish restaurants just off the Burke-Gilman Trail, this diminutive Cuban-meets-Creole hole-in-the-wall is an ideal stop for knackered cyclists craving a doorstep-sized sandwich made with crisp Cuban bread. The *lechón y chicharrones* (roast pork and crackling) and the shrimp po'boy, between them, ought to provide you with enough energy to cycle off to New Orleans and Havana – and back.

CAFE BESALU   BAKERY, CAFE $

Map p252 (☏206-789-1463; www.cafebesalu.com; 5909 24th Ave NW; pastries from $2.30; ⊘7am-3pm Wed-Sun; 🚌40) Slightly away from Ballard's 'downtown' streets, Besalu lures visitors to its isolated perch on 24th Ave with its French-style baked goods (in particular the croissants and quiches), which some bloggers have hailed as 'better than Paris.'

🏃 Neighborhood Walk
Old Ballard & Beyond

START CONOR BYRNE
END GOLDEN GARDENS PARK
LENGTH 2.5 MILES; 1½ TO TWO HOURS

Redbrick old Ballard is a low-rise version of Pioneer Square and dates from the same era (1890s to 1910s), when Ballard was a separate city with Ballard Ave NW as its 'downtown.' Most of the historic buildings lie in and around this thoroughfare.

To get acquainted with the neighborhood's historic side warm up in ❶**Conor Byrne** (p164) – today an Irish pub – one of Seattle's oldest still-operating taverns. The establishment's first liquor license was granted in 1904, when it was called the Owl, a name that endured through Prohibition, when it was briefly re-branded as a 'cafe.' Name changes aside, it still has its original mahogany bar.

Walk up to the intersection of 20th Ave NW and turn right. On your right is the ❷**Cors & Wegener Building**. Once the offices of the early local broadsheet *Ballard News*, this is one of the most impressive buildings in the area, dating from 1893. An early recipient of Ballard's historical revitalization program, it's now mostly shops, apartments and office space.

Older still is the ❸**Junction Building** (1890) just across the street. Now lacking its decorative 3rd-floor corner turret, the narrow edifice has had all number of reincarnations in its 125-year history from community hall to theater, shop and saloon. It currently houses Macleods Scottish pub.

Get back on Ballard Ave NW and turn right. At the next junction (with Vernon Pl) is the Second Empire baroque–style ❹**Scandinavian American Bank Building**, a fine example of the early-1900s tendency to flatter by imitation: its concrete surface is treated to look like stone. You can still see the 'Bank Building' sign embedded in the top corner. It once housed the flophouse Starlight Hotel but, since 2011, has been home to the more salubrious Ballard Inn.

Continue northwest along Ballard Ave. Of note on the left is the ❺**GS Sanborn**

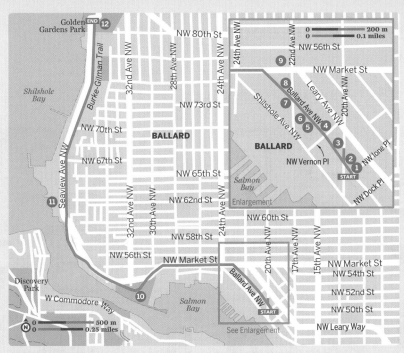

Building, Ballard's only example of Richardsonian Romanesque architecture, a style that was popular on the East Coast in the 1880s. It has a sandstone face and a 3rd-story arch, and housed some of Ballard's key businesses in the early 1900s, including a department store.

A little further on is a small wood-frame **6 house** at No 5341. Constructed around 1880 and predating the 1889 Great Fire, this is one of the oldest surviving buildings in Seattle, rescued and brought here from the International District in the 1970s. Rumor says it was once a bordello.

A great example of the attractive brickwork that embellishes many of the buildings along Ballard Ave, the **7 Portland Building** has housed all kinds of businesses since its construction, including taverns and dry-goods stores. It was given a historically sympathetic face-lift in 1985.

Opposite the Portland Building on the corner of 22nd Ave NW is a **8 Commemorative Bell Tower**. This is the original location of Ballard City Hall, sometimes called 'Hose Hall,' which also contained the jail and the fire-department hose company (hence the nickname). Weakened by earthquakes, the building was demolished in 1965, but the columns and bell were saved and made into this little landmark.

Ballard Ave NW ends at the intersection with NW Market St. Just to the right on the north side of the street stands the **9 Ballard Building**. Ballard's only major terracotta structure, it was built in the 1920s by the Fraternal Order of Eagles. It once held a community hospital and now houses shops, restaurants and cafes.

To truly understand Ballard, you have to prise yourself away from its historic core and digest a bit of its seafaring spirit. Continue west on NW Market St before veering left on NW 54th St. Here you'll find the entrance to the **10 Hiram M Chittenden Locks** (p156), as much an engineering marvel as a waterside attraction, with an interesting visitor center. Back outside the locks and its park, you can pick up the western segment of the Burke-Gilman Trail and follow it to where the ship canal opens out into Puget Sound. If hunger pangs attack, stop at **11 Ray's Boathouse** (p163) for excellent seafood and equitable views. Pass Shilshole Bay Marina on the Burke-Gilman's and head towards this walk's end point, **12 Golden Gardens Park** (p157), with its gorgeous sandy beach.

Seattle Outdoors

Maybe it's the lure of lofty snowcapped Mt Rainier or the sight of calm, kayak-able Lake Union – Seattle has the unnerving habit of turning traditionally sedentary office stiffs into fleece-donning, Lycra-wearing athletes. Wake up and smell the pine needles. They don't call it the Emerald City for nothing.

TUSHARKOLEY/SHUTTERSTOCK ©

BILL HINTON PHOTOGRAPHY / GETTY IMAGES ©

1. Running (p33)
There are good trails for runners, in the urban landscapes and the many city parks alike.

2. Mt Rainier National Park (p184)
Beguiling Mt Rainier offers bountiful activities and views, including this one from Paradise.

3. Discovery Park (p155)
Enjoy 534 acres of urban wilderness.

4. Rowing on Lake Union (p100)
Take to the water to explore a different side of Seattle.

5. Gas Works Park (p145)
A former power station, repurposed as green space.

KARL WEATHERLY / GETTY IMAGES ©

FRELARD

What do you get when you cross offbeat Fremont with Nordic-flavored Ballard? Frelard, according to some facetious Seattleites.

Seattle neighborhoods have always been indistinct, lacking official borders, and this ambiguity is no more apparent than in the warehouse district where western Fremont dissolves into eastern Ballard. Leary Way NW around 43rd and 45th Aves is where the demarcation gets a bit sticky, with some businesses claiming they're in Fremont, others saying they're in Ballard, and a significant portion in the middle say they don't really know – or care. Hale's Ales (p149), one of Seattle's finest microbreweries, is a classic case. Yelp puts it in Fremont, local paper the *Stranger* claims it's in Ballard. In 2015, the debate reached its logical conclusion when notable Seattle restaurateur Ethan Stowell opened a new pizza joint on Leary Way NW called Frelard Pizza Company. All hail the new neighborhood!

LARSEN'S DANISH BAKERY BAKERY $
(www.larsensbakery.com; 8000 24th Ave NW; pastries from $3; ☺5:30am-7:30pm Mon-Fri, 5:30am-7pm Sat, 6:30am-6pm Sun; ▣40) Keeping Nordic culture alive in Ballard is Larsen's Bakery, known for its Danish pastries, especially its *kringles* (pretzel-shaped sweet puff-pastry snacks).

LOCKSPOT CAFE SEAFOOD $
Map p252 (✆206-789-4865; www.thelockspot cafe.com; 3005 NW 54th St; mains $10-15; ☺8am-late; ▣40) The Lockspot is a throwback to old Ballard, before the attempted gentrification. Sit down with the potty-mouthed fishermen and antediluvian grandpas for classic greasy-spoon fare. Even better, order fish-and-chips from the walk-up window outside and take them over to the Hiram M Chittenden Locks to watch the boats go by.

FRESH FLOURS BAKERY, CAFE $
Map p252 (✆206-706-3338; www.freshflours seattle.com; 5313 Ballard Ave NW; pastries $3.50; ☺7am-5pm; ☎; ▣40) With Stumptown Coffee (imported from Portland, OR) and almond croissants so flaky they can seriously damage your laptop, Fresh Flours is a leading player in a strong field of Ballard cafes. The tiny tea cookies hint at a Japanese influence.

★BASTILLE CAFE & BAR FRENCH $$
Map p252 (www.bastilleseattle.com; 5307 Ballard Ave NW; mains $17-29; ☺4:30pm-midnight Mon-Fri, 10am-3pm & 4:30pm-midnight Sat & Sun; ▣40) ✐ French but not at all faux, Bastille could easily pass for a genuine Parisian bistro if it weren't for the surfeit of American accents. First there's the decor: beautiful white tiles juxtaposed with black wood, mirrors and chandeliers. Then there's the menu: *moules* (mussels), *frites* (real French fries), rabbit pâté, oysters and steak (all sourced locally).

STONEBURNER MEDITERRANEAN $$
Map p252 (✆206-695-2051; www.stoneburner seattle.com; 5214 Ballard Ave NW; mains $12-25; ☺3-10pm Mon-Thu, 3-11pm Fri, 10am-11pm Sat & Sun; ▣40) Come and see homemade pasta prepared before your eyes in this new-ish restaurant affiliated with the swanky Hotel Ballard (p196). Pasta-rollers massage dough at workstations in full view of the diners waiting to enjoy the fruits of their labor in Stoneburner's vaguely Parisian-style bistro, a theme that doesn't look out of place in Ballard these days.

Pasta aside, the brunch breakfast pizza and creative vegetable dishes stand out.

WALRUS & THE CARPENTER SEAFOOD $$
Map p252 (✆206-395-9227; www.thewalrusbar. com; 4743 Ballard Ave NW; small plates $11-14; ☺4-10pm; ▣40) Puget Sound waters practically bleed oysters and – arguably – there isn't a better place to knock 'em back raw with a glass of wine or two than the Walrus, a highly congenial oyster bar named not after a Beatles song but a poem by Lewis Carroll in *Through the Looking Glass*. The accolades (like the customers) keep flying in.

LA CARTA DE OAXACA MEXICAN $$
Map p252 (✆206-782-8722; www.lacartade oaxaca.com; 5431 Ballard Ave NW; mains $10-25; ☺11:30am-3pm & 5-11pm Tue-Sat, 5-11pm Mon; ▣40) One of Seattle's better Mexican places, the Oaxaca mixes old hometown

favorites with dishes that don't often make it north of the Rio Grande. Anyone who has been to Guadalajara will know that the *birria* has nothing to do with beer and plenty to do with slow-cooked lamb accompanied by roll-your-own tortillas. Order it and get your fingers dirty.

The other standout dish is the *mole negro Oaxaqueño,* with its rich mole sauce, the measuring stick of any good Oaxacan restaurant.

LA ISLA
PUERTO RICAN $$

Map p252 (☑206-789-0516; 2320 NW Market St; mains $15-21; ☺11am-2am; ☐40) What started as a food stand at Fremont Sunday Market has become this always-packed little restaurant that offers (it claims) the only Puerto Rican cuisine in Washington. As a starter, try the *empanadillas* (little fried dough pockets filled with various savories).

Then proceed to the enormous *pernil* (pulled pork) platter ($17), a huge pile of juicy meat alongside saucy rice, beans, avocados and cheese, plus a couple of piquant sauces. It's hard to beat – you'll be eating it for hours and still be sad when it's gone.

GRACIA
MEXICAN $$

Map p252 (☑206-268-0217; www.gracia seattle.com; 5313 Ballard Ave NW; mains $15-30; ☺11:30am-midnight Mon-Sat, 10:30am-midnight Sun; ☐40) There's been a spike in Mexican eateries in Seattle of late and Gracia is typical of the trend with a lean, interesting menu advertising reimagined traditional dishes using Spanish subheads, eg *antojitos* (little whims), *botanos* (tapa-like snacks). Expect salt-of-the-earth specials including blue tortillas and Veracruz-style fish, along with some decent margarita-accompanying tacos (two for $8).

RAY'S BOATHOUSE
SEAFOOD $$$

Map p252 (☑206-789-3770; www.rays.com; 6049 Seaview Ave NW; mains $28-46; ☺5-8pm Sun-Thu, 5-9pm Fri & Sat; ☐44 from U District) Out in western Ballard near the Shilshole Bay Marina, Ray's is all about placid Olympic Peninsula views, nautical decor and an exhaustive fresh-fish menu. It offers tourists everything they imagine when they think about a nice dinner out in Seattle. Reservations are required and it isn't cheap, but if you can't get in for dinner, at least come for a drink on the sundeck.

CHINOOK'S AT SALMON BAY
SEAFOOD $$$

Map p252 (☑206-283-4665; 1900 W Nickerson St; mains $13-40; ☺11am-10pm Mon-Fri, 8am-10pm Sat & Sun; ☐Rapid Ride D-Line) Across the Ballard Bridge in the Fisherman's Terminal, Chinook's is where fish practically leap out of the water and into the kitchen. You can't get it much fresher than this, and the selection of fish and range of preparations is vast. Watch the fishing fleet coming in from the massive restaurant windows.

🍷⚓ DRINKING & NIGHTLIFE

Ballard is Seattle's beer capital – which is saying something in a city that helped kick-start North America's microbrewing obsession in the 1980s. New bars and restaurants seem to pop up in the space of a lunch break, with fresh competition (a mixture of carefully configured dive bars and trendy gastropubs) standing shoulder to shoulder with the real dive bars of yore. Ballard is also the vortex of Seattle's microbrewing – and, more recently, nano-brewing – revolution.

★POPULUXE BREWING
NANO-BREWERY

(☑206-706-3400; www.populuxebrewing.com; 826b NW 49th St; ☺4:30-9pm Thu, 4:30-10pm Fri, noon-10pm Sat, 1-8pm Sun; ☐Rapid Ride D-Line) 🍷 Microbreweries too large for you? Move down a notch to a nano-brewery. The latest beer craze in Seattle favors the really little guys, such as Populuxe, who carefully nurture their beer barrel by barrel before serving it in pints and growlers from their tiny tasting room in Ballard.

The menu of 10 ever-changing brews is impossible to predict; just bank on it being made with skill, know-how and a whole lotta love. Food carts park outside in the small 'garden,' where you can sit, sup and play cornhole on warm summer evenings.

NOBLE FIR
BAR

Map p252 (☑206-420-7425; www.thenoblefir.com; 5316 Ballard Ave NW; ☺4pm-midnight Tue-Thu, 4pm-1am Fri & Sat, 1-9pm Sun; ☐40) Almost qualifying as a travel bookstore as well as a bar, Noble Fir's notoriously strong ales (up to 14% ABV) might fill you with enough courage to plan a hair-raising trip to the deepest Amazon (the jungle not the dot com), or somewhere equally exotic.

The bright, laid-back bar has a corner nook given over to travel books and maps with packing cases on which to rest your drinks. Snuggle down, drink...and dream!

HATTIE'S HAT   BAR

Map p252 (☑206-784-0175; 5231 Ballard Ave NW; ☺10am-2am Mon-Fri, 9am-2am Sat & Sun; ☐40) As long as there's a Hattie's Hat, a bit of old Ballard will always exist. This classic old divey bar has been around in some guise or other since 1904. It was last revived with new blood in 2009 but hasn't lost its charm – a perfect storm of stiff drinks, fun-loving staff and cheap, greasy-spoon food.

SEXTON   BAR

Map p252 (www.sextonballard.com; 5327 Ballard Ave NW; ☺5-11pm Tue-Thu, 5pm-2am Fri & Sat, 10am-11pm Sun; ☐40) This place is definitively new-school Ballard with a drinks menu that has a strong bourbon and cocktail bias (it's a little pricey, so come during happy hour, from 5pm to 7pm). The interior sports intentionally worn wood and an offbeat bar top made out of old cassettes. Creative, small-plate-style food soaks up the booze.

CONOR BYRNE   PUB

Map p252 (☑206-784-3640; www.conorbyrne pub.com; 5140 Ballard Ave NW; ☺4pm-midnight Mon-Thu, 4pm-2am Fri-Sun; ☐40) A bit of old Ballard they chose to leave behind (or perhaps just forgot about), Conor Byrne is a raffish Irish pub bivouacked in an old terracotta-brick building that has been a bar of some sort since its inception in 1904 (it was briefly reincarnated as a 'cafe' during prohibition). It's best known for its Guinness and regular live music.

KING'S HARDWARE   BAR

Map p252 (☑206-782-0027; www.kingsballard. com; 5225 Ballard Ave NW; ☺3pm-2am Mon-Fri, noon-2am Sat & Sun; ☐40) King's Hardware is like a time capsule from old Ballard, before the hipsters descended – the walls are loaded with taxidermy, the scuffed wooden benches reek of marinated beer and the best in-house art is on people's bodies. You can soak up the hard liquor with some tangy in-house chicken wings.

BALLARD & THE RISE OF NANO-BREWERIES

If you've come to Seattle in search of good beer (smart move!) head directly to Ballard, where the beer-brewing industry commands a level of economic importance once reserved for boat-building and fishing.

At last count Ballard had 10 small-scale breweries, most of them conceived and ignited in the post-recessionary 2010s. Some breweries maintain their own on-site pubs (known as brewpubs), others merely host tap or tasting rooms. Irrespective of the serving arrangements, the latest (and hippest) trend in the Ballard beer universe is downsizing. Microbreweries are being increasingly challenged by nano-breweries, tiny local operations that prefer to ferment high-quality small-batch beers that emphasize fun and creativity over huge profit margins. Run by beer-lovers and hobbyists, and often operating out of garages and warehouses, their modus operandi is subtly different to well-established microbrewers. Instead of knocking out big-hitting flagship beers, the nanos rely on eternally changing seasonal menus of experimental brews and esoteric one-offs produced one or two barrels at a time. Nanos have been known to attract rock-band-like followings of committed beer lovers eager to share in their latest creative endeavors, be it a British-style IPA or a dark, chocolatey stout. With a tangible potluck feel, tap rooms are known for their incredibly laid-back atmosphere. Typical nanos might allow bring-your-own food, and they usually have liberal policies on pets and kids.

For a good introduction to Ballard's small-scale beer world head to venerable Populuxe Brewing (p163), where the limited-hours tasting room has a handful of indoor tables, a rotating menu of around 10 beers and – bonus – a local food truck stationed outside most nights. Should the weather cooperate, you can enjoy an alfresco game of cornhole with your pint parked on a nearby picnic table. Another good diminutive brewer on the cusp of Ballard and Fremont is Bad Jimmy's (p149).

JOLLY ROGER TAPROOM BAR
(206-782-6181; www.maritimebrewery.com; 1111 NW Ballard Way; ⏱noon-10pm Mon-Thu, noon-11pm Fri & Sat, noon-9pm Sun; 🚇Rapid Ride D-Line) A secret treasure tucked away off busy Leary Way, Maritime Pacific Brewing's Jolly Roger Taproom is a tiny, pirate-themed bar with a nautical chart painted onto the floor. These days it's less scurvy-barnacle and more placid-yachtsman, but the beer's still tops – and served in 20oz pints. There are about 15 taps, all serving Maritime Pacific brews, including Jolly Roger Christmas Ale.

MACLEOD'S PUB
Map p252 (206-687-7115; www.macleodsballard.com; 5200 Ballard Ave NW; ⏱4pm-2am; 🚇40) This Scottish-style pub sells the inevitable phone book's worth of whiskey varietals in a bar overlooked by the framed countenances of notable Scots. However, MacLeod's trump card might just lay in its adjacent eating room where they do *real* British fish-and-chips with mushy peas, or – for the ultimate Scottish touch – curry sauce.

BALLARD BEER COMPANY BEER
Map p252 (www.ballardbeercompany.com; 2050 NW Market St; ⏱noon-11pm Mon-Thu, noon-midnight Fri & Sat, noon-9pm Sun; 🚇40) If you really can't decide in which of Ballard's many breweries to rest your tired legs, you can sit on the fence at this new taproom-cum-bottle shop which offers a revolving selection of the neighborhood's best – as well as some local ciders as well.

⭐ ENTERTAINMENT

Ballard claims two of Seattle's most hallowed medium-sized live-music venues.

TRACTOR TAVERN LIVE MUSIC
Map p252 (206-789-3599; www.tractortavern.com; 5213 Ballard Ave NW; ⏱8pm-2am; 🚇40) One of Seattle's premier venues for folk and acoustic music, the Tractor books local songwriters and regional bands, plus quality touring acts. Music runs towards country, rockabilly, folk, bluegrass and old-time. It's an intimate place with a small stage and great sound; occasional square dancing is frosting on the cake.

SUNSET TAVERN LIVE MUSIC
Map p252 (206-784-4880; www.sunsettavern.com; 5433 Ballard Ave NW; 🚇40) One of the two pillars of Ballard's thriving live-music scene along with the Tractor, the recently remodeled Sunset sports a riotously red front bar (no cover) complete with an old-fashioned photo booth (that works) and a small but sizzling music space out back that books great dirty-rock shows of local and touring bands.

🛍 SHOPPING

Ballard is a fun place to browse, especially right along the core of Market St, where there's a little cluster of interesting shops, including a couple of encyclopedic record stores.

⭐BOP STREET RECORDS MUSIC
Map p252 (www.bopstreetrecords.com; 2220 NW Market St; ⏱noon-8pm Tue-Wed, noon-10pm Thu-Sat, noon-5pm Sun; 🚇40) Probably the most impressive collection of vinyl you're ever likely to see lines the heavily stacked shelves of Bop Street Records. The collection of half a million records covers every genre – they even have old-school 78s. No wonder rock stars and other serious musicians make it their first Seattle port of call.

CARD KINGDOM GAMES
Map p252 (www.cardkingdom.com; 5105 Leary Ave NW; ⏱11am-midnight Mon-Fri, 10am-midnight Sat & Sun; 🚇40) Attracting poker players, *Dungeons & Dragons* geeks, kids, board-game enthusiasts and tourists on the rebound from Vegas, Card Kingdom is the games emporium you've been dreaming about. There are plenty of organized activities here, including an on-site games parlor, but you can drop by any time it's open to browse the shelves or play a hand.

The attached Cafe Mox is a popular nook for coffee-sipping chess players.

SONIC BOOM RECORDS MUSIC
Map p252 (206-297-2666; www.sonicboommusic.com; 2209 NW Market St; ⏱10am-10pm Mon-Sat, 10am-7pm Sun; 🚇40) Sonic Boom has a slightly less encyclopedic record collection than Bop Street Records across the street, but it sells concert tickets for local

venues and hosts its own live music most weeks.

BALLARD FARMERS MARKET   MARKET

Map p252 (⊙10am-3pm Sun; 🚇40) Seattle's most popular Sunday market is a genuine produce-only farmers market that sets up in Ballard Ave NW.

MONSTER ART & CLOTHING   ART, CLOTHING

Map p252 (www.monsterartandclothing.com; 5000 20th Ave NW; ⊙10:30am-6:30pm; 🚇40) Local art and clothing shop that sometimes combines both in inspired screen-printed T-shirts.

WILD AT HEART   ADULT

(📞206-782-5538;   www.wildatheartxxonline. com; 1111 NW Leary Way; ⊙noon-10pm Mon-Sat, noon-7pm Sun; 🚇Rapid Ride D-Line) This women-owned shop sells sex toys, fetish-wear, clubwear, lingerie and DVDs. Heavy drapes on the windows keep out prying eyes.

SECRET GARDEN BOOKSHOP   BOOKS

Map p252 (📞206-789-5006; www.secretgarden books.com; 2214 NW Market St; ⊙10am-8pm Mon-Fri, 10am-7pm Sat, 11am-5pm Sun; 🚼; 🚇40) The children's collection at this bookstore, especially the fiction, is excellent, and the staff will order you anything they don't have.

BUFFALO EXCHANGE   CLOTHING

Map p252 (📞206-297-5920; 2232 NW Market St; ⊙11am-7pm Mon-Sat, 11am-6pm Sun; 🚇40) Founded over 40 years ago, the Buffalo Exchange is actually a national chain with nearly 50 US stores specializing in the hipper end of the used clothes market.

🏃 SPORTS & ACTIVITIES

BALLARD BIKE CO   CYCLING

Map p252 (📞206-789-1678; www.dutchbike seattle.com; 4905 Leary Ave NW; bike rental per day $45; ⊙11am-7pm Mon-Fri, 11am-5pm Sat & Sun; 🚇40) The recently renamed Dutch Bike Co has moved premises (a block away), but continues to rent out bikes from their shop close to the west end of the Burke-Gilman cycling trail.

STONE GARDENS:
THE CLIMBERS GYM   CLIMBING

Map p252 (📞206-781-9828; www.stonegardens. com; 2839 NW Market St; ⊙6am-11pm Mon-Fri, 9am-10pm Sat & Sun; 🚇40) This climbing gym has 14,000 sq ft of climbing surface on more than 100 routes. The gym also has weights, lockers and showers. Courses, from beginner climber to belaying, are also offered. The drop-in rate is $17 ($14 for children).

Georgetown & West Seattle

GEORGETOWN | WEST SEATTLE

Neighborhood Top Five

1 **Museum of Flight** (p169) Seeing how Homo sapiens got from the Wright Brothers to Concorde in the space of just 66 years at this illustrious, entertaining and subtly educational museum.

2 **Alki Beach Park** (p170) Slowing down the rhythm a notch on a weekend summer's afternoon on Alki Beach.

3 **Georgetown** (p39) Going on a pub crawl amid the redbrick bars and beer-stained history of this bohemian enclave.

4 **Easy Street Records & Café** (p175) Spending a pleasurable afternoon in the cafe, bar and vinyl-stuffed aisles of West Seattle's legendary record store.

5 **Art Attack** (p171) Investigating surreal and abstract art creations in Georgetown's fabulous monthly arts event.

For more detail of this area see Maps p254 and p255

Lonely Planet's Top Tip

Even Seattle's most rain-hardened brethren would admit that West Seattle is best saved for a sunny day. Visit this hilly, beach-embellished neighborhood in spring or summer and join in the high jinks on ebullient Alki Beach.

✕ Best Places to Eat

➡ Bakery Nouveau (p172)

➡ Fonda la Catrina (p171)

➡ Brass Tacks (p172)

➡ Spud Fish & Chips (p172)

For reviews, see p171 ➡

☕ Best Drinking & Nightlife

➡ Conservatory (p173)

➡ Easy Street Records & Café (p175)

➡ Machine House Brewery (p173)

➡ Jules Maes Saloon (p173)

➡ Elliott Bay Brewery & Pub (p174)

For reviews, see p173 ➡

🔒 Best Places to Shop

➡ Easy Street Records & Café (p175)

➡ Fantagraphics Bookstore & Gallery (p174)

➡ Georgetown Records (p174)

For reviews, see p174 ➡

Explore: Georgetown & West Seattle

Located south of downtown and its industrial extension, SoDo, the neighborhoods of Georgetown and West Seattle feel more detached, cut off from the city center by the glassy expanse of Elliott Bay and SoDo's utilitarian warehouses. Since transportation connections to and from downtown are better than those between the neighborhoods themselves, they're often visited separately. Georgetown can be incorporated with a visit to the Museum of Flight, while West Seattle works as a pleasant summer weekend beach sortie.

Located 3 miles south of Seattle proper, Georgetown is an old neighborhood with a scrappy yet independent artistic sensibility whose coolness has still only been partially discovered. Once you get here (regular buses from downtown take 20 minutes), navigation is easy. Most of Georgetown's pubs, hip bars, funky shops and restaurants are clustered on Airport Way S.

There are plenty of Seattleites who would more likely visit Hawaii than spend a day catching rays in West Seattle. But, although this island-like enclave might feel peripheral in the minds of many urbanites, it's actually only – ahem – 15 minutes from downtown by water taxi. Not that everyone dismisses it. Indeed, among a certain type of Seattleite, West Seattle beckons like a proverbial Coney Island, courtesy of sandy Alki Beach, the city's best excuse to get undressed in public and pretend you're in California.

Spread over a peninsula, the neighborhood spins on two hubs: the de-facto downtown called 'the Junction' at California Ave SW and SW Alaska St (whose indie record store and one-in-a-million bakery alone are worth the visit), and the famous beach and its promenade. Free shuttles from the water-taxi dock connect with both.

Local Life

➡ **Seattle's backyard** When the sun's out, Alki Beach (p170) and its adjacent promenade become Seattle's communal backyard and a good place to play 'guess which neighborhood they're from' with the passing faces.

➡ **Arty inclinations** Mingle with minstrels, painters, posers and beer aficionados as Georgetown exhibits its playful side during its monthly 'Art attack' (p171).

Getting There & Away

➡ **Bus** Metro buses 106 and 124 run frequently from downtown to Georgetown. The 124 carries on to the Museum of Flight. Rapid Ride C-Line runs from downtown to West Seattle.

➡ **Water taxi** Hourly water taxis leave Pier 50 from the downtown waterfront to Seacrest Park in West Seattle. There's no weekend service in the winter.

ELENA_SUVOROVA / SHUTTERSTOCK ©

TOP SIGHT
MUSEUM OF FLIGHT

Chronicling flight history from Kitty Hawk to Concorde, the city that spawned Boeing coughs up one of the nation's finest aviation museums. It's a multifarious affair gluing together a sweep of flying-related memorabilia in several hangar-sized galleries. The exhibits include some of the most ingenious human-made objects that have defied gravity: picture nefarious V2 rockets, Apollo lunar modules and aerodynamic gliders.

DON'T MISS

➡ Aviation Pavilion
➡ X-Pilot simulators
➡ Full Fuselage Trainer
➡ 1903 *Wright Flyer*

PRACTICALITIES

➡ Map p254, A3
➡ 9404 E Marginal Way S, Boeing Field
➡ adult/child $21/13, 5-9pm 1st Thu of month free
➡ ⊘9am-5pm
➡ 🚌124

Great Gallery

The museum's centerpiece is a humongous gallery filled with historic aircraft that overhang exhibits on the history of flight. If you're short on time, jump-cut to the **Tower**, a mock-up of an air traffic control tower overlooking the still operational Boeing Field. Another must is a replica of the Wright Brothers' original 1903 *Wright Flyer*. Nearby, **X-Pilot simulators** pitch you into a WWII dogfight for an extra $9 per person.

Red Barn

Saved in the 1970s when it was floated upriver from its original location 3km away, this two-story red barn dating from 1909 was Boeing's original manufacturing space. It is filled with the early history of flight, with a strong bias toward the Boeing business.

Aviation Pavilion & Space Gallery

The new Aviation Pavilion opened in 2016 and is accessible via a modernist bridge over E Marginal Way. It displays half a dozen iconic planes that you can look inside, including a British Airways **Concorde**; the first jet-powered **Air Force One**, used by presidents Eisenhower, Kennedy, Johnson and Nixon; and a **Boeing 727** prototype. The adjacent Space Gallery was built in 2012 to house the decommissioned **Full Fuselage Trainer** of the Space Shuttle. It costs an extra $30/25 per adult/child to explore the crew compartment.

◉ SIGHTS

◉ Georgetown

MUSEUM OF FLIGHT   MUSEUM
See p169.

HAT 'N' BOOTS   LANDMARK
Map p254 (6427 Carleton Ave S) These two sculptures of a giant cowboy hat and boots are one of those only-in-America roadside attractions that originally embellished a Georgetown gas station in the 1950s – the hat was the pay kiosk, and the boots were the ladies and gents toilets. Obsolete by the 1990s, they lay rotting until foresighted community activists rescued and relocated them to this small local park. Full refurbishments were completed in 2010, meaning the comical cowboy behemoths now look as kitschy as they did in 1954.

GEORGETOWN STEAM PLANT   LANDMARK
Map p254 (✆206-763-2542; 6605 13th Ave S; ⊙10am-2pm 2nd Sat of month; 🚌124) **FREE**
The Georgetown Steam Plant, built in 1906, has one of the last working examples of the large-scale steam turbines that doubled the efficiency of electricity production and shifted the public's view of electricity from a luxury to a standard part of modern living. The plant ceased operations in 1972 and in 1980 was declared a Historic American Engineering Record site.

It's now an education-oriented museum. Note: visiting hours are limited to one day per month.

GEORGETOWN ARTS &
CULTURAL CENTER   ARTS CENTER
Map p254 (✆206-851-1538; www.georgetown artcenter.org; 5809 Airport Way S; ⊙11am-5pm Mon, 10am-4pm Tue & by appointment; 🚌124)
A former dance studio, this community-friendly arts center hosts rotating exhibitions as well as studio space, classes and workshops. It's best visited during Georgetown's monthly 'Art Attack' when it hosts art shows often with an artist in residence.

KRAB JAB STUDIO   GALLERY
Map p254 (www.krabjabstudio.com; 5628 Airport Way S; ⊙1-6pm Fri & Sat) You never know what you're going to get at this small gallery inside the old redbrick Rainier beer factory in Georgetown, which leans heavily toward 'fantasy art.'

At last visit they were displaying a sculpture called *I am the Walrus* depicting scenes from the Beatles song. Krab Jab opens extended hours during Georgetown's 'Art Attack' (6pm to 9pm second Saturday of the month).

TOTALLY BLOWN
GLASSWORKS   ARTS CENTER
Map p254 (✆206-768-8944; www.totallyblown glass.com; 5607 Corson Ave S; ⊙10:30am-4pm Wed-Fri, 10:30am-3:30pm Sat; 🚌124) This glassworks studio and shop makes all its work in-house; if you've never seen a glass-blowing demonstration, it's worth checking out. The studio welcomes spectators whenever it's open and is a popular stop during the monthly 'Art Attack.'

◉ West Seattle

DUWAMISH HEAD   LANDMARK
Map p255 (🚌775 from Seacrest Dock) Popular for its views of Elliott Bay and downtown, this relatively tranquil spot was once painted with a different hue. In 1907 a huge amusement park, Luna Park, opened here. In its days as a loud and over-the-top attraction, the park covered more than 10 acres and hosted the 'longest bar on the bay.' This grand assertion unfortunately led to claims of debauchery and carousing, and the park was eventually closed in 1913 by the conservative powers-that-were.

All that's left of the park are its ruined foundation pillars, visible at low tide.

ALKI BEACH PARK   BEACH, PARK
Map p255 (🚌775 from Seacrest Dock) Alki Beach has an entirely different feel from the rest of Seattle: this 2-mile stretch of sand could almost fool you into thinking it's California, at least on a sunny day, except for the obvious lack of...Californians. There's a bike path, volleyball courts on the sand, and rings for beach fires.

Look for the **miniature Statue of Liberty**, donated by the Boy Scouts. There's also a **pylon** marking Arthur Denny's landing party's first stop in 1851, which for some reason has a chip of Massachusetts' Plymouth Rock embedded in its base.

LOG HOUSE MUSEUM   MUSEUM
Map p255 (✆206-938-5293; www.loghousemu-seum.info; 3003 61st Ave SW; donations accepted; ⊙noon-4pm Thu-Sun; 🚌775 from Seacrest Dock)

GEORGETOWN SECOND SATURDAY ART ATTACK

Georgetown's industrial art scene pulls together on the second weekend of each month at the Georgetown Second Saturday Art Attack. This is the best time to visit the neighborhood's myriad galleries, some of which have rather sporadic opening hours. Almost the entire commercial strip takes part in the monthly event, which runs from 6pm to 9pm and exhibits work in cafes, pubs, galleries and studios. Complimentary drinks and snacks are often laid on.

A unique Georgetown feature is its free 'art ride' bus that runs up and down Airport Way S every 15 minutes between 6pm and 9.30pm. Many of the best galleries inhabit the former Rainier Brewery, including Krab Jab Studio (p170), a shared work space, gallery and shop specializing in fantasy art. The Conservatory (p173) is a cafe with Viennese airs that often hosts authentic live figure-painting. Other places worth visiting are the Miller School of Art (p175) and Georgetown Arts & Cultural Center (p170).

A historical curiosity in Seattle's oldest neighborhood, this museum was built in 1903 from Douglas fir trees as a carriage house for the currently disused Homestead Restaurant a block away. When all around it was moved or demolished to lay out West Seattle, the house miraculously survived and now sits amid a dense urban grid rather than dense forest. It serves as a small museum with revolving historical exhibitions.

ALKI POINT LIGHTHOUSE   LIGHTHOUSE
Map p255 (☑206-217-6123; www.cgauxseattle. org; 3201 Alki Av SW; ⊙1-4pm Sat & Sun May-Sep; ☑775 from Seacrest Dock) FREE The US Coast Guard maintains this lighthouse, which dates from 1913. It has limited seasonal hours but free tours are available when it's open. Check the website for the most up-to-date information.

HIGH POINT   LANDMARK
(cnr SW Myrtle St & 35th Ave; ☑21) This intersection marks the highest point in Seattle, 518ft above sea level. Views from the road crossing aren't astounding, but they get better if you shift over to the nearby **Myrtle Reservoir Park**.

DUWAMISH LONGHOUSE & CULTURAL CENTER   CULTURAL CENTER
(☑206-431-1582; www.duwamishtribe.org; 4705 W Marginal Way SW; ⊙10am-5pm Mon-Sat; ☑Rapid Ride C-Line) Cultural center for Seattle's main Native American tribe built out of cedar wood and located beside the Duwamish River. It's used mainly for cultural events, but displays some historical information and indigenous artifacts.

✖ EATING

West Seattle has two separate eating nexuses: the seaside boulevard backing Alki Beach and the businesses spread along California Ave SW around the so-called 'Junction' with SW Alaska St.

Nearly all of Georgetown's eating joints are on or adjacent to Airport Way S.

West Seattle excels in fish-and-chips; Georgetown serves some good pub grub.

✖ Georgetown

SQUARE KNOT DINER   DINER $
Map p254 (☑206-762-9764; 6015 Airport Way S; breakfast from $6; ⊙6am-11pm; ☑124) A comforting and not too kitschy diner in the middle of Georgetown with booths and a wraparound counter with screw-down stools. The food is no-nonsense – think burgers, breakfasts, hot sarnies and over-dressed salads – but it's cherished by repeat visitors for its epic vanilla milkshake made with Porter beer from the 9lb Hammer (p174) bar next door.

★FONDA LA CATRINA   MEXICAN $$
Map p254 (☑206-767-2787; www.fondalacat rina.com; 5905 Airport Way S; tacos & tamales $9; ⊙11am-11pm Mon-Fri, 10am-midnight Sat, 10am-10pm Sun; ☑124) The search to find a decent Mexican restaurant in Seattle comes to an end in Georgetown in the busy confines of Fonda la Catrina, where Day of the Dead iconography shares digs with Diego Rivera–like murals and – more importantly – fabulous food. Offering way beyond the

standard taco-burrito-enchilada trilogy, this place puts soul into its Latino cooking.

The highlight? One of the best *mole poblanos* this side of the Rio Grande.

BRASS TACKS   AMERICAN $$

Map p254 (☑206-397-3821; www.georgetown brass.com; 6031 Airport Way S; mains $14-25; ⊙11am-10pm Tue & Wed, 11am-11pm Thu-Sat, 10am-3pm Sun; ▣124) Of all the redbrick drinking houses that line Georgetown's Airport Way S, Brass Tacks is the most 'gourmet' place. Here you can sit at the bar and imbibe your beer with creative meat dishes while listening to the resident jazz trio. The standout dish? Not meat, but the brussels sprouts fried with blue cheese, lemon aioli and garlic.

VIA TRIBUNALI   PIZZA $$

Map p254 (☑206-464-2880; www.viatribunali. net; 6009 12th Ave S; pizze $15-19; ⊙11am-11pm Mon-Thu, 11am-midnight Fri, 4pm-midnight Sat, 3-10pm Sun; ▣124) This small Seattle-founded chain operates in four of the city's hipper sanctums (including Capitol Hill and Fremont) plus a couple of foreign enclaves (NYC and Portland, OR). It deals not in pizzas but *pizze*: crisp-crusted Italian pies that are true to the food's Neapolitan roots.

The extensive wine list is 90% Italian and offers some good accompaniments to pizza – try the sparkling red Lambrusco. Come during happy hour (4pm to 6pm) for $6 *pizze* and $3 beer.

✕ West Seattle

★BAKERY NOUVEAU   BAKERY $

Map p255 (www.bakerynouveau.com; 4737 California Ave SW; baked goods from $1.50; ⊙6am-7pm Mon-Fri, 7am-7pm Sat & Sun; ▣Rapid Ride C-Line) No discussion of Seattle's best bakery omits Bakery Nouveau. The crumbly, craggy almond and chocolate croissants are as addictive as other substances far worse for your health.

MARINATION MA KAI   HAWAIIAN, KOREAN $

Map p255 (☑206-328-8226; www.marination mobile.com; 1660 Harbor Ave SW; snacks $3-12; ⊙11am-8pm Mon-Thu, 9am-9pm Fri & Sat, 9am-8pm Sun; ▣Seacrest Dock) What do you get when you cross Hawaiian cuisine with the food of Korea? A Pacific marriage made in heaven if the fish tacos and kimchi quesadillas at Marination Ma Kai are anything to go by.

A former food truck that has sprouted foundations and spawned four brick-and-mortar food outlets, this place right next to the water-taxi dock in West Seattle offers fast service and unique fusion food, but is still true to its mobile roots.

SUNFISH   SEAFOOD $

Map p255 (☑206-938-4112; 2800 Alki Ave SW; fish & chips $6-11; ⊙11am-9pm Tue-Sun; ▧; ▣775 from Seacrest Dock) You haven't really been to Alki until you've tried the fish-and-chips and, for locals, there are two institutions: Spud Fish & Chips and this one. Options include cod, halibut, salmon, fried oysters and clam strips – or combinations thereof. Sit at one of the outdoor tables and enjoy the boardwalk feel.

SPUD FISH & CHIPS   SEAFOOD $

Map p255 (☑206-938-0606; www.alkispud. com; 2666 Alki Ave SW; fish & chips $6-16; ⊙11am-9pm; ▣775 from Seacrest Dock) Spud is as much a piece of West Seattle history as the Log House Museum or the Alki Point Lighthouse, having been in the fish-and-chip business since 1935. The two pieces of battered cod and hand-cut fries is the default dinner, though it also does oysters, clams, prawns and halibut. The downstairs lobby is an intriguing photo-museum of local history.

PHOENECIA AT ALKI   MEDITERRANEAN $$

Map p255 (☑206-935-6550; www.phoenecia westseattle.com; 2716 Alki Ave SW; mains $12-22; ⊙5-10pm Sun-Thu, 5-11pm Fri & Sat; ▣775 from Seacrest Dock) Mediterranean and Middle Eastern food, particularly artisan pizza, is the focus at long-standing Alki Beach staple, Phoenecia. The owner is Lebanese, but the flavors are pulled from as far afield as Italy and Morocco and combined with a bounty of fresh local seafood.

SALTY'S ON ALKI   STEAK, SEAFOOD $$$

Map p255 (☑206-937-1600; www.saltys.com; 1936 Harbor Ave SW; mains $26-46; ⊙11am-9pm Mon-Fri, 8:45am-9pm Sat, 9:30am-9pm Sun; ▣Seacrest Dock) Salty's isn't actually on Alki Beach; rather it is on the other side of Duwamish Head facing Elliott Bay. In any case, the view of the Seattle skyline combined with the deluxe steak-and-seafood menu make this a big enough lure for people all over Seattle. Eschewing the fish-and-chips frugality of the rest of West Seattle, this place is distinctly upmarket.

Choose from a range of succulent steaks or a long list of expertly prepared seafood, both local (crab and salmon) and not-so-local (lobster and rockfish).

🍷 DRINKING & 🍸 NIGHTLIFE

Head to Georgetown, former home of the Rainier beer factory, for a fine selection of redbrick drinking houses, most of which give at least a passing nod to the neighborhood's gritty industrial past.

West Seattle has the beachy charm of a vacation community and is *the* place to go in summer for an ice-cold beer with a beach view. It also has a great record store (p175) where you can sup a beer while you browse.

🍸 Georgetown

★CONSERVATORY   CAFE
Map p254 (☎206-420-3037; www.theconserva toryseattle.com; 5813 Airport Way S; ⊗8am-6pm; 📶; 📵124) Hit this bohemian cafe on the right night and you'll feel as if you've slipped into a Freudian dream and woken

up in 19th-century Vienna. The Conservatory, with its random art easels, mini-skeletons and piles of dusty books, models itself on the European coffee shops of the 1800s. Far more than just a cafe, it hosts regular figure-drawing sessions and other esoteric art happenings.

It's particularly evocative during Georgetown's monthly 'Art Attack.'

MACHINE HOUSE BREWERY   MICROBREWERY
Map p254 (☎206-432-6025; www.machine housebrewery.com; 5840 Airport Way S; ⊗3-9pm Wed-Fri, noon-9pm Sat, noon-6pm Sun; 📵124) If you want to enjoy a beer in Georgetown's erstwhile redbrick Rainier beer factory, head to this minimalist tap room and microbrewery where old-fashioned hand-pumps dispense classic British-style ales that are big on taste but not too high in alcohol per volume. Bonus: it's kid-friendly and shows British soccer games on the big screen.

JULES MAES SALOON   BAR
Map p254 (☎206-957-7766; 5919 Airport Way S; ⊗10am-2am; 📵124) You can pretty much imbibe the beer off the wallpaper in Seattle's oldest surviving pub: it's been offering liquor since 1888, when the city was a youthful 37 years old. Once a speakeasy and allegedly haunted, it still manages a shaky juxtaposition of traditional saloon (pinball

---

A NEIGHBORHOOD BUILT ON BEER

Georgetown's reputation for bohemian bars with blue-collar inclinations rests on solid foundations. The domineering redbrick building that overlooks the commercial strip of Airport Way S was once the center of operations for Rainier beer. Colored by an illustrious history, the Rainier Brewery was founded in 1883 by John Clanser and Edward Sweeny, who had noticed how well hops thrived in the valley. In the early days it was staffed mostly by Germans and Belgians, a fact not particularly evident in the Rainier beer we drink today, but after Prohibition the nation acquired an insatiable taste for the cool golden liquid.

Rainier quickly morphed into the sixth-largest brewery in the world and the neon 'R' sign – now on show at the Museum of History & Industry (p98) – became a pre–Space Needle Seattle icon. When the beer industry was consolidated in the 1970s, the company underwent various takeovers, and the famous brewery closed in 1999 when production shifted to California. But it wasn't all woe. The closure marked the inauspicious start of Georgetown's beatnik renaissance. With parts of the brewery divided up into artist studios, a different kind of drinker started frequenting the neighborhood bars and new businesses opened up to serve them. Nonetheless, some of Georgetown's old-school bars survive, including Jules Maes Saloon, Seattle's oldest drinking hole, founded in 1888, which still sells Rainier beer in bottles.

In 2013, amid a wave of nostalgia, a replica of the iconic 'R' sign was reinstated atop the erstwhile beer factory in recognition of its place in Seattle's history.

and other vintage games) and modern bar (punk rock and tattoos).

SMARTY PANTS
BAR

Map p254 (206-762-4777; www.smartypants seattle.com; 6017 Airport Way S; ⊙11am-midnight Mon-Fri, 9am-midnight Sat, 9am-4pm Sun; 124) This redbrick industrial hangout for scooterists and sport-bike riders has vintage motorcycles propped up in the windows, a hearty sandwich menu ($7 to $9; plus a weekend brunch) and an obvious fondness for two-wheeled mischief of all types. Wednesday is Bike Night, when fans watch the week's recorded races.

ALL CITY COFFEE
CAFE

Map p254 (206-767-7146; 1205 S Vale St; ⊙6am-7:30pm Mon-Fri, 7am-7pm Sat, 8am-7pm Sun; 124) Georgetown's go-to coffee bar serves locally produced Café Vita coffee amid old 1970s office furniture and bizarre 'trashion' art that makes use of half-wrecked skateboards.

9LB HAMMER
BAR

Map p254 (206-762-3373; 6009 Airport Way S; ⊙5pm-2am; 124) This darkened beer hall with its obligatory pool tables is one of Georgetown's more rugged haunts, but the place is generous with the pours and the peanuts. A mixed crowd of workers, hipsters, punks and bikers vacillates between energetic and rowdy.

West Seattle

ELLIOTT BAY BREWERY & PUB
BREWERY

Map p255 (206-932-8695; www.elliottbaybrew ing.com; 4720 California Ave SW; ⊙11am-midnight Mon-Sat, 11am-11pm Sun; Rapid Ride C-Line) Long and narrow, with a loft at the back of the room and a beer garden outdoors, this comfortable brewpub makes a nice retreat after a day at Alki Beach. All the beers are organic and range from the light Luna Weizen to the heavy-hitting Demolition IPA.

The food goes way outside the conventional 'pub grub' box with a pan-seared tofu sandwich and a quinoa garbanzo salad. It even offers burgers topped with beets and blue cheese.

OUTWEST BAR
GAY & LESBIAN

(206-937-1540; 5401 California Ave SW; ⊙4pm-midnight Mon-Thu, 4pm-2am Fri & Sat, 4-10pm Sun; Rapid Ride C-Line) Proof that

you don't need to gravitate to Capitol Hill to enjoy a good gay-friendly neighborhood bar is this laid-back place with cocktails, burgers, DJs and regular karaoke. It's about a mile south of the 'Junction' on California Ave SW.

WEST 5
COCKTAIL BAR

Map p255 (www.westfive.com; 4539 California Ave SW; ⊙11am-midnight Mon-Thu, 11am-1am Fri, 10am-1am Sat, 10am-midnight Sun; Rapid Ride C-Line) Looking like a cross between a diner and a cocktail lounge, West 5's curious formula obviously works – it's been in business since 1966. The long skinny space close to West Seattle's downtown nexus is particularly admired for its mac 'n' cheese, meatloaf and generous happy hour (4pm to 6pm).

SHOPPING

West Seattle's shopping district is clustered around 'the Junction' (corner of SW Alaska St and California Ave SW). Georgetown's art and antique shops line Airport Way S.

Both neighborhoods have excellent independent record stores.

Georgetown

GEORGETOWN RECORDS
MUSIC

Map p254 (206-762-5638; www.georgetown records.net; 1201 S Vale St; ⊙11:30am-8pm Mon-Sat, 11:30am-5pm Sun; 124) This amazing record store had the guts to open in 2004 when vinyl sales were close to an all-time low. With the format now returning to its pre-1990s glory, it's an excellent place to go to score rare picture-cover 45in singles from obscure British 1970s punk bands (and plenty more besides).

Bonuses: it share digs with the equally fantastic Fantagraphics Bookstore & Gallery, hosts in-store performances, and is part of the Georgetown 'Art Attack.'

FANTAGRAPHICS BOOKSTORE & GALLERY
BOOKS

Map p254 (206-658-0110; www.fantagraphics. com; 1201 S Vale St; ⊙11:30am-8pm Mon-Sat, 11:30am-5pm Sun; 124) Founded in the 1970s on the East Coast, this cool alt-comic and graphic-book publisher moved to Seattle in the late '80s and opened this one-of-a-kind bookstore-gallery in 2006. Stocked with quirky books, comics and magazines, and furnished in an exhibition space that hosts monthly shows and readings, it's well worth making a pilgrimage out to Georgetown for.

Don't miss the Damaged Room, with out-of-print and steeply discounted books.

KIRK ALBERT
VINTAGE FURNISHINGS HOMEWARES
Map p254 (www.kirkalbert.com; 5517 Airport Way S; ☺11am-6pm Wed-Sat; ☐124) Not so much stocked as curated, this funky, beautiful store represents the obsessions and tastes of its owner, a designer with a strongly original aesthetic. Come to browse and leave inspired.

🏠 West Seattle

★EASY STREET RECORDS & CAFÉ MUSIC
Map p255 (☑206-938-3279; www.easystreet online.com; 4559 California Ave SW; ☺9am-9pm; ☐Rapid Ride C-Line) Pearl Jam once played at Easy Street, arguably Seattle's most multifarious record store, and the business continues to sponsor regular events. Inside, young kids with elaborate tattoos mingle with graying ex-punks under a montage of retro parking signs and old Nirvana posters. Proving itself to be an invaluable community resource, Easy Street has its own on-site cafe selling food, coffee and beer.

The vegetarian 'Soundgarden burger' goes down nicely with a locally brewed Pike Place IPA and a little bit of Led Zeppelin on the side.

🏃 SPORTS & ACTIVITIES

FLIP FLIP DING DING PINBALL PARLOR
Map p254 (☑206-508-0296; 6012 12th Ave S; ☺noon-midnight Mon-Fri, 4pm-midnight Sat & Sun; ☐124) If golf can qualify as a sport then so can pinball. The game is currently undergoing a renaissance in Seattle (computer games be damned!) and its popularity is exemplified in places such as this wonderfully named bar/pinball emporium, which opened in 2014. Boisterous tournaments kick off most weekends.

RAINIER GLASS STUDIO COURSE
Map p254 (☑206-557-7883; www.rainierglass studio.com; 6006 12th Ave S; classes from $125; ☺11am-7pm Wed-Sun; ☐124) Glass art is quickly becoming synonymous with Seattle (thank Dale Chihuly) and this new nook is a good place to browse, participate or watch the masters in action. It's run by an ex-student of the famous Pilchuck Glass School near Seattle and offers classes in glassblowing as well as an opportunity to fashion your own glass art with an expert.

ALKI KAYAK TOURS CYCLING, KAYAKING
Map p255 (☑206-953-0237; www.kayakalki. com; 1660 Harbor Ave SW; kayaks/bikes per hour $15/10; 🚢Seacrest Dock) You can rent bicycles, stand-up paddle boards and kayaks (March to October) from this outlet whose boathouse is right next to West Seattle's water-taxi dock should you wish to explore Alki by human-powered means. It also offers instruction in water activities and guided kayak excursions (from $49 for two hours).

MILLER SCHOOL OF ART COURSE
Map p254 (www.millerschoolart.com; 1226a S Bailey St; ☐124) To tap into Georgetown's artistic sensibilities, join an art class under the auspices of professional artist Mark Miller. He offers beginners and experimental classes plus painting with hired models. Materials are provided. Prices work out at approximately $25 per hour.

SCHOOL OF ACROBATICS
& NEW CIRCUS ACTS COURSE
Map p254 (☑206-652-4433; www.sancaseattle. org; 674 S Orcas St; drop-ins $15-30; ♿; ☐124) Ever dreamed of running away to join the circus? To prepare yourself, run first of all to Georgetown and book into this innovative school where you can practice the esoteric arts of the high trapeze and juggling. Of interest to visitors are the drop-in classes, especially the two-hour 'Intro to Circus' (2:30pm Saturday; $30).

There's also a slew of kids' activities.

WEST SEATTLE GOLF COURSE GOLF
Map p255 (☑206-935-5187; 4470 35th Ave SW; green fees $35-40) With 18 holes and superior views across Elliott Bay, this is one of the area's best public courses.

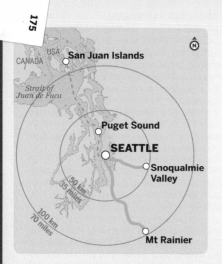

Day Trips from Seattle

Bainbridge Island p177
Worth visiting for the ferry journey alone, Bainbridge is like a detached Seattle suburb where life moves at a distinctly slower pace.

Whidbey Island p177
Gentle green island escape packed with pioneer history, winding lanes and an aura of peace that seems a million miles from downtown Seattle.

Snoqualmie Valley p179
A pastoral agricultural heaven east of Seattle that's renowned for its supersonic waterfall and misty mountainous *Twin Peaks* nostalgia.

Olympia p181
The state capital is smaller and slower paced than Seattle, but has a salubrious collegiate feel and an envelope-pushing music scene.

La Conner p182
Tiny Northwest town that has reinvented itself as an arts community with a strong culinary tradition and a nationally renowned tulip festival.

Mt Rainier p184
The USA's fifth-tallest mountain outside Alaska is an omnipresent Seattle sentinel when the weather's clear and, since 1899, has been encased in an enviably managed national park.

Bainbridge Island

Explore
Bainbridge Island is a popular destination for visitors but also home to over 23,000 Bainbridgers, many of whom commute daily to Seattle. The best way to get there is to do as they do and take the commuter ferry from downtown Seattle, a journey that is often held up as being a secret city highlight allowing you to gaze wistfully upon the Seattle skyline framed by mountains, water and broccoli green islands. With its lanes, lawns and white picket fences, Bainbridge contrasts pleasantly with the clamor of the city. Prepare to stroll around lazily, tour some waterfront cafes, taste unique wines at the Bainbridge Vineyards, 4 miles north of the urban hub of Winslow, and maybe rent a bike and cycle around the invitingly flat countryside.

The Best...
➝**Activity** Bainbridge Vineyards
➝**Place to Eat** Café Nola
➝**Place to Drink** Harbour Public House

Getting There & Away
➝**Washington State Ferries** (Map p232) run several times a day from Pier 52 on Seattle's Waterfront (adult $8.20, car and driver $18.20, bicycle surcharge $1).

Need to Know
➝**Area Code** ⌨206
➝**Location** Bainbridge Island is 9 miles west of Seattle, or 35 minutes on the ferry.
➝**Tourist Office** Get all your island info at the **Bainbridge Island Chamber of Commerce** (⌨206-842-3700; www. visitbainbridge.com; 395 Winslow Way E; ⊙9am-5pm Mon-Fri).

 **EATING & DRINKING**

There are tons of places to eat including upscale restaurants, cafes and delis, and some very special ice-cream shops.

MORA ICED CREAMERY　　ICE CREAM $
(⌨206-855-1112;　　www.moraicedcreamery. com; 139 Madrone Lane; single scoop $4.50; ⊙11:30am-9pm Mon-Thu, to 9:30pm Fri & Sat) Luscious ice creams and sorbets made locally on Bainbridge Island come in cones, cups or pints – and, as a bonus, it's all low-fat.

CAFÉ NOLA　　CAFE $$
(⌨206-842-3822; 101 Winslow Way; mains $14-34; ⊙11:30am-3pm & 5-9:30pm Mon-Fri, 9:30am-3pm & 5:30-9:30pm Sat & Sun) One highlight of a visit to Bainbridge is a meal at this popular bistro, serving a classy blend of Mediterranean and Northwest cooking.

HARBOUR PUBLIC HOUSE　　PUB FOOD $$
(⌨206-842-0969; 231 Parfitt Way; mains $12-19; ⊙11am-11pm Sun-Thu, to midnight Fri & Sat) After your bike ride, sit back and quaff microbrews at this lively public house. Seafood dishes, including the steamed mussels in beer ($15) and a calamari appetizer ($12), are recommended.

🏃 ACTIVITIES

BAINBRIDGE VINEYARDS　　WINE
(⌨206-842-9463;　　www.bainbridgevineyards. com; 8989 NE Day Rd; ⊙tastings noon-5pm Sat-Sun, weekdays by appointment) **FREE** Bainbridge Vineyards near Winslow is a good destination for cyclists or wine-lovers who don't mind a walk – the winery has moved to a place at the edge of its vineyards, about 4 miles north of town on Hwy 305. On Sundays at 2pm there's a tour around the vineyards.

Whidbey Island

Explore
Whidbey Island is an idyllic emerald escape beloved of stressed-out Seattleites. While not as detached or nonconformist as the larger San Juan archipelago further north (there's a bridge connecting it to adjacent Fidalgo Island), life is certainly slower, quieter and more pastoral here. Having six

WORTH A DETOUR

VASHON ISLAND

More rural and countercultural than Bainbridge, Vashon Island has resisted sub-urbanization – a rare accomplishment in the Puget Sound area. Much of Vashon is covered with farms and gardens; the small community centers double as commercial hubs and artists' enclaves. Cascade views abound, with unencumbered vistas of Mt Rainier and north to Baker.

Vashon is a good island to explore by bicycle or car, lazily stopping to pick berries or fruit at a 'U-pick' garden or orchard. You can also hike in one of the county parks.

There are two ways of getting to Vashon Island from Seattle: the **King County Water Taxi** (www.kingcounty.gov/transportation/kcdot/watertaxi/vashon.aspx; Pier 50, Seattle) from Pier 50 on the waterfront ($6.25, 25 minutes) or the car ferry from Fauntleroy in West Seattle (passenger $5.30, car and driver $23.20, 15 minutes).

state parks is a bonus, along with a plethora of B&Bs, two historic fishing villages (Langley and Coupeville), famously good mussels and a thriving artists' community.

Approaching from Seattle, you'll likely dock at Clinton on the south coast from where you can work north diverting through the small settlement of Langley and then heading on to Coupeville (encased in Ebey's Landing National Historical Reserve) and, ultimately, Deception Pass State Park on the island's northern tip. Rather than retracing your steps, it's possible to return to Seattle by tracking back across Fidalgo Island and cruising east on Hwy 20.

The Best...

→**Sight** Ebey's Landing National Historical Reserve (p179)

→**Place to Eat** Christopher's (p179)

→**Place to Drink** Toby's Tavern (p179)

Getting There & Away

→**Ferry** Services from Washington State Ferries run between Mukilteo, 25 miles north of Seattle and Clinton on the island (car and driver $10.80, passenger free). The crossing takes 20 minutes.

→**Bus** Frequent services are offered by **Seatac Shuttles** (☑877-679-4003; www. seatacshuttle.com) to nine locations on Whidbey Island from Sea-Tac (one way $41). Prepaid reservations are required.

Getting Around

Island Transit (☑360-678-7771; www.island transit.org) is a community-financed scheme running buses daily except Sunday, from the Clinton ferry dock to Greenbank, Coupeville, Oak Harbor and Deception Pass. Other routes reach the Keystone ferry dock and Langley on weekdays. Service is hourly and free.

Need to Know

→**Area Code** ☑360

→**Location** Whidbey Island is 26 miles north of Seattle with a journey time of one hour including drive and ferry.

→**Tourist Office** There's a **visitor information center** (☑360-678-5434; www. centralwhidbeychamber.com; 23 NW Front St; ☺10am-5pm) in the town of Coupeville.

◉ SIGHTS

DECEPTION PASS STATE PARK   PARK

(☑360-675-2417; 41229 N State Hwy 20) Deception Pass State Park straddles the eponymous steep-sided water chasm that flows between Whidbey and Fidalgo Islands, and incorporates lakes, islands, campsites and 27 miles of hiking trails. This area is also one of the best places in Washington to spot orcas from the shore, so keep an eye out to sea!

ISLAND COUNTY HISTORICAL SOCIETY MUSEUM   MUSEUM

(908 NW Alexander St; $4; ☺10am-5pm May-Sep, to 4pm Fri-Mon Oct-Apr) The island's most comprehensive museum has plenty of local historical testimonies showcased in meticulous and well-presented display cases. Also on offer are self-guided walking-tour maps of Coupeville's vintage homes. The helpful staff can also enlighten you on the highlights of Ebey's Landing National Historical Reserve.

WHIDBEY'S GREENBANK
BERRY FARM FARM
(www.greenbankfarm.com; Hwy 525, off Wonn Rd; ⊙10am-5pm) Go 10 miles south of Coupeville to find this winery-style farm that's open daily for touring, tasting and picnicking. Don't miss a stop in the cafe for the island's best fruit pies (slices $5).

 **EATING & DRINKING**

CHRISTOPHER'S SEAFOOD **$$**
(📞360-678-5480; www.christophersonwhidbey.com; 103 NW Coveland St; mains $16-25; ⊙11:30am-2pm & 5pm-close) The mussels and clams are the best in town (no mean feat in Coupeville), and the seafood alfredo pasta is wonderfully rich.

KNEAD & FEED BAKERY **$$**
(4 Front St; meals $10-18; ⊙9am-3pm Mon-Sat) A Coupeville classic with views over the water from homey, rustic wood tables. Upstairs is for pastries and coffee while full meals (from American breakfasts to sandwiches and soups) are served downstairs. Don't miss the clam chowder or marionberry pie!

TOBY'S TAVERN PUB FOOD **$$**
(www.tobysuds.com; 8 Front St; mains $15-23; ⊙11am-9pm Sun-Thu, to 10pm Fri & Sat) A quintessential Coupeville dive bar housed in a vintage mercantile building dating from the 1890s; even the polished back bar was originally shipped here from around Cape Horn in 1900. Quaff home-produced microbrews and enjoy a menu spearheaded by local classics such as fantastic mussels, clam strips, and halibut and chips, while listening to the jukebox or shooting pool.

CAFE LANGLEY MEDITERRANEAN **$$**
(www.cafelangley.com; 113 1st St; lunch around $10, dinner $16-24; ⊙11:30am-2:30pm & 5-8:30pm Mon & Wed-Sat, to 3pm Sun) Mediterranean cuisine, with a few deft Northwestern seafood infusions (eg mussels) thrown in for good measure. Located in the settlement of Langley.

USELESS BAY COFFEE ROASTERS CAFE
(121 Second St; ⊙7:30am-4:30pm) You'll notice the rustic smell of roasting beans long before you see this place in Langley. The vast, industrial-meets-1950s diner interior spills out to outdoor picnic tables. The coffee is great as are the burgers and sandwiches (around $10). Any food preferences from gluten- to dairy-free are very well catered to.

Snoqualmie Valley

Explore

East of Seattle's Eastside, the Snoqualmie Valley has long been a photogenic backwater of dairy farms, lush orchards and produce gardens surrounded by steep alpine peaks. Although suburbs are quickly taking

EBEY'S LANDING NATIONAL HISTORICAL RESERVE

This National Historical Reserve was the first of its kind in the nation when it was created in 1978 in order to preserve Whidbey Island's historical heritage from the encroaching urbanization that had already partly engulfed Oak Harbor. Ninety percent privately owned, **Ebey's Landing** (📞360-678-6084; www.nps.gov/ebla; 162 Cemetery Rd) comprises 17,400 acres encompassing working farms, four historic blockhouses, two state parks and the town of Coupeville itself. A series of interpretive boards shows visitors how the patterns of croplands, woods (or the lack of them) and even roads reflect the activities of those who have peopled this scenic landscape, from its earliest indigenous inhabitants to 19th-century settlers.

The Island County Historical Society Museum (p178) in Coupeville distributes a brochure on suggested driving and cycling tours through the reserve. Highly recommended is the 3.6-mile **Bluff Trail** that starts from a small parking area at the end of Ebey Rd. The energetic can walk or cycle here from Coupeville (approximately 2.5 miles along a quiet road), thus crossing the island at one of its narrowest points.

Other recreational activities here include scuba diving, boating and birdwatching – best along Keystone Spit on the southwestern tip of Crockett Lake.

over the valley, there's still enough of a low-key rural ambience to make it feel as if you're coming up for air after the tumult of Seattle.

This trip works best as a drive linking a quintet of small towns starting in the south in North Bend with its *Twin Peaks* TV nostalgia before progressing northwest through Snoqualmie (and its incredible waterfall), Carnation and Duvall, to Woodinville. Using the quieter Hwys 202 and 203, you'll log up 33 miles.

The Best...

➡ **Sight** Snoqualmie Falls

➡ **Place to Eat** Herbfarm

➡ **Place to Drink** Twede's

Getting There & Away

➡ **Bus** Run by King's County Metro (p219), bus 208 runs from Seattle to North Bend on weekdays.

➡ **Car** By road, take I-90 east out of Seattle turning off at exit 31 for North Bend.

Need to Know

➡ **Area Code** ☑425

➡ **Location** Snoqualmie is 31 miles east of Seattle (30 to 40 minutes' driving time).

➡ **Tourist Office** The main tourist information center is the **Snoqualmie Valley Visitors Center** (www.snovalley. org; 38767 SE River Street) in the town of Snoqualmie.

⊙ SIGHTS

The following sights are arranged south to north starting in North Bend.

NORTH BEND   TOWN

North Bend, on Hwy 202 just off I-90, is *Twin Peaks* country, the setting for David Lynch's surreal TV series from the early 1990s. It also sports the **Northwest Railway Museum** (www.trainmuseum.org; 38625 SE King St; ⊙10am-5pm) **FREE** housed in a Victorian-era train depot, that displays the history of rail in the area.

SNOQUALMIE   TOWN

Continue along Hwy 202 to the little town of Snoqualmie, where you'll find antique shops and a store devoted to Northwest wines.

Just north of town, **Salish Lodge & Spa** (☑800-826-6124, 425-888-2556; www.salish lodge.com; 6501 Railroad Ave; d from $195; ☎⊛) is a beautiful resort that sits atop 268ft Snoqualmie Falls. *Twin Peaks* fans know the hotel as the Great Northern; the exterior of the lodge appeared in the opening credits, and an observation point near the parking lot offers the same view. Visitors can also see the falls from the lodge's dining room or hike to them along a winding trail.

CARNATION   TOWN

Hwy 203 branches off from 202 at Fall City; follow it north to Carnation, where the Snoqualmie and Tolt Rivers meet at John McDonald Park. This is a great place for a riverside picnic, swim or hike. Carnation was once the center of the valley's dairy industry, and several farms here sell fruit and vegetables at roadside stands.

DUVALL   TOWN

Duvall, about 25 miles north of North Bend along Hwys 202 and 203, has a rural small-town atmosphere despite its recent growth spurt. Wander Main St and check out the shops and nurseries.

WOODINVILLE   TOWN

Head west on Woodinville–Duvall Rd for about 10 miles to reach Woodinville, home of several good wineries. There's a trail along the Sammamish River, if you fancy walking it off. From here it's a quick drive along I-405 back to Seattle.

✕ EATING

TWEDE'S   AMERICAN $$

(137 W North Bend Way; burgers from $10.50; ⊙6:30am-8pm) North Bend's former Mar T's Cafe, now called Twede's, was the diner with the famous cherry pie and cups of joe in *Twin Peaks*; a fire gutted it in 2000, but it has been rebuilt and is still a good place for lunch or a mediocre slice à la mode.

★HERBFARM   AMERICAN $$$

(14590 NE 145th St; dinner $180-200; ⊙7pm Thu-Sat, 4:30pm Sun) At this legendary, very-very-upscale restaurant in Woodinville, nine-course dinners are drawn from the gardens and farm itself, as well as small local growers, and matched with locally produced wines.

WORTH A DETOUR

FUTURE OF FLIGHT AVIATION CENTER & BOEING TOUR

One of the Seattle area's most worthwhile outlying sights is the **Future of Flight Aviation Center & Boeing Tour** (☑1-800-464-1476; www.futureofflight.org; 8415 Paine Field Blvd; adult/child $20/14; ◷8:30am-5:30pm, tours 9am-3pm) in the city of Everett, 25 miles north of Seattle. Serving as a good complement to Georgetown's Museum of Flight, the center, aside from its museum, offers a tour of the real working Boeing factory where the famous airplanes are made. The huge complex is the world's most voluminous building, meaning that the 90-minute tours involve plenty of traveling around, some of it by bus.

Future of Flight can be combined with a visit to Whidbey Island; the complex is situated on the mainland 2 miles south of the Mukilteo ferry dock. Alternatively you can take an organized tour direct from Seattle with **Tours Northwest** (☑20 6-768-1234; www.toursnorthwest.com), who pick up from downtown hotels. It charges $79/59 per adult/child, including admission. No cameras are allowed.

Olympia

Explore

Small in size but big in clout, state capital Olympia is a political, musical and outdoor powerhouse that punches well above its 48,000-strong population. Look no further than the street-side buskers on 4th Ave, the smartly attired bureaucrats marching across the lawns of the resplendent state legislature or the Gore-Tex-clad outdoor fiends overnighting before rugged sorties into the Olympic Mountains.

Dedicate several hours to admire the expansive legislative campus both inside and out before strolling down to the watery docks of Percival Landing allowing stops to sample the local coffee and oysters. Those with a penchant for alt-rock music genres should hit the dive bars and secondhand-guitar shops of downtown, places that, in the 1990s, were the original pulpits for riot-grrrl and grunge.

The Best...

➡**Sight** Washington State Capitol

➡**Place to Eat** Traditions Cafe & World Folk Art (p182)

➡**Place to Drink** Batdorf & Bronson (p182)

Getting There & Away

➡**Bus** Three Greyhound buses a day link Olympia to Seattle ($11, 1½ hours).

➡**Train** Amtrak Cascade and Coast Starlight trains stop at Centennial Station in Lacey. Five trains a day link Olympia with Seattle ($18). Bus 64 goes between the station and downtown hourly 6:30am to 7:30pm.

Need to Know

➡**Area Code** ☑360

➡**Location** The city of Olympia is 61 miles southwest of Seattle.

➡**Tourist Office** The **State Capitol Visitor Center** (☑360-704-7544; www.visitolympia.com; 103 Sid Snyder Ave SW; ◷10am-3pm Mon-Fri, 11am-3pm Sat & Sun) offers information on the capitol campus, the Olympia area and Washington State. Note the limited opening hours.

◉ SIGHTS

WASHINGTON STATE CAPITOL LANDMARK
(☑360-902-8880; 416 Sid Snyder Ave SW; ◷7am-5:30pm Mon-Fri, 11am-4pm Sat & Sun) **FREE** Olympia's capitol complex is set in a 30-acre park overlooking Capitol Lake with the Olympic Mountains glistening in the background. The campus's crowning glory is the magnificent **Legislative Building**. Completed in 1927, it's a dazzling display of craning columns and polished marble, topped by a 287ft dome that is only slightly smaller than its namesake in Washington, DC. Tours are available.

As well as the Legislative Building, visitors are welcome to peek inside both the Supreme Court or Temple of Justice, flanked by sandstone colonnades and lined inside by yet more marble, and the Capitol Conservatory, which hosts a large collection of tropical and subtropical plants.

The oldest building on the campus is the Governor's Mansion, built in 1908. The home of the governor is open for tours only on Wednesday; call to reserve a space. Outdoor attractions include the Vietnam War Memorial, a sunken rose garden, a replica of the Roman-style fountain found in Copenhagen's Tivoli Park, plus a Story Pole carved by Chief William Shelton of the local Snohomish tribe in 1938. The manicured grounds are an attraction in themselves, and a well-marked path zigzags down to Capitol Lake, where it connects with more trails.

STATE CAPITAL MUSEUM   MUSEUM
(☑253-272-3500; 211 21st Ave SW; $2; ⊙10am-4pm Tue-Sat, from noon Sun) This premier museum is housed in the 1920s Lord Mansion, a few blocks south of the campus, and preserves the general history of Washington State from the Nisqually tribe to the present day. At the time of research it was undergoing renovations.

PERCIVAL LANDING PARK   PARK
When Olympia was founded, its narrow harbor was a mudflat during low tides, but after years of dredging, a workable harbor was established. This park is essentially a boardwalk that overlooks the assembled pleasure craft and provides informative display boards describing Olympia's past as a shipbuilding port and a center of the lumber and cannery trades.

✕ EATING & DRINKING

Few places in the Pacific Northwest have as many good vegetarian or veg-friendly restaurants as Olympia. The city is also renowned for its delicate Olympic oysters, myriad ethnic eateries and cheap brunches.

TRADITIONS CAFE &
WORLD FOLK ART   HEALTH FOOD $
(☑360-705-2819; www.traditionsfairtrade.com; 300 5th Ave SW; sandwiches $9-10; ⊙9am-6pm Mon-Fri, 10am-6pm Sat, 11am-5pm Sun; ☑) ✐ This fair-trade hippy enclave offers fresh salads (lemon-tahini, smoked salmon etc), sandwiches (meat, veggie and vegan), a few Mexican and Italian plates, coffee drinks, herbal teas and local ice cream. Attached is an eclectic folk-art store. Check the website for music, poetry nights and more.

DARBY'S CAFÉ   DINER $
(211 5th Ave SE; lunch mains around $10; ⊙7am-9pm Wed-Fri, 8am-9pm Sat & Sun; ☑) This glorified greasy spoon on 5th isn't very greasy at all and pays equal respect to vegetarians and vegans. Unfussy food is served at a leisurely pace and without frills (often by tattooed waitstaff), but the breakfast scrambles, hash browns, and biscuits and gravy have garnered a loyal following.

The decor is self-described as 'halfway between a diner and a dive,' but you can call it 'quirky.'

SPAR CAFE BAR   PUB, DINER $
(114 4th Ave E; breakfast $5-9, lunch $7-12; ⊙7am-midnight) A legendary local cafe and eating joint now owned by Portland's McMenamin brothers, who have maintained its authentic wood-panel interior. You could spend all morning here eating brunch, shooting pool, admiring the cigar collections and discussing the latest music trends. Come back later for some of the real thing – live.

OYSTER HOUSE   SEAFOOD $$
(320 W 4th Ave; seafood dinners $15-25; ⊙11am-11pm, to midnight Fri & Sat) As you'd guess, this place specializes in Olympia's most celebrated cuisine, the delicate Olympia oyster, best served panfried and topped with a little cheese and spinach. Try them with the surprisingly delicious potato skins in a booth overlooking the placid harbor.

BATDORF & BRONSON   CAFE
(Capitol Way S; ⊙6am-7pm Mon-Fri, 7am-6pm Sat & Sun) ✐ Olympia's most famous coffee outlet is notably good, even in the caffeine-fueled Pacific Northwest. If you like your morning brew fair trade, shade grown and certified organic, this is the place to come. For travelers with an insatiable caffeine addiction, head down to the company's new roasting house for expert banter.

La Conner

....

Explore

Home of outlandishly colorful tulip fields and an out-of-the-box artist's community (abstract writer Tom Robbins lives here if that's any measuring stick), La Conner is arguably northwest Washington's most enticing small town, full of riverside charm, classy B&Bs and arty, boutique-style shops. Once a forgotten port, tourism has saved the day; it's now a favorite rural retreat for nature-loving Seattleites.

The zenith of La Conner's cultural calendar is the annual **tulip festival** (www.tulipfestival.org; ☉Apr). This is either the best or worst time to visit, depending on your traffic tolerance levels.

Start your exploration in the town itself perusing a trio of interesting museums before heading into the surrounding countryside for large doses of flower power, most notably at the Roozengaarde Display Garden.

....

The Best...
➡ **Sight** Roozengaarde Display Garden
➡ **Place to Eat** Seeds Bistro & Bar
➡ **Place to Drink** La Conner Brewing Co (p184)

....

Getting There & Away
➡ **Car** The quickest way to get from Seattle to La Conner is to drive north on I-5 before branching west at exit 221.
➡ **Bus** The Bellair Airporter Shuttle (p214) stops at the La Conner-Whitney gas station 4 miles north of La Conner. You can take a local bus or walk from here.

....

Need to Know
➡ **Area Code** ☑360
➡ **Location** La Conner is 66 miles north of Seattle (just over 1½ hours driving).
➡ **Tourist Office** Pick up helpful maps at **La Conner Chamber of Commerce** (www.laconnerchamber.com; Morris St; ☉10am-4pm Mon-Fri, 11am-2pm Sat).

◉ SIGHTS

★ROOZENGAARDE
DISPLAY GARDEN   GARDENS
(www.tulips.com; 15867 Beaver Marsh Rd, Mt Vernon; $5; ☉9am-6pm Mon-Sat, 11am-4pm Sun) Halfway between La Conner and Mt Vernon, this renowned bulb producer has color-drenched fields of blooms as well as a truly spectacular display garden with an

eye-boggling array of bulb varieties blooming in unison. With Mt Baker and a Dutch-inspired windmill glimmering in the background, photo opportunities abound! It's well worth the admission price and crowds.

MUSEUM OF NORTHWEST ART   MUSEUM
(www.monamuseum.org; 121 S 1st St; ☉10am-5pm Tue-Sat, noon-5pm Sun & Mon) **FREE** This art gallery endeavors to portray the 'special Northwest vision' through the works of representative artists. The ground floor is dedicated to changing shows by regional artists, while the upstairs space houses pieces from the permanent collection.

**SKAGIT COUNTY
HISTORICAL MUSEUM**   MUSEUM
(www.skagitcounty.net/museum; 501 S 4th St; adult/child $5/4; ☉11am-5pm Tue-Sun) Perched atop a hill that affords impressive views of Skagit Bay and the surrounding farmlands, this place presents indigenous crafts, dolls, vintage kitchen implements and other paraphernalia used by the region's early inhabitants.

✕ EATING & DRINKING

CALICO CUPBOARD   BAKERY $
(www.calicocupboardcafe.com; 720 S 1st St; ☉7:30am-4pm Mon-Fri, to 5pm Sat & Sun) The size of the cinnamon buns here beggars belief, and their quality (there are four specialist flavors) is equally good. Factor in a 10-mile run through the tulip fields before you tackle one and you should manage to stave off instant diabetes. The rest of the goods are also highly addictive. Try the bread pudding, flans, omelets or light lunches.

If the line is too long here, there's another branch in Anacortes.

SEEDS BISTRO & BAR   MODERN AMERICAN $$
(☑360-466-3280; www.seedsbistro.com; 623 Morris St; mains $12-26; ☉11am-9pm; ☑) Calling itself the 'seediest place in the valley,' farm-to-table Seeds serves all the fresh produce, fish and meats you'd hope for, all in brunch-cafe-style friendliness. The menu includes everything from creative salads to Samish Bay oysters and char-broiled pork tenderloin, and vegetarians and gluten-free folks are well catered for.

Finish your meal with a slice of homemade berry pie.

The best time to visit is happy hour (3pm to 6pm daily) when you can sample several $8 to $10 plates of the restaurant's specialties.

LA CONNER BREWING CO BREWERY
(www.laconnerbrewery.com; 117 S 1st St; ⏰11:30am-10pm Sun-Thu, to 11pm Fri & Sat) A polished pine pub that manages to combine the relaxed atmosphere of a cafe with the quality beers (including IPA and stout) of an English drinking house. Bonuses include wood-fired pizzas (from $10), fresh salads and six homebrews on tap.

Mt Rainier

Explore

The USA's fourth-highest peak (outside Alaska), majestic Mt Rainier is also one of its most beguiling. Encased in a 368-sq-mile national park (the nation's fifth national park when it was inaugurated in 1899), the mountain's snowcapped summit and forest-covered foothills boast numerous hiking trails, swaths of flower-carpeted meadows and an alluring peak that presents a formidable challenge for aspiring climbers.

🛈 PARK INFORMATION

For information on Mt Rainier National Park check out the National Park Service website at www.nps.gov/mora, which includes downloadable maps and descriptions of 50 park trails.

Park entrance fees are $20 per car and $10 for pedestrians and cyclists (those under 17 are admitted free), and are valid for seven days from purchase. A $40 annual pass admits the passholder and accompanying passengers for 12 months from date of purchase.

The driving loop around the mountain is 147 miles (driving time is about five hours without stops) and the main roads are usually open mid-May through October.

The park's Nisqually entrance in its southwestern corner is its most developed (and hence most visited) area.

Hwy 706 enters the park about an hour and a half's drive southeast of Seattle, just past Ashford and adjacent to the Nisqually River. After the entry tollbooth, a well-paved road continues east past Longmire, the park's first orientation point, to the elevated alpine meadows of Paradise, where you'll find the area's biggest and best information center–museum.

The Best...
→**Sight** Paradise (p185)
→**Place to Eat** Copper Creek Inn (p186)
→**Place to Drink** Mountain Goat Coffee (p186)

Getting There & Away
→For the most part you're best off driving yourself, although there are also tour options out of Seattle.
→**Car** Drivers should head south of Seattle on Hwy 167 and Hwy 161 and enter the park at the Nisqually entrance on Hwy 706.

Getting Around
Between June and September the **Paradise Shuttle** runs between Longmire and Paradise Friday to Sunday. There's an onward link to Ashford outside the park gates on Saturday and Sunday only. The shuttle runs every 45 minutes on Friday and every 20 minutes on Saturday and Sunday.

Need to Know
→**Area Code** 🗷360
→**Location** 92 miles (two hours) southeast of Seattle.
→**Tourist Office** In Longmire, the museum (p185) can field basic questions. The Henry M Jackson Visitor Center (p185) in Paradise is the best place to get answers.

🔘 SIGHTS

Of the park's four entrances, Nisqually is the most accessible from Seattle and the only one open year-round. Also popular is

HIKING IN MT RAINIER NATIONAL PARK

Rainier's textbook long-distance hike is the 93-mile **Wonderland Trail** that completely circumnavigates the mountain with a cumulative elevation gain of 21,400ft. Longmire is its most popular starting point, with the majority of hikers tackling the route over 10 to 12 days in a clockwise direction in July or August. There are 18 backcountry campsites en route.

For a shorter hike from Longmire you can test your mettle on the precipitous **Eagle Peak Trail**, a steep 7.2-mile out-and-back hike. A more laid-back look at some old-growth forest and pastoral meadows is available on the signposted **Trail of the Shadows Loop**, a 0.8-mile trail that begins across the road from the museum and is wheelchair accessible for the first 0.4 miles.

Paradise, situated at 5400ft, has a much shorter hiking season than Longmire (snow can persist into late June), but its wildflower pastiche, which includes avalanche lilies, western anemones, lupines, mountain bog gentians and paintbrushes, make the experience spectacular.

The Paradise area is crisscrossed with trails of all types and standards, some good for a short stroll (with the kids), others the realm of more serious hikers. To get a close-up of the Nisqually Glacier follow the 1.2-mile **Nisqually Vista Trail**. For something more substantial hike the 5-mile **Skyline Trail**.

Intrepid day-hikers can continue up the mountain from Panorama Point via the **Pebble Creek Trail** to the permanent snowfield track that leads to **Camp Muir**, the main overnight bivouac spot for climbing parties. At 10,000ft, this hike is not to be undertaken lightly. Take sufficient clothing and load up with a good supply of food and water.

the Ohanapecosh (o-*ha*-nuh-peh-*kosh*) entrance in the park's southeastern corner accessed by the small settlement of Packwood, 12 miles to the southwest on US 12.

★ **PARADISE**   AREA

Aside from hiding numerous trailheads and being the starting point for most summit hikes, Paradise guards the iconic Paradise Inn (built in 1916) and the massive, informative **Henry M Jackson Visitor Center** (☑360-569-6571; ⊙10am-7pm mid-Jun–Sep, to 5pm May & Oct, weekends only in winter), that holds a cutting-edge museum with hands-on exhibits on everything from flora to glacier formation and shows a must-see 21-minute film entitled *Mount Rainier: Restless Giant*.

Park naturalists lead free interpretive hikes from the visitor center daily in summer, and snowshoe walks on winter weekends.

The daughter of park pioneer James Longmire unintentionally named this high mountain nirvana, when she exclaimed what a paradise it was on visiting this spot for the first time in the 1880s. Suddenly, the high-mountain nirvana had a name, and a very apt one at that. One of the snowiest places on earth, 5400ft-high

Paradise remains the park's most popular draw, with its famous flower meadows backed by dramatic Rainier views on the days (a clear minority annually) when the mountain decides to take its cloudy hat off.

LONGMIRE INFORMATION CENTER & MUSEUM   HISTORIC BUILDING

(☑360-569-6575; ⊙9am-4:30pm May-Jul) The National Park Inn has stood here since 1917 – built in classic 'parkitecture' style – and is complemented by a small store, park offices, the tiny, free Longmire Museum and a number of important trailheads. James Longmire first came here in 1883 and noticed the hot mineral springs that bubbled up in a lovely meadow opposite the present-day National Park Inn.

The next year he established Longmire's Medicinal Springs, and in 1890 he built the Longmire Springs Hotel.

✖ EATING

Fresh produce from the surrounding fields and seafood from Washington's shores are served with pride all around town.

★COPPER CREEK INN   AMERICAN $$
(www.coppercreekinn.com; 35707 SR 706 E,
Ashford; breakfast from $8, burgers $10, dinner
mains $12-29; ☺7am-9pm) Forget the historic
inns. This is one of the state's great rural
restaurants, and breakfast is an absolute
must if you're heading off for a lengthy
hike inside the park. Situated just outside
the Nisqually entrance, the Copper Creek
has been knocking out pancakes, wild
blackberry pie and its own home-roasted
coffee since 1946.

NATIONAL PARK INN   AMERICAN $$
(mains $16-22; ☺7am-8pm) Hearty hiking
fare is served at this homely Longmire
inn-restaurant and – in the absence of
competition – it's surprisingly good. Try
the pot roast or the chicken with honey
glaze, and don't miss the huge blackberry
cobbler with ice cream that will require

a good 2-mile hike along the Wonderland
Trail (which starts just outside the door)
to work off.

PARADISE INN   AMERICAN $$
(brunch $27, dinner mains $17-31; ☺7am-8pm
Jun-Sep) The huge stone fireplace is the
highlight of this dining room and it easily
overshadows the food. Seared local salmon
and crab mac 'n' cheese are the most entic-
ing options.

MOUNTAIN GOAT COFFEE   CAFE, BAKERY $
(105 E Main St, Packwood; ☺7am-5pm) While
cops eat doughnuts, the park rangers of
Packwood seem to prefer muffins. Stop in
at this cozy morning spot for the best cof-
fee in town (they roast their own beans),
baked goods and perhaps an informative
chat with a friendly, khaki-clad officer.

🛏 Sleeping

In common with many US cities, Seattle's sleeping options are plentiful and varied. Want to drive up to a motor inn and park your car where you can see it through the window? You can do that. Rather slink up in a limo and throw your fancy bag to the overworked bellhop? You can do that too, as well as everything in between.

Finding Deals

Hotel prices in Seattle vary considerably; don't be put off by quoted rack rates. For the best deals, search around online. Room prices can vary wildly depending on: season (up to 50% off the rack rates from November to March; peak season is generally May through August); day of the week (weekends are usually cheaper); time of booking (earlier is usually better); hotel capacity (the fuller the hotel, the more expensive it is); whether there are festivals or events going on in town; and luck (are they throwing a deal?). Most places offer special AAA (auto club) rates. Some offer a third night for free. For more details on hotels, see the website www.visitseattle.org. Alternatively, the Seattle Bed & Breakfast Association (www.lodgingin seattle.com) has a searchable list of affiliated B&Bs; navigate to the 'Specials' page for info on packages and deals.

Note that Seattle hotel rooms are subject to a room tax of 15.6% (less for most B&Bs and historical properties), which will be tacked onto the final bill.

Free Extras

Everyone likes a freebie. It's par for the course to offer free high-speed wireless internet service in Seattle hotels these days. Most establishments also have a computer terminal available in the lobby for guests to use free of charge. Free city bikes are increasingly available in environmentally conscious hotels. Pineapple Hospitality's five establishments (Hotel Five (p193), Maxwell (p194), Palladian (p192), University Inn (p195) and Watertown (p195)) all loan out sturdy two-wheeled machines for short journeys. The same quintet also puts out plates of cupcakes and urns of coffee in its lobbies around 5pm daily.

Gyms and/or cardio rooms are available in most downtown hotels, and some also have small pools. The swish Fairmont Olympic Hotel (p190) has a health club staffed with personal trainers. Last, and most important, you'll find few hotels in Seattle that won't lend you that most useful of Pacific Northwest props – an umbrella.

Hotel Parking

Essentially all downtown hotels charge extra for parking, if they have it. (It's been said that half the population of Portland, OR, consists of people who couldn't find a place to park in Seattle and, searching in ever-widening circles, eventually wound up in Portland, where they stayed.) Usual parking rates start at around $20 a night, but check when booking as you can end up paying up to $45 a night just for your car. Many hotels downtown don't offer parking but can direct you to paid lots nearby. Otherwise, look for street meters and paid parking garages downtown, or off-street parking elsewhere.

NEED TO KNOW

Prices Ranges
The following price ranges refer to a standard double room in high season, not including tax or extra fees such as parking and breakfast.

$	less than $100
$$	$100–$250
$$$	more than $250

Useful Websites
➡ **Lonely Planet** (www.lonelyplanet.com/seattle) Recommendations and bookings.

➡ **Visit Seattle** (www.visitseattle.org) Deals available through the 'Lodging' page of the official Seattle/King County website.

➡ **Seattle Bed & Breakfast Association** (www.lodginginseattle.com) Portal of the city's 20 best B&Bs.

Lonely Planet's Top Choices

Edgewater (p192) A piece of rock-and-roll history jutting out over Puget Sound.

Hotel Monaco (p190) A boutique in the heart of downtown where no room is exactly the same.

Maxwell Hotel (p194) Free cupcakes, bike-lending, pool, gym, mosaics and jolly comfortable beds.

Fairmont Olympic Hotel (p190) Seattle's grand dame is a perfect mix of comfort, tradition and good taste.

Best by Budget

$
Moore Hotel (p192) Cheap, historic and perfectly comfortable option on the cusp of downtown.

Hotel Hotel Hostel (p196) Fremont's only non-B&B accommodations – a kind of hipster hostel.

City Hostel Seattle (p192) Hostel with private options and good wall art in Belltown.

Green Tortoise Hostel (p190) Seattle's favorite backpacker haunt.

$$
Edgewater (p192) Hotel steeped in rock history that juts out over Elliott Bay.

Hotel Max (p192) Boutique hotel with an art and music theme on the cusp of Belltown and downtown.

University Inn (p195) Close to the university, but a long way from austere student digs.

Palladian Hotel (p192) Big boutique hotel in Belltown with funky rock-star wall art.

$$$
Hotel Monaco (p190) Lavish downtown hotel with refreshingly down-to-earth service.

Fairmont Olympic Hotel (p190) Seattle's jazz-age giant rolls out the red carpet in downtown.

Arctic Club (p191) Commodious throwback to the age of the gold rush.

Best Pet-friendly Hotels

Alexis Hotel (p191) Visiting dogs are given a welcome bowl of distilled water and accommodated in designer doggie beds.

Hotel Monaco (p190) Pets are welcomed at no extra charge and with no size restrictions.

Hotel Vintage Park (p191) Offers pet-sitting services and personalized doggie itineraries.

Hotel 1000 (p191) Provides special dog beds, bowls and treats for a small one-off $40 pet fee.

Best Neighborhood Accommodations

Hotel Ballard (p196) Positively grandiose hotel and reason alone to visit Ballard, if you can afford it.

Watertown Hotel (p195) Boutique hotel in the U District that's a big step up from standard student digs.

Hotel Hotel Hostel (p196) Cheap hotel-hostel in keeping with the quirky spirit of Fremont.

Georgetown Inn (p196) Motel-style accommodations with personal touches in arty Georgetown.

Where to Stay

Neighborhood	For	Against
Downtown, Pike Place & Waterfront	Highest concentration of hotels of all types. Best neighborhood for absolute luxury. Fantastic central location.	Many places are expensive. Driving can be a nightmare and parking usually costs extra.
Pioneer Square, International District & SoDo	Close to sports grounds, downtown and the waterfront.	A noisy, rambunctious neighborhood at night that's a bit edgy for some. There's a dearth of non-chain economical hotels.
Belltown & Seattle Center	Plenty of economical hotel options within close walking distance of all Seattle's main sights.	Noisy at night with a boozy bar scene and some panhandling.
Queen Anne & Lake Union	Some great midrange options in Lower Queen Anne a stone's throw from Seattle Center.	Lacking options in Queen Anne proper. Lake Union has a lot of noisy building works and will do for some time yet.
Capitol Hill & First Hill	Excellent selection of high-quality, well-run B&Bs. Adjacent to Seattle's most exciting nightlife.	Lack of hotel choices in Capitol Hill. A little removed from downtown.
The CD, Madrona & Madison Park	Close to downtown.	Despite their proximity to downtown, these largely residential districts are bereft of decent accommodations options.
The U District	Three fantastic affordable boutique hotels adjacent to the pulsating life of 'the Ave.'	A little isolated from the downtown core and other major sights.
Green Lake & Fremont	Fun neighborhoods to hang out in with plenty of eating options and good bus and walking-trail access.	Options are limited to one budget hotel-hostel and the odd B&B.
Ballard & Discovery Park	Lovely spanking-new boutique hotel, exciting but laid-back nightlife and great restaurants.	Dearth of choices. Isolated from downtown and other neighborhoods.
Georgetown & West Seattle	Cheap, motel-style places close to a hip strip.	Few options and it's close to nowhere – except Georgetown.

🛏 Downtown, Pike Place & Waterfront

GREEN TORTOISE HOSTEL   HOSTEL **$**
(☎206-340-1222; www.greentortoise.net; 105 Pike St; dm from $35; @🛜; 🚉Westlake) Seattle's backpacker central – and what a location right across the street from Pike Place Market! Once pretty crusty, the Tortoise moved to the Elliot Hotel Building a few years back and now offers 30 bunk rooms and 16 European-style rooms (shared bath and shower). Free breakfast includes waffles and eggs.

The hostel offers a free dinner three nights a week and there are weekly events such as open-mic nights.

W HOTEL SEATTLE   HOTEL **$$**
(☎206-264-6000; www.whotels.com; 1112 4th Ave; r from $245; P❄@🛜🏊; 🚉University St) Seattle's W, like W hotels worldwide, offers comprehensive, upscale facilities with an abstract touch. The dark, minimalist Living Room bar out front sets the tone, though with 415 rooms spread over 26 floors this is no intimate boutique hotel. Bonuses include sofas to recline on in every room and a huge gym and spa. It's also pet-friendly.

MAYFLOWER PARK HOTEL   HOTEL **$$**
(☎206-623-8700; www.mayflowerpark.com; 405 Olive Way; r from $169; P❄@🛜; 🚉Westlake) If you're coming to Seattle to shop, this is the hotel for you. Attached by indoor walkway to the Westlake Center, it's also handy for taking the monorail out to Seattle Center for an event. The lobby bar is a nice hideaway for a drink. They also have bathrobes, complimentary newspapers and a noted in-house Mediterranean restaurant called Andaluca.

PENSIONE NICHOLS   GUESTHOUSE **$$**
(☎206-441-7125; www.pensionenichols.com; 1923 1st Ave; d/apt $180/280; 🛜🏊; 🚉Westlake) For a homey stay right near Pike Place, this cozy guesthouse is hard to beat. Interior rooms are quiet, but still bright with skylights, while deluxe rooms offer street views. Apartment suites sleep four to six and boast full kitchens. There are great water views from the common room, where continental breakfast is served.

⭐HOTEL MONACO   BOUTIQUE HOTEL **$$$**
(☎206-621-1770; www.monaco-seattle.com; 1101 4th Ave; d/ste $339/399; P@🛜🏊; 🚉University St) 🐾 Whimsical, with dashes of European elegance, the downtown Monaco is a classic Kimpton hotel whose rooms live up to the hints given off in the illustrious lobby. Bed down amid the stripy wallpaper and heavy drapes and reap the perks (complimentary bikes, free wine-tasting, in-room yoga mats).

⭐FAIRMONT OLYMPIC HOTEL   HOTEL **$$$**
(☎206-621-1700; www.fairmont.com/seattle; 411 University St; r from $279; P❄@🛜♿; 🚉University St) Built in 1924, the Fairmont Olympic is listed with the National Register of Historic Places, so it's not too surprising that it feels like a museum of old money. Regular remodels – including a $25-million makeover in 2016 – haven't destroyed the period glamor of its architecture

With 450 rooms and every imaginable service, this place is certainly a splurge, but it's worth exploring even if you don't stay here – have an oyster at Shuckers, the oak-paneled hotel bar, or pose like royalty on the Versailles-worthy main staircase.

FOUR SEASONS HOTEL SEATTLE   LUXURY HOTEL **$$$**
(☎206-749-7000; www.fourseasons.com/seattle; 99 Union St; r/ste from $405/890; P❄@🛜🏊; 🚉University St) 🐾 You can expect swish, five-star luxury from the Four Seasons with exemplary beyond-the-call-of-duty service to go with it; indeed, the personal touches are more akin to an intimate B&B than a 147-room hotel. The look is contemporary Northwest and is complemented by the setting – downtown and close to the water.

Bonuses include an infinity pool and the lauded on-site restaurant, The Goldfinch Tavern. It's popularly considered to be one of Seattle's best hotels.

HYATT AT OLIVE 8   HOTEL **$$$**
(☎206-971-7426; www.olive8.hyatt.com; 737 Olive Way; r $300; P❄@🛜♿; 🚉Westlake) 🐾 Encased in a sleek 39-story tower that was completed in 2009, the Olive 8 is managed by the Hyatt chain and is best described as swish, ultra-modern and, above all, green (it was the first LEED-certified hotel in Seattle). The hotel shares the tower with residential apartments, an arrangement that has its advantages – the on-site fitness club is huge and there's a good lap pool.

Rooms are suitably luxurious with comfy beds, superfast wi-fi and fluffy bathrobes.

ARCTIC CLUB
HOTEL $$$

(206-340-0340; www.thearcticclubseattle.com; 700 3rd Ave; r from $249; P@; Pioneer Sq) This plush hotel is housed in a famous downtown building renowned for its carved walrus heads, aka the Arctic Club, a now defunct association for Klondike vets who struck it rich in the 1897 gold rush. Currently under the ownership of Doubletree hotels, it has been upgraded to lure in equally rich contemporary clients with a wood-paneled gentleman's-club feel not far removed from its original incarnation.

You can relax in rooms adorned with photos of dapper young Arctic explorers, or take advantage of the on-site gym and business center. The ground-floor *Juno* restaurant serves solid Northwest food.

HOTEL 1000
HOTEL $$$

(206-957-1000; www.hotel1000seattle.com; 1000 1st Ave; r from $305; P@; University St) If you love the clean lines and simple elegance of IKEA, but you happen to have just won the lottery, you might design a hotel like this. Leather-clad egg chairs cuddle around a concrete-and-steel tube fireplace in the lounge; rooms have bedside tables made of chrome and wood, and bathrooms have granite counters and freestanding tubs that fill from the ceiling.

Each room has art reflecting guests' taste (you tell them what kind of art you like when you book or check in and they adjust the art in the room) and a 40in HDTV with surround sound. Some have a private bar, and some are pet-friendly. There is also virtual golf.

HOTEL VINTAGE PARK
HOTEL $$$

(206-624-8000; www.hotelvintagepark.com; 1100 5th Ave; r from $310; P@; University St) The rooms at this wood-paneled, gay-friendly hotel are a little smaller than at some other downtown hotels and they get a bit of street noise, but it's a pleasant place to stay, especially if you get a west-facing room. The theme is wine: rooms are named after Washington vineyards and wineries, and there's wine tasting in the lobby every afternoon.

ALEXIS HOTEL
HOTEL $$$

(206-624-4844; www.alexishotel.com; 1007 1st Ave; r/ste from $280/310; P@; University St) Run by the Kimpton Hotel group, the Alexis is a boutique hotel that is positively lavish, with huge rooms, thick carpets, gleaming bathrooms and some luxury extras – a steam room and fitness center, for instance. The hotel's pet-friendly moniker is taken seriously; visiting dogs get bowls of distilled water on arrival.

Thick double-glazed windows keep out the cacophony of downtown just outside the front door.

PARAMOUNT HOTEL
HOTEL $$$

(206-292-9500; www.paramounthotelseattle.com; 724 Pine St; r from $266; P@; Westlake) The Paramount has 146 large rooms that, like the lobby areas, are furnished with heavy antiques perhaps meant to give the relatively new hotel an old-world feel. The downstairs restaurant-bar, Dragonfish, has a 'sushi happy hour' and is a convenient place to meet for a drink before hitting the town.

RENAISSANCE SEATTLE HOTEL
HOTEL $$$

(206-583-0300; www.renaissanceseattle.com; 515 Madison St; r from $269; P@; University St) With 552 rooms set in a 28-floor tower, this gigantic hotel (part of the Marriott chain) has a boutique-like sheen with a relaxing lobby lounge, sparkling modern decor and a fitness center far better equipped than your standard hotel cardio-room. Extra bells and whistles are provided with a decent in-house restaurant, but beware of hidden extras: eg parking ($34) and wi-fi ($12.50).

Online deals can bring the rates down significantly.

INN AT THE MARKET
BOUTIQUE HOTEL $$$

(206-443-3600; www.innatthemarket.com; 86 Pine St; r with/without water view from $375/350; P@; Westlake) Right in the heart of Pike Place Market, this 71-room boutique hotel has elegant, good-sized rooms, many with large windows or small balconies. There's an awesome communal terrace offering views onto market activity and Puget Sound. A swimming pool is available at a nearby gym; parking costs $32.

🛏 Pioneer Square, International District & SoDo

HI AT THE AMERICAN HOTEL
HOSTEL $

(206-622-5443; www.americanhotelseattle.com; 520 S King St; dm from $35; @; International District/Chinatown) Seattle's HI hostel is handily positioned next to King St station and other transport hubs, though it's a 2km walk to Pike Place Market. Set in an old building in the disheveled ID it fits the bill if you don't mind the edgy – sometimes noisy – street life. Rooms are clean, if utilitarian, and staff are eager to please.

BEST WESTERN PIONEER SQUARE HOTEL
HOTEL **$$**

(☎206-340-1234; www.pioneersquare.com; 77 Yesler Way; r $168-268; P @ ?; Occidental Mall) Rooms and common areas at this historical hotel feature period decor and a comfortable atmosphere. The only hotel in the historical heart of Seattle, it can't be beaten for location – as long as you don't mind some of the saltier characters who populate the square in the off hours. Nightlife, restaurants and shopping are just steps from the door.

SILVER CLOUD HOTEL
HOTEL **$$$**

(☎206-204-9800; www.silvercloud.com; 1046 1st Ave S; r from $250; P ✳ @ ? ⊠; Stadium) Sports fans are in luck – this relatively new hotel is smack in the middle of the action, across the street from Safeco Field (p75) and next to CenturyLink Field (p75). Rooms are spacious and modern, with refrigerator and microwaves, an iPod dock on the alarm clock, and Aveda bath products.

A free shuttle service takes guests practically anywhere within 2 miles. And in warm weather you can splash around in the rooftop pool.

🛏 Belltown & Seattle Center

MOORE HOTEL
HOTEL **$**

(☎206-448-4851; www.moorehotel.com; 1926 2nd Ave; d with private/shared bath from $124/97; ?; Westlake) Old-world and allegedly haunted, the hip and whimsical Moore is undoubtedly central Seattle's most reliable bargain, offering fixed annual prices for its large stash of simple but cool rooms (some have shared bathrooms). Bonuses – aside from the dynamite location – are the cute ground-floor cafe, and zebra and leopard-skin patterned carpets.

CITY HOSTEL SEATTLE
HOSTEL **$**

(☎206-706-3255; www.hostelseattle.com; 2327 2nd Ave; dm/d from $32/99; @ ?; Westlake) One of three excellent budget hostels to

adorn central Seattle, this well-located, boutique 'art hostel' has colorful murals painted by local artists splashed on the walls of every room. There's also a common room, hot tub, in-house movie theater and all-you-can-eat breakfast.

Dorms have either four or six beds and some are female only. There are also several private rooms.

★EDGEWATER
HOTEL **$$**

(☎206-728-7000; www.edgewaterhotel.com; Pier 67, 2411 Alaskan Way; r $150-250; P ✳ @ ?; 13) Fame and notoriety has stalked the Edgewater. Perched over the water on a pier, it was once the hotel of choice for every rock band that mattered, including the Beatles, the Rolling Stones and, most infamously, Led Zeppelin, who took the 'you can fish from the hotel window' advertising jingle a little too seriously and filled their suite with sharks.

These days, the fishing – if not Led Zeppelin – is prohibited, but the rooms are still deluxe with a capital D. If you want to splurge, ask for 'The Beatles Suite' replete with luxury and fab four memorabilia.

★HOTEL MAX
BOUTIQUE HOTEL **$$**

(☎206-441-4200; www.hotelmaxseattle.com; 620 Stewart St; r from $229; P ✳ @ ? 🐾; Westlake) It's tough to get any hipper than a hotel that has a whole floor dedicated to Seattle's indie Subpop record label (they who unleashed Nirvana on an unsuspecting world). The 5th floor pays homage to the music with giant grunge-era photos and record-players with selective vinyl albums in every room. The art theme continues throughout the hotel (there's a Warhol in the lobby).

Other bonuses include a fully-equipped gym, special offers on Zip cars and a pet-friendly policy.

PALLADIAN HOTEL
BOUTIQUE HOTEL **$$**

(☎206-448-1111; www.palladianhotel.com; 2000 2nd Ave; r $160-275; ✳ ? 🐾; Westlake) Run by the Kimpton Group as an upscale boutique hotel, the Palladian's vintage neo-classical façade lives up to its name. The interior decor is more whimsical. The biggest eye-catchers are the portraits of cultural icons – Bill Gates and Jimi Hendrix among them – depicted in imperial garb on the walls (they're also reproduced on pillow cases).

Ultra-cool rooms come with armoires, yoga mats, retro phones and flat-screen TVs mounted on easels. Even better are the free-to-borrow bikes, complementary wine-tasting (daily at 5pm) and speakeasy-style cocktail bar called Penny Royal.

HOTEL FIVE   BOUTIQUE HOTEL **$$**

(☏206-448-0924; www.hotelfiveseattle.com; 2200 5th Ave; r $123-165; P❀🐾; 🖥13) Probably the least generic and most interesting of Belltown's upper crust options, this trendy hotel mixes retro-'70s furniture with sharp color accents to produce something dazzlingly modern. The ultra-comfortable beds are a valid cure for insomnia, while the large reception area invites lingering, especially when they lay out the complimentary cupcakes and coffee in the late afternoon.

Look out for regular deals, including a 'stay two nights and get the third night free'.

HOTEL ÄNDRA   BOUTIQUE HOTEL **$$**

(☏206-448-8600; www.hotelandra.com; 2000 4th Ave; r from $200; P❀🐾🖥; 🚇Westlake) It's in Belltown (so it's trendy) and it's Scandinavian-influenced (so it has lashings of minimalist style), plus the Ändra's fine location is complemented by attractive woody decor, subtle color accents, well-stocked bookcases, fluffy bathrobes, Egyptian-cotton bed linen and a complimentary shoe-shine. The Lola (p90) restaurant next door handles room service. Say no more.

ACE HOTEL   HOTEL **$$**

(☏206-448-4721; www.acehotel.com; 2423 1st Ave; r with private/shared bath from $219/119; P❀🐾🖥; 🖥13) The original locale of the highly stylized Ace Hotel chain, this place sports nouveau-industrial decor, sliding barn-door bathrooms and Pendleton wool blankets. True to its original ethos, the hotel is economical but trendy, especially if you don't mind sharing a bathroom. Enhancing the hipster appeal, some rooms come with record players. Continental breakfast is free, but parking costs $26.

BELLTOWN INN   HOTEL **$$**

(☏206-529-3700; www.belltown-inn.com; 2301 3rd Ave; r from $159; ❀@🐾; 🚇Westlake) The reliable Belltown Inn is a popular midrange place to stow your suitcase – good on the basics, if a little light on embellishments. That said, there's a roof terrace, free bike

rentals and some rooms have kitchenettes. Both Downtown and the Seattle Center are within easy walking distance.

BEST WESTERN EXECUTIVE INN   HOTEL **$$**

(☏206-448-9444; www.bestwestern.com; 200 Taylor Ave N; r from $138; P❀@🐾; 🚏Seattle Center) In the shadow of the Space Needle, the Executive Inn has a terrifying, almost brutalist facade but is perfectly decent inside. Pillow-top beds, in-room coffee and tea, microwaves and refrigerators, room service, a fitness room and a sports lounge are available, and it's a pick-up point for the Quick Shuttle (p213) to Vancouver.

WARWICK HOTEL   HOTEL **$$$**

(☏206-443-4300; www.warwickwa.com; 401 Lenora St; r from $289; @🐾🏊; 🚇Westlake) One of five Warwicks in the US (the most famous is in New York), Seattle's offering looks rather stuffy, but actually it isn't. Rooms, with HBO connection and Lavazza coffee-makers, are airier and more open than the disorientating lobby suggests and there's a Gallic-accented restaurant on site. In the basement lie a small but useful pool and gym.

WESTIN HOTEL SEATTLE   HOTEL **$$$**

(☏206-728-1000; www.westinseattle.com; 1900 5th Ave; r from $329; P❀@🐾🏊; 🚇Westlake) This impossible-to-miss, two-cylinder luxury business hotel has an astounding 900 rooms, some of which contain Jacuzzis and a range of workout equipment. There's a heated pool, an exercise room, a gift shop, a business center, and a large airport-like lobby – not to mention great views and a popular restaurant.

INN AT EL GAUCHO   HOTEL **$$$**

(☏206-728-1133; www.elgaucho.com; 2505 1st Ave; ste from $259; P❀@🐾; 🖥13) In 17 suites decorated '50s-style, above the type of anachronistic steakhouse that harks back to the good ole' days when vegetarians were eaten by the wealthy as snacks between meals, the Inn at El Gaucho offers a particularly oversized, swaggering American luxury. Plasma-screen TVs, complementary cookies and wine-tasting, 'Rain System' showers and buttery leather couches are par for the course.

And if that fails to bring out your inner lounge lizard, El Gaucho restaurant will serve you steak in bed.

SLEEPING QUEEN ANNE & LAKE UNION

🛏 Queen Anne & Lake Union

★ MAXWELL HOTEL BOUTIQUE HOTEL $$
(☎206-286-0629; www.themaxwellhotel.com; 300 Roy St; r from $240; P✹@🗢🏊; 🚌Rapid Ride D-Line) Located in Lower Queen Anne, the Maxwell's huge designer-chic lobby with its floor mosaic and funky furnishings welcomes you with aplomb. Upstairs, the slickness continues in 139 gorgeously modern rooms with hardwood floors and Scandinavian bedding. There's a small pool, gym, free bike rentals and complimentary cupcakes.

MEDITERRANEAN INN HOTEL $$
(☎206-428-4700; www.mediterranean-inn.com; 425 Queen Anne Ave N; r from $199; P✹@; 🚌Rapid Ride D-Line) There's something about the surprisingly un-Mediterranean Med Inn that just clicks. Maybe it's the handy Lower Queen Anne location, or the genuinely friendly staff, or the kitchenettes in every room, or the small downstairs gym, or the surgical cleanliness in every room. Don't try to define it – just go there and soak it up.

SILVER CLOUD INN LAKE UNION HOTEL $$
(☎206-447-9500; www.silvercloud.com; 1150 Fairview Ave N; r from $189; P✹@🗢🏊; 🚌Fairview & Campus Dr) Silver Cloud is a pleasant midrange Pacific Northwest chain (with 10 hotels in Seattle and Portland). This branch with 184 rooms overlooking Lake Union (p100) is stuffed with cost-saving extras such as a gym, indoor and outdoor pools, comp laundry facilities and complimentary breakfast, free shuttle service to downtown and (unusually for Seattle) free parking.

MARQUEEN HOTEL HOTEL $$
(☎206-282-7407; www.marqueen.com; 600 Queen Anne Ave N; r from $175; P✹@🗢; 🚌Rapid Ride D-Line) A classic old-school apartment building (built in 1918), the MarQueen has hardwood floors throughout and a variety of rooms, all with kitchenettes (left over from the building's days of housing apartments). The neighborhood is an under-visited gem, handy to various attractions. If hill walking isn't your thing, there is a courtesy van to take you to nearby sights.

Children 17 and under stay free with a parent. Note that there are no elevators in this three-story building.

HOLIDAY INN SEATTLE DOWNTOWN HOTEL $$
(☎206-728-8123; www.ihg.com; 211 Dexter Ave N; r from $145; P✹@🗢; 🚌Westlake & Denny) Balancing out the benefits of quality versus price in the clutch of chain hotels around the Space Needle (p80), this dependable Holiday Inn might just come out on top. It's well-kept, friendly and has all the basic comforts (including a cardio room). The location is ideal for Belltown, downtown and South Lake Union.

Note: despite its name this hotel isn't technically in downtown – it's in South Lake Union, a 10- to 15-minute walk away.

HAMPTON INN HOTEL $$
(☎206-282-7700; www.hamptoninnseattle.com; 700 5th Ave N; r from $209; P✹@🗢; 🚌3) A couple of blocks north of Seattle Center (p78), the Hampton Inn has 198 rooms, most of which have balconies. There's a wide variety of accommodations, from standards to two-bedroom suites with fireplaces. A cooked breakfast is included.

COURTYARD MARRIOTT HOTEL $$$
(☎206-213-0100; www.marriott.com; 925 Westlake Ave N; r $303; P✹@🗢🏊; 🚌Lake Union Park) Over on the southwest side of Lake Union, the Courtyard Marriott has all the big-hotel amenities you'd expect, including an indoor pool and a restaurant. It's set up to suit the business traveler, but it's comfy enough to justify not getting any work done. There's a small convenience store on site for impromptu snacks.

🛏 Capitol Hill & First Hill

★ BACON MANSION B&B B&B $$
(☎206-329-1864; www.baconmansion.com; 959 Broadway E; r $114-299; P@🗢; 🚌49) A 1909 Tudor mansion whose imposing exterior belies the quirky charm of its friendly hosts, this four-level B&B on a quiet residential street just past the Capitol Hill action has a grand piano in the main room that guests are invited to play. The 11 tastefully furnished rooms come in a variety of configurations, including a carriage house that's wheelchair-accessible; two of them have a shared bathroom.

The Bacon is one of the few accommodations in Seattle that allows guests to use marijuana products on the premises (with discretion).

SILVER CLOUD HOTEL –
SEATTLE BROADWAY HOTEL $$
(206-325-1400; www.silvercloud.com/seattle
broadway; 1100 Broadway; r from $229;
P❋@☎☮; Broadway & Marion) Capitol
Hill's only conventional hotel is a slick
abode that is part of a small regional chain.
Coming with a pool, restaurant, excellent
location and modern rooms verging on
the boutique, it's a steal if you can nab a
decent room rate outside of peak season.
Discounts are offered if you're using the
nearby medical facilities.

GASLIGHT INN B&B B&B $$
(206-325-3654; www.gaslight-inn.com; 1727
15th Ave; r shared/private bathroom from
$128/158; P@☎☮; 10) Set in a landmark-
listed Craftsman-style house in Capitol
Hill, the Gaslight Inn has eight rooms available, six of which have private bathrooms.
In summer, it's refreshing to dive into the
outdoor pool or just hang out on the sun
deck. No pets: the B&B already has a cat
and a dog.

11TH AVENUE INN B&B $$
(206-720-7161; www.11thavenueinn.com; 121
11th Ave E; r from $199; P❋@☎; Capitol Hill)
Formerly a boarding house and a dance
studio, this 1906 home has been a B&B
since 2003. Its facade is not the grandest
of Seattle's B&Bs, but you know what they
say about judging a book by its cover. The
11th Avenue Inn has nine rooms, each with
eclectic Victorian furnishings, oriental
rugs, handsome headboards and hand-
pressed Egyptian cotton sheets.

You won't go hungry here: breakfast
(included in the rates) is a full-course
sit-down affair in the Victorian dining
room, and you're invited to help yourself
to snacks and drinks throughout the day.
There's also a living room with stereo and
computer, and – big bonus – parking is
free. There's a three-night minimum stay.

INN AT VIRGINIA MASON HOTEL $$
(206-583-6453; www.innatvirginiamason.com;
1006 Spring St, First Hill; r from $199; P☎; 64)
On First Hill, just above the downtown
area near a complex of hospitals, this nicely
maintained older hotel caters to families
needing to stay near the medical facilities.
It also offers a number of basic rooms for
other visitors and has a nice rooftop garden
with a view from First Hill overlooking the
rest of the city.

There's an on-site cafe and discounts if
you are staying for medical reasons.

SORRENTO HOTEL HOTEL $$$
(206-622-6400; www.hotelsorrento.com; 900
Madison St; d from $269; P❋@☎☮; 64)
William Howard Taft, 27th US president,
was the first registered guest at the Sor-
rento, an imposing Italianate hotel known
since its birth in 1909 as the jewel of Seattle.
The combination of luxurious appointments,
over-the-top service and a pervasive sense of
class add up to a perfect blend of decadence
and restraint.

The beautiful Fireside Lounge is perhaps
the best place in Seattle to flop down with
a long drink.

Oh – and it's allegedly haunted.

🛏 U District

COLLEGE INN HOTEL $
(206-633-4441; www.collegeinnseattle.com;
4000 University Way NE; s/d from $75/85; @☎;
70) This pretty, half-timbered building
in the U District, left over from the 1909
Alaska-Yukon-Pacific Exposition, has 25
European-style guest rooms with sinks
and shared baths. Think 'student digs'
and you won't be disappointed. There's no
elevator.

★UNIVERSITY INN BOUTIQUE HOTEL $$
(206-632-5055; www.universityinnseattle.com;
4140 Roosevelt Way NE; r from $189; P❋@☎☮;
74) Located just one block from sister Pineapple hotel the Watertown, this spotless,
modern, well-located place is equally good
– especially when you factor in the waffles
served with the complimentary breakfast.
The hotel is four blocks from campus and
just three from the bustle of 'the Ave.' The
102 rooms come in three levels of plushness.

All of them offer such basics as a coffee maker, hair dryer and wi-fi; some have
balconies, sofas and CD players. There's a
Jacuzzi, an outdoor pool, laundry facilities
and a guest computer in the lobby. Attached
to the hotel is the recommended Portage Bay
Cafe (p134), and there's also a free shuttle to
various sightseeing areas.

WATERTOWN HOTEL BOUTIQUE HOTEL $$
(206-826-4242; www.watertownseattle.com;
4242 Roosevelt Way NE; r/ste $179/259;
P❋@☎☮☮; 74) Easy to miss because
it looks like one of those crisp new modern

apartment buildings, the Watertown has more of an arty-industrial feel than its sister hotel, the University Inn (p195). Bare concrete and high ceilings in the lobby make it seem stark and museum-like, but that translates to spacious and warmly furnished rooms with giant beds, swivel TVs and huge windows.

There's a seasonal pool, on-site cafe and exercise room. Guests can borrow bicycles or use the hotel's free shuttle to explore the area.

HOTEL DECA   BOUTIQUE HOTEL **$$**
(☑206-634-2000; www.hoteldeca.com; 4507 Brooklyn Ave NE; r from $206; P ✳ @ 🛜; 🖵70) The same architect who designed the Old Faithful Lodge in Yellowstone National Park built this hotel in 1931. Formerly the Meany Tower Hotel, the Deca has benefited from several renovations although it still pays homage to its early art-deco style. Its 16 stories offer boutique rooms with either a Cascade view or a downtown view.

There's access to a workout room, a bar and a restaurant, plus a coffee shop in the building.

🛏 Green Lake & Fremont

HOTEL HOTEL HOSTEL   HOTEL, HOSTEL **$**
(☑206-257-4543; www.hotelhotel.co/; 3515 Fremont Ave N; dm $28-32, d with private/shared bath $114/95; 🛜; 🖵5) Fremont's only real hotel is a good one, encased in a venerable old building replete with exposed brick and chunky radiators. In true Fremont fashion, Hotel Hotel is technically more of a hostel (with dorms), but it also passes itself off as an economical hotel on account of its private rooms with an assortment of shared and en-suite bathrooms.

The industrial-chic decor means it's comfortable without being fancy. A buffet breakfast is included in the price, and there is a common room and a kitchen.

9 CRANES INN   B&B **$$**
(☑206-855-5222; www.9cranesinn.com; 5717 Palatine Ave N, Phinney Ridge; r $149-269; P 🛜; 🖵5) A lovely four-room B&B up on Phinney Ridge near the zoo with sweeping views (if you get the Ballard View room), the 9 Cranes

has established a good reputation since its 2012 opening. It inhabits a pleasant, self-contained neighborhood near Green Lake that has long lacked good places to stay.

🛏 Ballard & Discovery Park

BALLARD INN   BOUTIQUE HOTEL **$$**
(☑206-789-5011; www.ballardinnseattle.com; 5300 Ballard Ave NW; r from $129; 🛜; 🖵40) This small, intimate hotel with a European feel (the Scandinavian influence?) offers a far cheaper alternative to the Hotel Ballard next door. The building, dating from 1902, is right on Ballard's main drag. Most rooms share bathrooms.

★**HOTEL BALLARD**   BOUTIQUE HOTEL **$$$**
(☑206-789-5012; www.hotelballardseattle.com; 5216 Ballard Ave NW; d $329; 🛜; 🖵40) Ballard's glittering designer hotel, which opened May 2013, exemplifies the neighborhood's upward rise. The seduction begins outside: Hotel Ballard has a lovely street profile, with its wrought-iron balconies blending in with the red-brick edifices of yore. Inside, it's even more opulent (upholstered headboards, funky chandeliers, super-streamlined bathtubs) but stays faithful to the neighborhood's Scandinavian heritage with Nordic murals.

Guests get free use of the equally fancy Olympic Athletic Club next door.

🛏 Georgetown & West Seattle

GEORGETOWN INN   HOTEL **$**
(☑206-762-2233; www.georgetowninnseattle. com; 6100 Corson Ave S; r $99-119; P ✳ 🛜; 🖵124) For a more in-depth look at Seattle, it's well worth spending a night or two in Georgetown especially during the 'Art Attack' (second Saturday of the month). This modest but comfortable hotel provides an ideal base. Rooms are pretty standard, but there's on-site parking, an excellent breakfast and 24/7 coffee and cookies. It's five minutes from the main strip.

Understand
Seattle

Seattle Today

The most unchanging thing about Seattle is that it keeps on changing. Fueled by an Amazon-led building frenzy and inspired by a new generation of technological wizards, it remains, economically speaking, one of the fastest-growing cities in the US. Stoking further regional pride, local NFL team, the Seahawks, won its first ever Super Bowl in 2014, while soccer's Sounders has developed a similar addiction to silverware. But, problems with inequality and worries about the culture-stifling effects of gentrification still create furrowed brows among locals.

Best on Film

Sleepless in Seattle (1993) Meg Ryan and Tom Hanks are irresistibly adorable in this riff on *An Affair to Remember*.

Singles (1992) Attractive slackers deal with apartment life and love.

Disclosure (1994) Semi-erotic thriller that juxtaposes steamy sex scenes with shots of Seattle's best sights.

Hype! (1996) An excellent time capsule of the grunge years.

Best in Print

Another Roadside Attraction (Tom Robbins; 1971) Robbins' wacky word carnival imagines Jesus alongside a flea circus at a pit stop.

Waxwings (Jonathan Raban; 2003) Travel writer Raban illuminates Seattle's recent high-tech boom in a novel that tells the parallel stories of two immigrants.

The Terrible Girls (Rebecca Brown; 1992) Experimental collection of short stories about lesbian relationships.

Heavier than Heaven (Charles R Cross; 2001) Moving portrait of Nirvana's Kurt Cobain.

The Sweet Smell of Success

In many ways, Seattle is like a prosperous sports team that manages to remain successful with the passing of time. When faced with the need to evolve and stay competitive, it just replaces one great squad of players with another. In the 1990s, the city nurtured international game-changers, Microsoft, grunge band Nirvana, and the innovative concept of microbrewed beer. In the 2010s, it has produced Amazon, Macklemore and a tech-savvy posse of craft spirit-makers. Amazon's massive Seattle campus in South Lake Union has created a whole new neighborhood, which has had an important ripple effect throughout the local economy; Macklemore has woken up the rest of America to a strain of socially conscious hip-hop that has long been popular in the Northwest; while the micro-distillery craze has applied Seattle's beer and coffee expertise to a whole new alcoholic genre (the city contains the highest percentage of micro-distilleries in the US).

Tackling Inequalities

Landmark legislation on marijuana and same-sex marriage has proved that Seattle doesn't lack progressive credentials. But, while the economy has boomed for some, it has remained a struggle for others. In an attempt to stall widening inequalities, the city council approved a radical new law in 2014, raising the minimum wage to $15 an hour, the highest rate in the US. With a roll-out spread over seven years, the full impact of the law won't be felt until 2021. Meanwhile, homelessness is still a worrying feature in downtown Seattle, a phenomenon that contrasts sharply with the sparkling new tech towers of South Lake Union (SLU) and the adjacent Denny Triangle. Dominated by the Amazon campus, SLU has added 50 new buildings and seen its working population grow by 50%

in the last decade, but the expansion is far from over. A dozen new skyscrapers are planned over the next few years, many of them earmarked for luxury apartments.

Transportation Revolution

In the last three years, the gridlock appears to have finally been broken in Seattle's ongoing transportation crisis. For those not addicted to the motorcar, getting from A to B has suddenly become a whole lot easier with the introduction of an extended light-rail line (costing $1.9 billion), a new streetcar and a comprehensive bike-sharing scheme. Registering less success is the much delayed Alaska Viaduct replacement tunnel, where work has been regularly stalled due to 'injuries' sustained by the temperamental drilling machine, 'Bertha.' As a result, the tunnel's opening ceremony has been put back two years to 2018. The subsequent redevelopment of the long overshadowed waterfront has, meanwhile, been given fresh impetus by Pike Up, a project to extend iconic Pike Place Market for the first time in 40 years.

Grassroots Trends

While Seattle's macro-businesses count their millions, its micros continue to quietly set trends at the grassroots level. A recent increase in the sale of print books has buoyed the city's robust contingent of bookstores, so much so that, in 2015, online retail giant Amazon opened its first brick-and-mortar bookstore in the U District. On the coffee scene, Starbucks has started surfing coffee's third wave with a new roastery in Capitol Hill offering high-end coffee that's roasted in-house. Vinyl records and the stores that ply them continue to prosper and provide an excellent excuse to hang around in Seattle's creative neighborhoods and dip a barometer into the underground music scene. The boldest and most controversial retail trend of the last few years is the birth and subsequent proliferation of pot shops, though, with still no official sanction for marijuana-friendly cafes, the dream of a 'New Amsterdam' has yet to be realized.

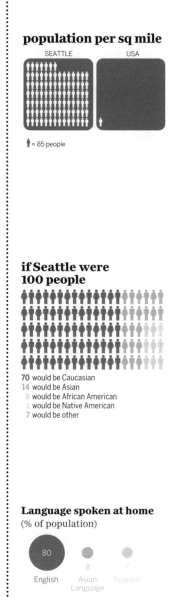

population per sq mile

SEATTLE   USA

♦ ≈ 85 people

if Seattle were 100 people

70 would be Caucasian
14 would be Asian
8 would be African American
1 would be Native American
7 would be other

Language spoken at home
(% of population)

80
English

8
Asian Language

7
Spanish

4
Other European Language

1
Other

History

In the pantheon of world cities, 166-year-old Seattle is still in its kindergarten years. Although indigenous groups have lived in and around Puget Sound for 12 millennia, the region was still covered in thick forest when the first colonial settlers bushwhacked their way through in 1851. And so began a historical trajectory marked by a mixture of bravery, folly, fire, rebirth, bust, boom and an explosion of urban growth almost unparalleled in US history. Hold tight!

Native Peoples of Puget Sound

When the accumulated ice of the great polar glaciers of the Pleistocene Epoch lowered sea levels throughout the world, the ancestors of Native Americans migrated from Siberia to Alaska via a land bridge across the Bering Strait. By this reckoning, the present tribes of Puget Sound arrived here 11,000 or 12,000 years ago, before the glaciers receded.

Unlike the Plains tribespeople living inland, who were primarily nomadic hunter-gatherers, the inhabitants of the Pacific Northwest were tied to the rivers, lakes and sea. The tribe living on the site of today's Seattle was called the Duwamish. They and other tribal groups along Puget Sound – notably the Suquamish, Coast Salish and Chinook – depended on catching salmon, cod and shellfish. On land, they hunted deer and elk, more for their hides than for their flesh. Though each group had its own dialect, coastal tribes communicated through a language called Lushootseed, which indigenous people today struggle to keep from extinction.

Extended family groups lived together in longhouses, which were constructed over a central pit-like living area. The social structure in these self-sustaining tribal villages was quite stratified, with a class of chiefs holding the majority of wealth and power. Social and religious rituals were dominated by a strict clan system. Wealth was measured in goods such as blankets, salmon and fish oil. Such commodities were consumed and to some degree redistributed in ceremonial feasts in which great honor accrued to the person who gave away these valued items.

Puget Sound tribespeople evolved complex cultural, social and economic structures, which the invasion of Euro-American settlers in the mid-

History Books

....

The Good Rain (1991), Timothy Egan

....

Stepping Westward (1991), Sallie Tisdale

....

Vanishing Seattle: Images of America (2006), Clark Humphrey

TIMELINE	9000–11,000 BC	AD 1792	1851
	The ancestors of the Duwamish, Suquamish, Coast Salish and Chinook tribes arrive in Puget Sound.	British sea captain George Vancouver sails through the Straits of Juan de Fuca and Georgia.	The Denny party arrives at Alki Point and settles in Puget Sound, already home to the Duwamish people.

1800s almost erased. Today the Duwamish tribe maintains a longhouse (p171) and cultural center on the Duwamish River near West Seattle.

New York Pretty Soon

Arthur and David Denny were native New Yorkers who, in 1851, led a group of settlers across the Oregon Trail with the intention of settling in the Willamette Valley near Portland. On the way, they heard stories of good land and deep water ports along Puget Sound. When the Denny party arrived in Portland in the fall, they decided to keep going north. The settlers landed on Alki Point, in present-day West Seattle in November 1851 and staked claims. The group named their encampment Alki-New York (the Chinookan word *alki* means 'pretty soon' or 'by and by'). After a winter of wind and rain, the group determined that their fledgling city needed a deeper harbor and moved the settlement a couple of miles northeast to the mudflats across Elliott Bay. The colony was renamed Seattle for the Duwamish chief Sealth, who was the friend of an early merchant.

Luther Collins staked a land claim near Georgetown on September 14, 1851, two weeks before the Denny party arrived at Alki. Technically, it is he, not Denny, who was Seattle's first settler.

Birth of the City

The heart of the young city beat in the area now known as Pioneer Square. Although there was a small but deep harbor at this point in Elliott Bay, much of the land immediately to the south was mudflats, ideal for oysters but not much else. The land to the north and east was steep and forested. The early settlers (whose names now ring as a compendium of street names and landmarks: Denny, Yesler, Bell, Boren) quickly cleared the land and established schools, churches, civic institutions and Seattle's first industry – Yesler's sawmill. From the start, the people who settled Seattle never doubted that they were founding a great city. The original homesteads were quickly plaited into city streets, and trade, not farming or lumbering, became the goal.

Since it was a frontier town, the majority of Seattle's male settlers were bachelors. One of the town's founders (and sole professor at the newly established university), Asa Mercer, went back to the East Coast with the express purpose of inducing young, unmarried women to venture to Seattle. Fifty-seven women made the journey and married into the frontier stock.

The Great Fire & the Regrading of Seattle

Frontier Seattle was a thrown-together village of wooden storefronts, log homes and lumber mills. Tidewater lapped against present-day 1st Ave S, and many of the buildings and the streets that led to them were on stilts. No part of the original downtown was more than 4ft above the bay at high tide, and the streets were frequently a quagmire.

1889	1897	1910	1932
The Great Fire sweeps through the city, gutting its core and destroying the mostly wooden storefronts and log homes on stilts.	The Klondike gold rush is sparked by the arrival of the ship *Portland*. The city's population doubles by 1900.	Seattle begins to grow up. Its population reaches a quarter million, making it a clear contender for the preeminent city of the Pacific Northwest.	A shantytown called 'Hooverville,' after President Hoover, forms south of Pioneer Square. Made up of lean-tos and shacks, it houses hundreds of unemployed squatters.

On June 6, 1889, an apprentice woodworker accidentally let a pot of boiling glue spill onto a pile of wood chips in a shop on 1st Ave and Madison St. The fire quickly spread through the young city, with boardwalks providing an unstoppable conduit for the flames. By the end of the day, 30 blocks of the city had burned, gutting the core of downtown.

What might have seemed a catastrophe was in fact a blessing, as the city was rebuilt with handsome structures of brick, steel and stone. This time, however, the streets were regraded and ravines and inlets filled in. This raised the new city about a dozen feet above the old. In some areas the regrading meant building on top of older ground-level buildings and streets. People had to cross trenches to get from one side of the street to another. Buildings were constructed around the notion that the first floor or two would be buried when the city got around to filling in the trenches.

The transformation inspired by the Great Fire fueled another great rebuilding project. One of Seattle's original seven hills, Denny Hill, rose out of Elliott Bay north of Pine St. Its steep face limited commercial traffic, though some hotels and private homes were perched on the hilltop. City engineers determined that if Seattle's growth were to continue, Denny Hill had to go. Between 1899 and 1912, the hill was sluiced into Elliott Bay.

KLONDIKE GOLD RUSH

Seattle's first real boom came when the ship *Portland* docked at the waterfront in 1897 with its now-famous cargo: two tons of gold newly gleaned from northern Canadian goldfields. The news spread quickly across the USA; within weeks, thousands of fortune seekers from all over the world converged on Seattle, the last stop before heading north. That summer and fall, 74 ships left Seattle bound for Skagway, Alaska, and on to the goldfields in Dawson City, Yukon.

In all, more than 40,000 prospectors passed through Seattle. The Canadian government demanded that prospectors bring a year's worth of supplies, so they wouldn't freeze or starve to death midway. Outfitting the miners became big business in Seattle. The town became the banking center for the fortunes made in the Yukon. Bars, brothels, theaters and honky-tonks in Pioneer Square blossomed.

Many of Seattle's shopkeepers, tavern owners and restaurateurs made quick fortunes in the late 1890s – far more than most of the prospectors. Many who did make fortunes in Alaska chose to stay in the Northwest, settling in the thriving port city on Puget Sound.

Seattle grew quickly. The Klondike gold rush provided wealth, and railroads brought in a steady stream of immigrants, mostly from Eastern Europe and Scandinavia. Seattle controlled most shipping trade with Alaska and increasingly with nations of the Pacific Rim. Company-controlled communities like Ballard sprang up, populated almost exclusively with Scandinavians who worked in sawmills. A new influx of Asian immigrants, this time from Japan, began streaming into Seattle, establishing farms and fishing fleets.

1942	1954	1962	1975
Japanese Americans are ordered to evacuate Seattle; they are detained under prison conditions in a relocation center for the duration of the war.	Boeing Air Transport, launched 40 years prior and already a pioneer in commercial airline flight, announces production of the 707.	The World's Fair takes place. The headliner on opening night is singer John Raitt. His 12-year-old daughter, Bonnie, holds his sheet music.	Bill Gates and Paul Allen start Microsoft, a move that helps power the Seattle economy into the 21st century and beyond.

The War Years

Seattle's boom continued through WWI, when lumber was in demand. The opening of the Panama Canal brought increased trade to Pacific ports, which were free from wartime threats. Shipyards opened along Puget Sound, bringing shipbuilding close to the forests of the Northwest.

WWII brought other, less positive, developments to Seattle. About 7000 Japanese residents in the city and the nearby areas were forcibly removed from their jobs and homes. They were sent to the nearby 'relocation center,' or internment camp, in Puyallup, then on to another camp in Idaho where they were detained under prison conditions for the duration of the war. This greatly depleted the Japanese community, which up to this point had built a thriving existence farming and fishing in Puget Sound. In all, an estimated 110,000 Japanese across the country, two-thirds of whom were US citizens, were sent to internment camps. Upon their release, many declined to return to the homes they'd been forced to abandon.

HISTORY THE WAR YEARS

Boeing & Postwar Seattle

The Boeing Airplane Company was founded and named by William E Boeing and his partner Conrad Westervelt in 1916. Boeing tested his first plane, the *B&W*, in June 1916 by taking off from the middle of Lake Union. For years, Boeing single-handedly ruled Seattle industry. After WWII, the manufacturer diversified its product line and began to develop civilian aircraft. In 1954 Boeing announced the launch of the 707, and the response was immediate and overwhelming. The world found itself at the beginning of an era of mass air travel, and Boeing produced the jets that led this revolution in transportation. By 1960, when the population of Seattle topped one million, one in 10 people worked for Boeing, and one in four people worked in jobs directly affected by Boeing.

But the fortunes of Boeing weren't always to soar. A combination of overstretched capital (due to cost overruns in the development of the 747) and a cut in defense spending led to a severe financial crisis in the early 1970s, known as the 'Boeing Bust.' Boeing was forced to cut its workforce by two-thirds; in one year, nearly 60,000 Seattleites lost their jobs. The local economy went into a tailspin for a number of years.

In the 1980s increased defense spending brought vigor back to aircraft production lines, and expanding trade relations with Pacific Rim nations brought business to Boeing too. But, in September 2001, the world's largest airplane manufacturer, the company as synonymous with Seattle as rain, relocated 50% of its HQ staff to digs in Chicago. However, the Boeing factory has stayed put in Seattle, where the company remains the city's biggest employer with a workforce of 80,000.

Seattle's Boom Industries

Lumber: 1852–89

Gold: 1897–1905 (Klondike)

Shipbuilding: 1911–18

Airplanes: 1945–70 (Boeing)

Dot com: 1995–2000 (Microsoft)

Online retail: 2008–present-day (Amazon)

1991	1999	2001	2012
The formerly underground style of music known as grunge goes mainstream, with Pearl Jam's *Ten* and Nirvana's *Nevermind* hitting record-store shelves.	Seattle is rocked by the World Trade Organization riots. Microsoft is declared a monopoly and enters into lengthy negotiations over the future of its business.	On February 28, an earthquake measuring 6.8 on the Richter scale hits Seattle, toppling several historical buildings and causing more than $2 billion in damage.	Washington State passes landmark laws legalizing the limited sale and use of marijuana, and permitting same-sex marriage.

Way of Life

Surprisingly elegant in places and coolly edgy in others, Seattle is notable for its technological know-how, passion for books, and long-standing green credentials. Although it has fermented its own pop culture in recent times, it has yet to create an urban mythology like Paris or New York. But it is the future rather than the past that's more important here. Seattle's lifestyle is organic. Rather than trying to live up to its history, it's scanning the horizon for what happens next.

What is a Seattleite?

To avoid faux pas, don't compare Seattle with Portland, don't say grunge (it's 'the Sub Pop thing'), and don't mention the relocation of the Seattle SuperSonics basketball team to Oklahoma.

Every city has its stereotypes and Seattle is no different. Those who have never been here imagine it as a metropolis of casually dressed, latte-supping urbanites who drive Priuses, vote Democrat, consume only locally grown food, and walk around with an unwavering diet of Nirvana-derived indie rock programmed into their i-players. To the people who live here, the picture is a little more complex. Seattle has a rich multicultural history and is home to Native American, African American, Asian American and growing Ethiopian American populations. The city's African American population is 8.4% – higher than every West Coast city except Los Angeles – and its Asian American population (14%) is even higher, 10% above the national average.

Living beneath overcast skies for much of the year, the locals brightened the mood by opening up cafes, reasoning that drinking liberal doses of caffeine in a cozy social environment was more fun than hiking in the rain. Seattleites have reinvented coffee culture, sinking into comfortable armchairs, listening to Ray Charles albums on repeat and nurturing mega-sized locally made coffee mugs large enough to last all day.

Seattle's geographic setting, a spectacular combination of mountains, ocean and temperate rainforest, has earned it the moniker 'Emerald City.' When you look out of your office window on sunny days and see broccoli-green Douglas fir trees framing a giant glacier-covered volcano, it's not hard to feel passionate about protecting the environment. The green culture has stoked public backing for Seattle's rapidly expanding public-transportation network and an almost religious reverence for local food.

In contrast to the USA's hardworking eastern seaboard, life out west is more casual and less frenetic. Idealistically, westerners would rather work to live than live to work. Indeed, with so much winter rain, Seattleites will dredge up any excuse to shun the nine-to-five treadmill and hit the great outdoors. The first bright days of summer prompt a mass exodus of hikers and cyclists making enthusiastically for the wilderness areas for which the region is justly famous.

Upon taking office in 2014, Seattle mayor Ed Murray became the first married gay mayor of a US city.

Creativity is a longstanding Northwestern trait, be it redefining the course of modern rock music or reconfiguring the latest Microsoft operating system. The city that once saw one in 10 of its workforce employed at aviation giant Boeing has long been obsessed with creative engineering – and this skill has been transferred to other genres.

Rather than making do with hand-me-downs, Seattle's mechanically minded coffee geeks took apart imported Italian coffee machines in the early 1990s and reinvented them for better performance. Similarly, they have experimented boldly with British-style beer, using locally grown hops, and have opened up their own whiskey distilleries. More recently, techies with taste have turned their hand to craft cider, small-batch gin and ice-cream micro-creameries.

Dealing with Success

Despite its achievements and importance to the region, Seattle still has the mellow sense of modesty and self-deprecation that characterizes the Northwest. The attitude peaked in the 1950s and '60s, with the wild anti-boosterism of newspaper columnist Emmett Watson, an opponent of Seattle's rapid urban growth plan who invented a series of tongue-in-cheek aphorisms that played down Seattle's lures in the hope that the city would remain small. Such wryness colored the way the nation perceives Seattle, and the popularization of the anti-glamorous continued into the 1990s with grunge, a trend whose success still seems to mortify the city.

Seattle has long made a habit of turning its clever homemade inventions into global brands. But the city has always had an uncomfortable relationship with the success it has struggled to achieve. Ask an average Seattleite how they rate Starbucks and they might express barely concealed pride one minute and tell you they never drink there the next. Similar sentiments are reserved for business behemoths Microsoft, Boeing and Amazon. Macklemore might be Seattle's biggest contemporary music icon and a cool proponent of modern hip-hop, but go into a trendy Seattle record store in Capitol Hill and you'll often find his records filed in the 'pop music' section.

Two of Seattle's most successful citizens, Bill Gates and Paul Allen, also happen to be its two largest public figures. And they symbolize a certain aspect of the city's contradictory attitude toward its own success. Both undeniably ambitious and indisputably successful, Gates and

Seattle Brands that Went Global

Amazon

Starbucks

Microsoft

REI

Costco

Nordstrom

Boeing

WAY OF LIFE DEALING WITH SUCCESS

POLITICS & SOCIAL ISSUES

Washington is arguably the most socially progressive state in the US and one of only two (the other is Oregon) where same-sex marriage, assisted suicide and marijuana usage are all legal. King County, where Seattle makes up the bulk of the population, has voted Democrat in presidential elections since the 1980s, with Barack Obama enjoying 70% of the popular vote in 2012. Similarly, Seattle has had a Democratic mayor since 1969. The city elected the first female mayor in US history, Bertha Knight Landes, who served from 1926 to 1928. (Ironically, it hasn't elected another woman to the office since.)

Seattle has often stood at the forefront of the push for 'greener' lifestyles, in the form of car clubs, recycling programs, organic restaurants and biodiesel whale-watching tours. Former mayor Greg Nickels (2002–10) was an early exponent of ecofriendly practices and advocated himself as a leading spokesperson on climate change. Another recent mayor, Michael McGinn (2010–14) was also an environmental activist and former state chair of the Sierra Club.

Seattle is one of the country's more gay-friendly cities, with most bars and nightlife centered on Capitol Hill. Journalist and media pundit Dan Savage has long been a high-profile local voice. You can read his weekly column in the Stranger, an alternative free newspaper that picked up a Pulitzer Prize in 2012. Current Seattle mayor Ed Murray is gay and married.

Allen are seen simultaneously as points of civic pride and as shameless capitalists who are totally alien to the prevailing Seattle culture.

Arts

Seattle is an erudite city of enthusiastic readers with more bookstores per capita than any other US city. It has also, somewhat ironically, produced – and remains HQ to – the world's biggest online retailer, Amazon.com, founded in 1995 as an online bookstore. Not surprisingly, numerous internationally recognized writers have gravitated here, among them Tom Robbins, Jonathan Raban and Sherman Alexie. David Guterson – author of the wonderfully evocative *Snow Falling on Cedars* (1994), set on a fictional Puget Sound island – was born in Seattle, graduated from the University of Washington and now lives on Bainbridge Island.

Seattle's visual arts are also dynamic. From Native American and Asian to contemporary American, its cultural strands meet and transfuse on canvas, in glass and in sculpture.

Literature

In the 1960s and '70s, western Washington attracted a number of counterculture writers. The most famous of these (and the best!) is Tom Robbins, whose books, including *Another Roadside Attraction* (1971) and *Even Cowgirls Get the Blues* (1976), are a perfect synthesis of the enlightened braininess, sense of mischief and reverence for beauty that add up to the typical mellow Northwest counterculture vibe.

Having, among other things, a fondness for the Blue Moon tavern in common with Robbins, poet Theodore Roethke taught for years at the University of Washington, and along with Washington native Richard Hugo he cast a profound influence over Northwest poetry.

Raymond Carver, the short-story master whose books include *Will You Please Be Quiet, Please?* (1976) and *Where I'm Calling From* (1988), lived near Seattle on the Olympic Peninsula. Carver's stark and grim vision of working-class angst profoundly affected other young writers of his time. His second wife, Tess Gallagher, also from Port Angeles and a UW alumnus, is a novelist and poet whose books include *At the Owl Woman Saloon* (1997).

Noted British travel writer Jonathan Raban, who has lived in Seattle since the early 1990s, has written such books as *Coasting* (1987), *Hunting Mister Heartbreak* (1990) and *Driving Home: An American Journey* (2011). His novel *Waxwings* (2003) is an account of two families of Seattle immigrants.

Seattle has two daily newspapers, the *Seattle Post-Intelligencer*, founded in 1863, and the *Seattle Times*, founded in 1993. The *Post-Intelligencer* ended print publication in 2009 but still runs an active website (www. seattlepi.com).

Sherman Alexie is a Native American author whose short-story collection *The Lone Ranger and Tonto Fistfight in Heaven* (1993) was among the first works of popular fiction to discuss reservation life. In 1996 he published *Indian Killer,* a chilling tale of ritual murder set in Seattle, to great critical acclaim. His recent *War Dances,* a collection of poetry and stories, won the 2010 PEN/Faulkner Award for fiction.

The misty environs of western Washington seem to be a fecund habitat for mystery writers. Dashiell Hammett once lived in Seattle, while noted writers JA Jance, Earl Emerson and Frederick D Huebner currently call the Northwest home.

One peculiar phenomenon is the relatively large number of cartoonists who live, or have lived, in the Seattle area. Lynda Barry *(Ernie Pook's Comeek, Cruddy)* and Matt Groening (creator of *The Simpsons)* were students together at Olympia's Evergreen State College. Gary Larson, whose *Far Side* animal antics have netted international fame and great fortune, lives in Seattle. A good number of underground comic-book artists live here, too, among them the legendary Peter Bagge *(Hate)*, Jim Woodring *(The Frank Book)*, Charles Burns *(Black Hole)* and Roberta Gregory *(Naughty Bits)*. It could well have something to do with the fact that Fantagraphics, a major and influential publisher of underground comics and graphic novels, is based here.

Cinema & Television

Seattle has come a long way as a movie mecca since the days when Elvis starred in the 1963 film *It Happened at the World's Fair,* a chestnut of civic boosterism. Films with Seattle as their backdrop include *Tugboat Annie* (1933); *Cinderella Liberty* (1974), a steamy romance with James Caan and Marsha Mason; and *The Parallax View* (1974) with Warren Beatty. Jessica Lange's movie *Frances,* about the horrible fate of outspoken local actor Frances Farmer (she was jailed on questionable pretenses, then institutionalized for years and eventually lobotomized), was filmed here in 1981. Debra Winger's hit *Black Widow* (1986) shows many scenes shot at the University of Washington.

John Cusack starred in *Say Anything* (1989), Michelle Pfeiffer and Jeff Bridges did it up in *The Fabulous Baker Boys* (1989), and Sly Stallone and Antonio Banderas flopped in *Assassins* (1995), all partly filmed in and around Seattle. Horror hit *The Ring* (2002) and JLo vehicle *Enough* (2002) both had a few scenes shot in Seattle and on local ferries.

The two most famous (until recently) Seattle movies happened when the city was at the peak of its cultural cachet in the '90s: *Singles* (1992), with Campbell Scott, Kyra Sedgwick, Matt Dillon and Bridget Fonda, captured the city's youthful-slacker vibe. (Incidentally, both *Singles* and *Say Anything* were directed by Cameron Crowe, who is married to Nancy Wilson from Seattle rock band Heart.) And then there was *Sleepless in Seattle,* the 1993 blockbuster starring Tom Hanks, Meg Ryan and, perhaps more importantly, Seattle's Lake Union houseboats. As a Seattle-based film phenomenon, however, nothing tops the tween-vampire soap opera *Twilight* and its sequels, set in the town of Forks, WA.

TV's *Northern Exposure,* filmed in nearby Roslyn, WA, and *Frasier* both did a lot to boost Seattle's reputation as a hip and youthful place to live. The creepy, darker side of the Northwest was captured in the moody *Twin Peaks.* And let's not forget ABC's phenomenally popular hospital drama, *Grey's Anatomy.*

Theater

Seattle has one of the most dynamic theater scenes in the country. There are reportedly more equity theaters in Seattle than anywhere in the US, except New York City. This abundance of venues provides the city with a range of classical and modern dramatic theater.

In addition to quality professional theater hosting touring Broadway shows, the city offers a wide array of amateur and special-interest troupes, including both gay and lesbian theater groups, puppet theaters, children's theater troupes, cabarets and plenty of alternative theaters staging fringe plays by local playwrights. Of particular esoteric interest are Pike Place's Market Theater and Fremont's Atlas Theater (both showing improv comedy), Belltown's Jewel Box Theater (burlesque) and the CD's artist-run New City Theater (stripped-down Shakespeare and the like).

Several Native American languages are spoken and taught in Seattle, such as the Duwamish dialect Lushootseed, a branch of the Salishan language family.

WAY OF LIFE ARTS

Music

Music is as important to Seattle as coffee, computers or airplanes. The jazz era produced Ray Charles, rock delivered Hendrix, and the '70s coughed up crusty hard-rock merchants Heart. Then, in the early 1990s, a generation of flannel-shirted urban slackers tired of being ignored by the mainstream threw away their '80s fashion manuals and turned up the volume on their guitars to 11. Suddenly, the city wasn't just exporting individual artists, it had invented a whole new musical genre: grunge.

The Jazz Age

Born in Texas in 1928, jazz singer Ernestine Anderson moved to Seattle at age 16 and became a product of the fertile jazz scene spearheaded by Ray Charles and Quincy Jones.

At its peak in the 1940s, when many GIs were based in Seattle, S Jackson St – in what is now 'Little Saigon,' an eastern outpost of the International District – and its environs had more than 20 raucous bars with music, dancing and bootleg liquor. Although the city never rewrote the jazz songbook with its own genre or style, it provided a fertile performance space for numerous name artists. Charlie Parker, Lester Young and Duke Ellington all passed through and, in 1948, a young, unknown, blind pianist from Florida named Ray Charles arrived to seek his fortune. Later that year, the 18-year-old Charles met 15-year-old trumpeter and Seattle resident Quincy Jones in the Black Elk's Club on S Jackson and the creative sparks began to fly.

Seattle's jazz scene had died down by the 1960s, when S Jackson embraced tight-lipped sobriety, and the young and hip turned their attention to rock and roll (enter Hendrix stage left). Benefiting from regular revivals in the years since, a small jazz scene lives on in Belltown, where two venues – Dimitriou's Jazz Alley (p93) and Tula's (p94) – still attract international talent.

From Hendrix to Heart

Musical Alumni of Garfield High School

Jimi Hendrix

Quincy Jones

Ernestine Anderson

Ben Haggerty (Macklemore)

Seattle lapped up rock and roll like every other US city in the late '50s and early '60s, but it produced few rockers of its own, save the Fleetwoods (from nearby Olympia), who had a string of hits from 1959 to 1966. No one took much notice when a poor black teenager named Johnny Allen Hendrix took to the stage in the basement of a local synagogue in the Central District (CD) in 1960. Hendrix' band fired him mid-set for showing off – a personality trait he would later turn to his advantage. Ignored and in trouble with the law, Hendrix served briefly in the US army before being honorably discharged. After a stint in Nashville, he gravitated to New York, where he was 'discovered' playing in a club by Keith Richards' girlfriend. Encouraged to visit London, the displaced Seattleite was invited by bassist Chas Chandler to play in a new nightclub for his mates Eric Clapton and the Beatles, whose jaws immediately hit the floor.

Heart was another band that had to travel elsewhere – in its case, to Canada – to gain international recognition. The band recorded its first album in Vancouver and followed it up with a second, which produced the hard-rock million-seller 'Barracuda.' Enjoying a comeback in the mid-1980s, Heart is probably best remembered for the soft-rock hit 'These Dreams.'

Grunge – Punk's West Coast Nirvana

Synthesizing Generation X angst with a questionable approach to personal hygiene, the music popularly categorized as 'grunge' first dive-bombed onto Seattle's scene in the early 1990s like a clap of thunder on a typically wet and overcast afternoon. The anger had been fermenting for years – not purely in Seattle but also in its sprawling satellite towns and suburbs. Some said it was inspired by the weather, others cited the Northwest's geographic isolation. It didn't really matter. Armed with dissonant chords and dark, sometimes ironic lyrics, a disparate collection of bands stepped sneeringly up to the microphone to preach a new message from a city that all of the touring big-name rock acts serially chose to ignore. There were Screaming Trees from collegiate Ellensburg, the Melvins from rainy Montesano, Nirvana from the timber town of Aberdeen, and the converging members of Pearl Jam from across the nation.

Historically, grunge's roots lay in West Coast punk, a musical subgenre that first found a voice in Portland, OR, in the late 1970s, led by the Wipers, whose leather-clad followers congregated in legendary dive bars such as Satyricon. Another musical blossoming occurred in Olympia, WA, in the early 1980s, where DIY musicians Beat Happening invented 'lo-fi' and coyly mocked the corporate establishment. Mixing in elements of heavy metal and scooping up the fallout of an itchy youth culture, Seattle quickly became the alternative music's pulpit, spawning small, clamorous venues where boisterous young bands more interested in playing rock music than 'performing' could lose themselves in a melee of excitement and noise. It was a raucous, energetic scene characterized by stage-diving, crowd-surfing and barely tuned guitars, but, armed with raw talent and some surprisingly catchy tunes, the music filled a vacuum.

A crucial element in grunge's elevation to superstardom was Sub Pop Records, an independent Seattle label whose guerrilla marketing tactics created a flurry of hype to promote its ragged stable of cacophonous bands. In August 1988, Sub Pop released the seminal single 'Touch Me I'm Sick' by Mudhoney, a watershed moment. The noise got noticed, most importantly by the British music press, whose punk-savvy journalists quickly reported the birth of a 'Seattle sound,' later christened grunge by the brand-hungry media. Suitably inspired, the Seattle scene began to prosper, spawning literally hundreds of new bands, all cemented in the same DIY, anti-fashion, audience-embracing tradition. Of note were sludgy Soundgarden, who later went on to

Green River was an early grunge band whose members went on to bigger things. Mark Arm and Steve Turner started Mudhoney, and Jeff Ament and Stone Gossard set up Pearl Jam.

Songs about Seattle

'Frances Farmer Will Have Her Revenge on Seattle,' Nirvana (1993)

'Aurora,' Foo Fighters (1999)

'Belltown Ramble,' Robyn Hitchcock (2006)

'The Town,' Macklemore (2009)

GRUNGE TOP FIVE PLAYLIST

Superfuzz Bigmuff (Sub Pop), Mudhoney Released in 1988, the catchy debut single 'Touch Me I'm Sick' became an instant classic.

Nevermind (Geffen), Nirvana Grunge anthem 'Smells Like Teen Spirit' became, and remains, one of the most analyzed singles in the history of rock.

Ten (Epic), Pearl Jam The first studio album by one of rock's biggest groups took a while to peak but contained three hit singles.

Badmotorfinger (A&M), Soundgarden The hair-metal side of grunge.

Facelift (Columbia), Alice in Chains First offering from legendary grunge-metal band with the hidden harmonies.

MACKLEMORE & RYAN LEWIS

For decades Seattle's hip-hop (with the exception of Sir Mix-a-Lot) was little heard outside low-key house parties in the Central District and occasional exposure on local radio station KEXP. Then, in 2012, the music hit the mainstream when the song 'Thrift Shop' by Seattle duo Macklemore (real name Ben Haggerty) and Ryan Lewis went to number one in multiple countries and – perhaps more importantly in the internet age – garnered nearly one billion views on YouTube. Extolling the virtues of secondhand clothes over the normal rapper uniform of bling, 'Thrift Shop' (and its accompanying album *The Heist*) was a curious hit whose success was achieved the hard way. Macklemore and University of Washington alumnus Lewis were indie artists who produced and promoted their music with scant help from major record labels.

win two Grammys; metal-esque Alice in Chains; and the soon-to-be-mega Nirvana and Pearl Jam. By the dawn of the 1990s, every rebellious slacker with the gas money was coming to Seattle to hit the clubs. It was more than exciting.

What should have been grunge's high point came in October 1992, when Nirvana's second album, the hugely accomplished *Nevermind,* knocked Michael Jackson off the number-one spot, but the kudos ultimately killed it. After several years of railing against the mainstream, Nirvana and grunge had been incorporated into it. The media blitzed in, grunge fashion spreads appeared in *Vanity Fair* and half-baked singers from Seattle only had to cough to land a record contract. Many recoiled, most notably Nirvana vocalist and songwriter Kurt Cobain, whose drug abuse ended in suicide in his new Madison Park home in 1994. Other bands soldiered on, but the spark – which had burnt so brightly while it lasted – was gone. By the mid-1990s, grunge was officially dead.

Hip-Hop

Best Pike Place Market Buskers

....

Johnny Hahn *Alfresco pianist since 1986.*

....

Emery Carl *Hula-hooping guitarist.*

....

Morrison Boomer *Acoustic band.*

....

Jim Page *Folk and protest singer.*

....

Ronn Benway *Guitar-playing troubadour.*

Seattle's earliest hip-hop proponent was a DJ rather than a group. 'Nasty Nes' Rodriguez used to air a show called *Fresh Tracks* on KKFX radio in the early 1980s, which pushed the then unfashionable local rap talent to in-the-know kids with their ears tuned to New York. On his early playlist was the Emerald Street Boys, a rap trio from the CD neighborhood, and Sir Mix-a-Lot (real name Anthony Ray), whose breakthrough song 'Posse on Broadway,' released in 1987, gave a Seattle spin to the region's hip-hop by describing the intimate geography of Capitol Hill and the CD. Sir Mix-a-Lot went on to have a massive number one hit with 'Baby Got Back' in 1992, a bright if brief explosion on the national stage that wasn't immediately followed up.

Nonetheless, by the 2000s, hip-hop had successfully infiltrated Seattle's indie-rock universe and begun to have a more all-round impact. This was partly thanks to influential radio station KEXP (p93), which added local hip-hop artists into its airplay at all hours. But it was mostly due to the fact that the work coming out of the Pacific Northwest was overwhelmingly high quality and, as befits the region, generally positive and socially conscious. The probing intelligent lyrics of U-Dub (University of Washington) band the Blue Scholars were an important link to massive popularization of Northwest hip-hop in the 2010s, a process that culminated in the unprecedented rise of Macklemore in 2012.

Survival Guide

Transportation

ARRIVING IN SEATTLE

Seattle is served by **Sea-Tac International Airport**, located 13 miles south of downtown Seattle. It's one of the top 20 airports in the US with numerous domestic flights and good direct connections to Asia and a handful of European cities, including Paris and London.

Three railway arteries converge in Seattle from the east (the Empire Builder to Chicago), south (the Coast Starlight to Oregon and California) and north (the Cascades to Vancouver, Canada). These land-based journeys through the watery, green-tinged, mountainous Pacific Northwest landscape are spectacular and often surprisingly cheap.

Seattle's main road highway is the mega-busy I-5, which flows north–south along the West Coast. Points east are best served by cross-continental I-90,

which crosses the Cascade Mountains via Snoqualmie Pass. Regular boats arrive in Seattle from Victoria, Canada. It's also possible to arrive on a cruise liner.

Sea-Tac International Airport

Sea-Tac International Airport (SEA; ☑206-787-5388; www.portseattle.org/ Sea-Tac; 17801 International Blvd; ☎), shared with the city of Tacoma, is the arrival point for 42 million people annually.

There are **baggage storage facilities** (www.kensbaggage.com; suitcases, duffels & backpacks per day $7-11) in the airport as well as currency-exchange services. Car-rental agencies are located in the baggage-claim area.

You can dial ☑55 from any of the traveler information boards at the base of the

baggage-claim escalators for on-the-spot transportation information. There's also an information booth on the 3rd floor of the parking garage. For further details on ground transportation to and from the airport, check the Sea-Tac website (www.portseattle. org/seatac/ground).

Light Rail

The best option for making the 13-mile trek from the airport to downtown Seattle is with the Central Link light-rail line. It's fast and cheap and takes you directly to the heart of downtown as well as a handful of other stops along the way. In 2016, the line was extended to Capitol Hill and the U District.

Sound Transit (www. soundtransit.org) runs the Central Link service to the airport. Trains go every 15 minutes or better between 5am and just after midnight. Stops in town include the University of Washington,

---

CLIMATE CHANGE & TRAVEL

Every form of transport that relies on carbon-based fuel generates CO_2, the main cause of human-induced climate change. Modern travel is dependent on airplanes, which might use less fuel per kilometer per person than most cars but travel much greater distances. The altitude at which aircraft emit gases (including CO_2) and particles also contributes to their climate change impact. Many websites offer 'carbon calculators' that allow people to estimate the carbon emissions generated by their journey and, for those who wish to do so, to offset the impact of the greenhouse gases emitted with contributions to portfolios of climate-friendly initiatives throughout the world. Lonely Planet offsets the carbon footprint of all staff and author travel.

Capitol Hill, Westlake Center, Pioneer Square and SoDo. The ride between the two furthest points, the University of Washington and Sea-Tac, takes 44 minutes and costs $3.25.

Shuttle Bus

Shuttle Express (☑425-981-7000; www.shuttlexpress.com) has a pickup and drop-off point on the 3rd floor of the airport garage; it charges approximately $18 and is handy if you have a lot of luggage.

Taxi

Taxis are available at the parking garage on the 3rd floor. Fares to downtown start at $42.

Seattle Orange Cab (☑206-522-8800; www.orangecab.net)

Seattle Yellow Cab (☑206-622-6500; www.seattleyellowcab.com)

STITA Taxi (☑206-246-9999; www.stitataxi.com)

Private Vehicle

Rental-car counters are located in the baggage-claim area. Some provide pickup and drop-off service from the 1st floor of the garage, while others provide a shuttle to the airport. Ask when you book your car.

Driving into Seattle from the airport is fairly straightforward – just take I-5 north. It helps to find out whether your downtown exit is a left-hand or right-hand one, as it can be tricky to cross several lanes of traffic at the last minute during rush hour.

King Street Station

Amtrak serves Seattle's **King Street Station** (☑206-296-0100; www.amtrak.com; 303 S Jackson St). Three main routes run through town: the Amtrak Cascades

(connecting Vancouver, Seattle, Portland and Eugene), the very scenic Coast Starlight (connecting Seattle, Oakland and Los Angeles) and the Empire Builder (a cross-continental roller-coaster to Chicago).

The station is situated between Pioneer Square and the International District right on the cusp of downtown and has good, fast links with practically everywhere in the city.

Streetcar

The First Hill streetcar runs from near King Street Station through the International District and First Hill to Capitol Hill every 15 minutes. Fares are $2.25/1.50 per adult/child.

Light Rail

King Street Station is adjacent to the International District/Chinatown Central Link light-rail station, from where it is three stops (seven minutes) to the Westlake Center in downtown. Fares are $2.25/1.50 per adult/child.

The Piers

Nearly 200 cruise ships call in at Seattle annually. They dock at either Smith Cove Cruise Terminal (Pier 91), in the Magnolia neighborhood 2 miles north of downtown, or Bell Street Cruise Terminal (Pier 66). The latter is adjacent to downtown and far more convenient. Many cruise lines pre-organize land transportation for their passengers. Check ahead.

The **Victoria Clipper** (Map p238; ☑206-448-5000; www.clippervacations.com; 2701 Alaskan Way, Pier 69) ferry from Victoria, Canada, docks at Pier 69 just south of the Olympic Sculpture Park in Belltown. Washington State Ferries services from Bremerton and Bainbridge Island use Pier 52.

Bus

Metro buses 24 and 19 connect Pier 91 in Magnolia with downtown via the Seattle Center. Fares are a flat $2.75.

Shuttle Bus

Shuttle Express (☑425-981-7000; www.shuttlexpress.com) links the piers with Sea-Tac airport ($22) or downtown ($12).

Private Vehicle

If you are driving to Pier 52 for the car ferries, leave I-5 at exit 164A (northbound) or exit 165B (southbound).

Bus Stations

Various inter-city coaches serve Seattle and there is more than one drop-off point – it all depends on which company you are using.

Greyhound (Map p234; ☑206-628-5526; www.greyhound.com; 503 S Royal Brougham Way; 🚇Stadium) Connects Seattle with cities all over the country, including Chicago ($228 one way, two days, two daily), Spokane ($51, eight hours, three daily), San Francisco ($129, 20 hours, three daily) and Vancouver (Canada; $32, four hours, five daily). The company has its own terminal just south of the King St train station in SoDo, accessible on the Central Link light rail (stadium station).

Quick Shuttle (Map p238; ☑800-665-2122; www.quickcoach.com; 🚌) Fast and efficient with five to six daily buses to Vancouver ($43). Picks up at the Best Western Executive Inn in Taylor Ave N near the Seattle Center. Grab the monorail or walk to downtown.

Cantrail (www.cantrail.com) Amtrak's bus connector runs four daily services to Vancouver ($42) and picks up and drops off at King Street Station.

Bellair Airporter Shuttle (Map p232;📞866-235-5247; www. airporter.com) Runs buses to Yakima, Bellingham and Anacortes and stops at King Street Station (for Yakima) and the Washington State Convention Center (for Bellingham and Anacortes).

GETTING AROUND

Light Rail

Sound Transit (www. soundtransit.org) operates Link light rail. The first – and, as yet, only – Seattle line, Central Link, runs from Sea-Tac airport to the University of Washington via Westlake Station in downtown. There are 15 stations including stops in SoDo, the International District, Pioneer Square and Capitol Hill. Fares within the city limits are \$2.25. From downtown to the airport costs \$3. Trains run between 5am and 12:30am.

By 2021 it is expected that further lines will be built, north to Northgate, and east to Mercer Island and Bellevue.

Bus

Buses are operated by **King County Metro Transit** (📞206-553-3000; www.metro. kingcounty.gov), part of the King County Department of Transportation. The website prints schedules and maps and has a trip planner.

To make things simple, all bus fares within Seattle city limits are a flat \$2.75 at peak hours (6am to 9am and 3pm to 6pm weekdays). Off-peak rates are \$2.50. Those aged six to 18 pay \$1.50, kids under six are free, and seniors and travelers with disabilities pay \$1. Most of the time you pay or show your transfer when you board. Your transfer ticket is valid for three hours from time of purchase. Most buses can carry two to three bikes.

There are six Rapid Ride bus routes (A to F). Of interest to travelers are lines C (downtown to West Seattle) and D (downtown to Ballard). Rapid Ride buses are faster and more frequent (every 10 minutes).

Be aware that very few buses operate between 1:30am and 5am, so if you're a long way from home when the bars close, plan on calling a cab instead.

Streetcar

The revival of the **Seattle Streetcar** (www.seattle streetcar.org) was initiated in 2007 with the opening of the 2.6-mile South Lake Union line that runs between the Westlake Center and Lake Union. There are 11 stops and fares cost a standard \$2.25/1.50 per adult/child. Streetcars breeze by every 15 minutes from 6am to 9pm (slightly later on Friday and Saturday). A second 10-stop line opened in 2016 running from Pioneer Square via the International District and First Hill to Capitol Hill.

Plans for future streetcar lines are extensive, with links earmarked for Fremont, Ballard and the U District.

Bicycle

Seattle has a bike-sharing scheme called **Pronto** (📞844-677-6686; www.pronto cycleshare.com) covering most of the central area. There are 500 available bikes located in 54 docking stations. A 24-hour pass costs \$8 payable at machines at any stations. You can also rent helmets.

Bike lanes city-wide have improved exponentially since the introduction of Pronto in

STREETWISE

Seattle street addresses are confusing, and few visitors will have time to figure out how the system works. It's easier to use neighborhoods to indicate where things are found: '10th Ave in Queen Anne' indicates which 10th Ave is being referred to; likewise '1st Ave in Wallingford' as opposed to 1st Ave downtown. So it's important to get a working knowledge of Seattle's neighborhoods. With so many different numbering systems, it's the only easy way to make sense of the city.

Downtown is in the middle of the hourglass part of Seattle; Pioneer Square is to the south of it. Capitol Hill lies to the northeast, and the Central District/Madrona area to the east. The U District is north of Capitol Hill, across Lake Washington. Belltown, Seattle Center and Queen Anne are slightly northwest of downtown. Fremont, Wallingford and Green Lake are north, across Lake Union, and Ballard is off to the northwest. Georgetown is south, and West Seattle – well, that's easy.

Generally speaking, avenues run north and south, and streets run east and west. Yesler Way near Pioneer Square is the zero street for numbering addresses on downtown avenues; Western Ave is the zero street for addresses on streets. Usually Seattle's avenues have a directional suffix (6th Ave S), while its streets have directional prefixes (S Charles St); however, downtown streets and avenues have neither.

THIS CITY WAS MADE FOR WALKING

Yes, the monorail was highly revolutionary in 1962, and the streetcar will bring back pleasant memories of the 1930s if you're over 90, but on a pleasant clear spring day in Seattle, you can't beat the visceral oxygen-drinking act of walking. Because most of Seattle's through-traffic is funneled north–south along one of three main arteries – I-5, the Alaskan Way Viaduct and Aurora Ave N – the central streets aren't as manic as you'd imagine. In Belltown and Pioneer Square your worst hassle is a few innocuous panhandlers, in downtown the hills might slow your progress slightly, while on the waterfront you'll need to watch out for the seagulls – and the tourists! Seattle's most walkable neighborhoods are leafy Capitol Hill and Queen Anne. If you're really adventurous, ditch the car/bus/train and explore the U District, Fremont and Ballard on that entertaining alfresco people-watching bonanza, the Burke-Gilman Trail (p140).

2014. They are painted green and usually separated from traffic lanes. Pick up a copy of the *Seattle Bicycling Guide Map*, published by the City of Seattle's Transportation Bicycle & Pedestrian Program (www.cityofseattle.net/transportation/bikemaps.htm) and available at bike shops (or downloadable from the website). The website also has options for ordering delivery of the printed map (free of charge).

The best non-motor traffic route is the scenic Burke-Gilman Trail (p140), which passes through the northern neighborhoods of the U District, Wallingford, Fremont and Ballard. Other handy bike paths are the Ship Canal Trail on the north side of Queen Anne, Myrtle Edwards Park, Green Lake Park and the Cheshiahud Loop around Lake Union.

Seattle and all of King County require that cyclists wear helmets. If you're caught without one, you can be fined $30 to $80 on the spot. Most places that rent

bikes will rent helmets to go with them, sometimes for a small extra fee.

Boat

The most useful inter-neighborhood boat route is the water taxi (p168) that connects the downtown waterfront (Pier 50) with West Seattle (Seacrest Park). The water taxi runs hourly every day in the summer and weekdays only in the winter. The fare is $5.25 for the 10-minute crossing.

Taxi

You can hail a cab from the street, but it's a safer bet to call and order one. All Seattle taxi cabs operate at the same rate, set by King County. At the time of research the rate was $2.60 at meter drop, then $2.70 per mile. There may be an additional charge for extra passengers and baggage. Any of the following offer reliable taxi services:

Seattle Orange Cab (☎206-522-8800; www.orangecab.net)

Seattle Yellow Cab (☎206-622-6500; www.seattleyellowcab.com)

STITA Taxi (☎206-246-9999; www.stitataxi.com)

Car & Motorcycle

Seattle traffic is disproportionately heavy and chaotic for a city of its size, and parking is scarce and expensive. Add to that the city's bizarrely cobbled-together mishmash of skewed grids, the hilly terrain and the preponderance of one-way streets and it's easy to see why driving downtown is best avoided if at all possible.

TOURS

Seattle seems to excel in first-rate city tours undertaken by various means of transportation including buses, boats and even a specially adapted bus-boat. Non-daunting tours on foot are similarly popular. Some tours are neighborhood-specific, others cover a particular topic; several pull together the city's best sights.

Not surprisingly, the city calls upon an abundance of food tours, many of them centered on its proverbial larder, Pike Place Market. The culinary theme also extends to liquid refreshment with tours specializing in beer and coffee.

A couple of companies run unique tours of Seattle's spooky, but historically significant 'underground' buried beneath the streets of Pioneer Square. Calling on a well-established team of witty guides, they are riotously popular.

Directory A–Z

Customs Regulations

US Customs allows each person over the age of 21 to bring 1L of liquor, 100 cigars and 200 cigarettes duty-free into the USA. US citizens are allowed to import, duty-free, up to $800 worth of gifts from abroad, while non-US citizens are allowed to import $200 worth. If you're carrying more than $10,000 in US and foreign cash, traveler's checks, money orders etc, you need to declare the excess amount. There is no legal restriction on the amount that may be imported, but undeclared sums in excess of $10,000 will probably be subject to investigation. If you're bringing prescription drugs, make sure they're in clearly marked containers. For updates, check www.cbp.gov.

Discount Cards

If you're going to be in Seattle for a while and plan on seeing its premier attractions, consider buying a **Seattle CityPASS** (www.citypass.com/seattle; adult/child 4-12yr $101/74). Good for nine days, the pass gets you entry into five sights: the Space Needle, Seattle Aquarium, Argosy Cruises Seattle Harbor Tour, Museum of Pop Culture *or* Woodland Park Zoo, Pacific Science Center *or* Chihuly Garden & Glass. You wind up saving about 45% on admission costs and you never have to stand in line. You can buy one at any of the venues or online.

PRACTICALITIES

Smoking

Washington State law prohibits smoking in, or within 25ft of, all public buildings.

Newspapers & Magazines

Northwest Asian Weekly (www.nwasianweekly.com) Serving Washington State's Asian community.

Real Change (www.realchangenews.org) Weekly paper focused on the city's homeless community.

Seattle Daily Journal of Commerce (www.djc.com) Focuses on the region's business world.

Seattle Gay News (www.sgn.org) A weekly newspaper focusing on gay issues.

Seattle Magazine (www.seattlemag.com) A slick monthly lifestyle magazine.

Seattle Post-Intelligencer (www.seattlepi.com) The former morning daily, now online only.

Seattle Times (www.seattletimes.com) The state's largest daily paper.

Seattle Weekly (www.seattleweekly.com) Free weekly with news and entertainment listings.

The Stranger (www.thestranger.com) Irreverent and intelligent free weekly, formerly edited by Dan Savage of 'Savage Love' fame.

Electricity

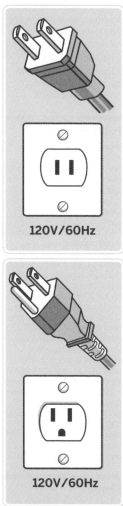

120V/60Hz

120V/60Hz

Emergency

Community Information Line	☑206-461-3200
Police, Fire & Ambulance	☑911
Seattle Police	☑206-625-5011
Washington State Patrol	☑360-596-2600

Internet Access

Seattle seems to be one big wi-fi hot spot. It's free nearly everywhere, in most hotels, many bars and all but a handful of coffee shops. You'll also find free wi-fi on some Sound Transit trains, all Rapid Ride buses and Washington State Ferries services (for the latter you must subscribe through Boingo).

LGBTIQ Travelers

Seattle is a progressive, liberally minded city with thriving gay and lesbian communities; census data shows that approximately 12.9% of the city's population identifies itself as gay or lesbian, and there doesn't tend to be much sexual-orientation-based hostility among the rest of the population.

In 2013, the city opened up a specific **LGBT Visitors Center** (Map p244; 614 Broadway E; ⊘9am-5pm Mon-Thu, 9am-6pm Fri; ⊠Capitol Hill) in Capitol Hill, only the second of its kind in the nation.

Some other resources and events to look out for:

Seattle Gay News (www.sgn.org) A weekly newspaper focusing on gay issues.

Outcity (www.outcity.com) A color magazine that focuses on the Pacific Northwest cities of Seattle; Portland, OR; Vancouver (Canada); and Victoria (Canada).

TWIST: Seattle Queer Film Festival (www.threedollarbill-cinema.org; ⊘Oct) Usually held in the third week of October.

Seattle Pride (☑206-322-9561; www.seattlepride.org; ⊘Jun) Seattle's pioneering lesbian- and gay-pride event (held every year since 1974) usually falls on the last Sunday in June and includes a huge downtown parade followed by PrideFest, during which numerous vendors and entertainers set up in the Seattle Center.

Medical Services

Know that all emergency rooms are obliged to receive sick or injured patients whether they can pay or not.

Clinics

If you're sick or injured, but not badly enough for a trip to the emergency room, try one of the following options:

Harborview Medical Center (☑206-744-3000; www.uwmedicine.org/harborview; 325 9th Ave; ⊠Broadway & Terrace) Full medical care, with emergency room.

US HealthWorks Medical Group (☑206-682-7418; 140 4th Ave N; ⑤Seattle Center) Walk-in clinic for nonemergencies.

Money

The US dollar is divided into 100 cents. US coins come in denominations of 1¢ (penny), 5¢ (nickel), 10¢ (dime), 25¢ (quarter), the practically extinct 50¢ (half-dollar) and the not-often-seen golden dollar coin.

Notes come in $1, $2, $5, $10, $20, $50 and $100 denominations.

ATMs

ATMs are easy to find: there's practically one per block in the busier commercial areas, as well as one outside every bank. Many bars, restaurants and grocery stores also have machines, although the service fees for these can be steep ($2 to $4, plus your own bank's fees). Getting money this way saves you a step – no need to change money from your own currency – and is a safer way to travel, as you only take out what you need as you go.

Changing Money

Banks and moneychangers will give you US currency based on the current exchange rate.

Travelex-Thomas Cook Currency Services (◷6am-8pm) The booth at the main airport terminal is behind the Delta Airlines counter.

Credit & Debit Cards

Major credit cards are accepted at most hotels, restaurants and shops throughout Seattle. Places that accept Visa and MasterCard generally also accept (and will often prefer) debit cards, which deduct payments directly from your check or savings account. Be sure to confirm with your bank before you leave that your debit card will be accepted in other states or countries. Debit cards from large commercial banks can often be used worldwide.

If your cards are lost or stolen, contact the issuing company immediately. Toll-free numbers for the main credit-card companies:

American Express ☏800-528-4800

Diners Club ☏800-234-6377

Discover ☏800-347-2683

MasterCard ☏800-627-8372

Visa ☏800-847-2911

Opening Hours

Banks 9am or 10am to 5pm or 6pm weekdays; some also 10am to 2pm Saturday

Businesses 9am to 5pm or 6pm weekdays; some also 10am to 5pm Saturday

Restaurants breakfast 7am to 11am, brunch 7am to 3pm, lunch 11:30am to 2:30pm, dinner 5:30pm to 10pm

Shops 9am or 10am to 5pm or 6pm (or 9pm in shopping malls) weekdays, noon to 5pm (later in malls) weekends; some places open till 8pm or 9pm

Post

At the time of research, rates for 1st-class mail within the US were 47¢ for letters up to 1oz and 34¢ for postcards. For package and international-letter rates, which vary, check with the local post office or with the online postal-rate calculator (http://ircalc.usps.gov). For other postal-service questions, call ☏800-275-8777 or visit the US Post Office website (www.usps.com).

Seattle's most convenient post office locations:

Main branch (Map p232; ☏206-748-5417; www.usps.com; 301 Union St; ◷8:30am-5:30pm Mon-Fri; ⓡWestlake)

Queen Anne (Map p240; 415 1st Ave N; ◷8:30am-6pm Mon-Fri, 9am-3pm Sat; ⓑ13)

University Station (Map p248; 4244 University Way NE; ◷8:30am-5:30pm Mon-Fri, 8:30am-3pm Sat)

Public Holidays

National public holidays are celebrated throughout the USA. On public holidays, banks, schools and government offices (including post offices) close and public transportation follows a Sunday schedule. Plan ahead if you're traveling during many holidays. Flights are full, highways are jammed and on Christmas and Thanksgiving, many grocery stores and restaurants close for the day.

New Year's Day January 1

Martin Luther King Jr Day Third Monday in January

Presidents' Day Third Monday in February

Memorial Day Last Monday in May

Independence Day (Fourth of July) July 4

Labor Day First Monday in September

Columbus Day Second Monday in October

Veterans' Day November 11

Thanksgiving Day Fourth Thursday in November

Christmas Day December 25

Taxes & Refunds

➡ Seattle's sales tax is 9.6% (a combination of Washington State taxes, King County taxes and city taxes).

➡ The hotel tax is 15.6%.

➡ There are no refunds available on sales taxes paid by travelers visiting the US.

Telephone

Phone numbers within the USA consist of a three-digit area code followed by a seven-digit local number. For long distance, dial ☏1 plus the three-digit area code plus the seven-digit number. To call internationally, first dial ☏011 then the country code and phone number.

Phone numbers in Seattle have a ☏206 area code. Even local calls made to the same area code require you to dial the full 10-digit number (no need to dial ☏1 first, though).

Toll-free numbers are prefixed with an ☏800, ☏877, ☏866 or ☏888 area code. Some toll-free numbers for local businesses or government offices only work within the state or the Seattle region, but most can be dialed from abroad. Just be aware that you'll be connected at regular long-distance rates, which could become a costly option if the line you're dialing tends to park customers on hold.

Time

Seattle is in the Pacific Standard Time zone:

➡ three hours behind New York (Atlantic Standard Time)

➡ eight hours behind London (Greenwich Mean Time)

➡ nine hours behind Paris (Central European Time)

➡ 17 hours behind Sydney (Australian Eastern Time)

In spring and summer, as in most of the time zones in the US, Pacific Standard Time becomes Pacific Daylight Time. Clocks are reset an hour forward in mid-March, and reset an hour back in early November.

Tourist Information

Visit Seattle (Map p232; ✆206-461-5800; www.visitseattle.org; cnr Pike St & 7th Ave; ⊙9am-5pm daily Jun-Sep, Mon-Fri Oct-May; ⊠Westlake) The main tourist information center is located in the Washington State Convention Center in downtown.

There's a helpful **Market Information Booth** (Map p232; ✆206-682-7453; cnr Pike St & 1st Ave; ⊙9am-6pm Mon-Sat, 9am-5pm Sun; ⊠Westlake) at the entrance to Pike Place Market.

The University of Washington has a small **visitor center** (Map p248; Odegaard Undergraduate Library; ⊙8:30am-5pm Mon-Fri; ⊠University of Washington).

There's a gay-specific **LGBT Visitors Center** (p217) in Capitol Hill.

Travelers with Disabilities

All public buildings (including hotels, restaurants, theaters and museums) are required by law to provide wheelchair access and to have appropriate restroom facilities available. Telephone companies provide relay operators for the hearing impaired. Many banks provide ATM instructions in braille. Dropped curbs are standard at intersections throughout the city.

Around 80% of Metro's buses are equipped with wheelchair lifts. Timetables marked with an 'L' indicate wheelchair accessibility. Be sure to let the driver know if you need your stop to be called and, if possible, pull the cord when you hear the call. Seeing-eye dogs are allowed on Metro buses. Passengers with disabilities qualify for a reduced fare but first need to contact **Metro Transit** (✆206-553-3000; www.metro.kingcounty.gov) for a permit.

Most large private and chain hotels have suites for guests with disabilities. Many car-rental agencies offer hand-controlled models at no extra charge. Make sure you give at least two days' notice. All major airlines, Greyhound buses and Amtrak trains allow guide dogs to accompany passengers and often sell two-for-one packages when attendants of passengers with serious disabilities are required. Airlines will also provide assistance for connecting, boarding and disembarking. Ask for assistance when making your reservation.

The following organizations specialize in the needs of travelers with disabilities:

Access-Able Travel Service (www.access-able.com) Full of information, with tips on scooter rental, wheelchair travel, accessible transportation and more.

Easter Seals of Washington (✆206-281-5700; www.easterseals.com/washington) Provides technology assistance, workplace services and camps for individuals with disabilities and special needs.

Society for Accessible Travel & Hospitality (✆212-447-7284; www.sath.org) Provides info for travelers with disabilities.

Visas

Foreigners needing visas to travel to the US should plan ahead. There is a reciprocal visa-waiver program (better known as ESTA) in which citizens of 38 countries may enter the USA for stays of 90 days or less with a passport but without first obtaining a visa. Currently these countries include Australia, Austria, Denmark, France, Germany, Italy, Japan, the Netherlands, New Zealand, Spain, Sweden, Switzerland and the UK. Under this program you must have a round-trip ticket that is nonrefundable in the USA.

Citizens of countries in the Visa Waiver Program have to register with the government online (https://esta.cbp.dhs.gov) three days before their visit. The registration is valid for two years and costs $14.

Note: Canadian citizens do not need a visa or a visa waiver to travel to the US.

Other travelers will need to obtain a visa from a US consulate or embassy. In most countries, the process can be done by mail. Visa applicants may be required to 'demonstrate binding obligations' that will ensure their return home. Because of this requirement, those planning to travel through other countries before arriving in the USA are generally better off applying for their US visa while they are still in their home country, rather than when they're already on the road.

The Non-Immigrant Visitors Visa is the most common visa. It is available in two forms: the B1 for business and the B2 for tourism or visiting friends and relatives. The validity period for US visitor visas depends on which country you're from. The length of time you'll be allowed to stay in the USA is determined by US immigration authorities at the port of entry. Non-US citizens with HIV should know that they can be excluded from entry to the USA.

For updates on visas and other security issues, you can visit the US Department of Homeland Security (https://www.cbp.gov/travel/international-visitors/esta), the US Department of State (www.travel.state.gov) and the Transportation Security Administration (www.tsa.gov).

Behind the Scenes

SEND US YOUR FEEDBACK

We love to hear from travelers – your comments keep us on our toes and help make our books better. Our well-traveled team reads every word on what you loved or loathed about this book. Although we cannot reply individually to your submissions, we always guarantee that your feedback goes straight to the appropriate authors, in time for the next edition. Each person who sends us information is thanked in the next edition – the most useful submissions are rewarded with a selection of digital PDF chapters.

Visit **lonelyplanet.com/contact** to submit your updates and suggestions or to ask for help. Our award-winning website also features inspirational travel stories, news and discussions.

Note: We may edit, reproduce and incorporate your comments in Lonely Planet products such as guidebooks, websites and digital products, so let us know if you don't want your comments reproduced or your name acknowledged. For a copy of our privacy policy visit lonelyplanet.com/privacy.

WRITER THANKS

Brendan Sainsbury

Thanks to all the untold bus drivers, chefs, hotel receptionists, tour guides and innocent by-standers who helped me during this research. Special thanks to my wife Liz and ten-year-old son Kieran for their company on the road.

Celeste Brash

Thanks to my husband Josh, my daughter Jasmine and her friend Garett for helping me out on the road, and to my son Tevai for holding the fort. Also thanks to friends Jackie, Sandra Bao, Chris Ashby and the Forster-Pilot clan for very helpful tips.

ACKNOWLEDGEMENTS

Cover photograph: Pike Place Market, Danita Delimont Stock/AWL.
Seattle Downtown Metro map courtesy of King County Metro Transit http://metro.king county.gov

THIS BOOK

This 7th edition of Lonely Planet's *Seattle* guidebook was researched and written by Brendan Sainsbury. Celeste Brash wrote the Day Trips from Seattle chapter. The previous edition was also written by Brendan and Celeste. This guidebook was produced by the following:

Destination Editor
Alexander Howard
Product Editor Joel Cotterell
Senior Cartographer Alison Lyall
Book Designer Clara Monitto
Assisting Editors Michelle Bennett, Kellie Langdon, Lauren O'Connell, Gabrielle Stefanos

Assisting Book Designers
Fergal Condon, Jessica Rose
Cover Researcher Naomi Parker
Thanks to Jennifer Carey, Evan Godt, Andi Jones, Marissa Lighthiser, Kate Mathews, Catherine Naghten, Martine Power, Kirsten Rawlings, Ross Taylor, Tony Wheeler, Dora Whitaker

See also separate subindexes for:

✕ EATING P225

🍷 DRINKING & NIGHTLIFE P226

☆ ENTERTAINMENT P227

🛍 SHOPPING P227

🏃 SPORTS & ACTIVITIES P228

🛏 SLEEPING P228

Index

🍴 EATING

🏃 SPORTS & ACTIVITIES

🛏 SLEEPING

Seattle Maps

Sights
- Beach
- Bird Sanctuary
- Buddhist
- Castle/Palace
- Christian
- Confucian
- Hindu
- Islamic
- Jain
- Jewish
- Monument
- Museum/Gallery/Historic Building
- Ruin
- Shinto
- Sikh
- Taoist
- Winery/Vineyard
- Zoo/Wildlife Sanctuary
- Other Sight

Activities, Courses & Tours
- Bodysurfing
- Diving
- Canoeing/Kayaking
- Course/Tour
- Sento Hot Baths/Onsen
- Skiing
- Snorkeling
- Surfing
- Swimming/Pool
- Walking
- Windsurfing
- Other Activity

Sleeping
- Sleeping
- Camping

Eating
- Eating

Drinking & Nightlife
- Drinking & Nightlife
- Cafe

Entertainment
- Entertainment

Shopping
- Shopping

Information
- Bank
- Embassy/Consulate
- Hospital/Medical
- Internet
- Police
- Post Office
- Telephone
- Toilet
- Tourist Information
- Other Information

Geographic
- Beach
- Gate
- Hut/Shelter
- Lighthouse
- Lookout
- Mountain/Volcano
- Oasis
- Park
- Pass
- Picnic Area
- Waterfall

Population
- Capital (National)
- Capital (State/Province)
- City/Large Town
- Town/Village

Transport
- Airport
- BART station
- Border crossing
- Boston T station
- Bus
- Cable car/Funicular
- Cycling
- Ferry
- Metro/Muni station
- Monorail
- Parking
- Petrol station
- Subway/SkyTrain station
- Taxi
- Train station/Railway
- Tram
- Underground station
- Other Transport

Note: Not all symbols displayed above appear on the maps in this book

Routes
- Tollway
- Freeway
- Primary
- Secondary
- Tertiary
- Lane
- Unsealed road
- Road under construction
- Plaza/Mall
- Steps
- Tunnel
- Pedestrian overpass
- Walking Tour
- Walking Tour detour
- Path/Walking Trail

Boundaries
- International
- State/Province
- Disputed
- Regional/Suburb
- Marine Park
- Cliff
- Wall

Hydrography
- River, Creek
- Intermittent River
- Canal
- Water
- Dry/Salt/Intermittent Lake
- Reef

Areas
- Airport/Runway
- Beach/Desert
- Cemetery (Christian)
- Cemetery (Other)
- Glacier
- Mudflat
- Park/Forest
- Sight (Building)
- Sportsground
- Swamp/Mangrove

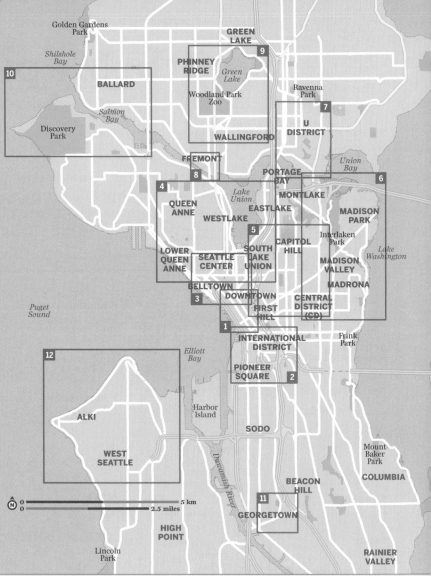

MAP INDEX

DOWNTOWN, PIKE PLACE & WATERFRONT Map on p232

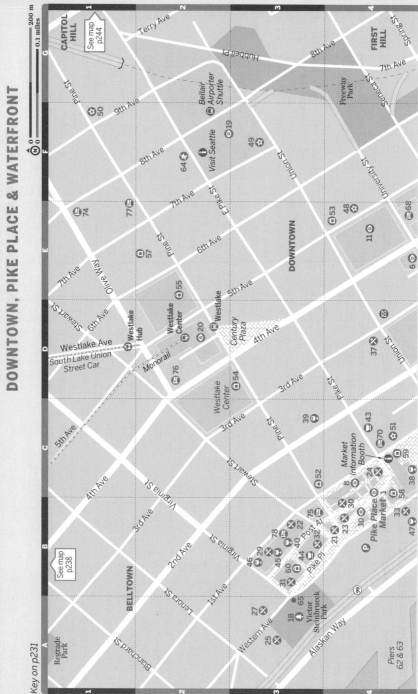

DOWNTOWN, PIKE PLACE & WATERFRONT

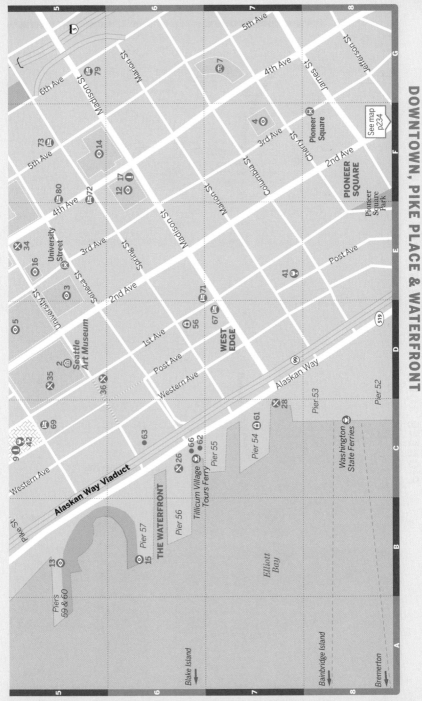

See map p234

Key on p236

PIONEER SQUARE, INTERNATIONAL DISTRICT & SODO

Bainbridge Island

Washington
State Ferries

Bremerton

Vashon Island

West Seattle

Columbia St

Post Ave

1st Ave

Cherry St

James St

Jefferson St

4th Ave

5th Ave

Terrace St

Dilling Way

See map
p232

Pier 50

Water Taxis

Pier 48

Alaskan Way Viaduct

99

20

65   25

42
39

10

1

47

48

56

22

26

15

Grand
Central
Arcade

Occidental
Mall

21
2 *Pioneer
Building*
14
13

*Smith
Tower*

60
29

3

32

24

41

11

S Washington St

S Main St

31

38

12   8

54   45

46

Washington State
Exhibition
Center

67

44

49

50

53

2nd Ave

Occidental Ave S

2nd Ave Extended S

Pioneer
Square

Yesler Way

PIONEER
SQUARE

18
40

3rd Ave S

4

35

S Jackson St

7

King St
Station
(Amtrak)

S King St

S Washington St

4th Ave S

5th & Jackson/
Japantown

17

Union
Station   66

62

Airport Way S

90

4th Ave S

5th Ave S

1st Ave S

S Railroad Way

Alaskan Way S

Occidental Ave S

Alaskan Way Viaduct

99

1st Ave S

S Royal Brougham Way

Utah Ave S

3rd Ave S

Stadium

S Atlantic St

S Atlantic St

Colorado Ave S

1st Ave S

Occidental Ave S

4th Ave S

S Massachusetts St

Inset (0.3mi)

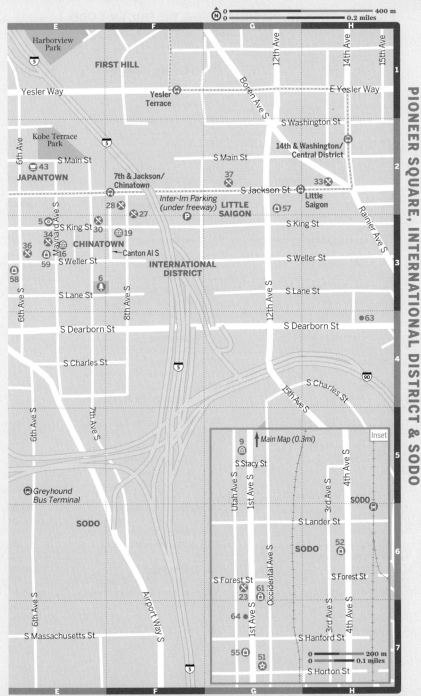

PIONEER SQUARE, INTERNATIONAL DISTRICT & SODO

PIONEER SQUARE & INTERNATIONAL DISTRICT

PIONEER SQUARE, INTERNATIONAL DISTRICT & SODO *Map on p234*

BELLTOWN & SEATTLE CENTER *Map on p238*

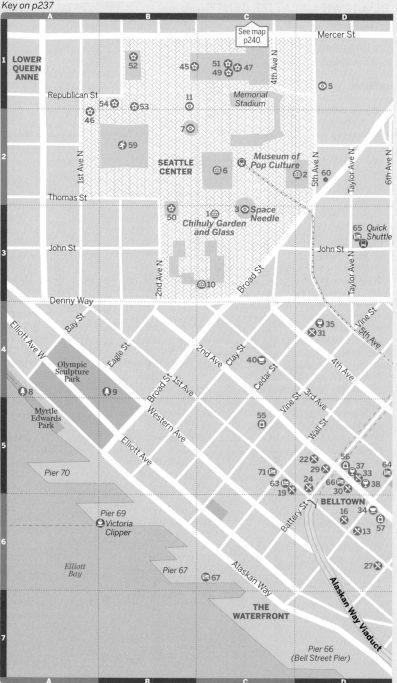

See map
p240

Mercer St

1

LOWER
QUEEN
ANNE

52

45

51
49
47

5

Republican St

54
46
53

11

Memorial
Stadium

4th Ave N

7

2

1st Ave N

59

SEATTLE
CENTER

6

Museum of
Pop Culture

2

60

5th Ave N

Taylor Ave N

6th Ave N

Thomas St

50

1

Chihuly Garden
and Glass

3 Space
Needle

3

John St

2nd Ave N

10

Broad St

John St

65 Quick
Shuttle

Taylor Ave N

Denny Way

Elliott Ave W

Bay St

4

Olympic
Sculpture
Park

Eagle St

2nd Ave

Clay St

40

Cedar St

Broad St
1st Ave

35
31

Vine St

4th Ave

5th Ave

3rd Ave

8

9

Myrtle
Edwards
Park

Western Ave

Elliott Ave

55

Wall St

5

Pier 70

71

22
29
24

63
19

56
37
33
66
30
38

64

Battery St

BELLTOWN

Pier 69
Victoria
Clipper

16
34
57

13

Elliott
Bay

Pier 67

67

Alaskan Way

27

6

THE
WATERFRONT

Alaskan Way Viaduct

Pier 66
(Bell Street Pier)

7

A   B   C   D

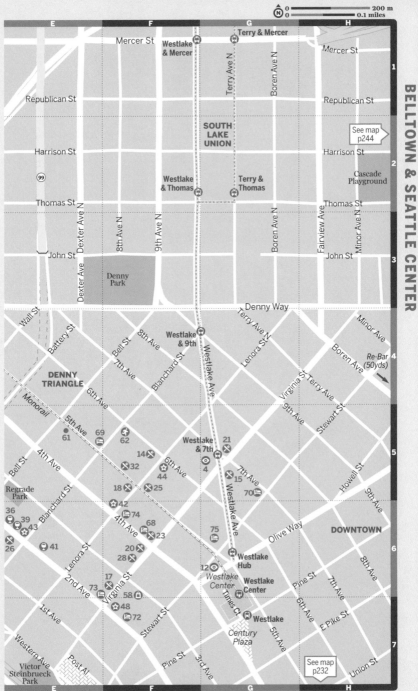

0   200 m
0   0.1 miles

Mercer St
Westlake & Mercer
Terry & Mercer
Mercer St

Republican St

SOUTH LAKE UNION

See map p244

Republican St

Harrison St

Harrison St

99

Westlake & Thomas

Terry & Thomas

Cascade Playground

Thomas St N

Dexter Ave N
Dexter Ave
8th Ave N
9th Ave N
Terry Ave N
Boren Ave N
Fairview Ave
Minor Ave N

Thomas St

John St

John St

Denny Park

Denny Way

Wall St

Battery St

Westlake & 9th

Terry Ave N

Lenora St

Minor Ave

Boren Ave

Re-Bar (50yds)

DENNY TRIANGLE

Bell St

8th Ave

7th Ave

Blanchard St

Westlake Ave

Virginia St

Terry Ave

Monorail

6th Ave

9th Ave

Stewart St

5th Ave

69   62

61

14

32

Westlake & 7th   21

4

7th Ave

Howell St

9th Ave

4th Ave

Bell St

Regrade Park

Blanchard St

18   25

44   6th Ave

15

70

36   39

43

26   41

42

74

68

23

75

Olive Way

DOWNTOWN

8th Ave

7th Ave

Lenora St

20

28

Westlake Ave

Westlake Hub

12

Westlake Center

Pine St

6th Ave

E Pike St

2nd Ave

17

73

58

48   72

Virginia St

Stewart St

Westlake Center

Times Ct

Westlake

5th Ave

Century Plaza

Pine St

3rd St

See map p232

Union St

1st Ave

Western Ave

Victor Steinbrueck Park

Post Al

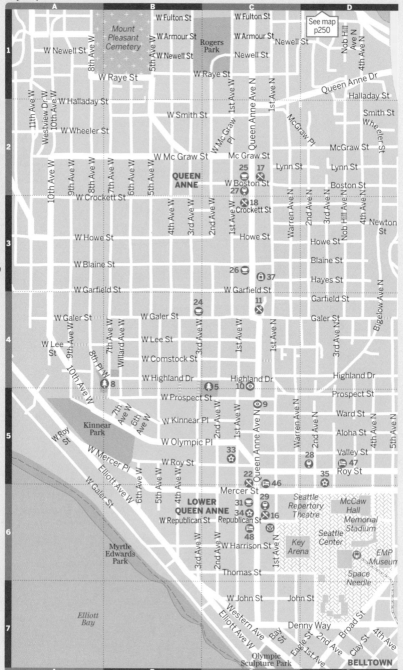

QUEEN ANNE & LAKE UNION

0 — 500 m
0 — 0.25 miles

E Hamlin St

E Edgar St

E Roanoke St

4 🌳
Gas Works
Park

14 ✕

Dexter Ave N

Westlake Ave N

8th Ave N

Waverly Pl N

Crockett St

99

Fairview Ave E

Minor Ave E

Yale Ave E

Eastlake Ave E

Franklin Ave E

Boylston Ave E

E Louisa St

38 📮

E Lynn St

EASTLAKE

Harvard Ave E

Lake
Union

42 ✕

WESTLAKE

Taylor Ave N

Aurora Ave N

99

E Boston St

20 ✕

E Newton St

E Howe St

E Blaine St

E Garfield St

Howe
St

Taylor Ave N

Galer St

Lee St

E Galer St

E Galer St

Westlake Ave N

Highland Dr

Prospect St

Taylor Ave N

6th Ave N

Fairview Ave N

49 🍴

I-5

Lakeview Blvd E

E Prospect St

Lakeview Pl E

Belmont Ave E

Boylston Ave E

Harvard Ave E

41 ✕

Fairview &
Campus Drive

Eastlake Ave E

43 🛏

9th Ave N

Aloha St

Lake
Union
Park

6 ⊙

1 🏛 Museum of History
& Industry

2 🏛

7 🌳

40 🚹

Valley St

Valley St

Lake Union
Park

Roy St

Minor Ave N

Belmont Ave E

44 🛏

15 ✕

Roy St

Westlake
& Mercer

Broad St

6th Ave N

Taylor Ave N

Mercer St

12 ✕

Terry &
Mercer

Republican St

SOUTH
LAKE UNION

Harrison St

Pontius Ave N

Yale Ave E

Eastlake Ave E

13 ✕

Bellevue Ave E

Summit Ave E

Boylston Ave E

CAPITOL
HILL

Melrose Ave E

99

19 ✕

21 🍴

Westlake Ave N

Terry Ave N

E Harrison St

I-5

E Thomas St

Westlake
& Thomas

Thomas St

23 🍴

Terry & Thomas

Cascade
Playground

45 🛏

Dexter Ave N

6th Ave N

Taylor Ave N

John St

3 ✕

Boren Ave N

Minor Ave N

John St

39 📮

36 📮

32 ⭐

E Olive Way

E Denny Way

Denny Way

Westlake & 9th

Wall St

6th Ave

8th Ave

See map
p238

Lenora St

Terry Ave

Boren Ave

Stewart St

Howell St

30 ✕

See map
p244

QUEEN ANNE & LAKE UNION *Map on p240*

CAPITOL HILL & FIRST HILL Map on p244

⊚ Sights (p110)
1 Frye Art Museum ... B8
2 Gay City Library ... B6
3 Jimi Hendrix Statue ... C6
4 Lakeview Cemetery ... D1
5 Seattle Asian Art Museum ... D1
  Sorrento Hotel ... (see 63)
6 St James Cathedral ... B8
7 St Mark's Cathedral ... C1
8 Stimson-Green Mansion ... B7
9 Volunteer Park ... D1
10 Volunteer Park Conservatory ... D1
11 Water Tower Observation Deck ... D2

⊗ Eating (p112)
12 Annapurna Cafe ... C5
13 Bimbo's Cantina ... C6
14 Bluebird Microcreamery ... D6
15 Cascina Spinasse ... D6
16 Coastal Kitchen ... D4
17 Eltana Wood-fired Bagel Cafe ... D6
18 Ernest Loves Agnes ... F3
19 Honeyhole ... C6
20 Lost Lake Cafe & Lounge ... C6
21 Mamnoon ... B6
22 Oddfellows Cafe ... C6
23 Osteria La Spiga ... D6
24 Poppy ... C3
25 Rione XIII ... D4
26 Rumba ... A6
27 Sitka & Spruce ... B6

⊙ Drinking & Nightlife (p115)
28 Baltic Room ... B6
  Caffé Vita ... (see 13)
29 Canterbury Ale House ... E3
30 Capitol Cider ... C6
31 Comet Tavern ... C6
32 Elysian Brewing Company ... D6
33 Espresso Vivace at Brix ... C3
34 Fuel Coffee ... F3
35 High Line ... C4
36 Linda's Tavern ... C6
37 Neighbours ... C6
38 Optimism Brewing Co ... C7
39 R Place ... B6
40 Starbucks Reserve Roastery & Tasting Room ... B6
41 Stumptown on 12th ... D7
42 Sun Liquor Distillery ... B6
43 Tavern Law ... D6
44 Victrola Coffee Roasters ... C6
45 Wildrose ... C6

⊙ Entertainment (p117)
46 Annex Theatre ... C6
47 Chop Suey ... C3
48 Neumo's ... C6
49 Northwest Film Forum ... D6
  Richard Hugo House ... (see 1)

⊞ Shopping (p118)
50 Ada's Technical Books & Cafe ... D4
51 Babeland ... C6
52 Crossroads Trading Co ... C4
53 Dilettante Chocolates ... C3
  Elliott Bay Book Company ... (see 22)
  Melrose Market ... (see 27)
54 Revival ... C4
  Throwbacks NW ... (see 14)
55 Twice Sold Tales ... C5
56 Urban Outfitters ... C4
  Wall of Sound ... (see 14)
  Zion's Gate Records ... (see 46)

⊛ Sports & Activities (p119)
57 Century Ballroom ... C6

⊟ Sleeping (p194)
58 11th Avenue Inn ... C5
59 Bacon Mansion B&B ... C2
60 Gaslight Inn B&B ... D5
61 Inn at Virginia Mason ... B7
62 Silver Cloud Hotel – Seattle Broadway ... C7
63 Sorrento Hotel ... B8

Key on p243

See map p246

E Madison St

500 m
0.25 miles

Washington Park Arboretum

E Galer St
E Lee St
26th Ave E
E 26th Ave E

25th Ave E
24th Ave E
23rd Ave E
22nd Ave E
21st Ave E
20th Ave E
19th Ave E
18th Ave E
17th Ave E
16th Ave E
15th Ave E

E Highland Dr
E Prospect St
E Aloha St
E Roy St
E Valley St
E Mercer St

E Aloha St
E Roy St
E Mercer St
E Republican St
E Harrison St
E Thomas St
E John St

Louisa Boren
Lookout
(150yds)

Lakeview
Cemetery
E Galer St

Volunteer
Park

E Ward St
E Valley St

CAPITOL HILL

Reservoir

Volunteer Park Rd

Volunteer Park Rd

E Highland Dr

E Galer St

E Prospect St

Federal Ave E

Harvard Ave E

Broadway E

E Aloha St

E Roy St

14th Ave E
13th Ave E
12th Ave E
11th Ave E
10th Ave E
Federal Ave E
E Republican St
E Harrison St
E Thomas St

Malden Ave E
Broadway E
Harvard Ave E

LGBT
Visitors
Center

Belmont Pl E
Belmont Ave E
Summit Ave E
Bellevue Ave E
Melrose Ave E

Summit Ave E
E Roy St
E Mercer St

Lakeview Blvd E
E Galer St
Eastlake Ave E
Fairview Ave E

EASTLAKE

Eastlake Ave E

Fairview &
Campus Drive

See map
p240

Lake
Union

Valley St
Yale Ave N

Mercer St
Harrison St

SOUTH
LAKE
UNION

Cascade
Playground

THE CD, MADRONA & MADISON PARK

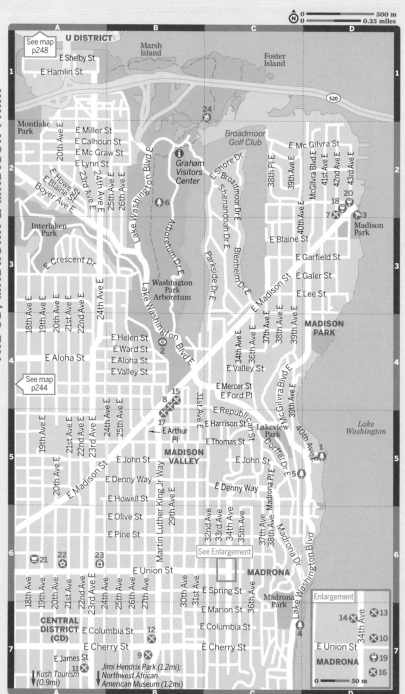

N
0 ———————— 500 m
0 ———————— 0.25 miles

See map p248

U DISTRICT

E Shelby St
E Hamlin St

Marsh Island

Foster Island

520

Montlake Park

20th Ave E
E Miller St
E Calhoun St
E Mc Graw St
E Lynn St

E Howe St
E Blaine St
Boyer Ave E
23rd Ave E
24th Ave E
25th Ave E
26th Ave E

Lake Washington Blvd E

24
🏛

Broadmoor Golf Club

E Mc Gilvra St

38th Pl E
39th Ave E
McGilvra Blvd E
41st Ave E
42nd Ave E
43rd Ave E

ℹ 6
Graham Visitors Center

E Shore Dr
Broadmoor Dr E
Shenandoah Dr E

Arboretum Dr E

18
20
7 🚻 3
Madison Park
40th Ave E

Interlaken Park

E Crescent Dr

24th Ave E

Washington Park Arboretum

Blenheim Dr E
Parkside Dr E

E Blaine St

E Garfield St
E Galer St
E Lee St

E Madison St

37th Ave E
39th Ave E

MADISON PARK

18th Ave E
19th Ave E
20th Ave E
21st Ave E
22nd Ave E

24th Ave E

Lake Washington Blvd E

E Helen St
E Ward St
E Aloha St
E Valley St

2

34th Ave E
36th Ave E

E Aloha St

See map p244

E Valley St
E Mercer St
E Ford Pl

McGilvra Blvd E
39th Ave E

Lake Washington

15
8 🏨
17
E Arthur Pl

31st Ave E

E Republican St
E Harrison St
E Thomas St

Lakeview Park

40th Ave E
Dorffel Dr E

1
🚻

19th Ave E
21st Ave E
22nd Ave E
23rd Ave E

24th Ave E
25th Ave E

E John St

E John St
5 🏨

20th Ave E

E Madison St

E Denny Way

Martin Luther King Jr Way

29th Ave E

E Denny Way

Madrona Pl E

E Howell St

E Olive St

E Pine St

MADISON VALLEY

Madrona Dr

32nd Ave E
33rd Ave E
34th Ave E
35th Ave

37th Ave E
38th Ave E

🖥 21
22 ★
23 🔒

E Union St

See Enlargement

MADRONA

Lake Washington Blvd

Enlargement

14 ❌ 13
34th Ave

18th Ave
19th Ave
21st Ave
22nd Ave
23rd Ave E
24th Ave
25th Ave
26th Ave
27th Ave

30th Ave
31st Ave

E Spring St

E Marion St

36th Ave

Madrona Park

❌ 10

CENTRAL DISTRICT (CD)

E Columbia St
12

E Columbia St

4
🚻

💧 19

MADRONA

❌ 16

E Cherry St

9 ❌

E Cherry St

E Union St

0 ——— 50 m

E James St

11

Kush Tourism (0.9mi)

Jimi Hendrix Park (1.2mi); Northwest African American Museum (1.2mi)

THE CD, MADRONA & MADISON PARK

THE CD, MADRONA & MADISON PARK

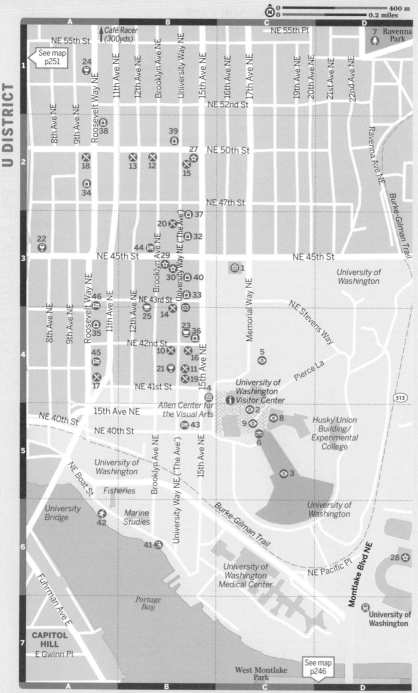

U DISTRICT

0 400 m
0 0.2 miles

NE 55th St

Café Racer
(300yds)

See map
p251

24

NE 55th Pl

7 Ravenna
Park

NE 52nd St

8th Ave NE
9th Ave NE
Roosevelt Way NE
11th Ave NE
12th Ave NE
Brooklyn Ave NE
University Way NE
15th Ave NE
16th Ave NE
17th Ave NE
19th Ave NE
20th Ave NE
21st Ave NE
22nd Ave NE

Ravenna Ave NE

Burke-Gilman Trail

38

39

27
NE 50th St

18

13   12

15

34

NE 47th St

37

20

32

22

44   29

NE 45th St

Brooklyn Ave NE
University Way NE ('The Ave')

30

1

NE 45th St

University of
Washington

40

Roosevelt Way NE

46

33

NE 43rd St

25   14

8th Ave NE
9th Ave NE
11th Ave NE
12th Ave NE
15th Ave NE

Memorial Way NE

NE Stevens Way

35

23   36

NE 42nd St

10   16

5

45

21   11

19

17

NE 41st St

Pierce La

4

University of
Washington
Visitor Center

15th Ave NE

Allen Center for
the Visual Arts

2

513

NE 40th St

NE 40th St

43

9   8

6

Husky Union
Building/
Experimental
College

University of
Washington

NE Boat St

University of
Washington

Brooklyn Ave NE

3

Fisheries

University
Bridge

Marine
Studies

42

University Way NE ('The Ave')

15th Ave NE

Burke-Gilman Trail

University of
Washington

41

28

University of
Washington
Medical Center

NE Pacific Pl

Montlake Blvd NE

University of
Washington

Fuhrman Ave E

Portage
Bay

CAPITOL
HILL
E Gwinn Pl

West Montlake
Park

See map
p246

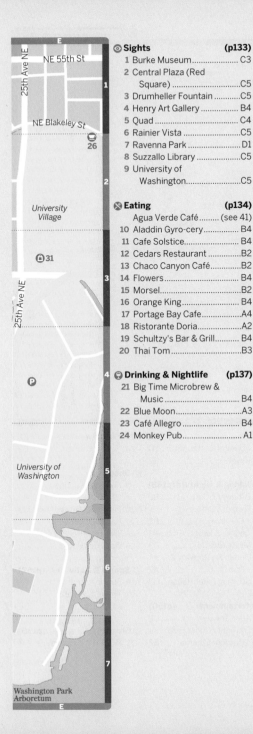

U DISTRICT

FREMONT

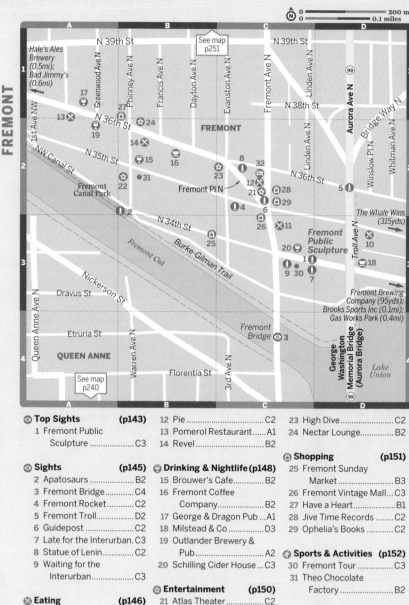

0   200 m
0   0.1 miles

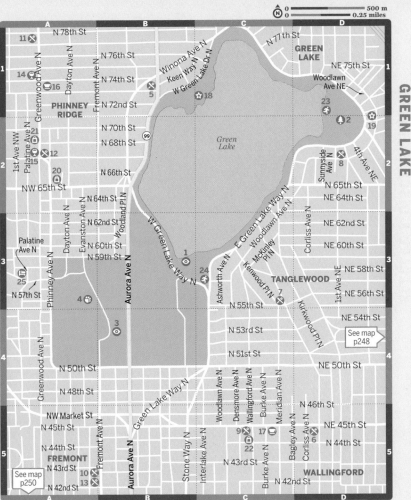

BALLARD & DISCOVERY PARK

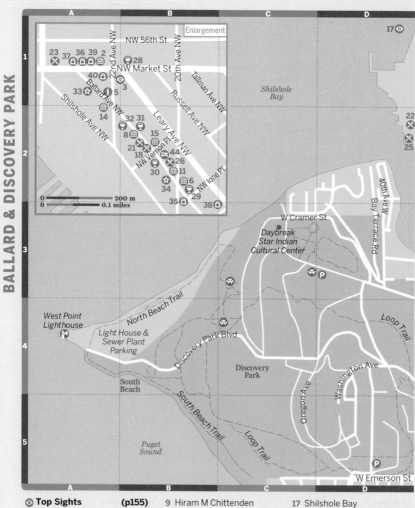

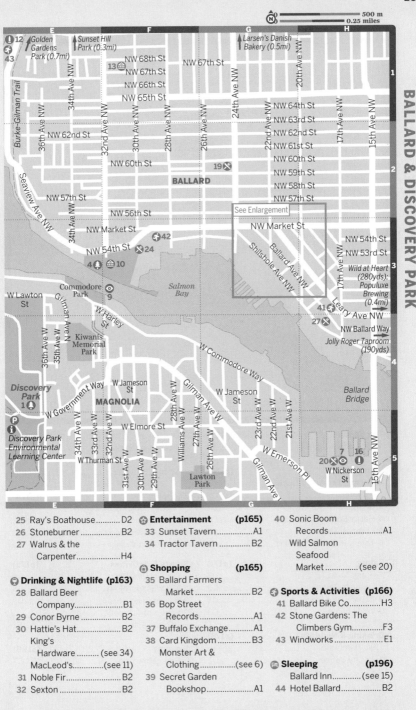

GEORGETOWN

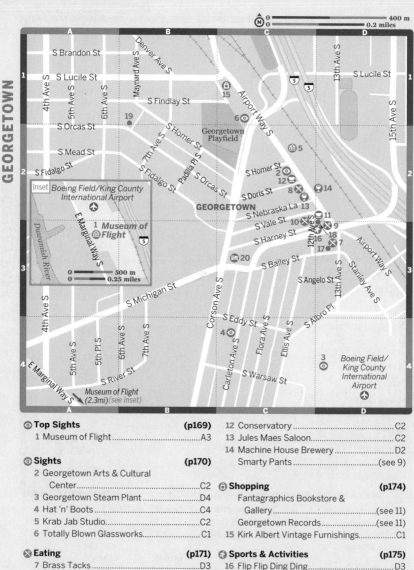